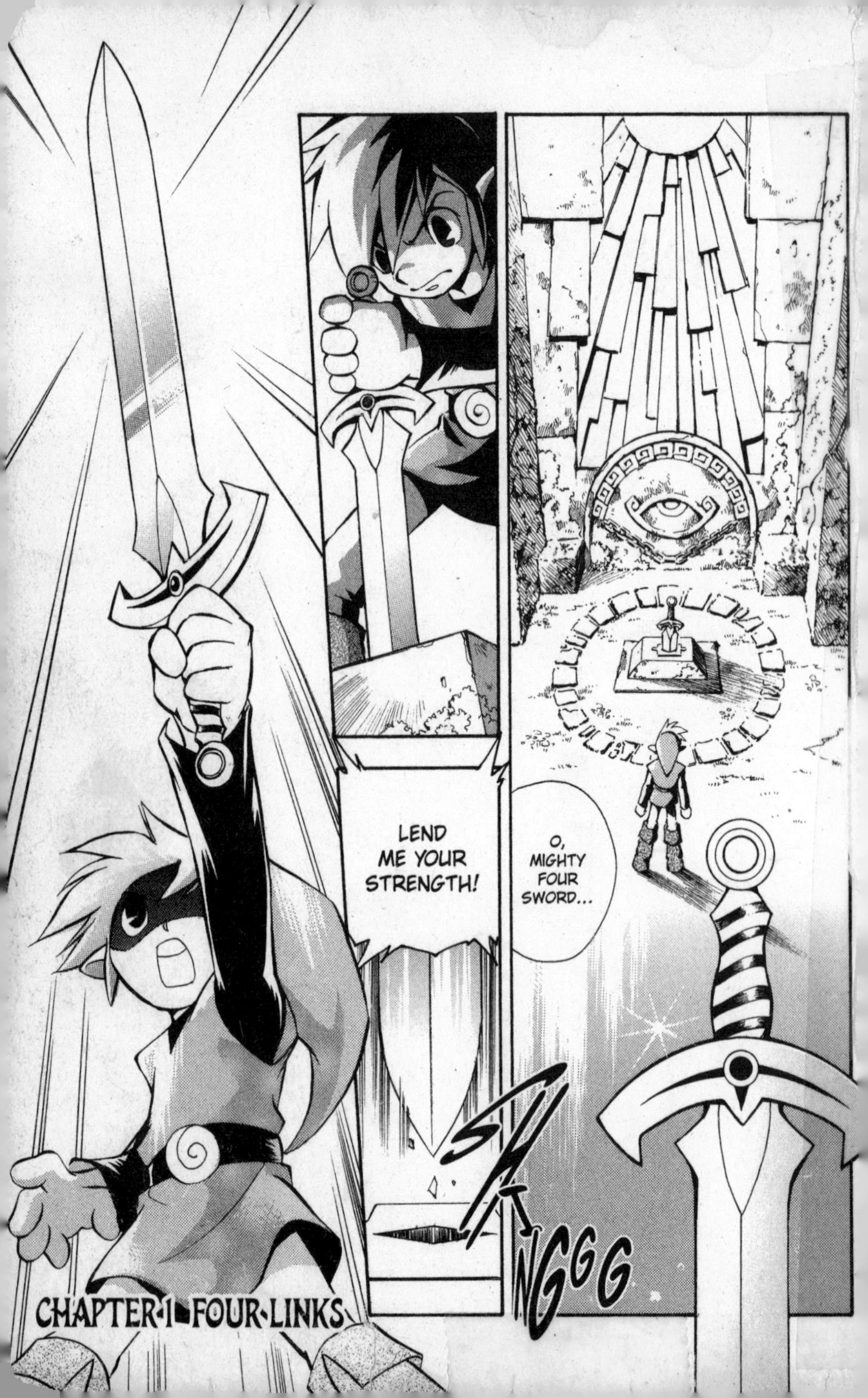
O, MIGHTY FOUR SWORD...
LEND ME YOUR STRENGTH!
SHANGGG
CHAPTER 1 FOUR LINKS

CHAPTER 1
FOUR LINKS

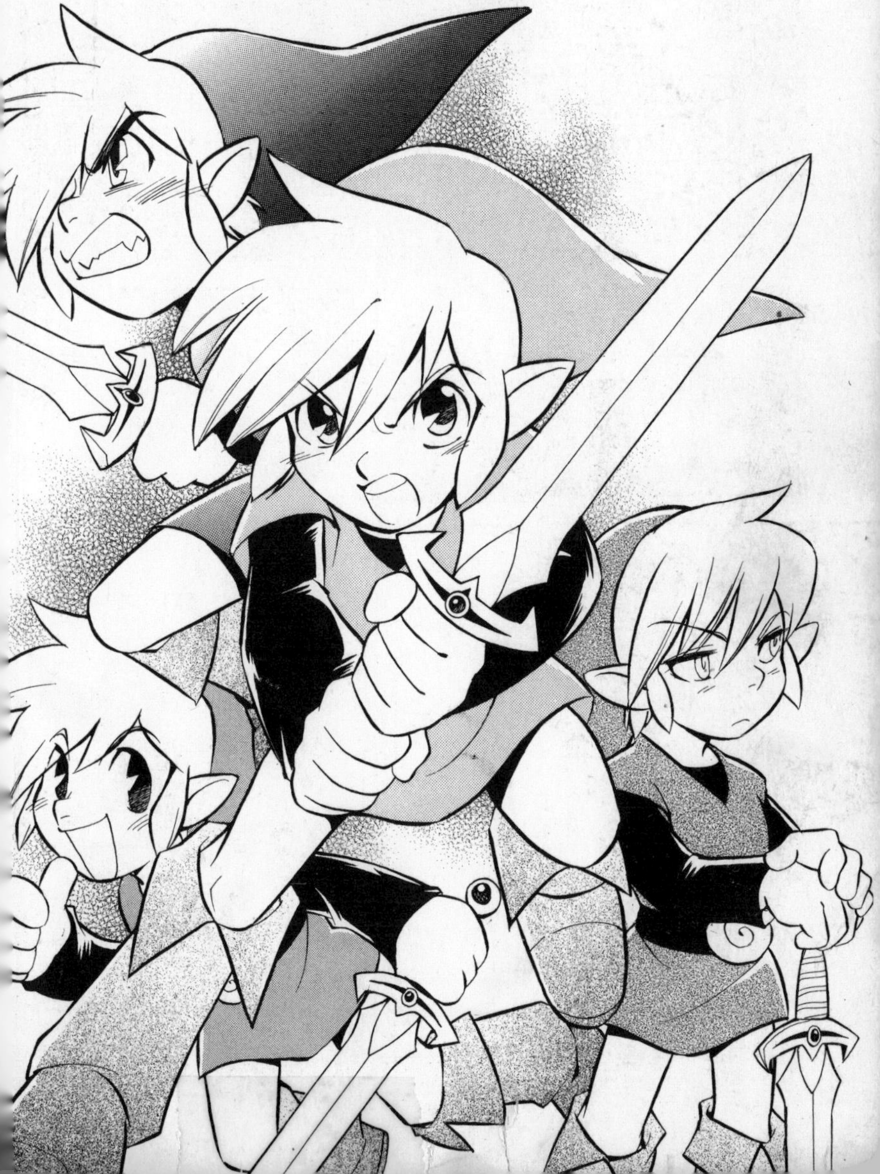

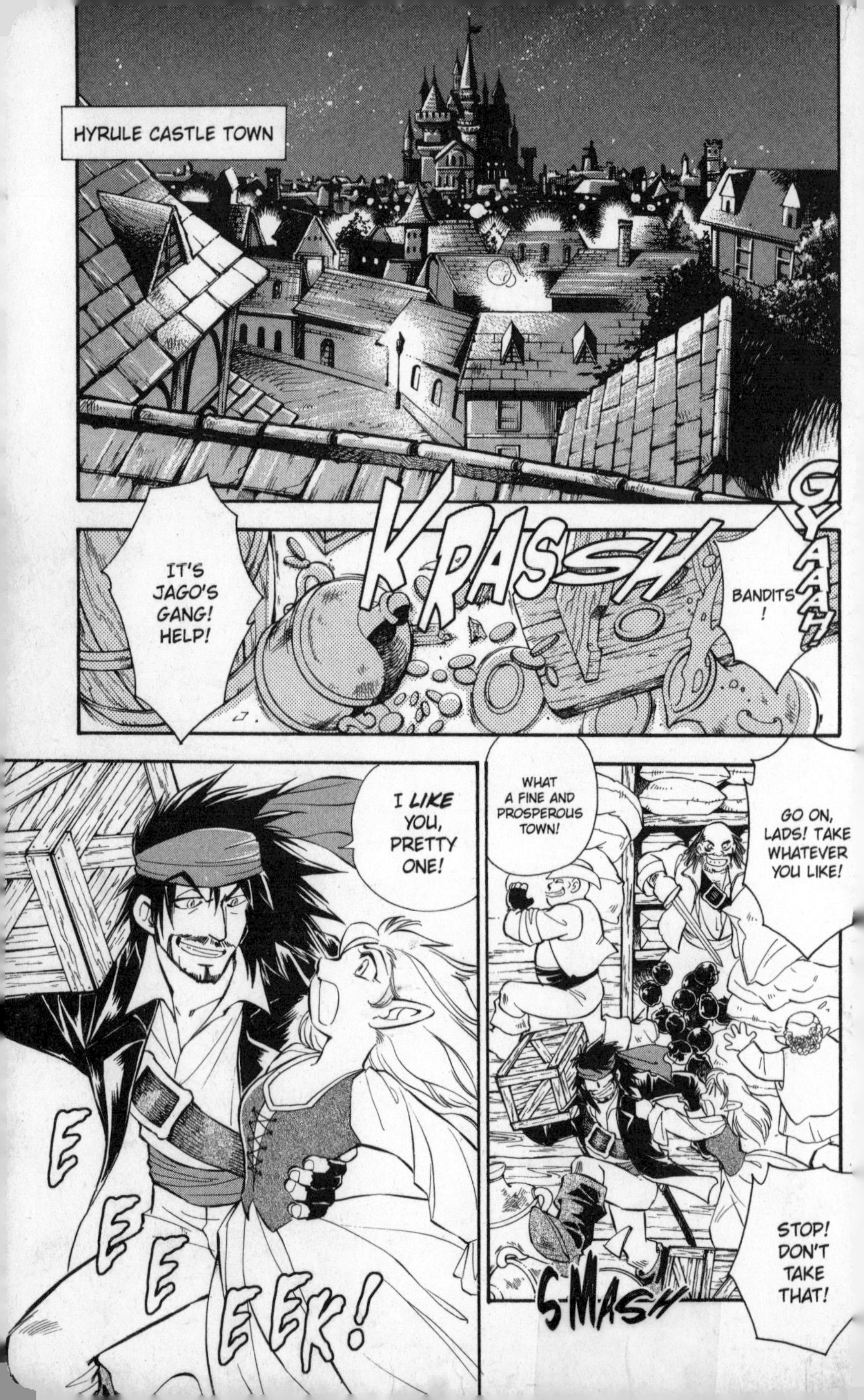
HYRULE CASTLE TOWN
GYAAAH
BANDITS!
KRASSH
IT'S JAGO'S GANG! HELP!
GO ON, LADS! TAKE WHATEVER YOU LIKE!
WHAT A FINE AND PROSPEROUS TOWN!
STOP! DON'T TAKE THAT!
SMASH
I *LIKE* YOU, PRETTY ONE!
EEEEEEK!

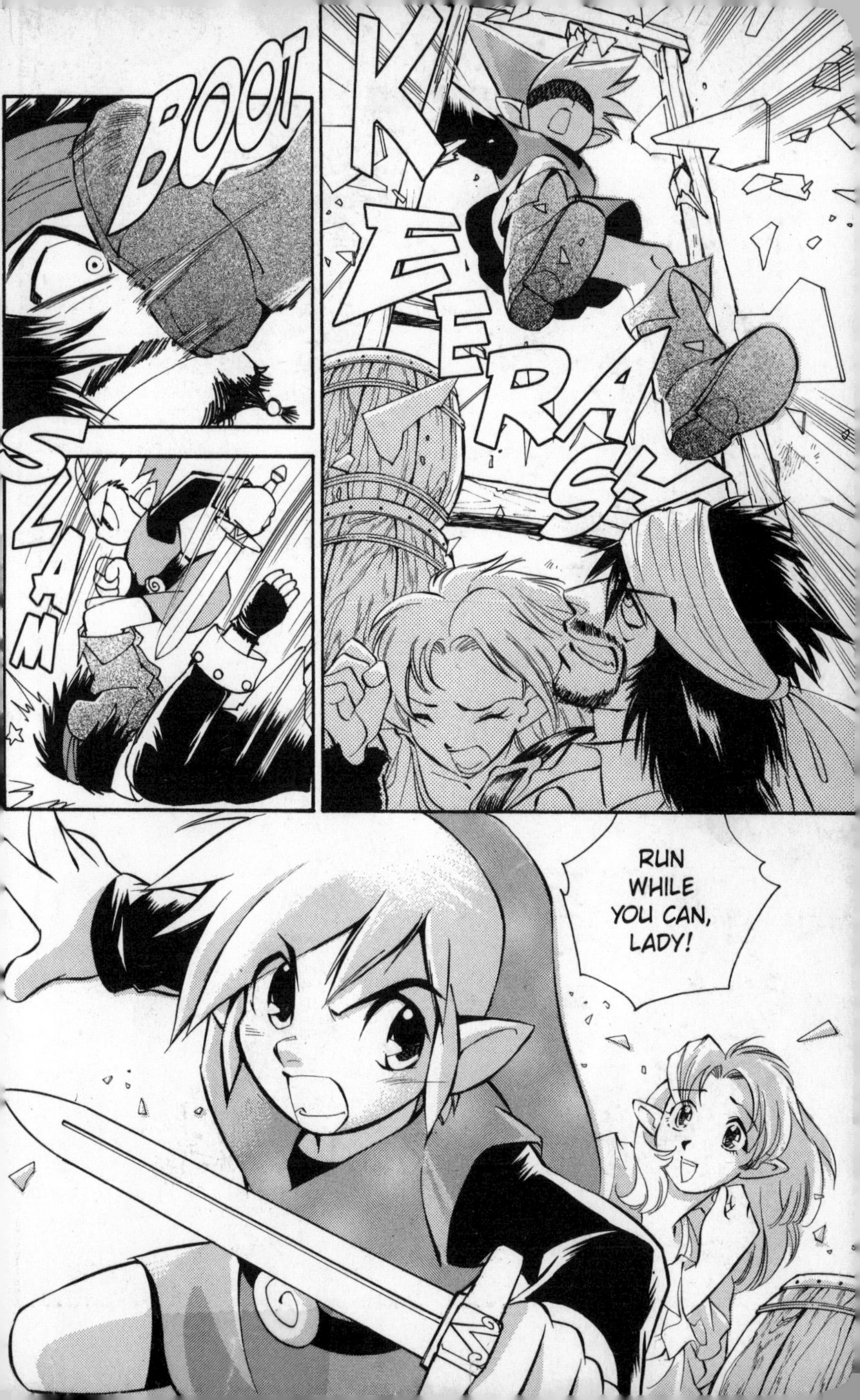
KEERASH
BOOT
SLAM
RUN WHILE YOU CAN, LADY!

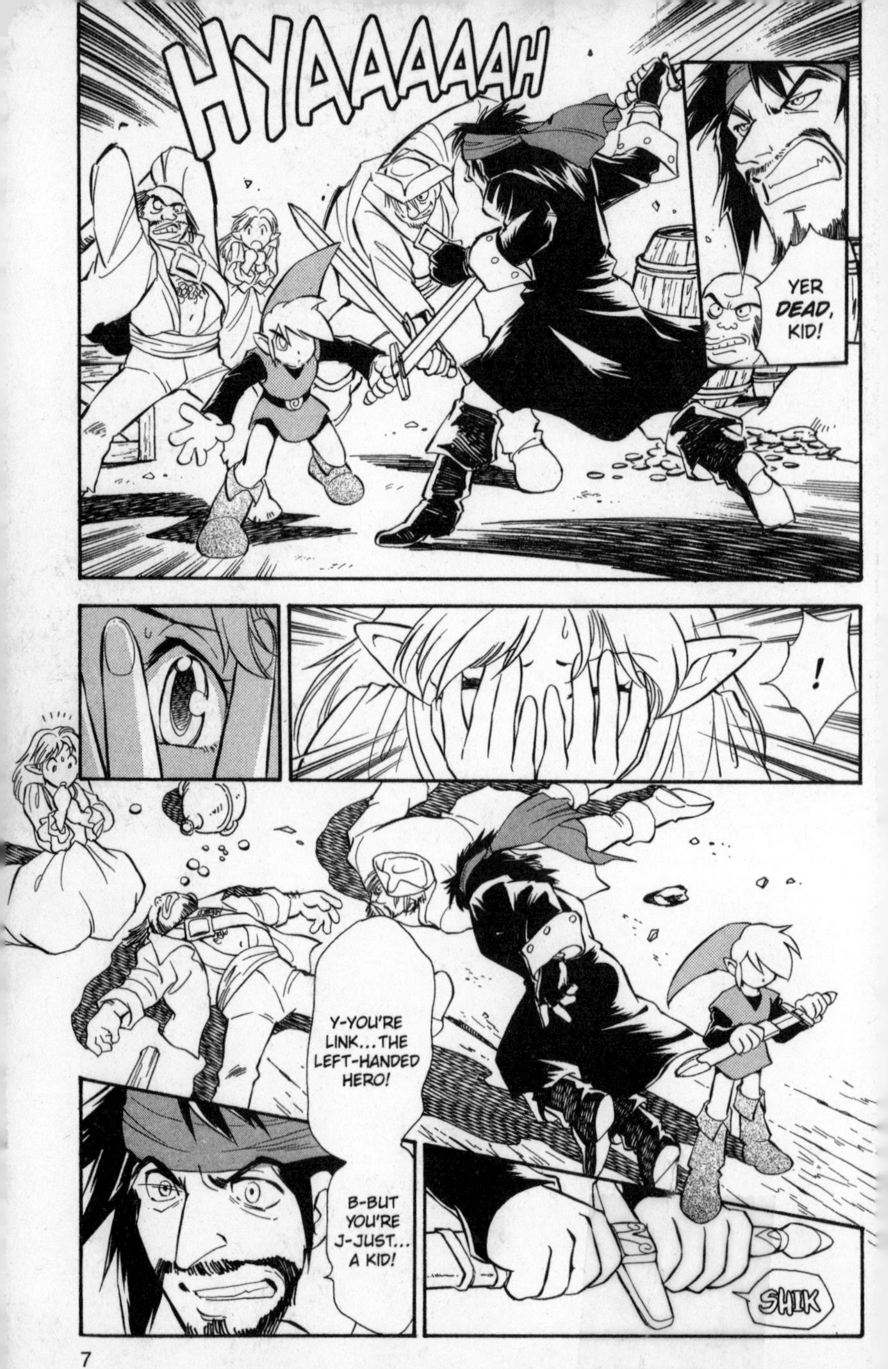
HYAAAAAH
YER DEAD, KID!
!
Y-YOU'RE LINK...THE LEFT-HANDED HERO!
SHIK
B-BUT YOU'RE J-JUST... A KID!

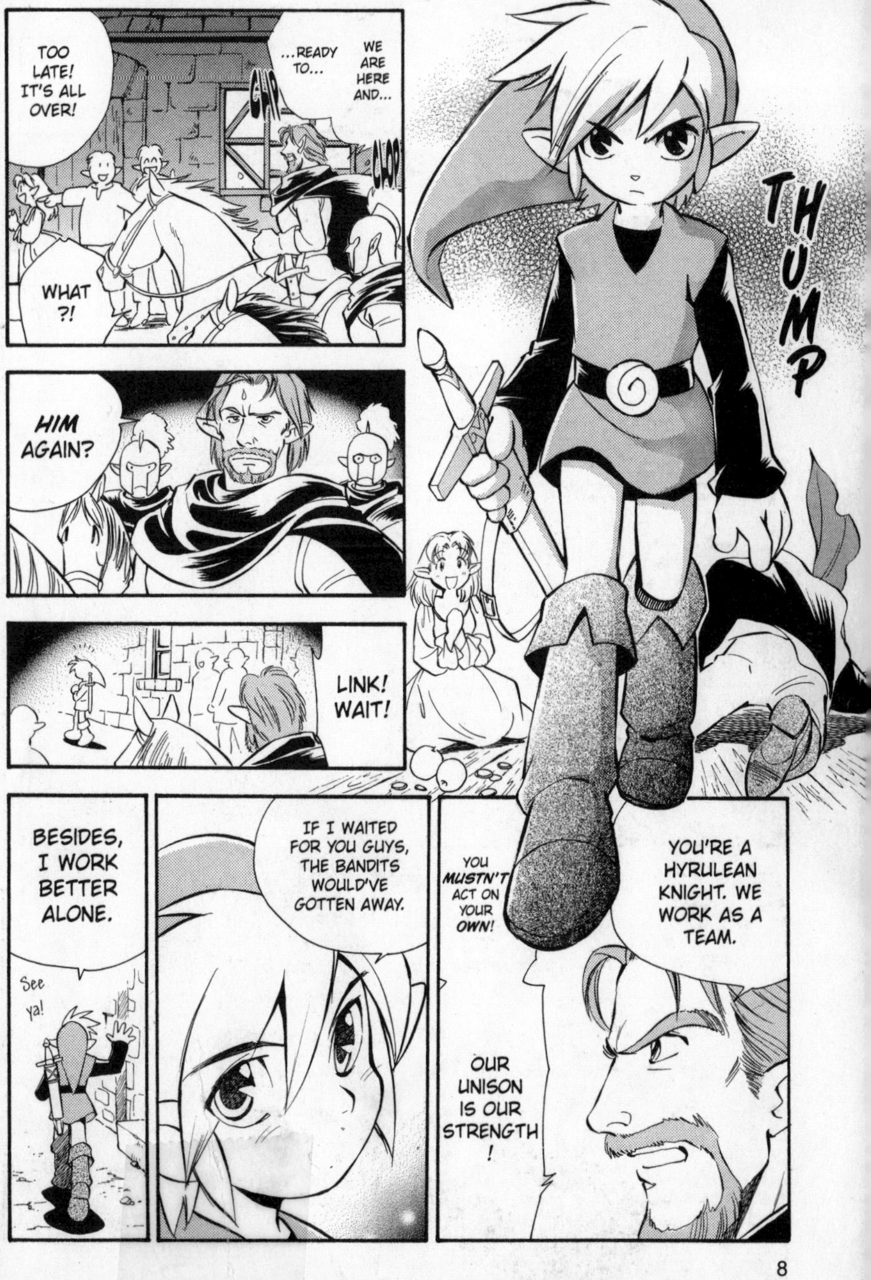
THUMP
WE ARE HERE AND...
...READY TO...
CLOP
CLOP
TOO LATE! IT'S ALL OVER!
WHAT ?!
HIM AGAIN?
LINK! WAIT!
YOU'RE A HYRULEAN KNIGHT. WE WORK AS A TEAM.
YOU MUSTN'T ACT ON YOUR OWN!
OUR UNISON IS OUR STRENGTH!
IF I WAITED FOR YOU GUYS, THE BANDITS WOULD'VE GOTTEN AWAY.
BESIDES, I WORK BETTER ALONE.
See ya!

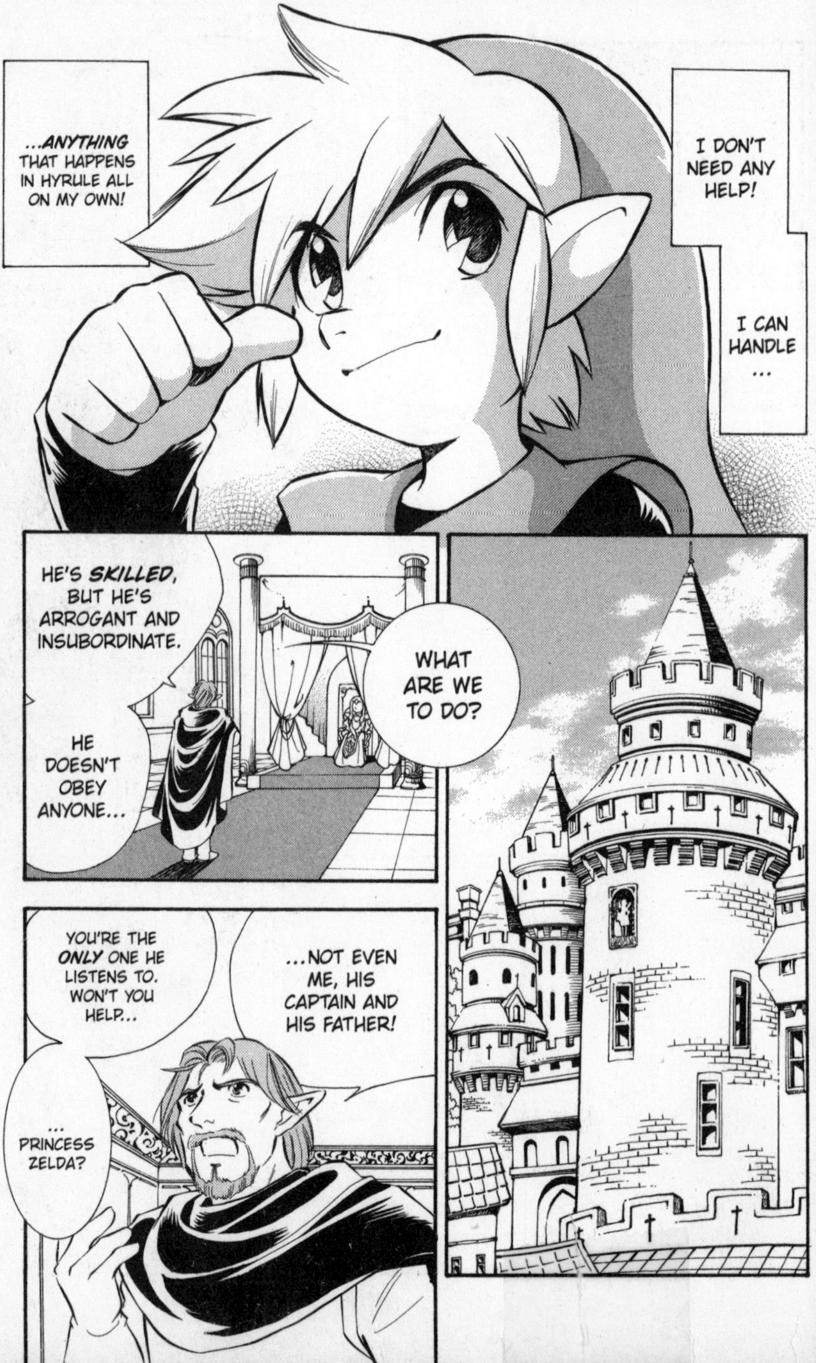
I DON'T NEED ANY HELP!
I CAN HANDLE ...
...ANYTHING THAT HAPPENS IN HYRULE ALL ON MY OWN!
WHAT ARE WE TO DO?
HE'S SKILLED, BUT HE'S ARROGANT AND INSUBORDINATE.
HE DOESN'T OBEY ANYONE...
...NOT EVEN ME, HIS CAPTAIN AND HIS FATHER!
YOU'RE THE ONLY ONE HE LISTENS TO. WON'T YOU HELP...
... PRINCESS ZELDA?

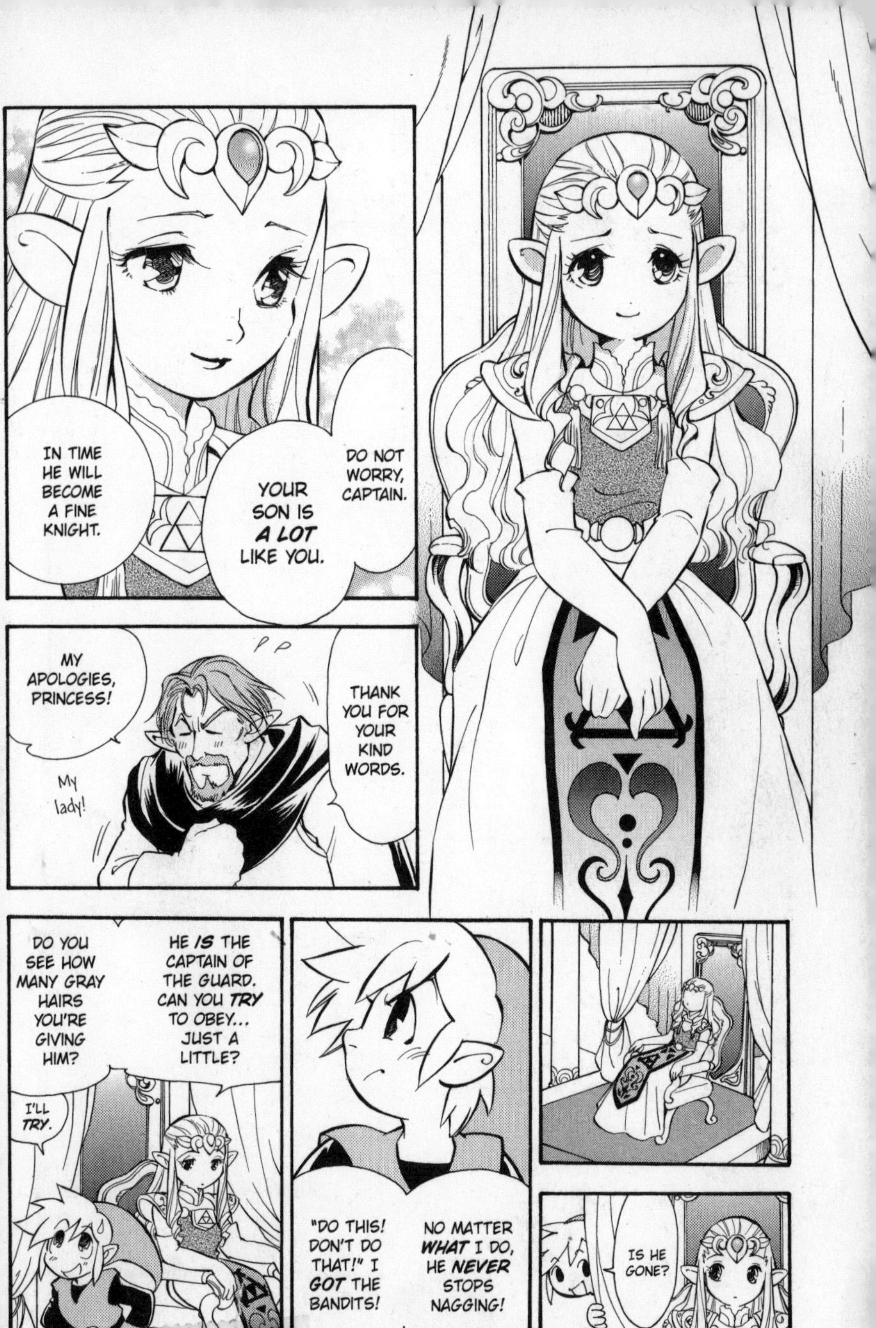
DO NOT WORRY, CAPTAIN.
YOUR SON IS *A LOT* LIKE YOU.
IN TIME HE WILL BECOME A FINE KNIGHT.
THANK YOU FOR YOUR KIND WORDS.
MY APOLOGIES, PRINCESS!
My lady!
IS HE GONE?
NO MATTER *WHAT* I DO, HE *NEVER* STOPS NAGGING!
"DO THIS! DON'T DO THAT!" I *GOT* THE BANDITS!
HE *IS* THE CAPTAIN OF THE GUARD. CAN YOU *TRY* TO OBEY... JUST A LITTLE?
DO YOU SEE HOW MANY GRAY HAIRS YOU'RE GIVING HIM?
I'LL *TRY*.

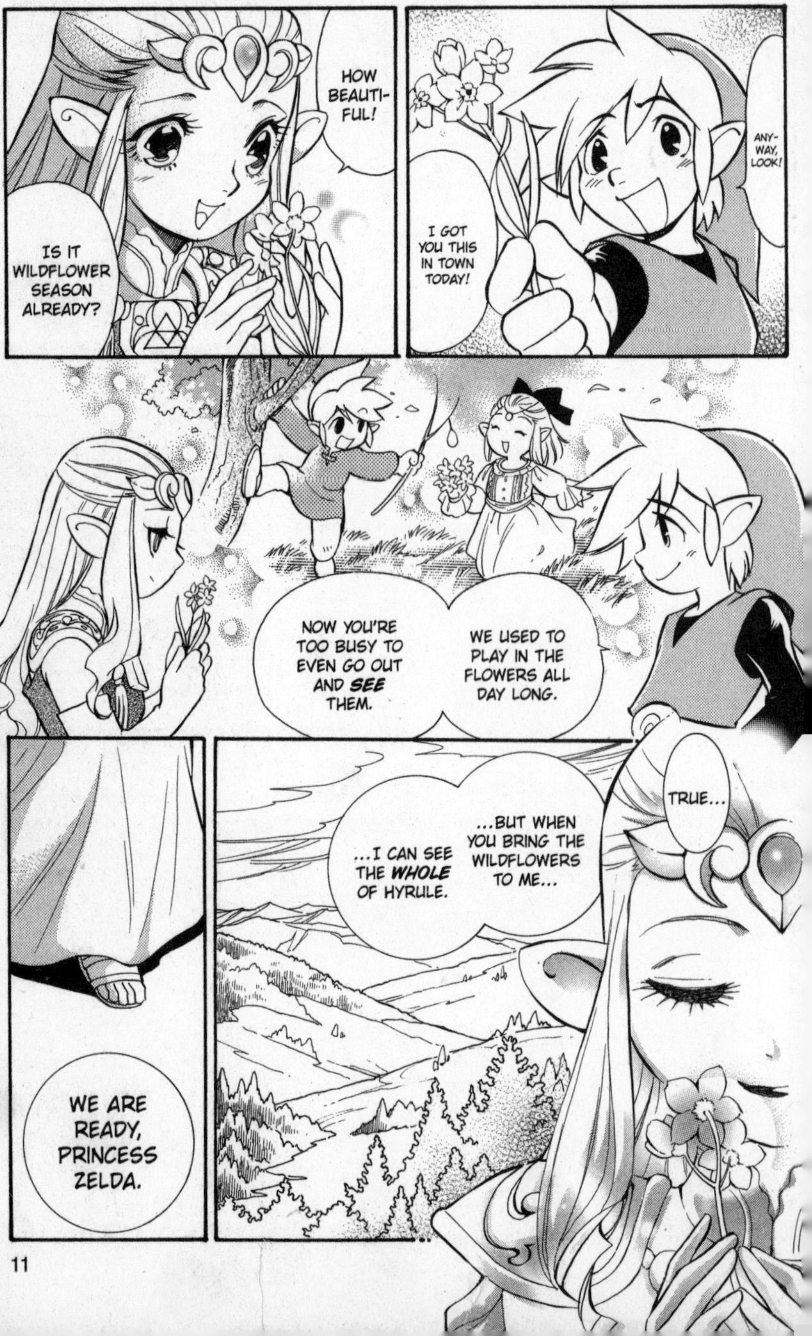
ANY-WAY, LOOK!
I GOT YOU THIS IN TOWN TODAY!
HOW BEAUTI-FUL!
IS IT WILDFLOWER SEASON ALREADY?
WE USED TO PLAY IN THE FLOWERS ALL DAY LONG.
NOW YOU'RE TOO BUSY TO EVEN GO OUT AND *SEE* THEM.
TRUE...
...BUT WHEN YOU BRING THE WILDFLOWERS TO ME...
...I CAN SEE THE *WHOLE* OF HYRULE.
WE ARE READY, PRINCESS ZELDA.

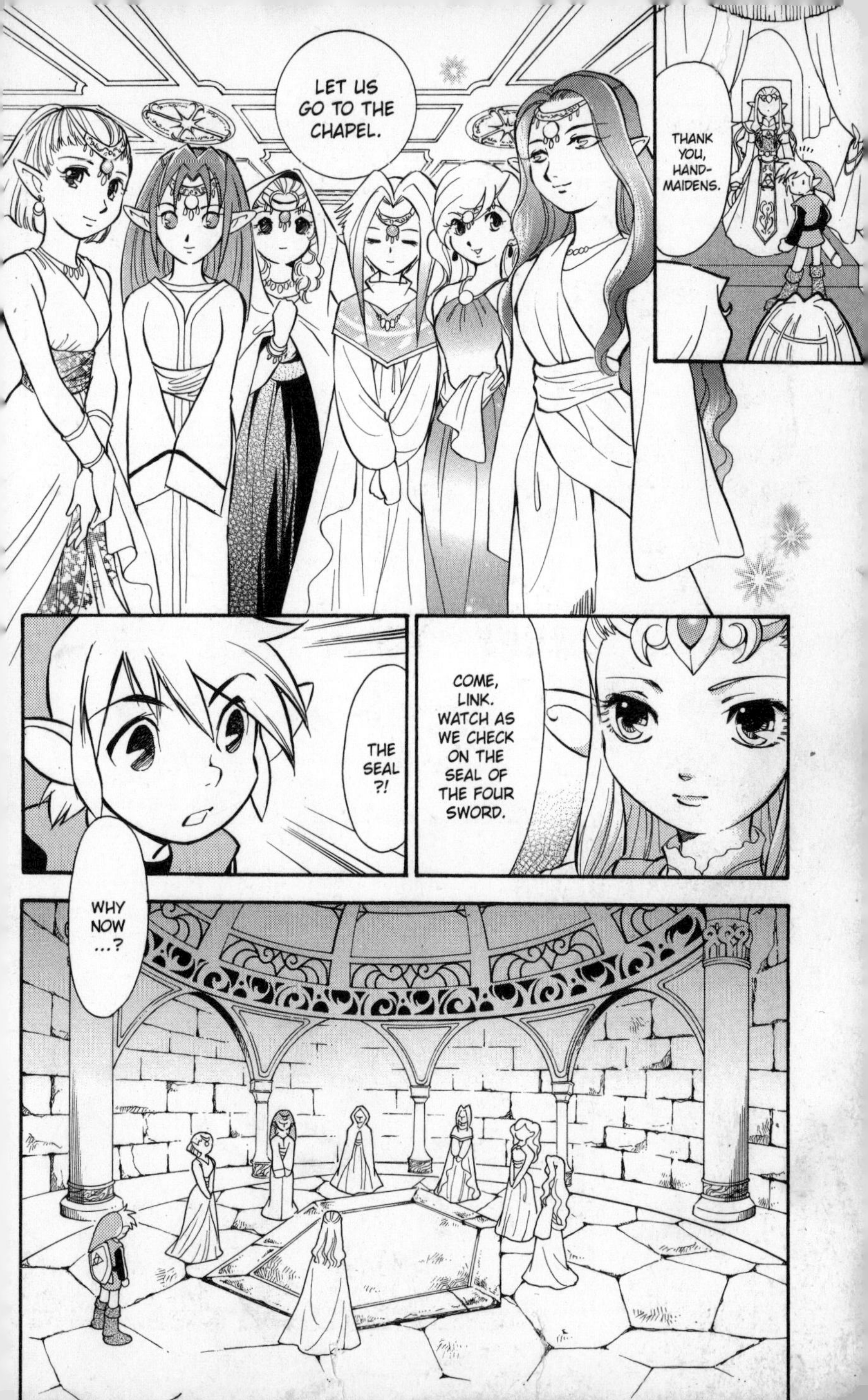
THANK YOU, HAND-MAIDENS.
LET US GO TO THE CHAPEL.
COME, LINK. WATCH AS WE CHECK ON THE SEAL OF THE FOUR SWORD.
THE SEAL ?!
WHY NOW ...?

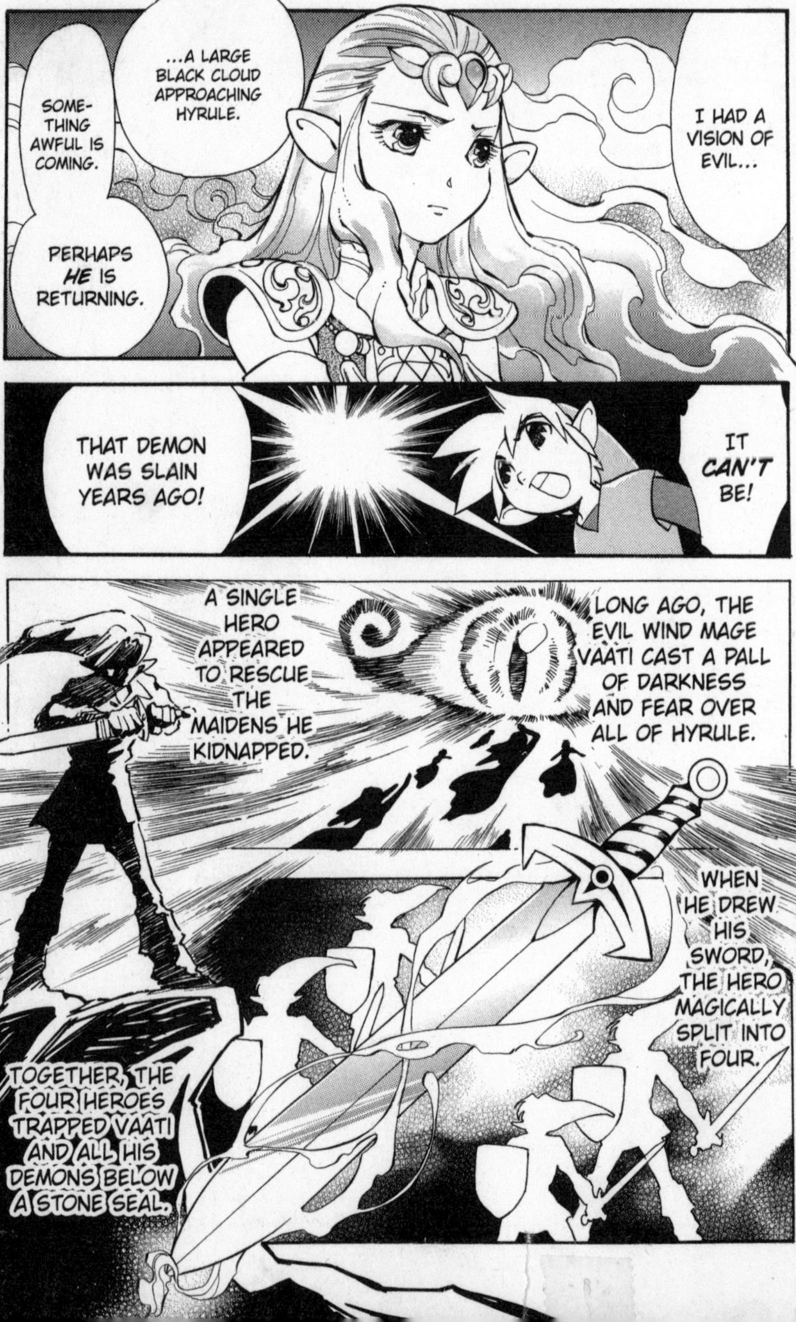
I HAD A VISION OF EVIL...
...A LARGE BLACK CLOUD APPROACHING HYRULE.
SOME-THING AWFUL IS COMING.
PERHAPS *HE* IS RETURNING.
IT *CAN'T* BE!
THAT DEMON WAS SLAIN YEARS AGO!
LONG AGO, THE EVIL WIND MAGE VAATI CAST A PALL OF DARKNESS AND FEAR OVER ALL OF HYRULE.
A SINGLE HERO APPEARED TO RESCUE THE MAIDENS HE KIDNAPPED.
WHEN HE DREW HIS SWORD, THE HERO MAGICALLY SPLIT INTO FOUR.
TOGETHER, THE FOUR HEROES TRAPPED VAATI AND ALL HIS DEMONS BELOW A STONE SEAL.

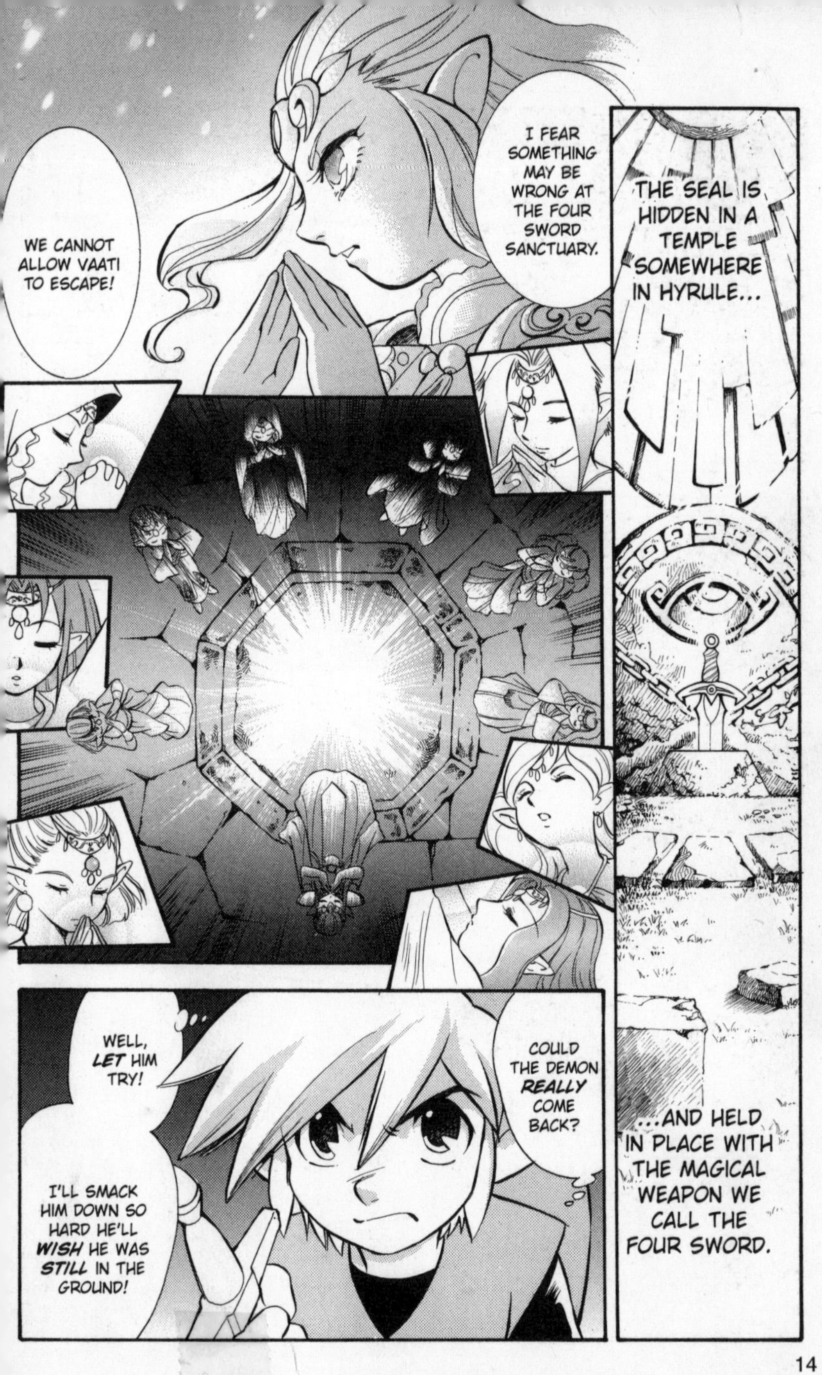
I FEAR SOMETHING MAY BE WRONG AT THE FOUR SWORD SANCTUARY.
WE CANNOT ALLOW VAATI TO ESCAPE!
THE SEAL IS HIDDEN IN A TEMPLE SOMEWHERE IN HYRULE...
...AND HELD IN PLACE WITH THE MAGICAL WEAPON WE CALL THE FOUR SWORD.
COULD THE DEMON REALLY COME BACK?
WELL, LET HIM TRY!
I'LL SMACK HIM DOWN SO HARD HE'LL WISH HE WAS STILL IN THE GROUND!

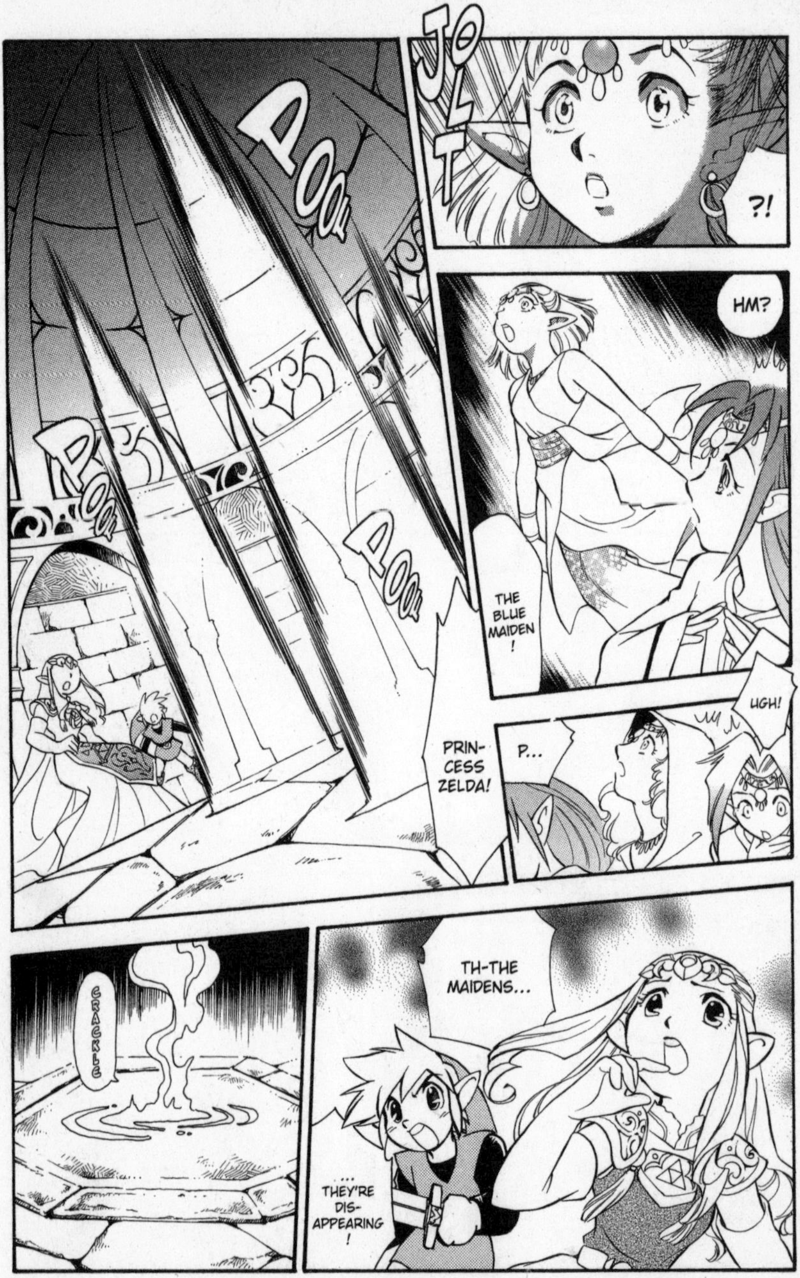
JOLT
?!
HM?
THE BLUE MAIDEN!
UGH!
P...
PRIN-CESS ZELDA!
DOOM
DOOM
DOOM
TH-THE MAIDENS...
...THEY'RE DIS-APPEARING!
CRACKLE

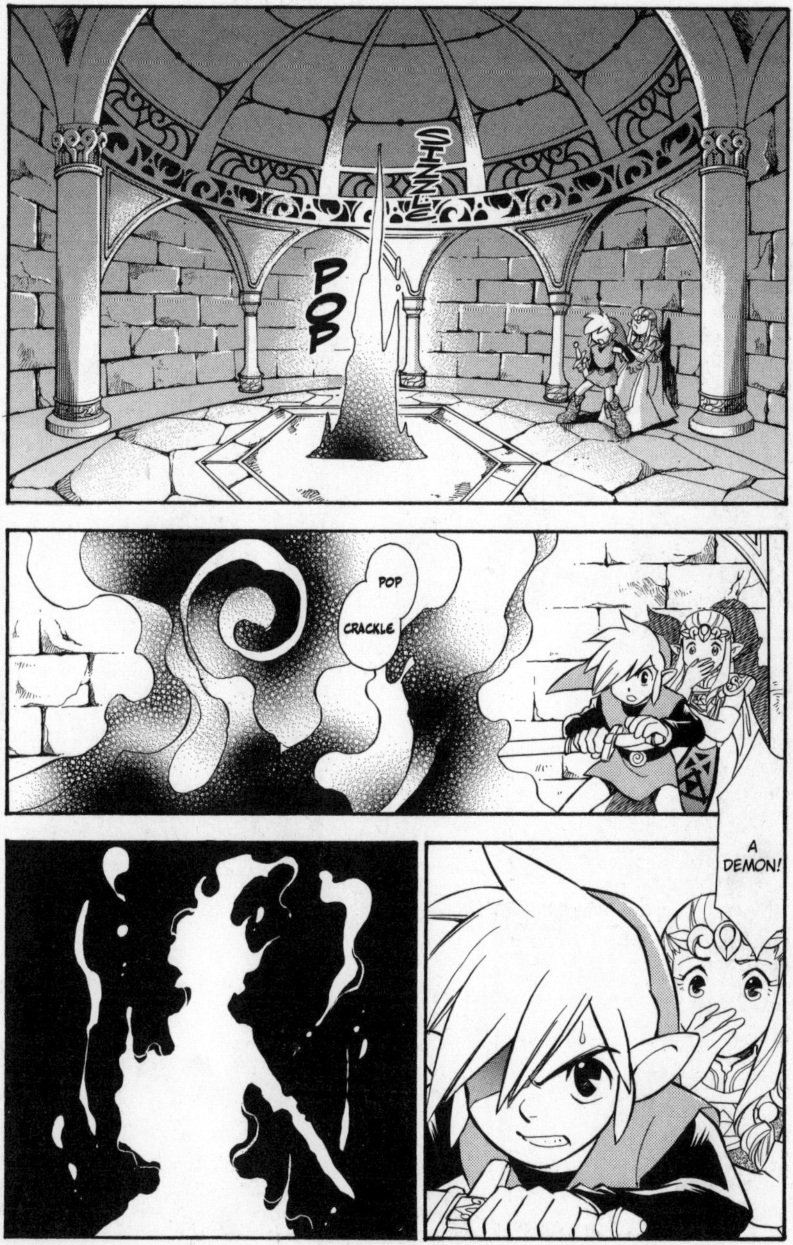
SHZZLE
POP
POP
CRACKLE
A DEMON!

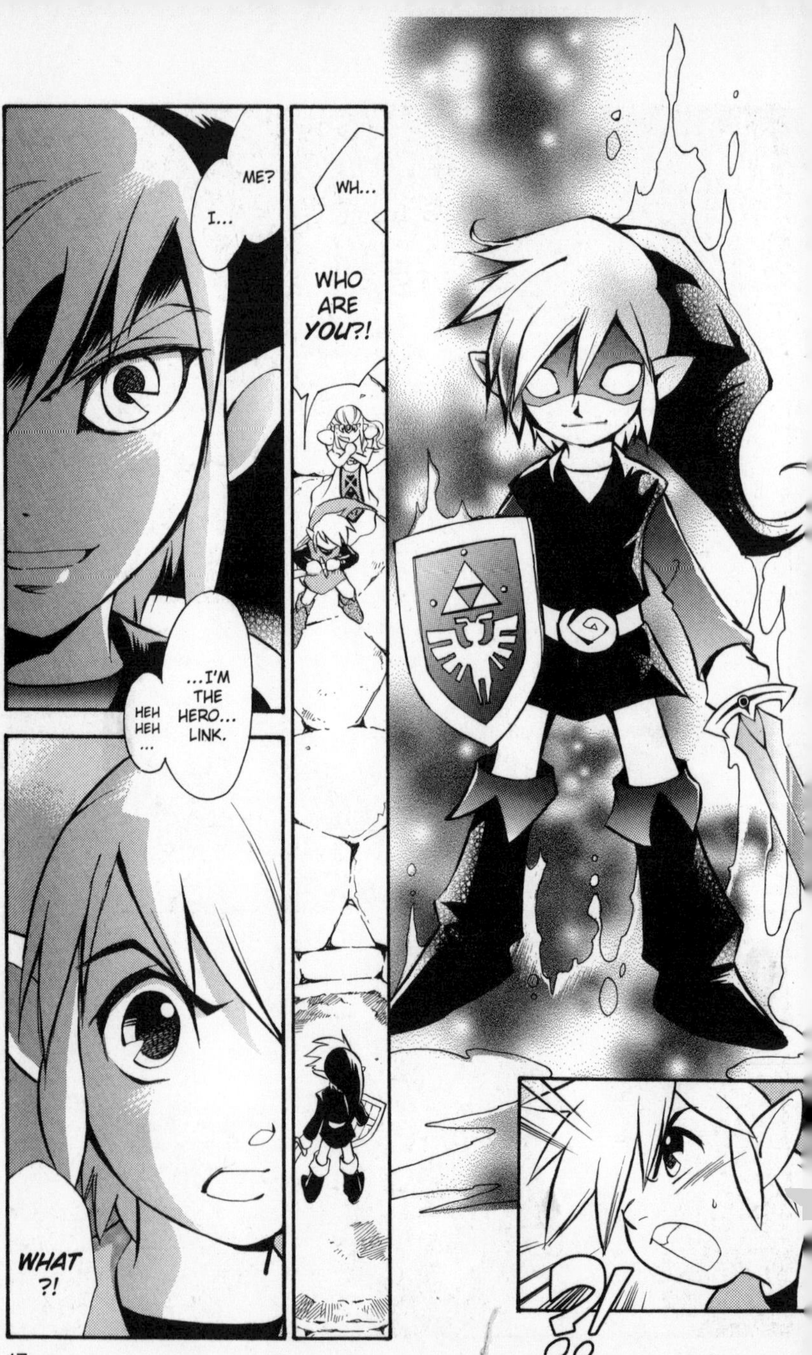
?!
WH...
WHO ARE YOU?!
I... ME?
...I'M THE HERO... LINK.
HEH HEH ...
WHAT ?!

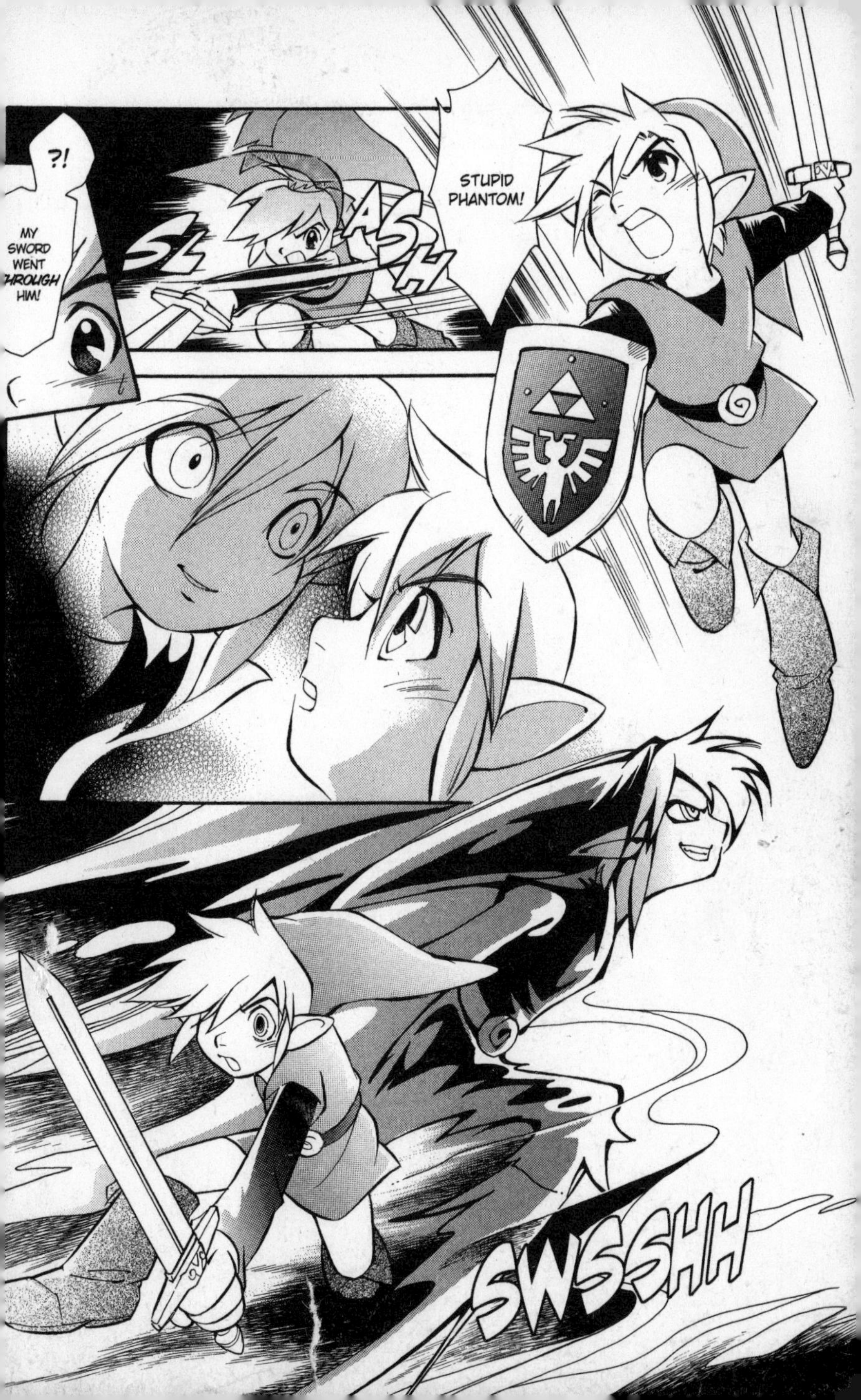
STUPID PHANTOM!
SLASH
?!
MY SWORD WENT THROUGH HIM!
SWSSHH

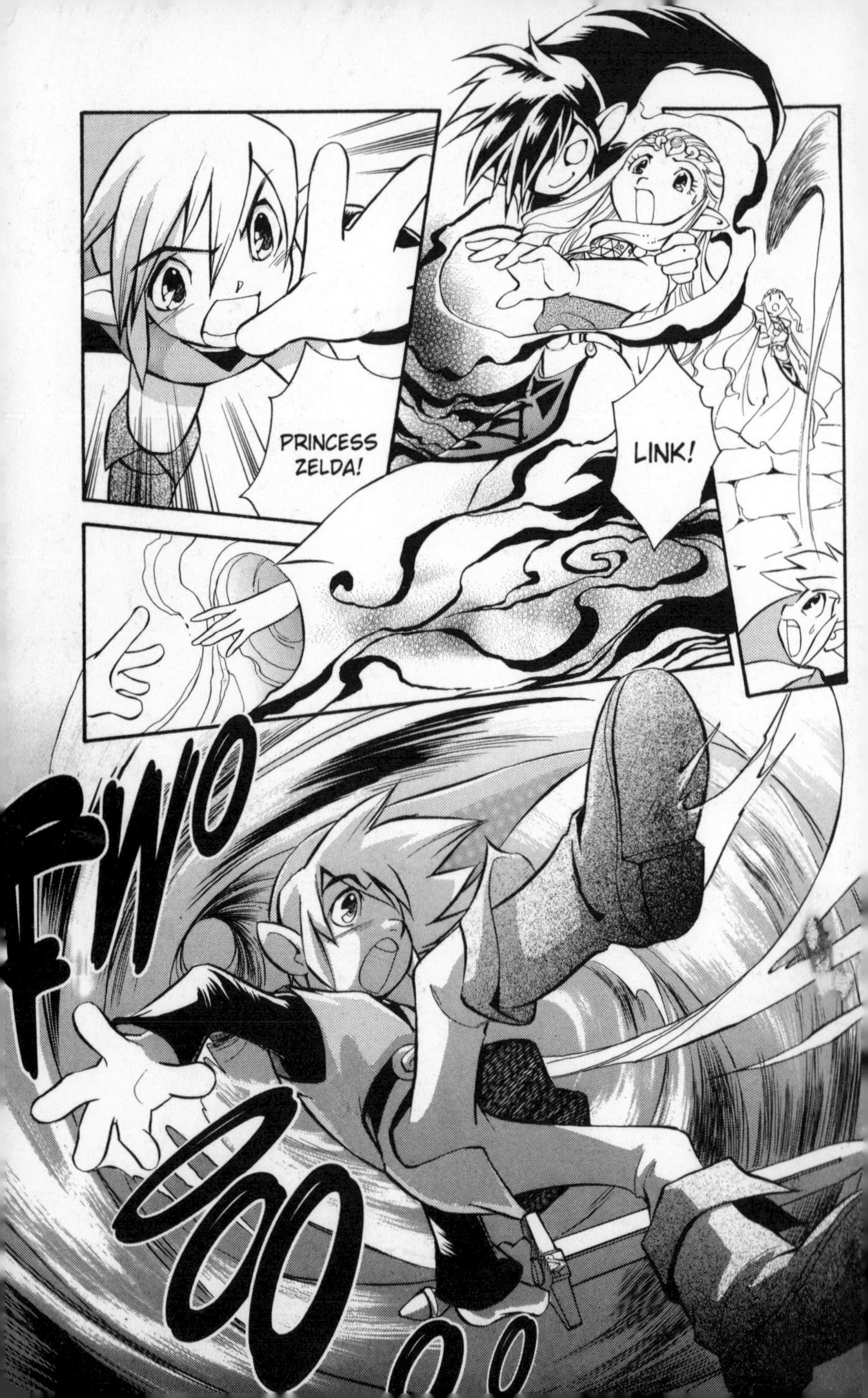
LINK!
PRINCESS ZELDA!
FWOOOOOO

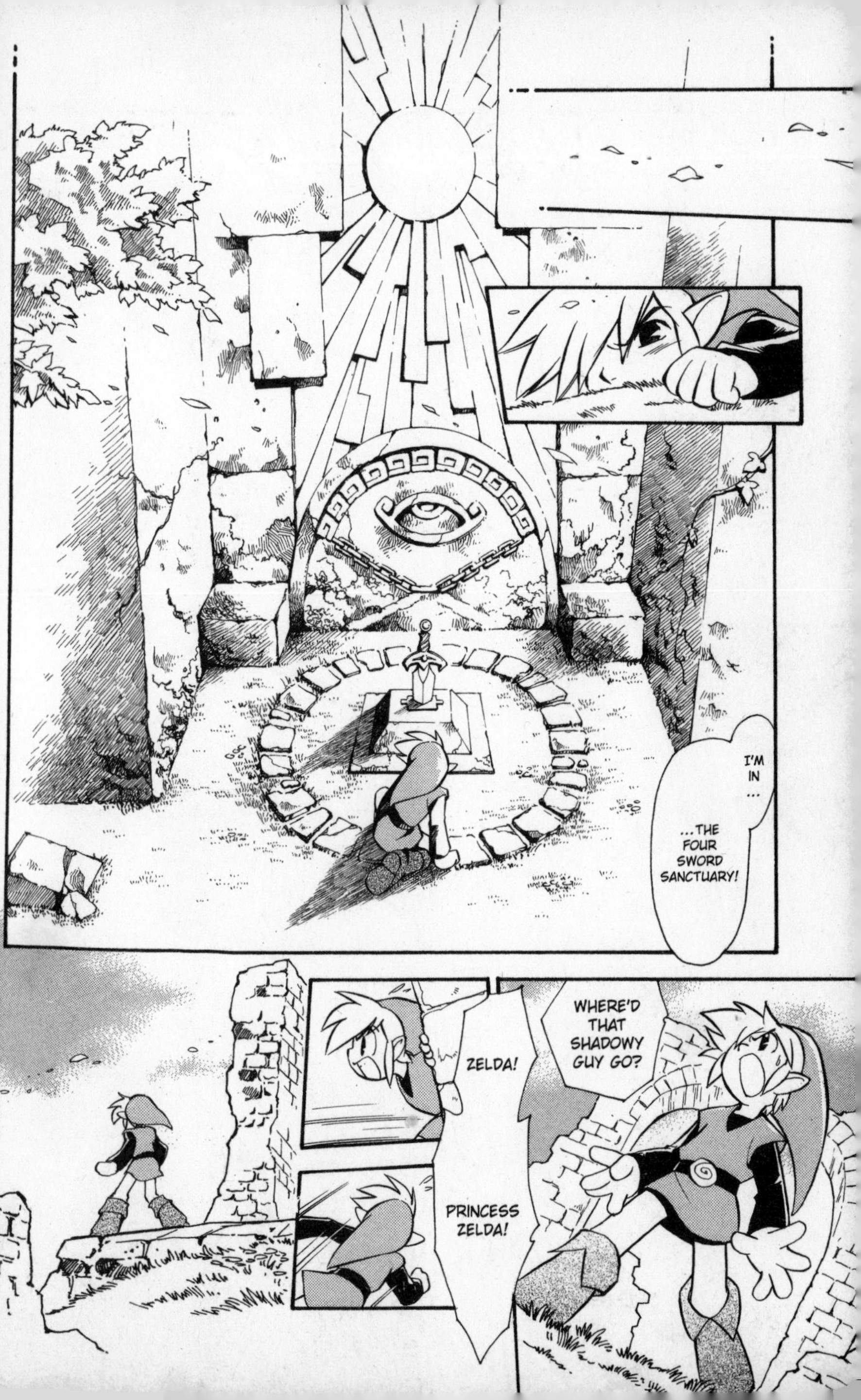
I'M IN ...
...THE FOUR SWORD SANCTUARY!
WHERE'D THAT SHADOWY GUY GO?
ZELDA!
PRINCESS ZELDA!

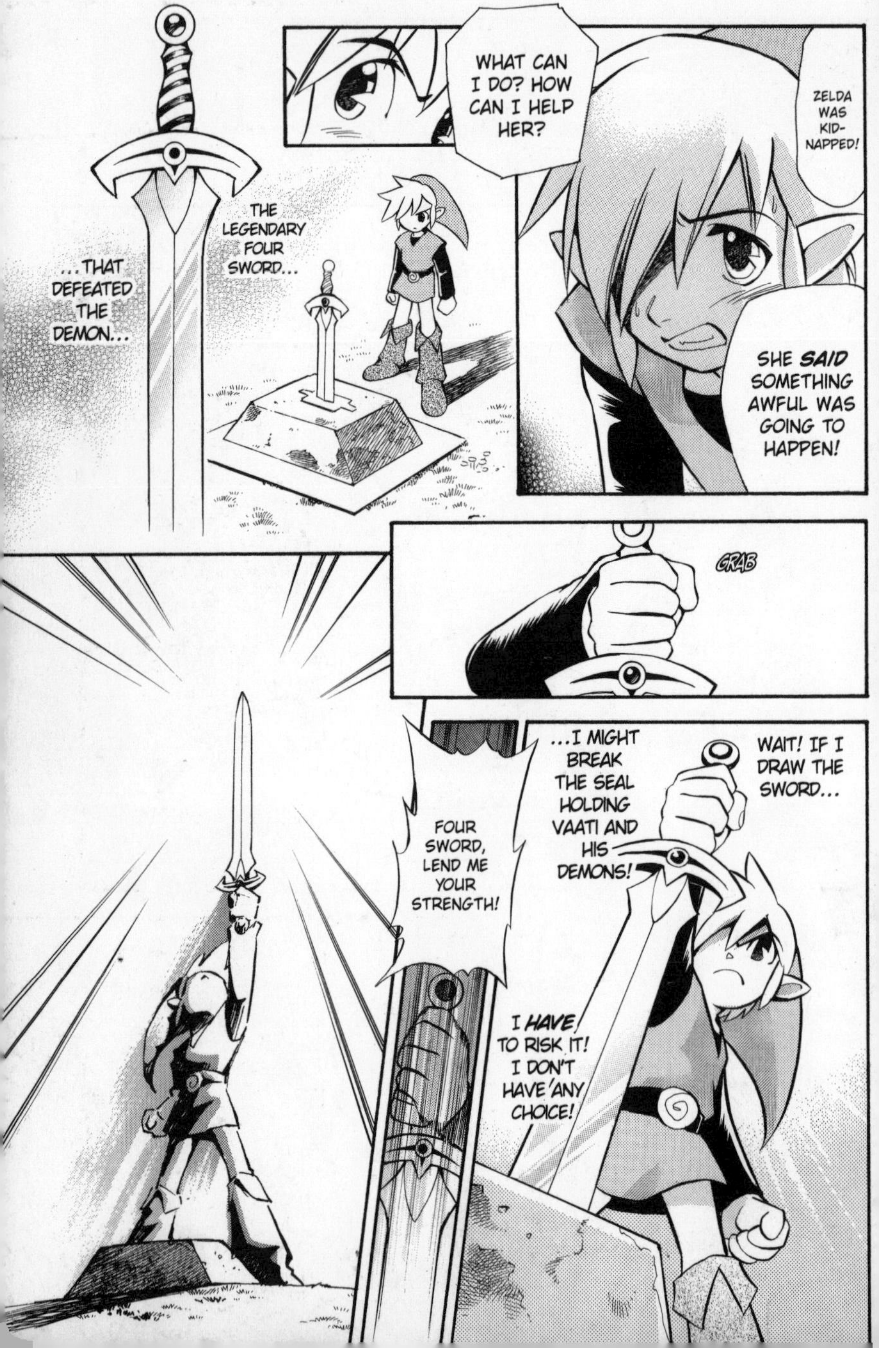
ZELDA WAS KID-NAPPED!
SHE SAID SOMETHING AWFUL WAS GOING TO HAPPEN!
WHAT CAN I DO? HOW CAN I HELP HER?
THE LEGENDARY FOUR SWORD...
...THAT DEFEATED THE DEMON...
GRAB
WAIT! IF I DRAW THE SWORD...
...I MIGHT BREAK THE SEAL HOLDING VAATI AND HIS DEMONS!
I HAVE TO RISK IT! I DON'T HAVE ANY CHOICE!
FOUR SWORD, LEND ME YOUR STRENGTH!

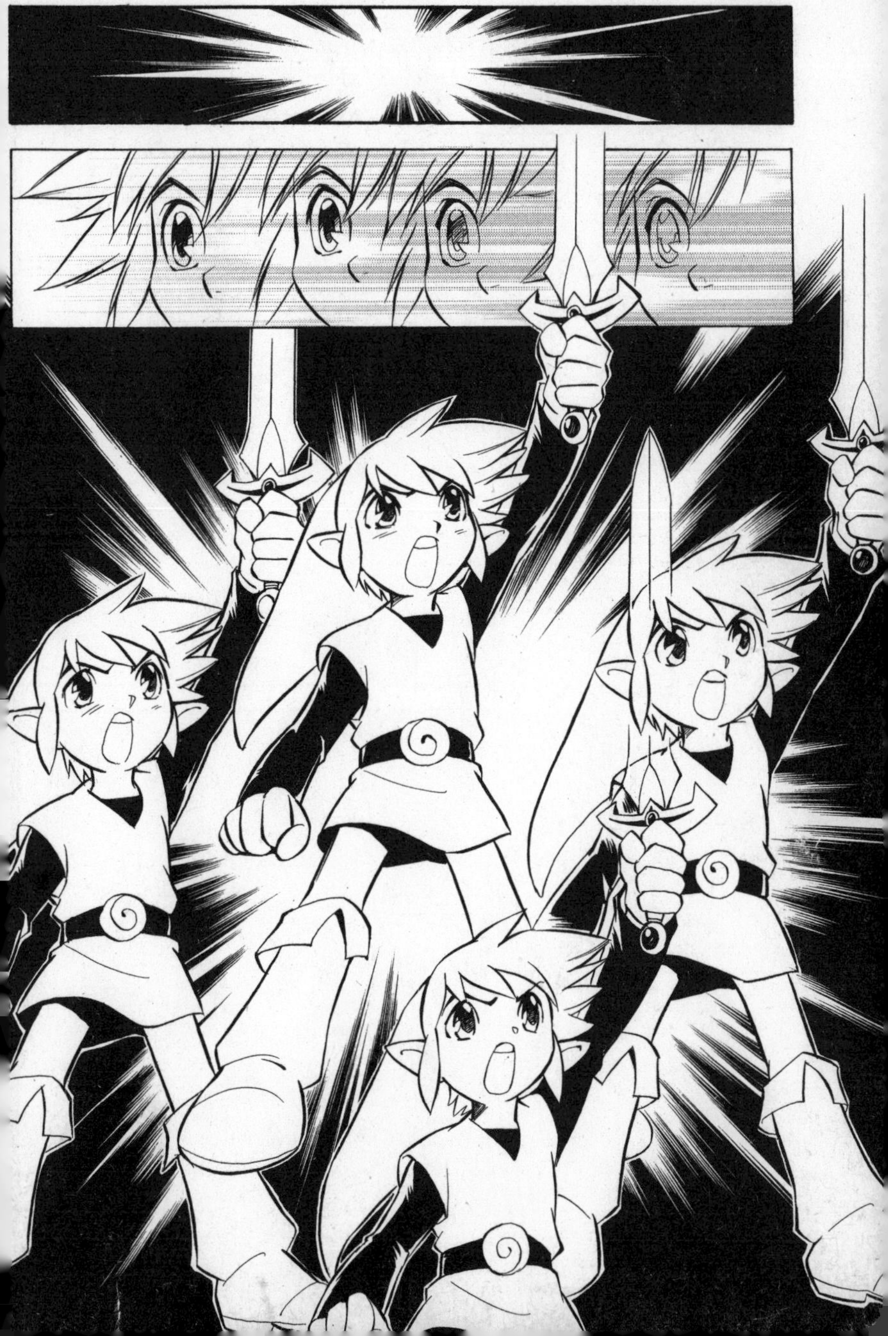

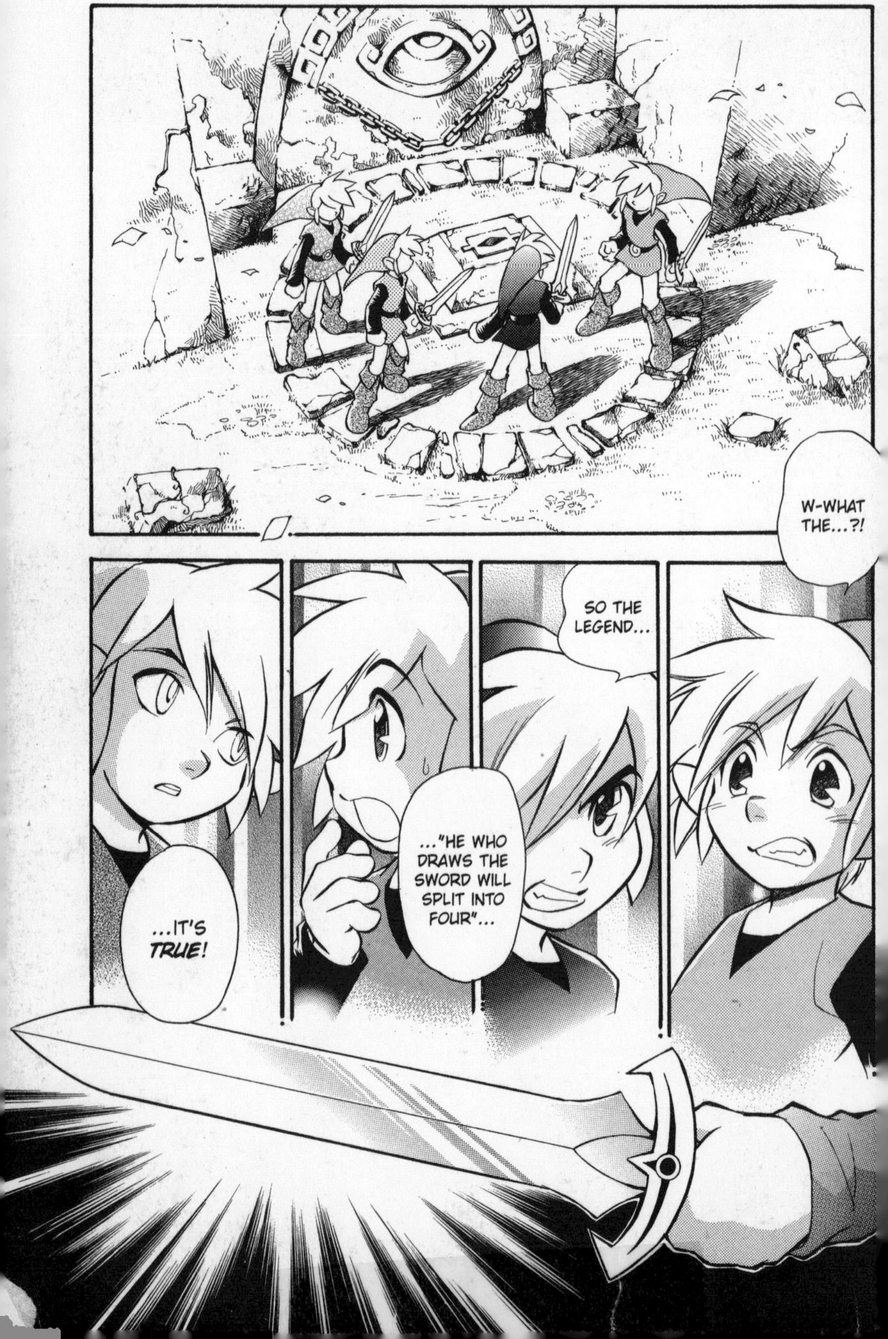
W-WHAT THE...?!
SO THE LEGEND...
..."HE WHO DRAWS THE SWORD WILL SPLIT INTO FOUR"...
...IT'S *TRUE*!

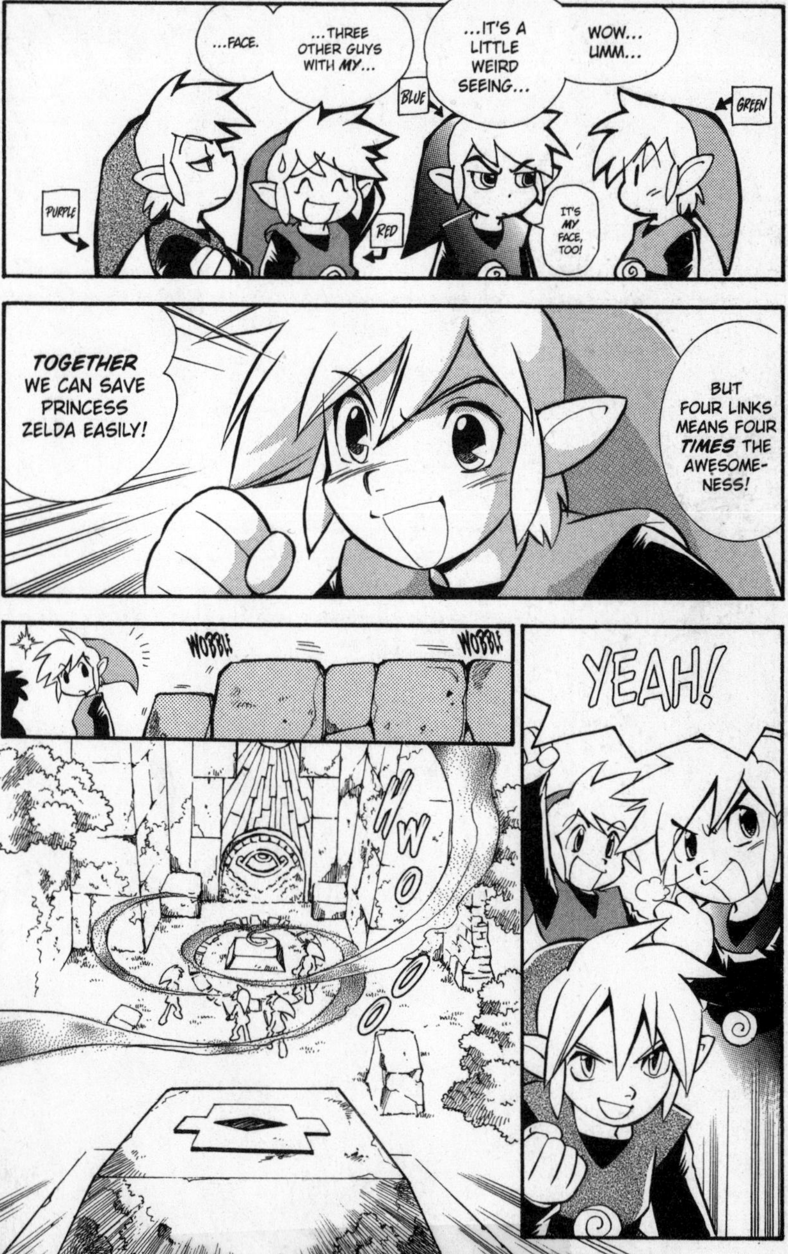
GREEN
WOW... UMM...
...IT'S A LITTLE WEIRD SEEING...
...THREE OTHER GUYS WITH *MY*...
...FACE.
BLUE
IT'S *MY* FACE, TOO!
RED
PURPLE
BUT FOUR LINKS MEANS FOUR *TIMES* THE AWESOMENESS!
TOGETHER WE CAN SAVE PRINCESS ZELDA EASILY!
YEAH!
WOBBLE
WOBBLE
HWOOO

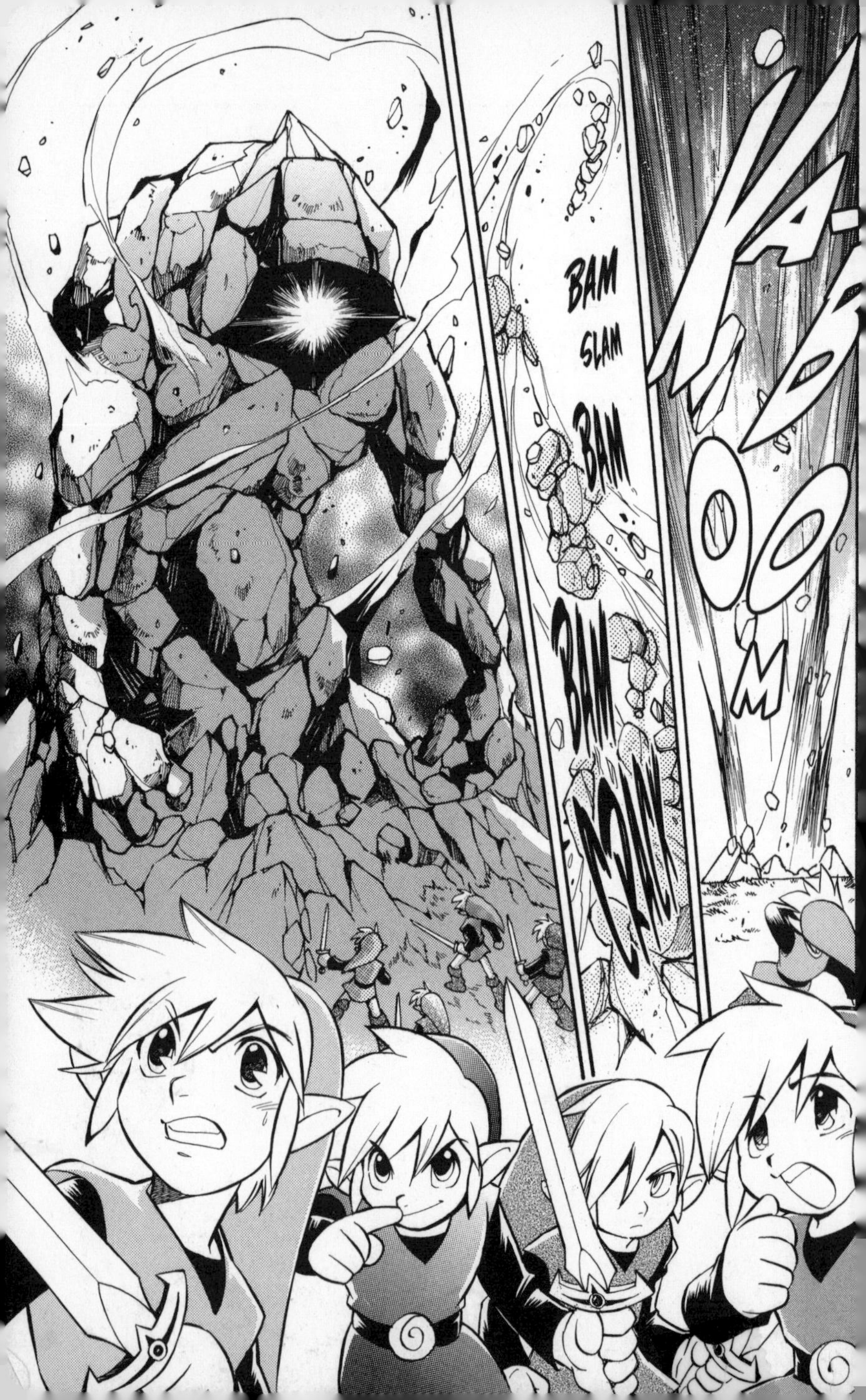
KA-BOOM
BAM
SLAM
BAM
BAM
BAM
CRACK

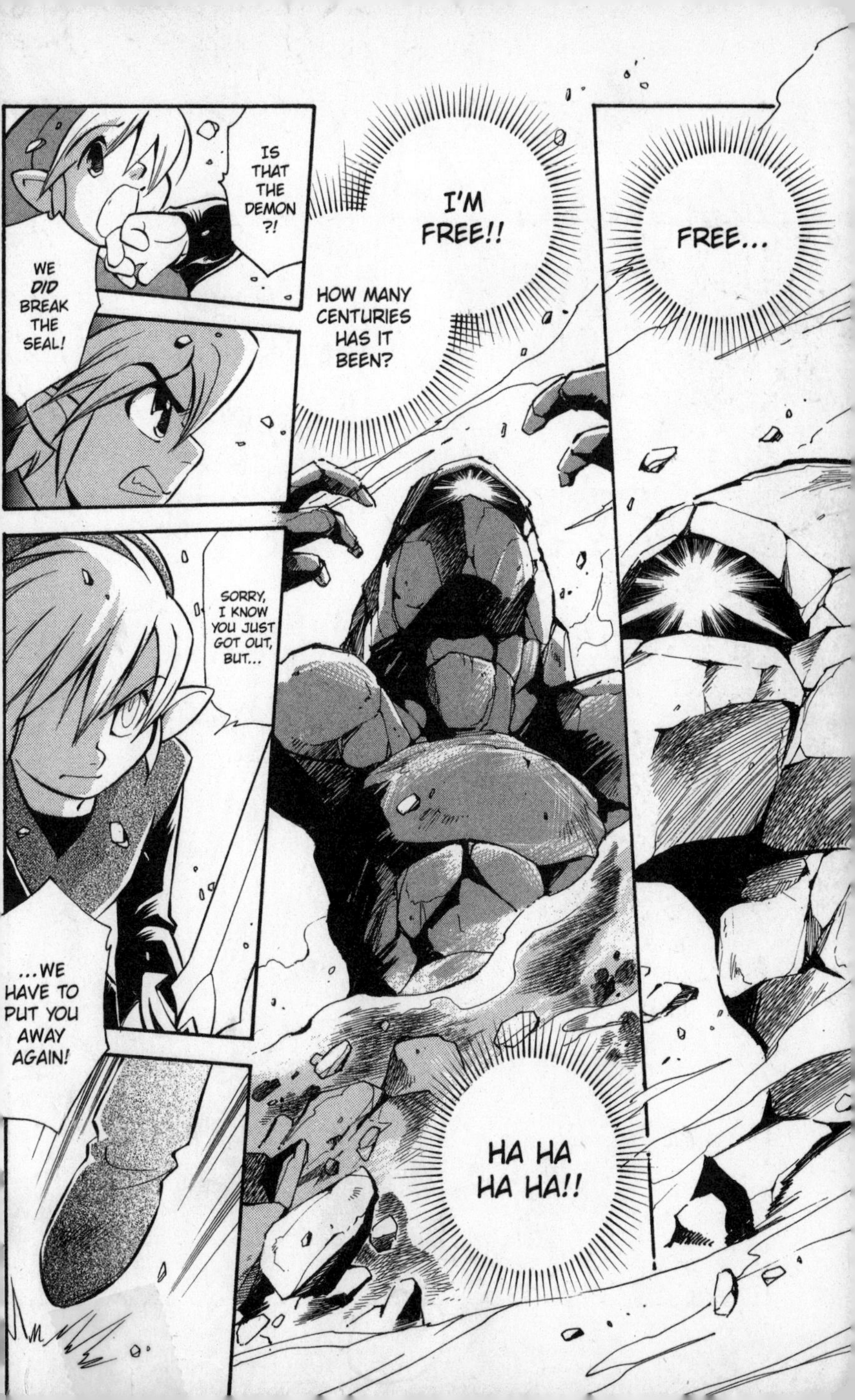
FREE...
I'M FREE!!
HOW MANY CENTURIES HAS IT BEEN?
HA HA HA HA!!
IS THAT THE DEMON?!
WE *DID* BREAK THE SEAL!
SORRY, I KNOW YOU JUST GOT OUT, BUT...
...WE HAVE TO PUT YOU AWAY AGAIN!

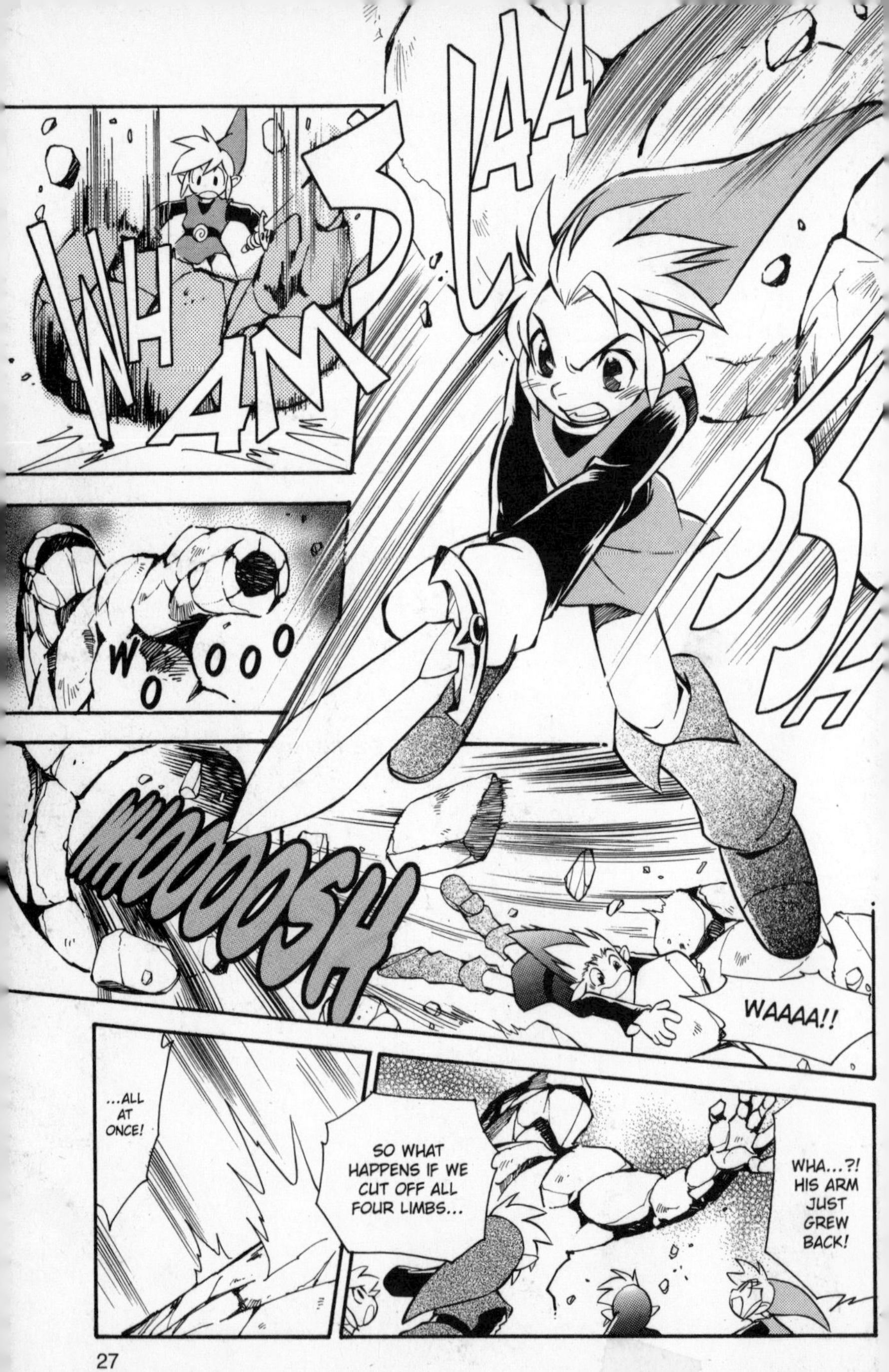
WHAM
WOOOO
WHOOOOSH
WAAAA!!
WHA...?! HIS ARM JUST GREW BACK!
SO WHAT HAPPENS IF WE CUT OFF ALL FOUR LIMBS...
...ALL AT ONCE!

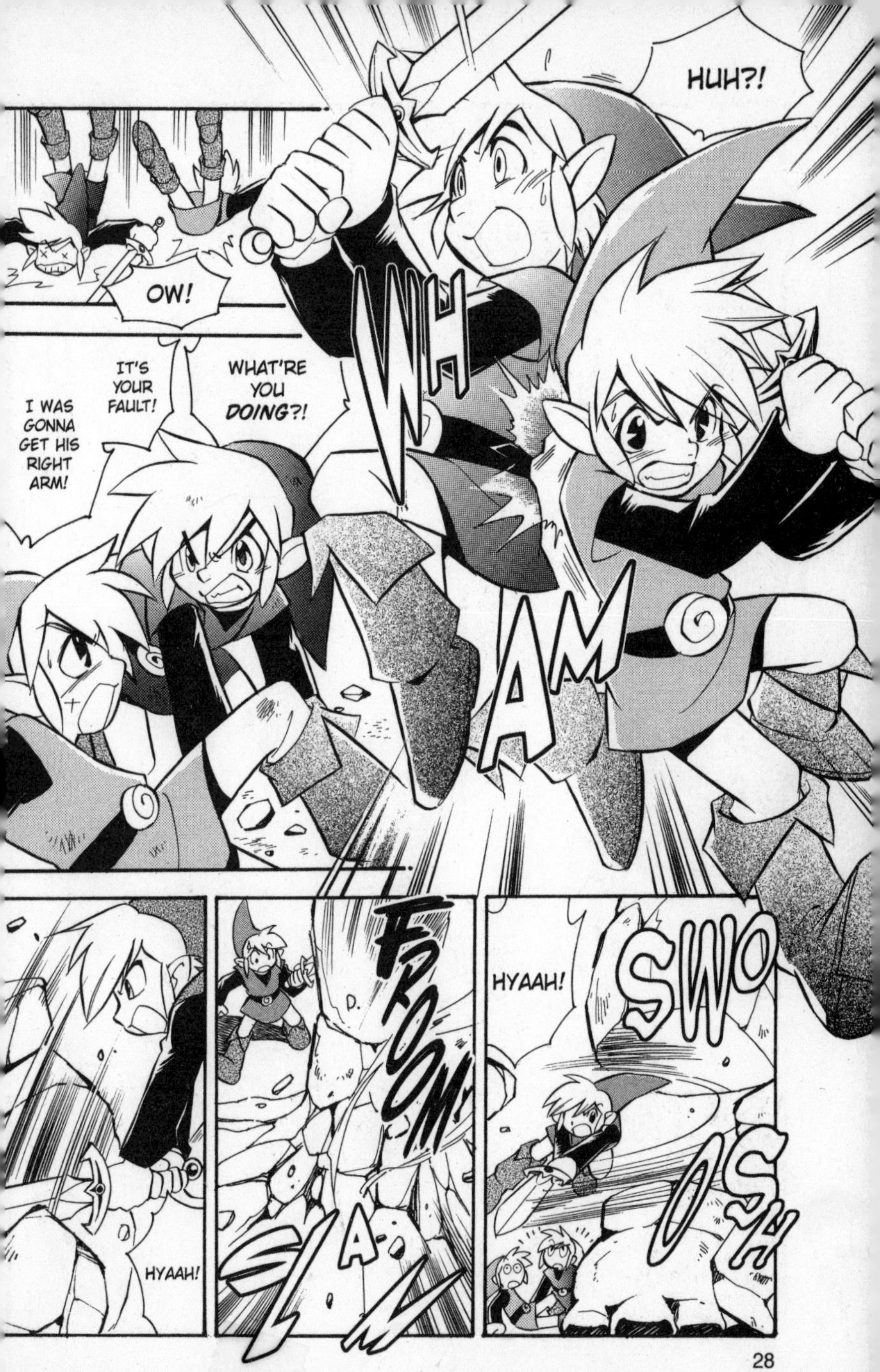
HUH?!
WHAM
OW!
WHAT'RE YOU DOING?!
IT'S YOUR FAULT!
I WAS GONNA GET HIS RIGHT ARM!
HYAAH!
SWOOSH
FROOM!
HYAAH!

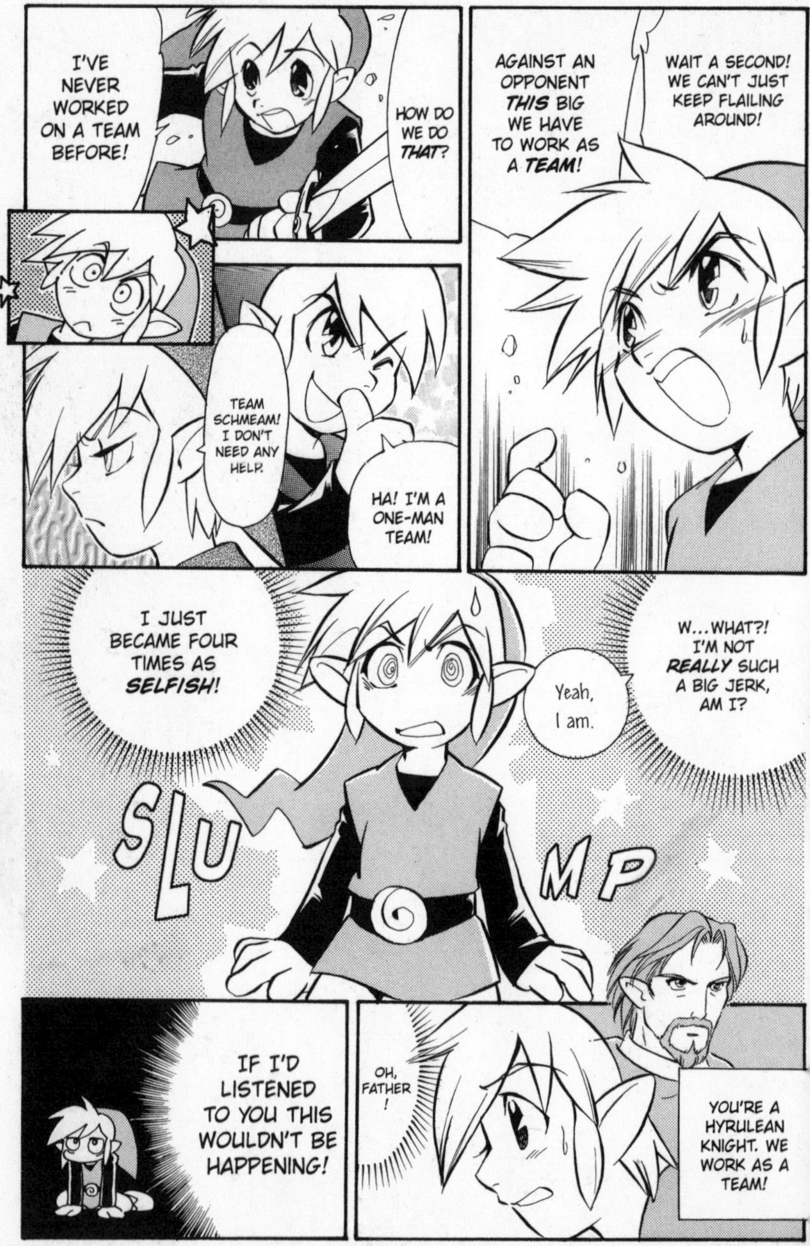
WAIT A SECOND! WE CAN'T JUST KEEP FLAILING AROUND!
AGAINST AN OPPONENT THIS BIG WE HAVE TO WORK AS A TEAM!
HOW DO WE DO THAT?
I'VE NEVER WORKED ON A TEAM BEFORE!
TEAM SCHMEAM! I DON'T NEED ANY HELP.
HA! I'M A ONE-MAN TEAM!
W...WHAT?! I'M NOT REALLY SUCH A BIG JERK, AM I?
Yeah, I am.
I JUST BECAME FOUR TIMES AS SELFISH!
SLUMP
YOU'RE A HYRULEAN KNIGHT. WE WORK AS A TEAM!
OH, FATHER!
IF I'D LISTENED TO YOU THIS WOULDN'T BE HAPPENING!

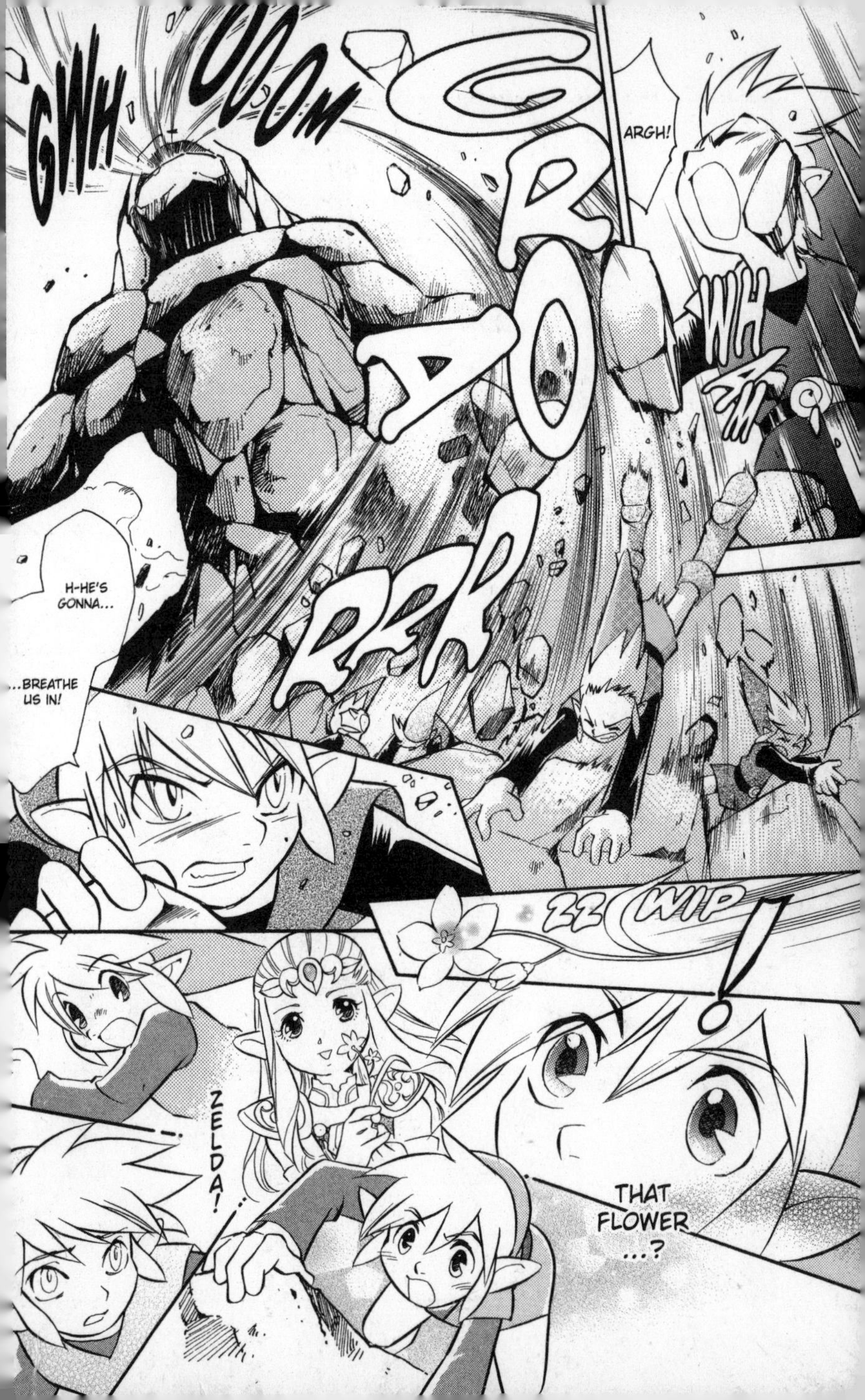
ARGH!
WHAM
H-HE'S GONNA...
...BREATHE US IN!
ZZWIP
!
THAT FLOWER ...?
ZELDA!

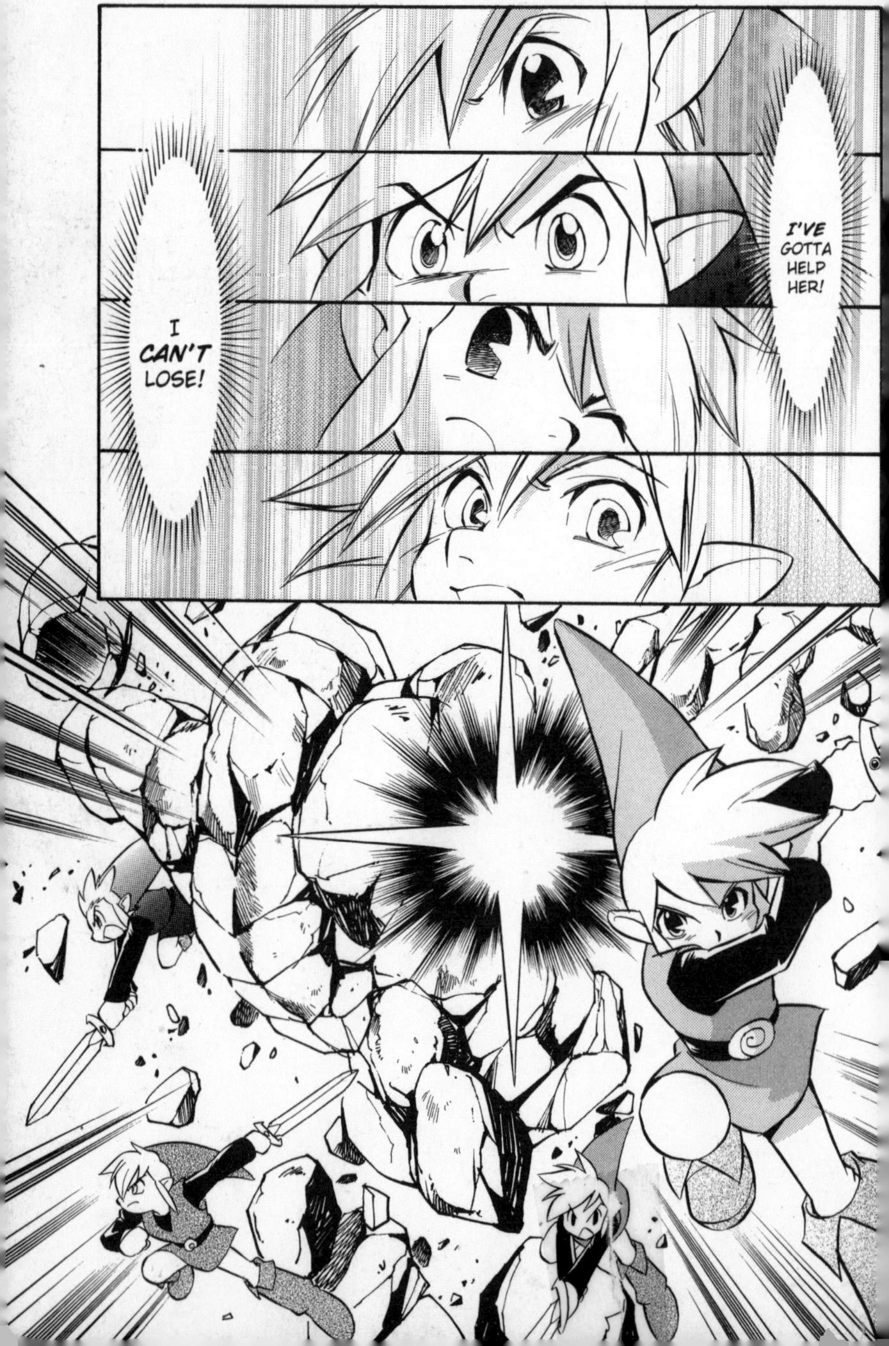
I'VE GOTTA HELP HER!
I CAN'T LOSE!

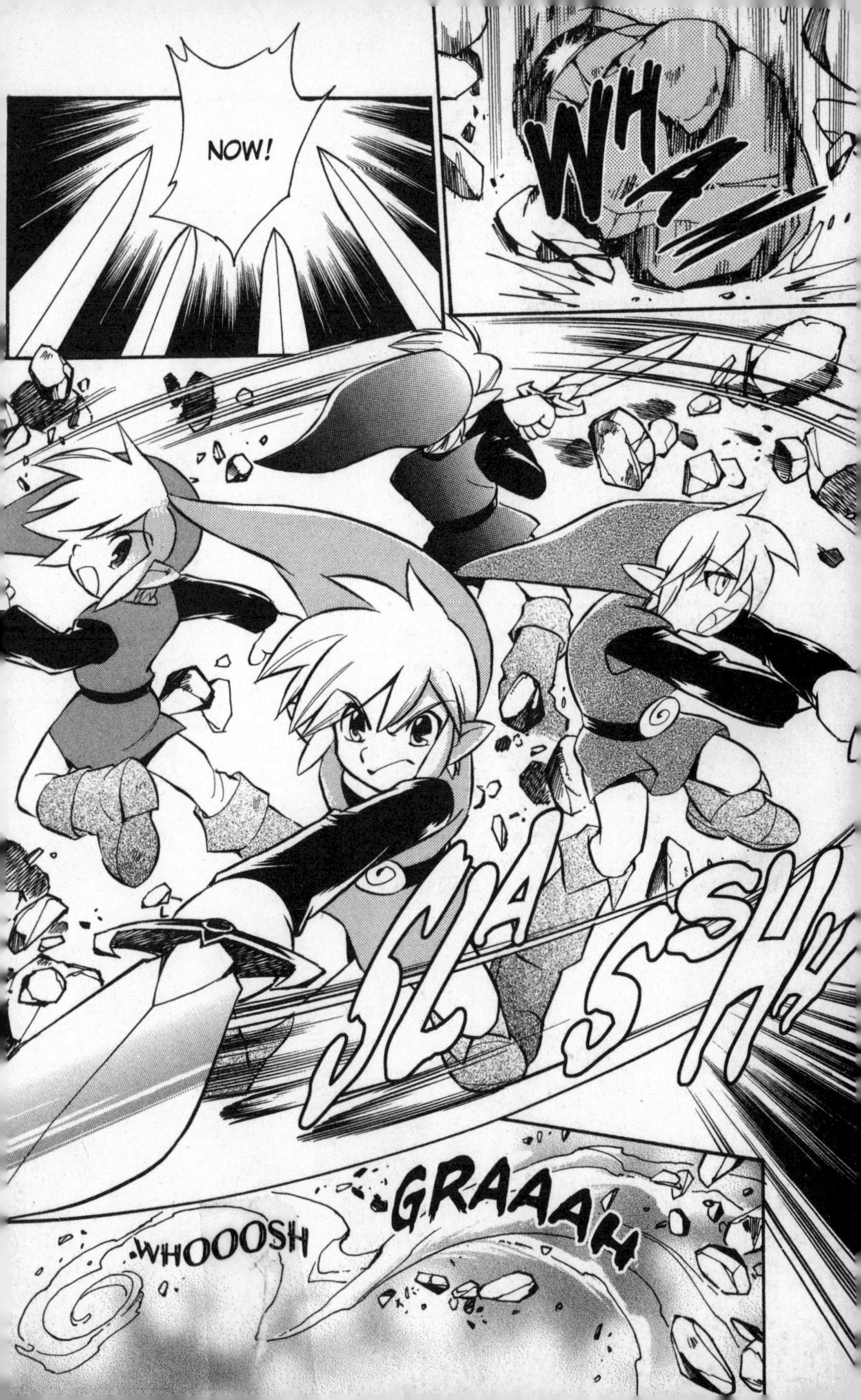
WHA
NOW!
SLASH
GRAAAH
WHOOOSH

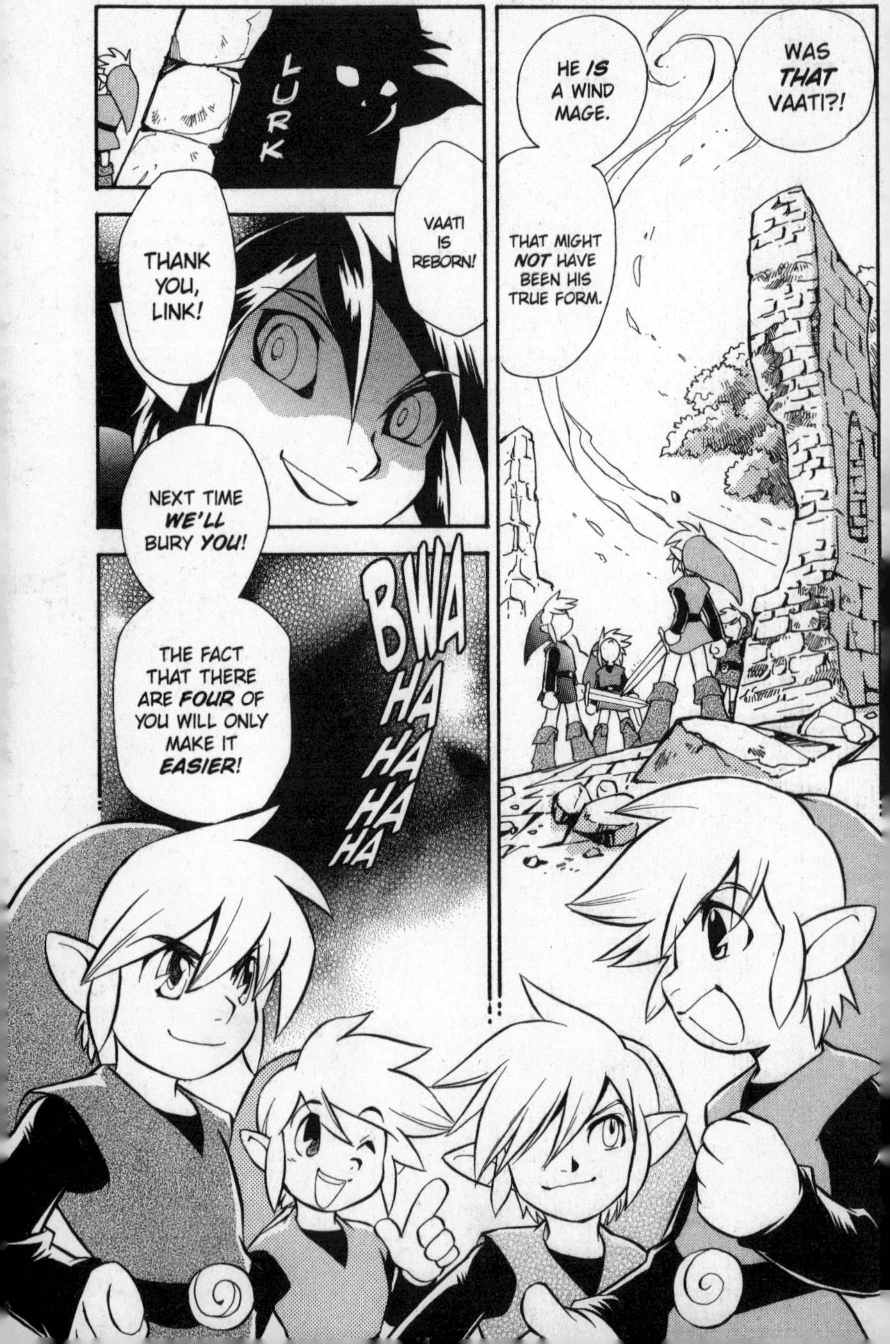
WAS *THAT* VAATI?!
HE *IS* A WIND MAGE.
THAT MIGHT *NOT* HAVE BEEN HIS TRUE FORM.
LURK
VAATI IS REBORN!
THANK YOU, LINK!
NEXT TIME *WE'LL* BURY *YOU*!
THE FACT THAT THERE ARE *FOUR* OF YOU WILL ONLY MAKE IT *EASIER*!
BWA HA HA HA HA HA

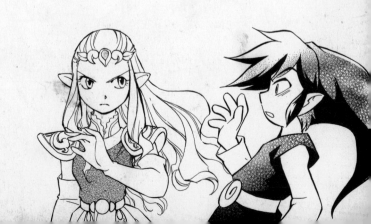

CHAPTER 2 THE FALL OF HYRULE CASTLE

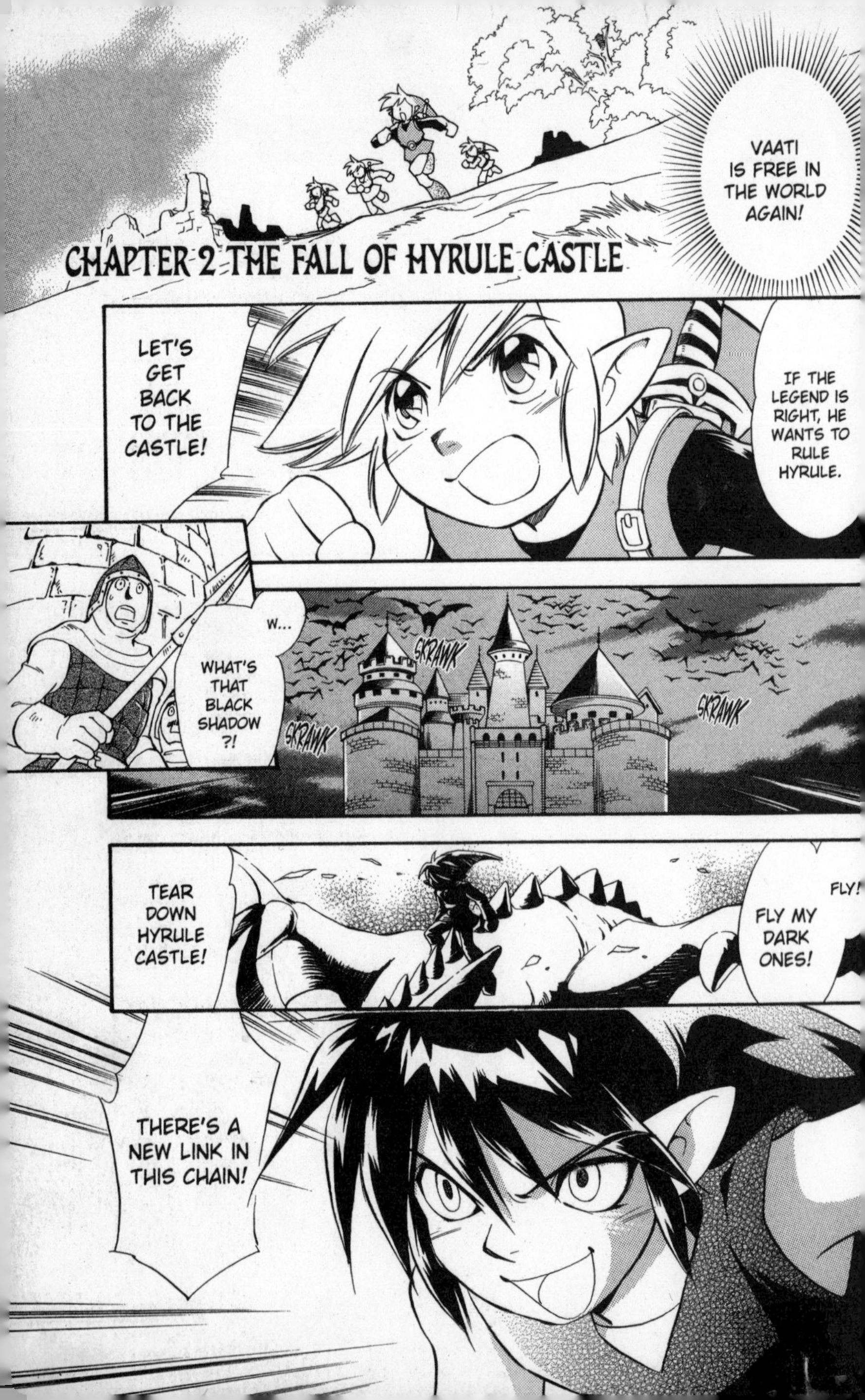
VAATI IS FREE IN THE WORLD AGAIN!
IF THE LEGEND IS RIGHT, HE WANTS TO RULE HYRULE.
LET'S GET BACK TO THE CASTLE!
SKRAWK
SKRAWK
SKRAWK
W...
WHAT'S THAT BLACK SHADOW ?!
FLY!
FLY MY DARK ONES!
TEAR DOWN HYRULE CASTLE!
THERE'S A NEW LINK IN THIS CHAIN!

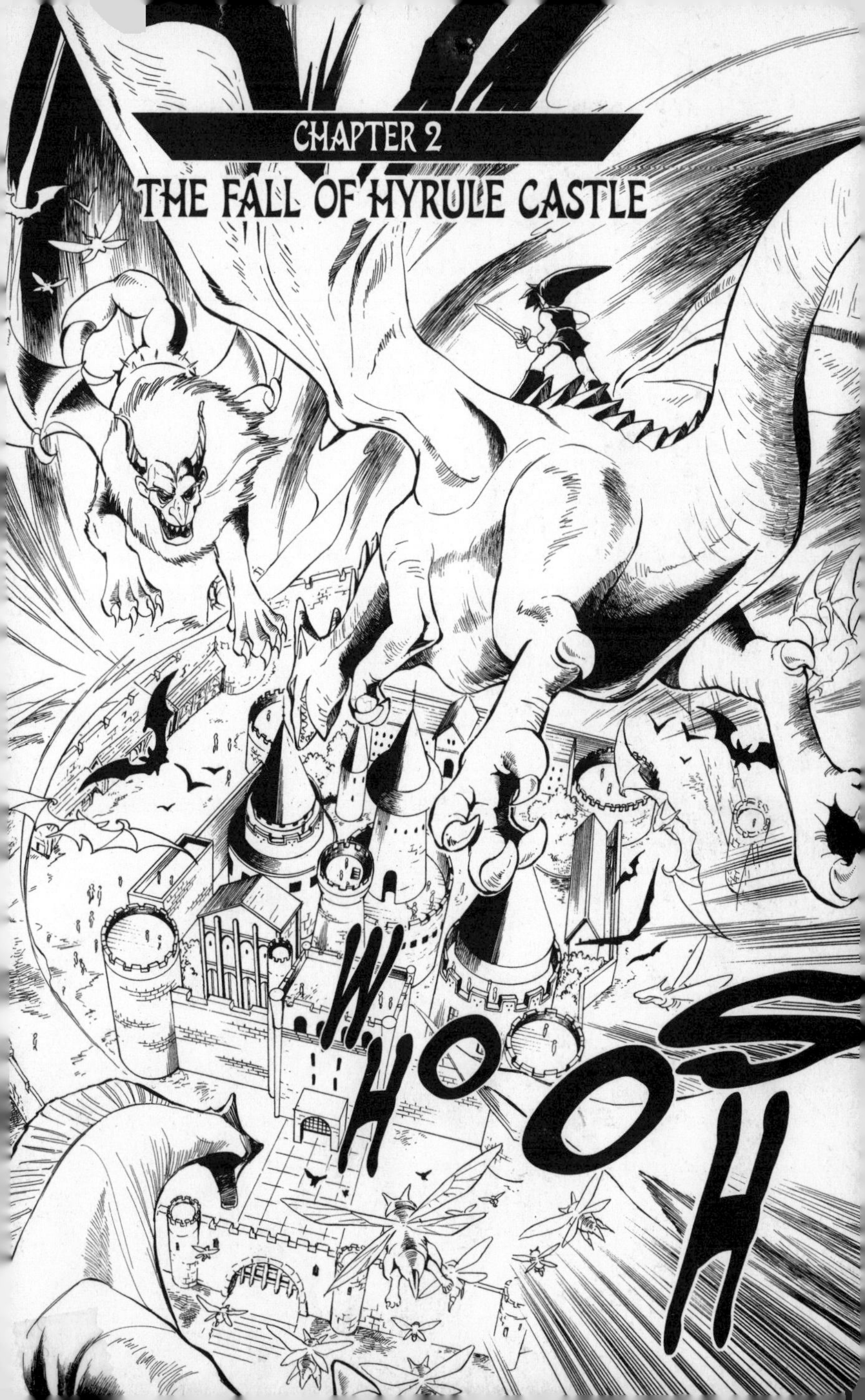
CHAPTER 2
THE FALL OF HYRULE CASTLE
WHOOSH

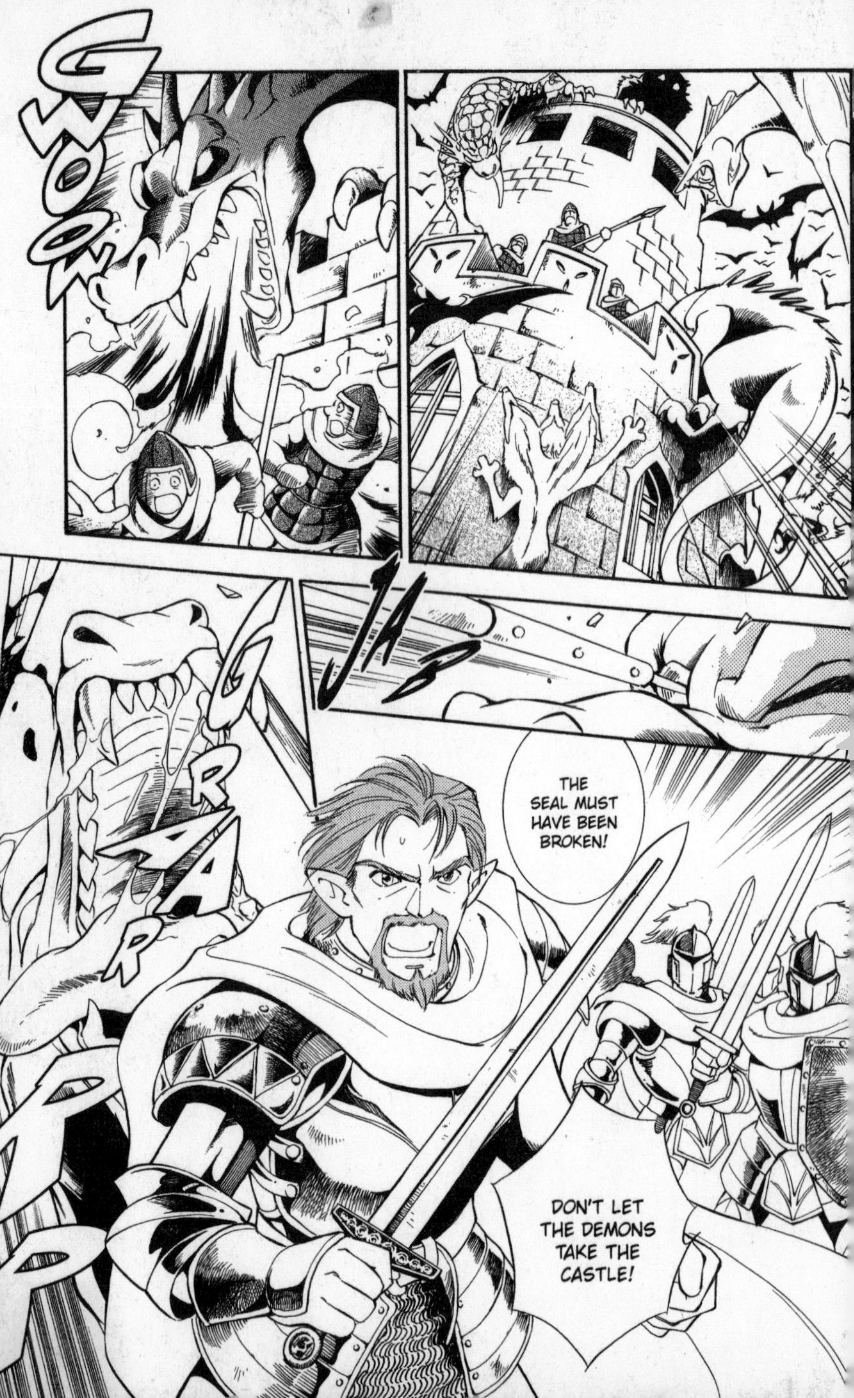
GWOOOW
JAB
GRAAR
THE SEAL MUST HAVE BEEN BROKEN!
DON'T LET THE DEMONS TAKE THE CASTLE!
RRR

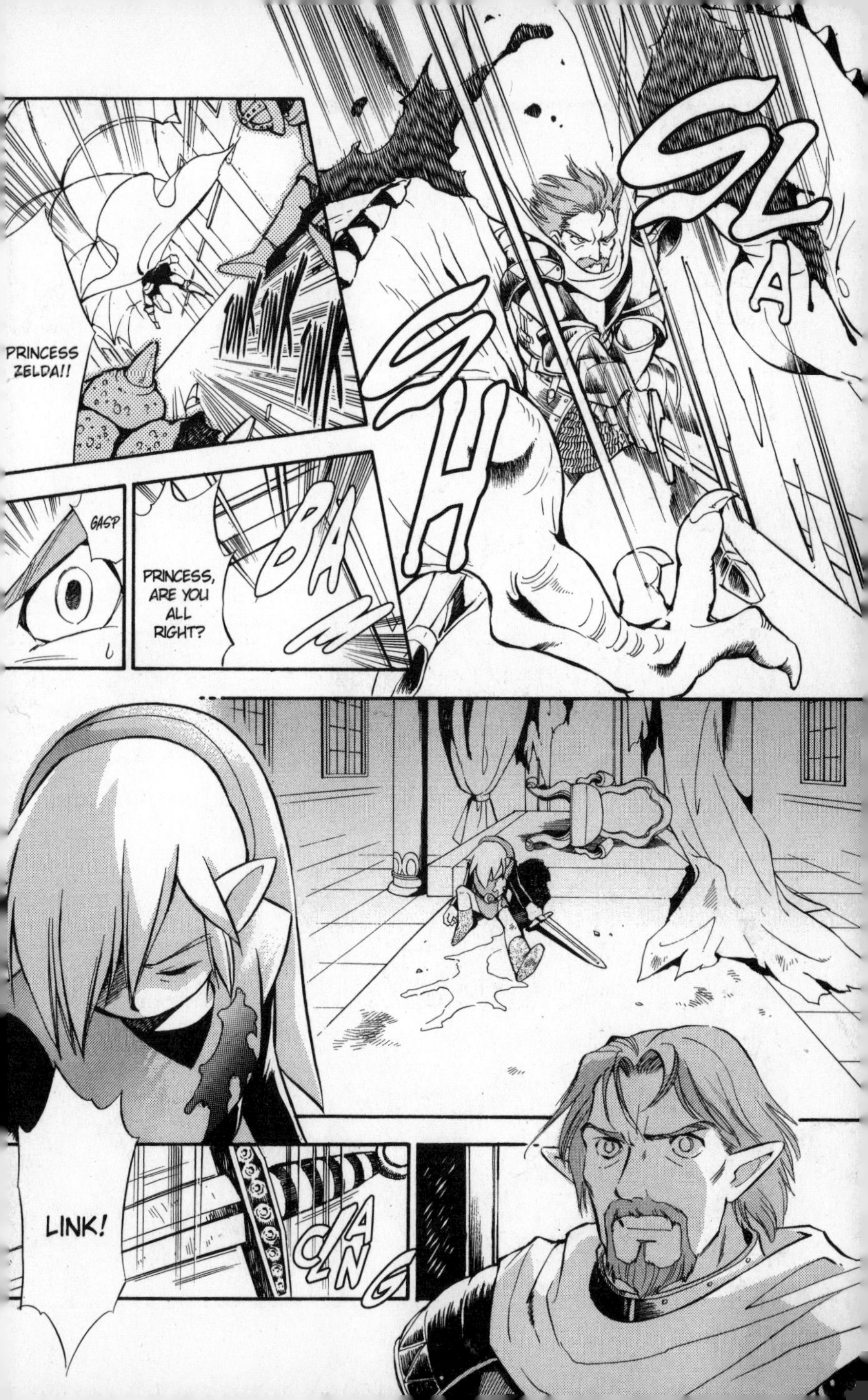
SLASH
PRINCESS ZELDA!!
BAM
PRINCESS, ARE YOU ALL RIGHT?
GASP
CLANG
LINK!

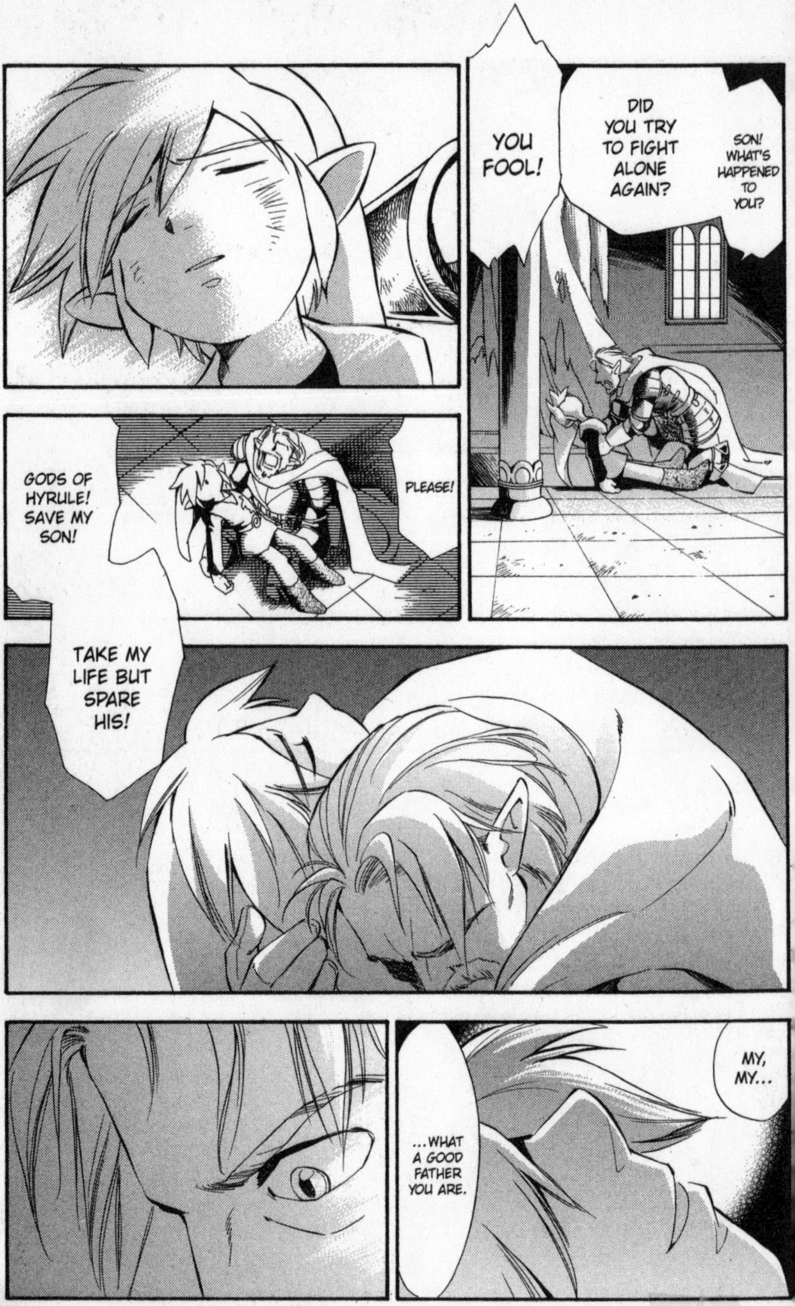
SON! WHAT'S HAPPENED TO YOU?
DID YOU TRY TO FIGHT ALONE AGAIN?
YOU FOOL!
PLEASE!
GODS OF HYRULE! SAVE MY SON!
TAKE MY LIFE BUT SPARE HIS!
MY, MY...
...WHAT A GOOD FATHER YOU ARE.

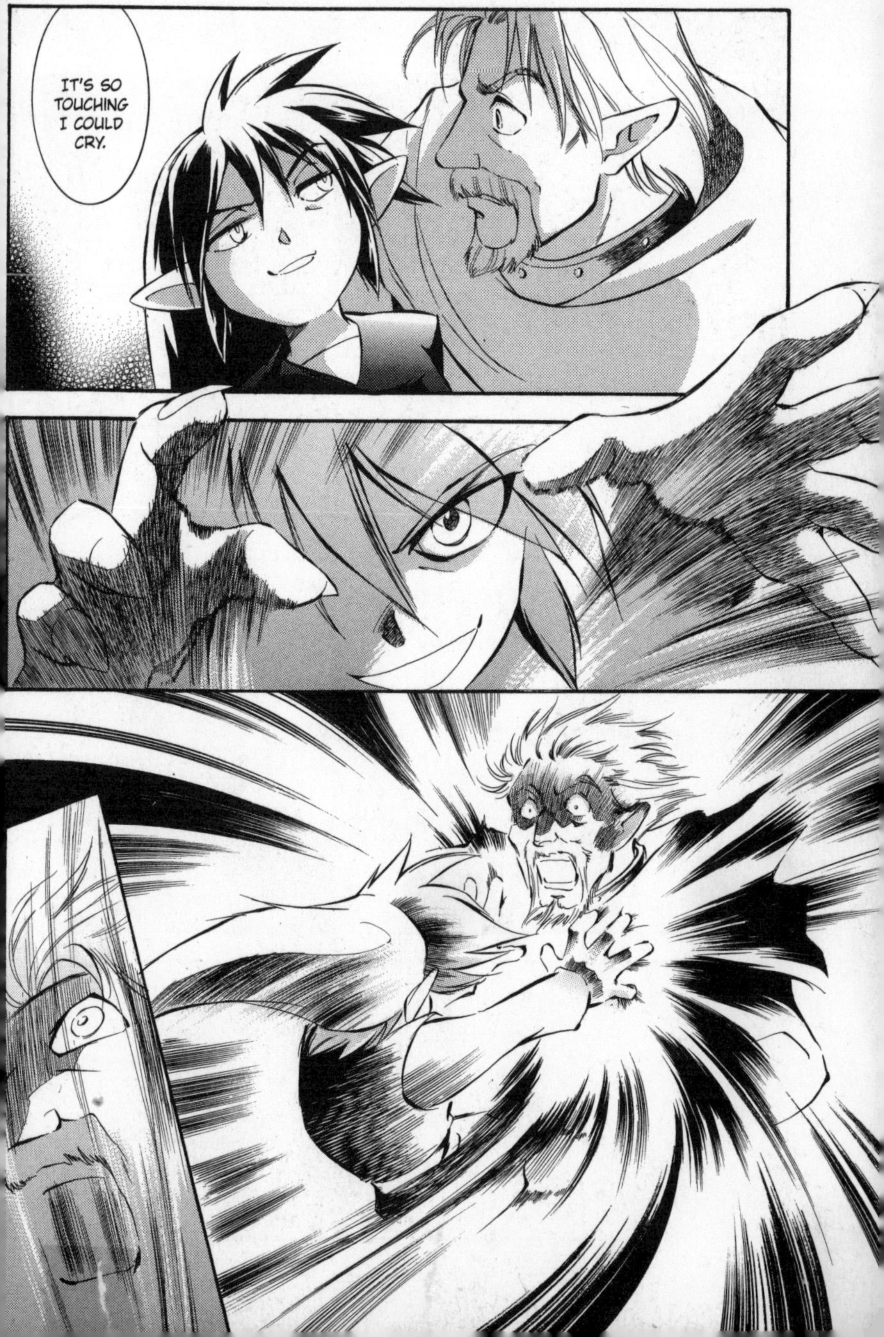
IT'S SO TOUCHING I COULD CRY.

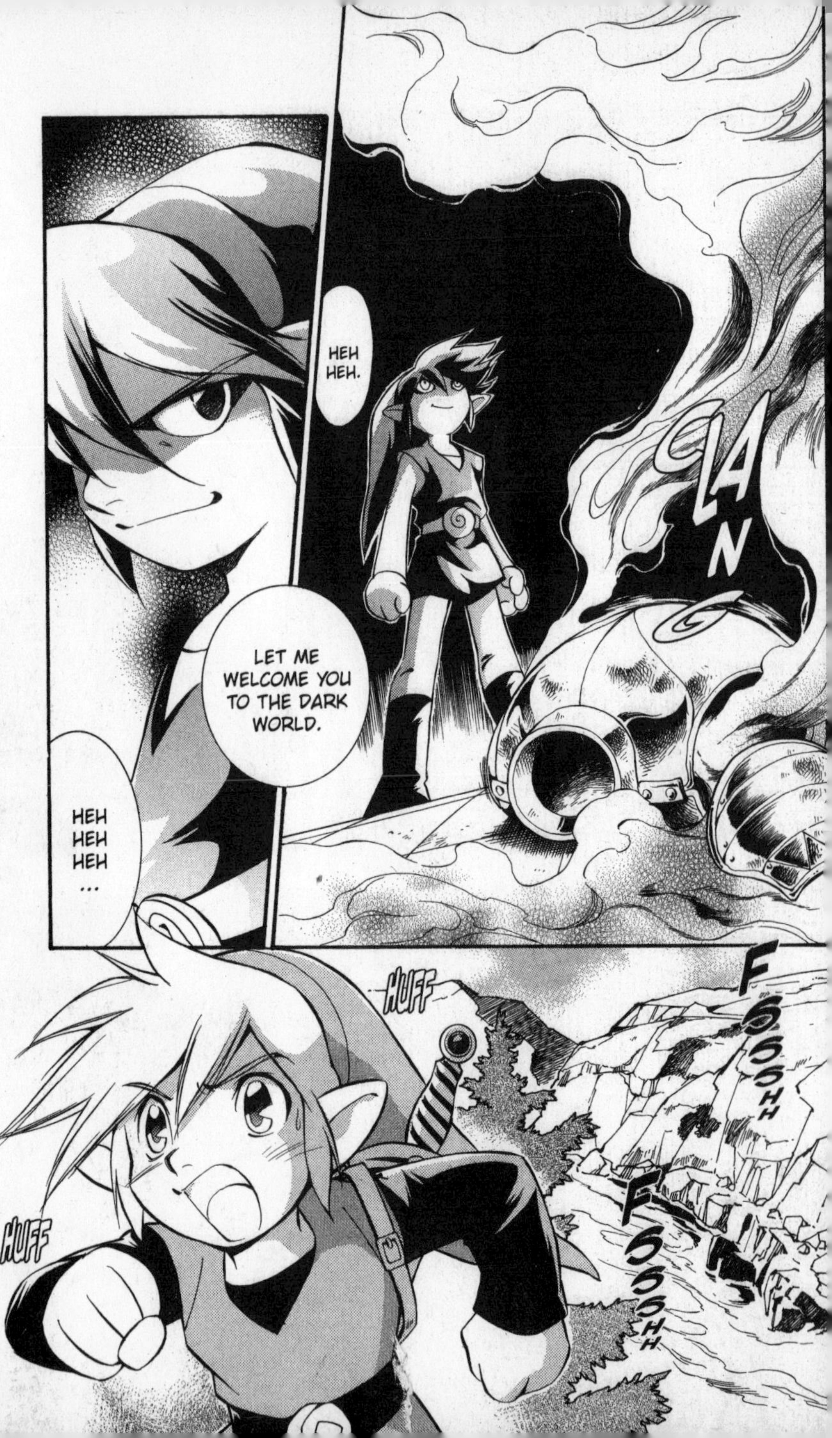
CLANG
HEH HEH.
LET ME WELCOME YOU TO THE DARK WORLD.
HEH HEH HEH ...
FSSSHH
FSSSHH
HUFF
HUFF

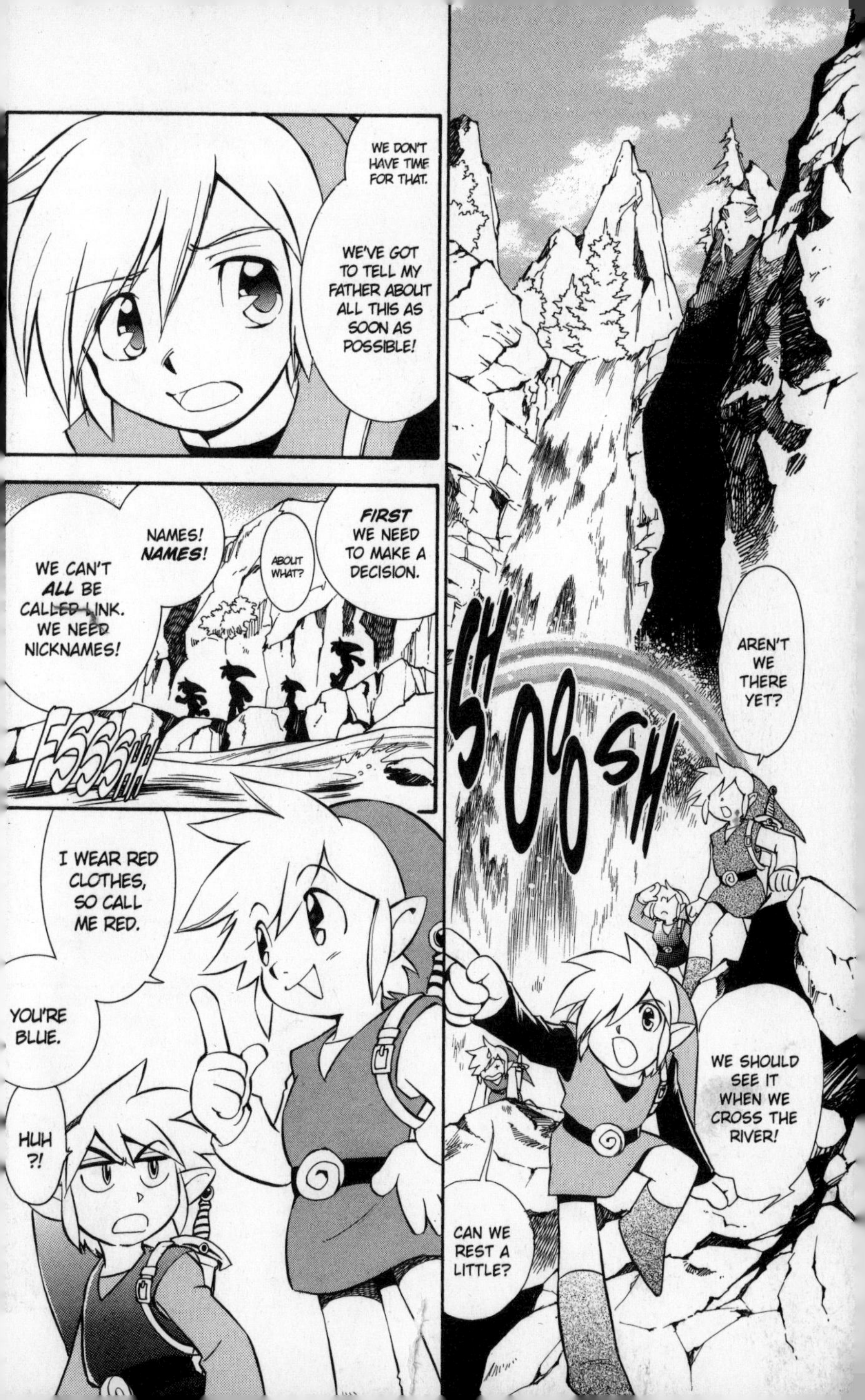
AREN'T WE THERE YET?
SHOOOOSH
WE SHOULD SEE IT WHEN WE CROSS THE RIVER!
CAN WE REST A LITTLE?
WE DON'T HAVE TIME FOR THAT.
WE'VE GOT TO TELL MY FATHER ABOUT ALL THIS AS SOON AS POSSIBLE!
FIRST WE NEED TO MAKE A DECISION.
ABOUT WHAT?
NAMES! NAMES!
WE CAN'T ALL BE CALLED LINK. WE NEED NICKNAMES!
FSSSHH
I WEAR RED CLOTHES, SO CALL ME RED.
YOU'RE BLUE.
HUH?!

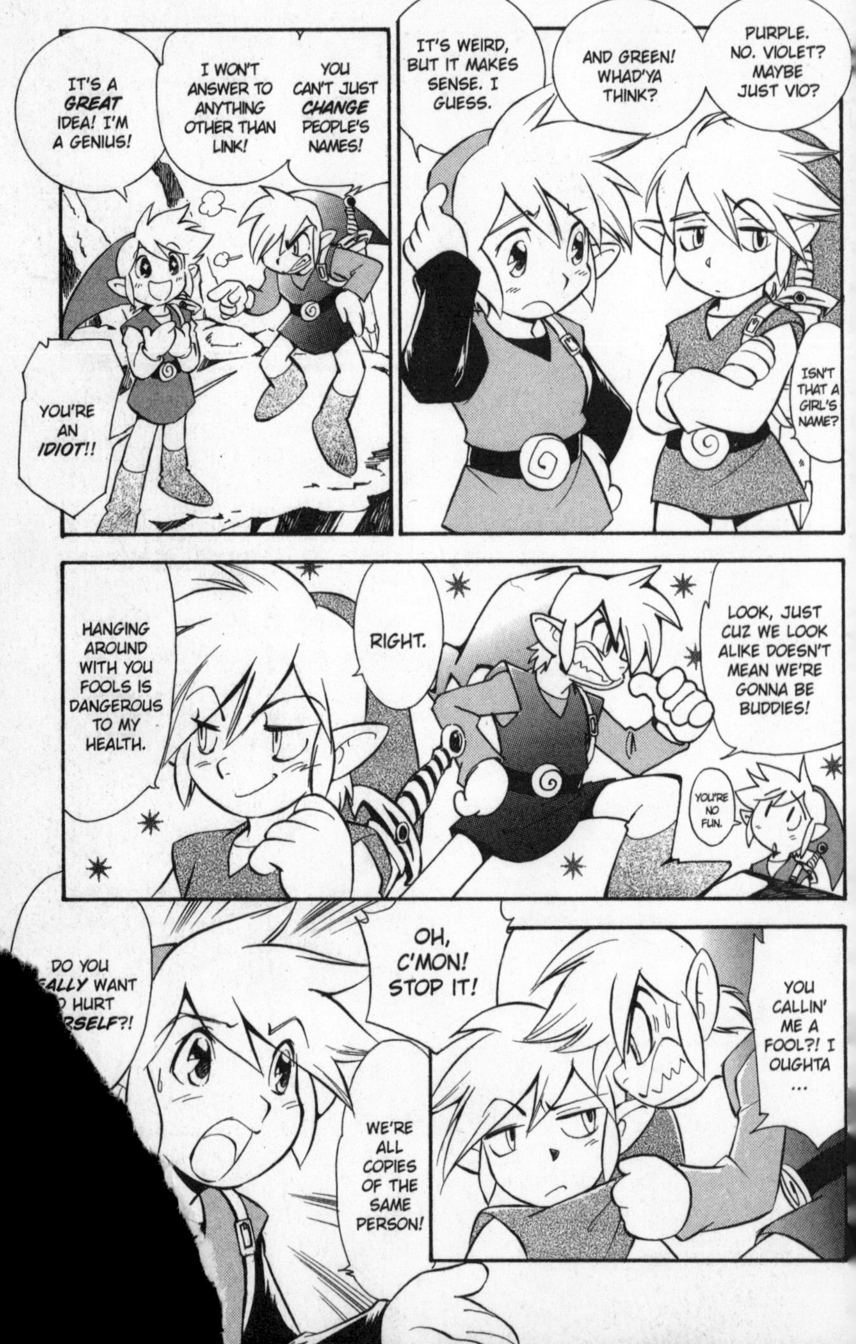
PURPLE. NO. VIOLET? MAYBE JUST VIO?
AND GREEN! WHAD'YA THINK?
IT'S WEIRD, BUT IT MAKES SENSE. I GUESS.
ISN'T THAT A GIRL'S NAME?
YOU CAN'T JUST **CHANGE** PEOPLE'S NAMES!
I WON'T ANSWER TO ANYTHING OTHER THAN LINK!
IT'S A **GREAT** IDEA! I'M A GENIUS!
YOU'RE AN **IDIOT**!!
LOOK, JUST CUZ WE LOOK ALIKE DOESN'T MEAN WE'RE GONNA BE BUDDIES!
YOU'RE NO FUN.
RIGHT.
HANGING AROUND WITH YOU FOOLS IS DANGEROUS TO MY HEALTH.
YOU CALLIN' ME A FOOL?! I OUGHTA ...
WE'RE ALL COPIES OF THE SAME PERSON!
OH, C'MON! STOP IT!
DO YOU …**EALLY** WANT …O HURT …**RSELF**?!

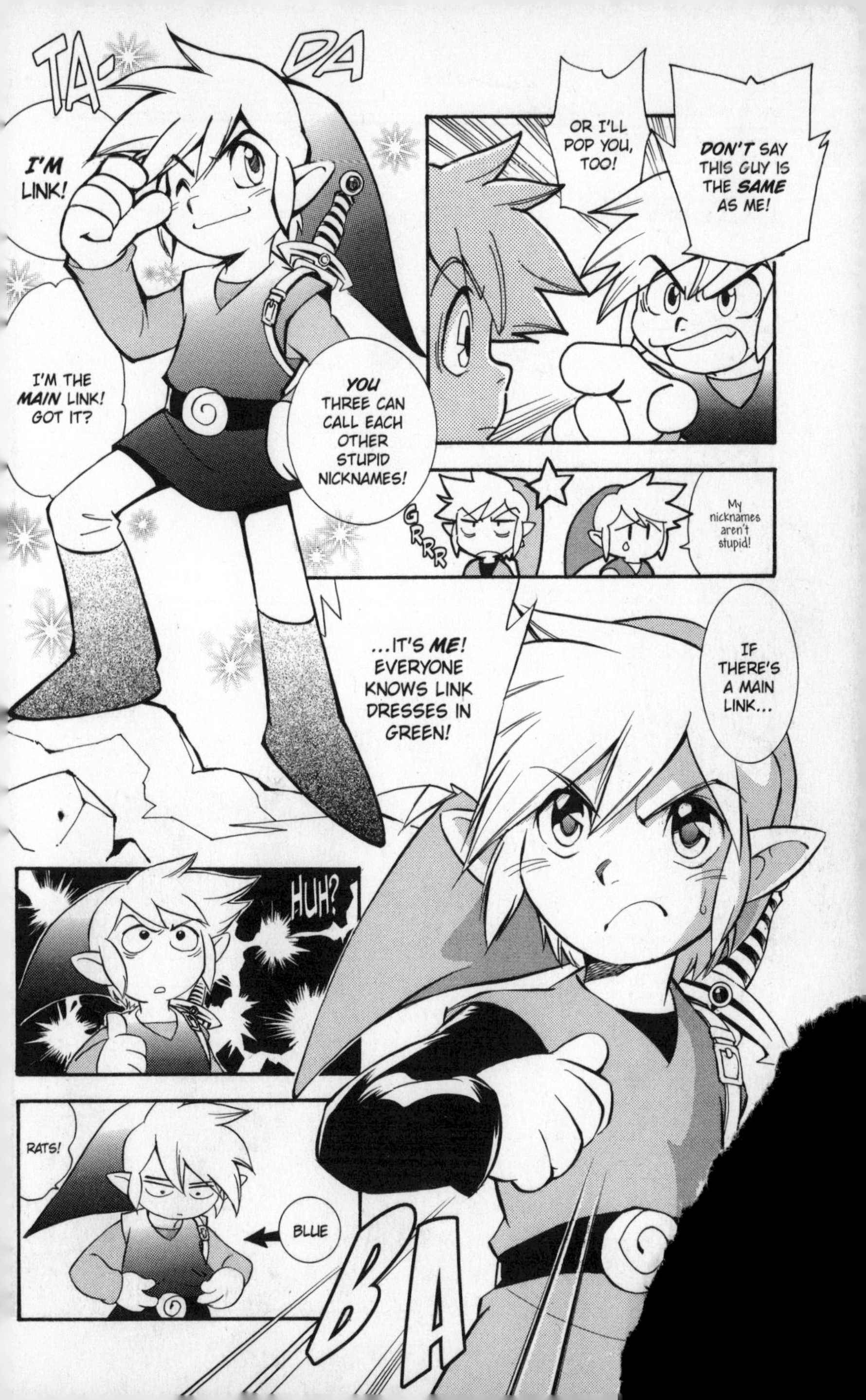
DON'T SAY THIS GUY IS THE SAME AS ME!
OR I'LL POP YOU, TOO!
TA-DA
I'M LINK!
I'M THE MAIN LINK! GOT IT?
YOU THREE CAN CALL EACH OTHER STUPID NICKNAMES!
My nicknames aren't stupid!
GRRR
IF THERE'S A MAIN LINK...
...IT'S ME! EVERYONE KNOWS LINK DRESSES IN GREEN!
BA
HUH?
RATS!
BLUE

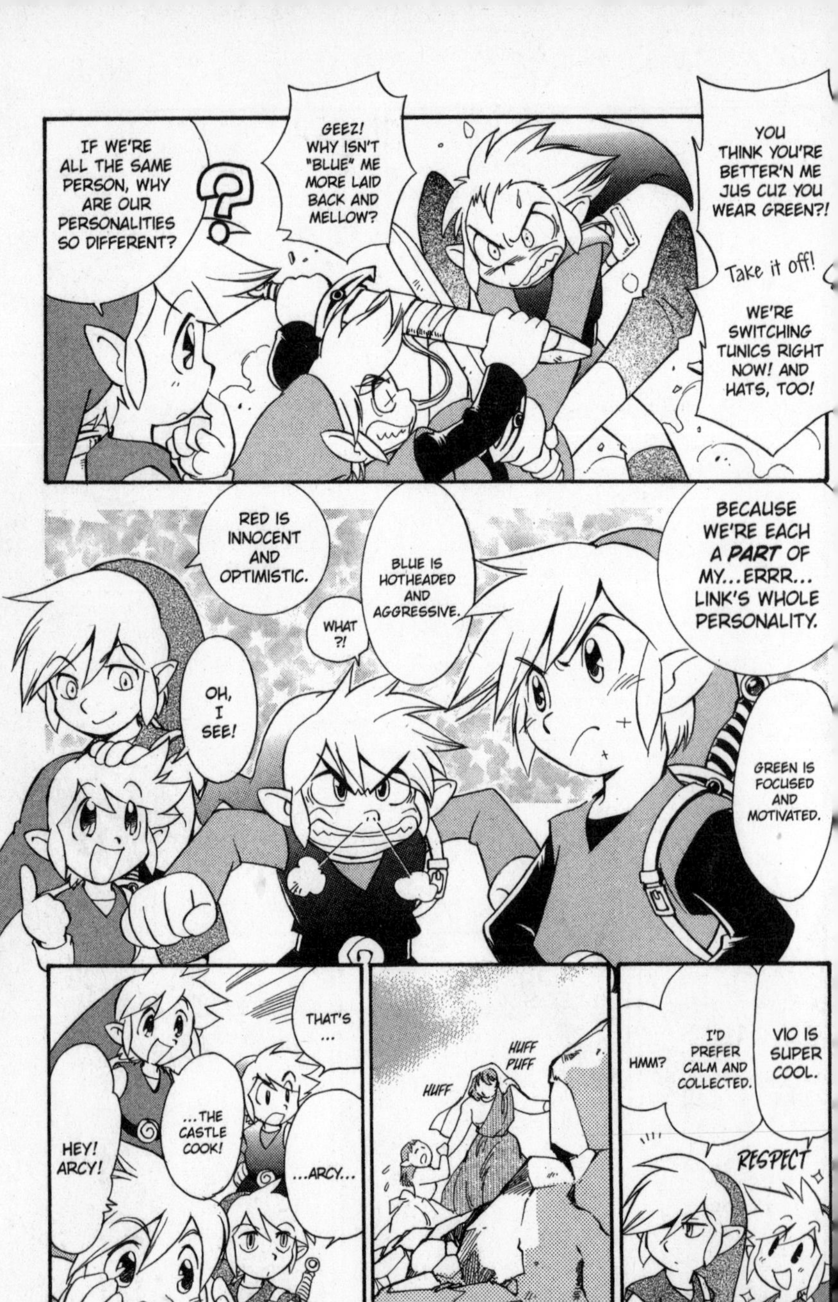

YOU THINK YOU'RE BETTER'N ME JUS CUZ YOU WEAR GREEN?!
Take it off!
WE'RE SWITCHING TUNICS RIGHT NOW! AND HATS, TOO!
GEEZ! WHY ISN'T "BLUE" ME MORE LAID BACK AND MELLOW?
IF WE'RE ALL THE SAME PERSON, WHY ARE OUR PERSONALITIES SO DIFFERENT?
BECAUSE WE'RE EACH A *PART* OF MY...ERRR... LINK'S WHOLE PERSONALITY.
GREEN IS FOCUSED AND MOTIVATED.
BLUE IS HOTHEADED AND AGGRESSIVE.
WHAT ?!
RED IS INNOCENT AND OPTIMISTIC.
OH, I SEE!
VIO IS SUPER COOL.
I'D PREFER CALM AND COLLECTED.
HMM?
RESPECT
HUFF PUFF
HUFF
THAT'S ...
...THE CASTLE COOK!
...ARCY...
HEY! ARCY!

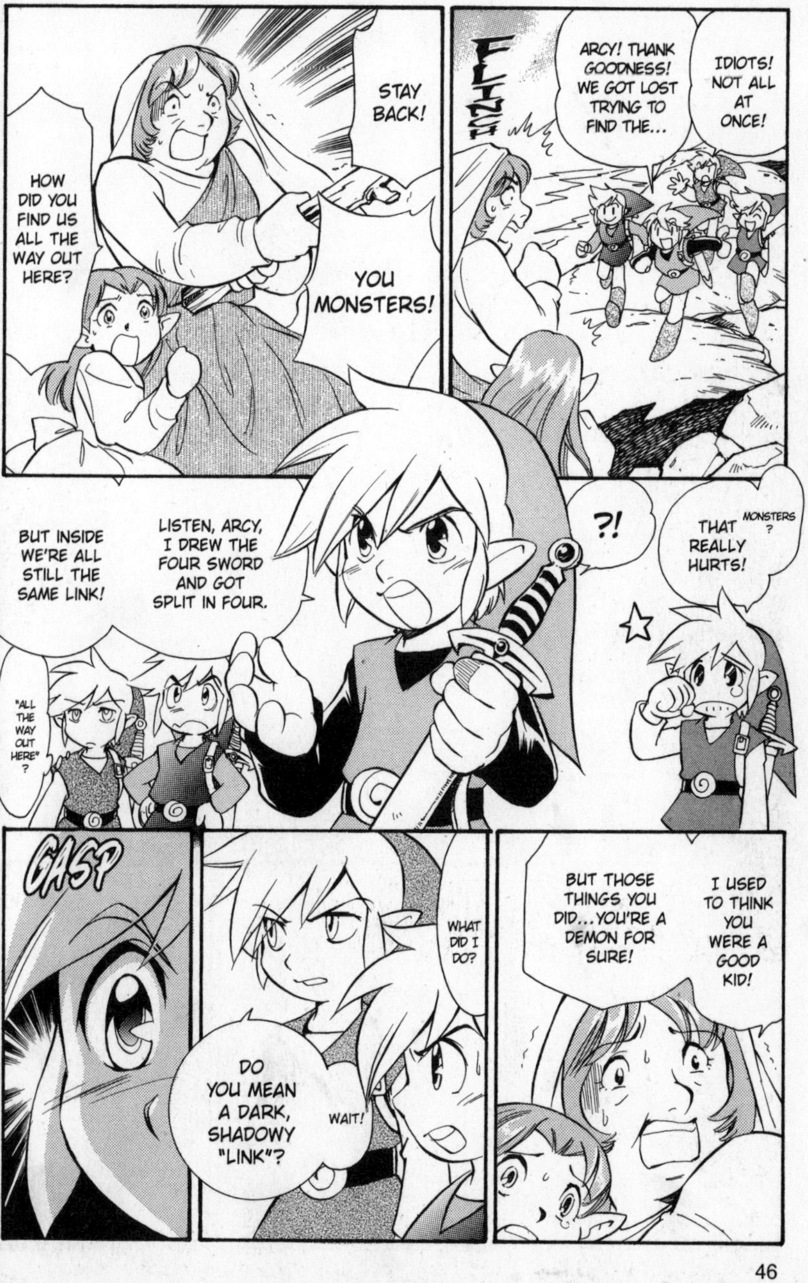
IDIOTS! NOT ALL AT ONCE!
ARCY! THANK GOODNESS! WE GOT LOST TRYING TO FIND THE...
FLINCH
STAY BACK!
YOU MONSTERS!
HOW DID YOU FIND US ALL THE WAY OUT HERE?
MONSTERS?
THAT REALLY HURTS!
?!
LISTEN, ARCY, I DREW THE FOUR SWORD AND GOT SPLIT IN FOUR.
BUT INSIDE WE'RE ALL STILL THE SAME LINK!
"ALL THE WAY OUT HERE"?
I USED TO THINK YOU WERE A GOOD KID!
BUT THOSE THINGS YOU DID...YOU'RE A DEMON FOR SURE!
WHAT DID I DO?
WAIT!
DO YOU MEAN A DARK, SHADOWY "LINK"?
GASP

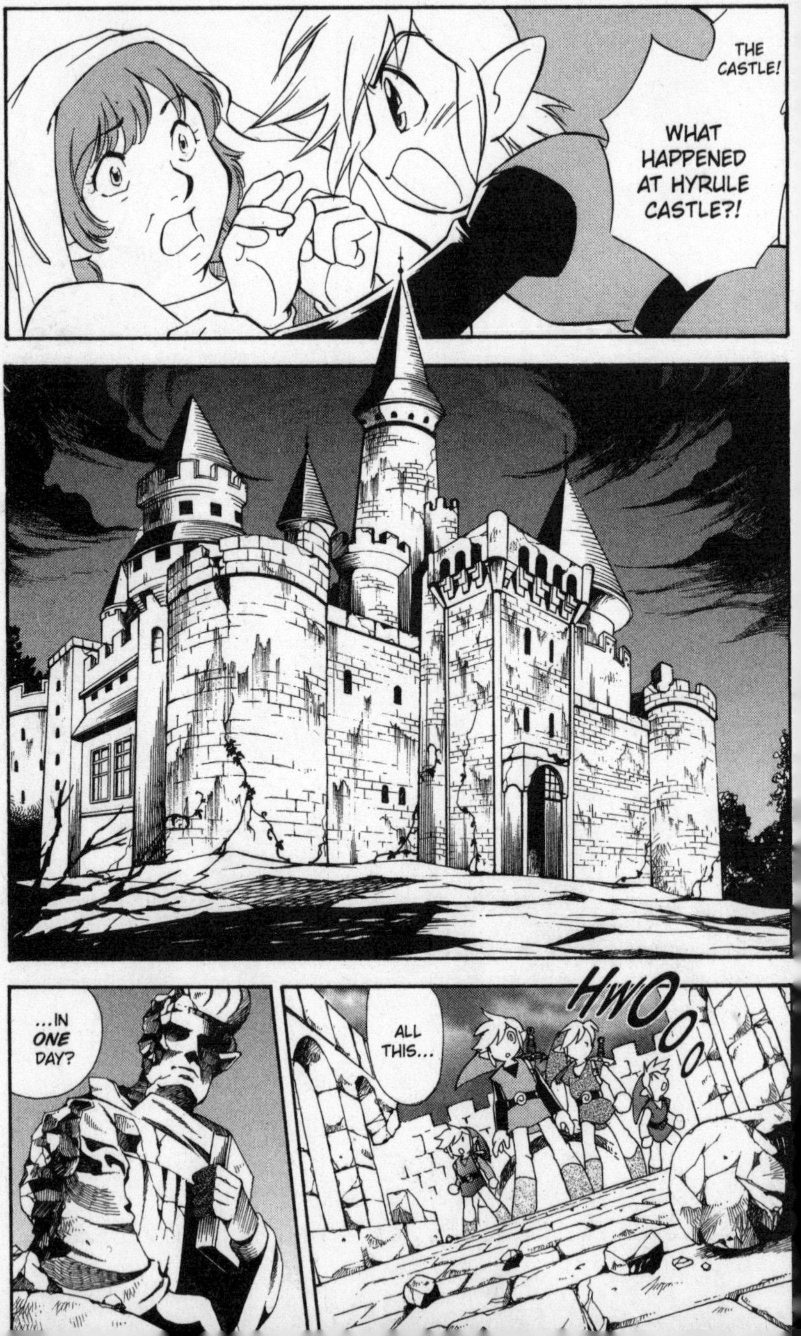
THE CASTLE!
WHAT HAPPENED AT HYRULE CASTLE?!
HWOOOO
ALL THIS...
...IN ONE DAY?

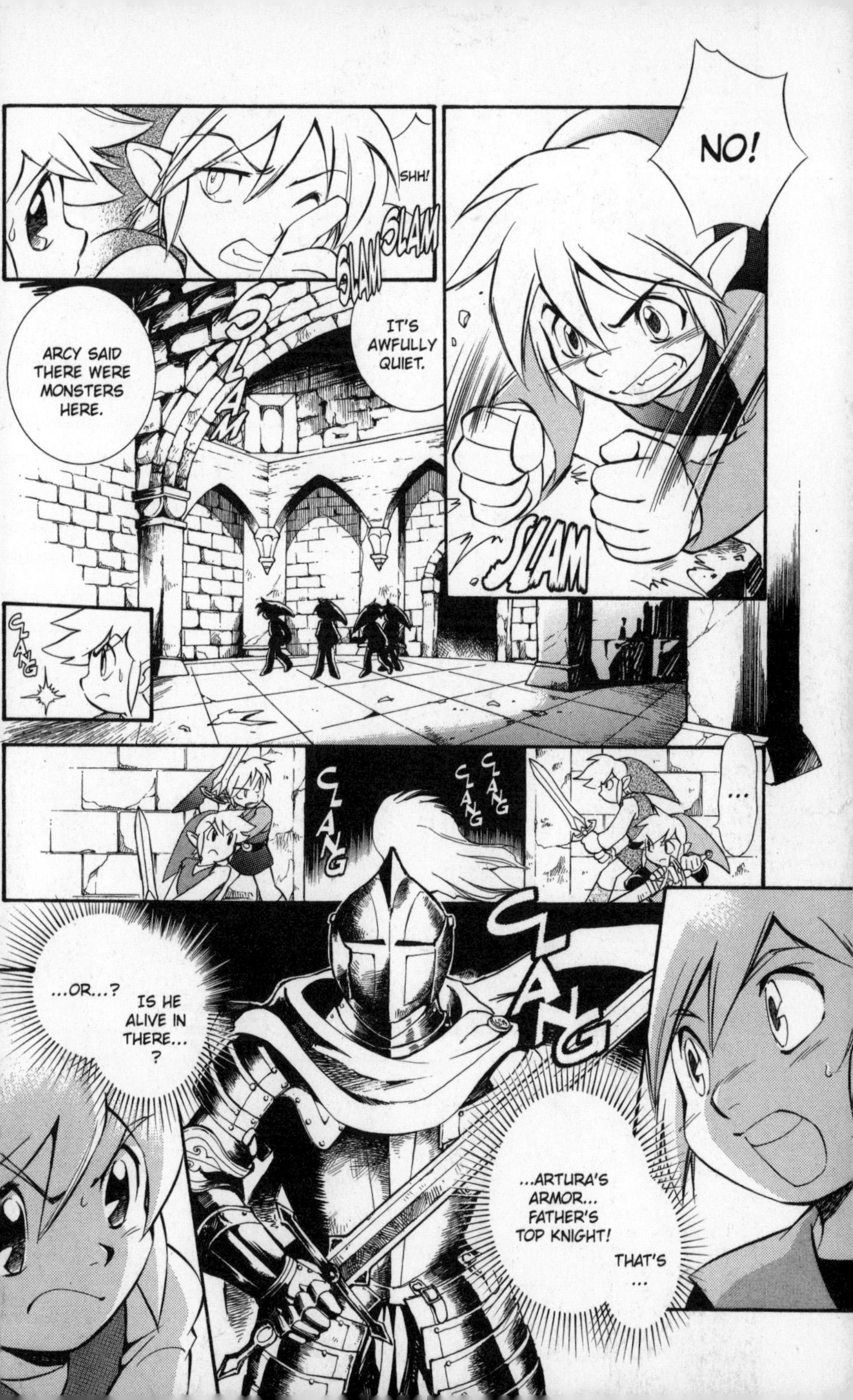
NO!
SLAM
SHH!
SLAM SLAM
SLAM
IT'S AWFULLY QUIET.
SLAM
ARCY SAID THERE WERE MONSTERS HERE.
CLANG
...
CLANG CLANG
CLANG
CLANG
...ARTURA'S ARMOR... FATHER'S TOP KNIGHT!
THAT'S ...
...OR...?
IS HE ALIVE IN THERE... ?

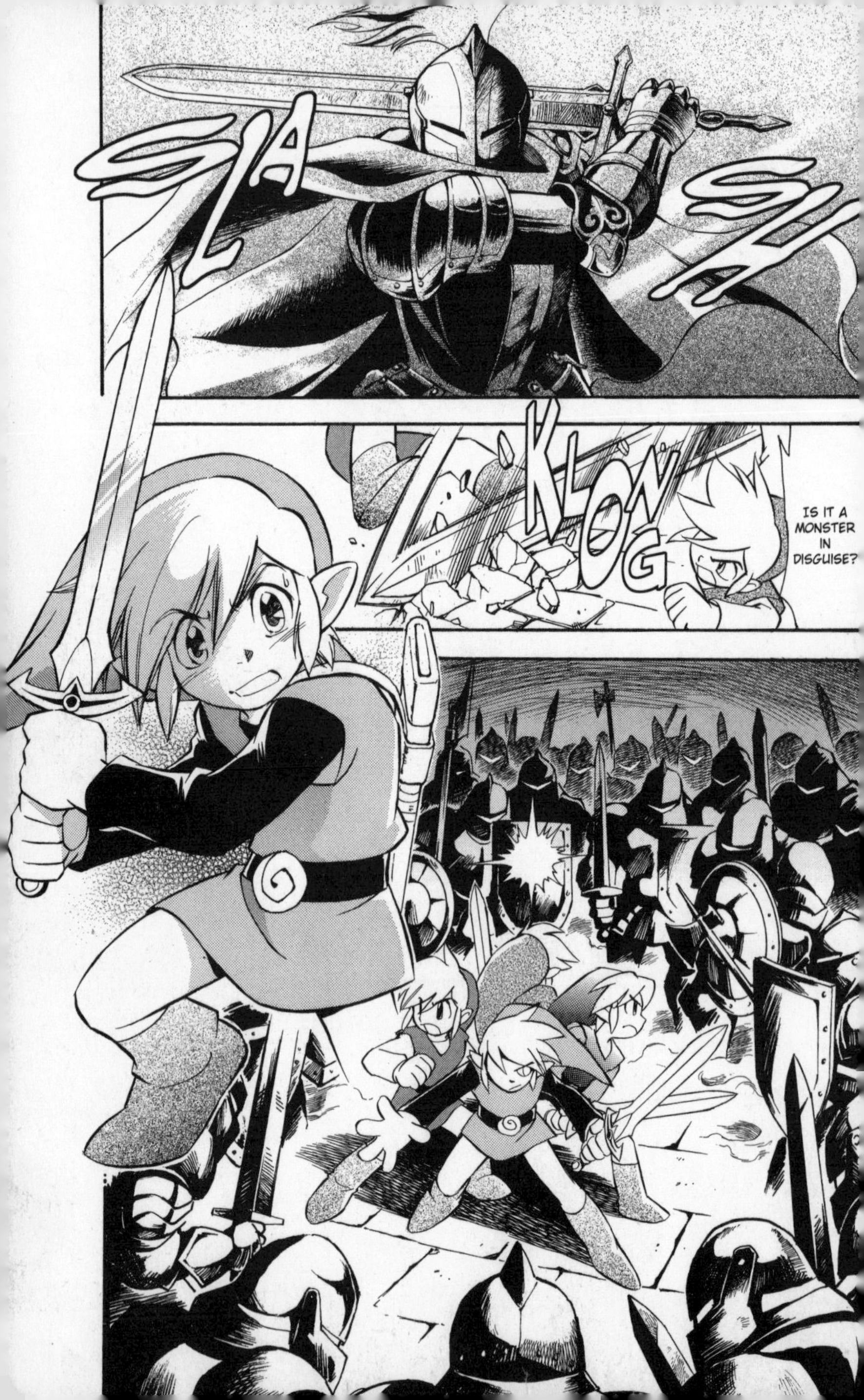
SLASH
IS IT A MONSTER IN DISGUISE?
KLONG

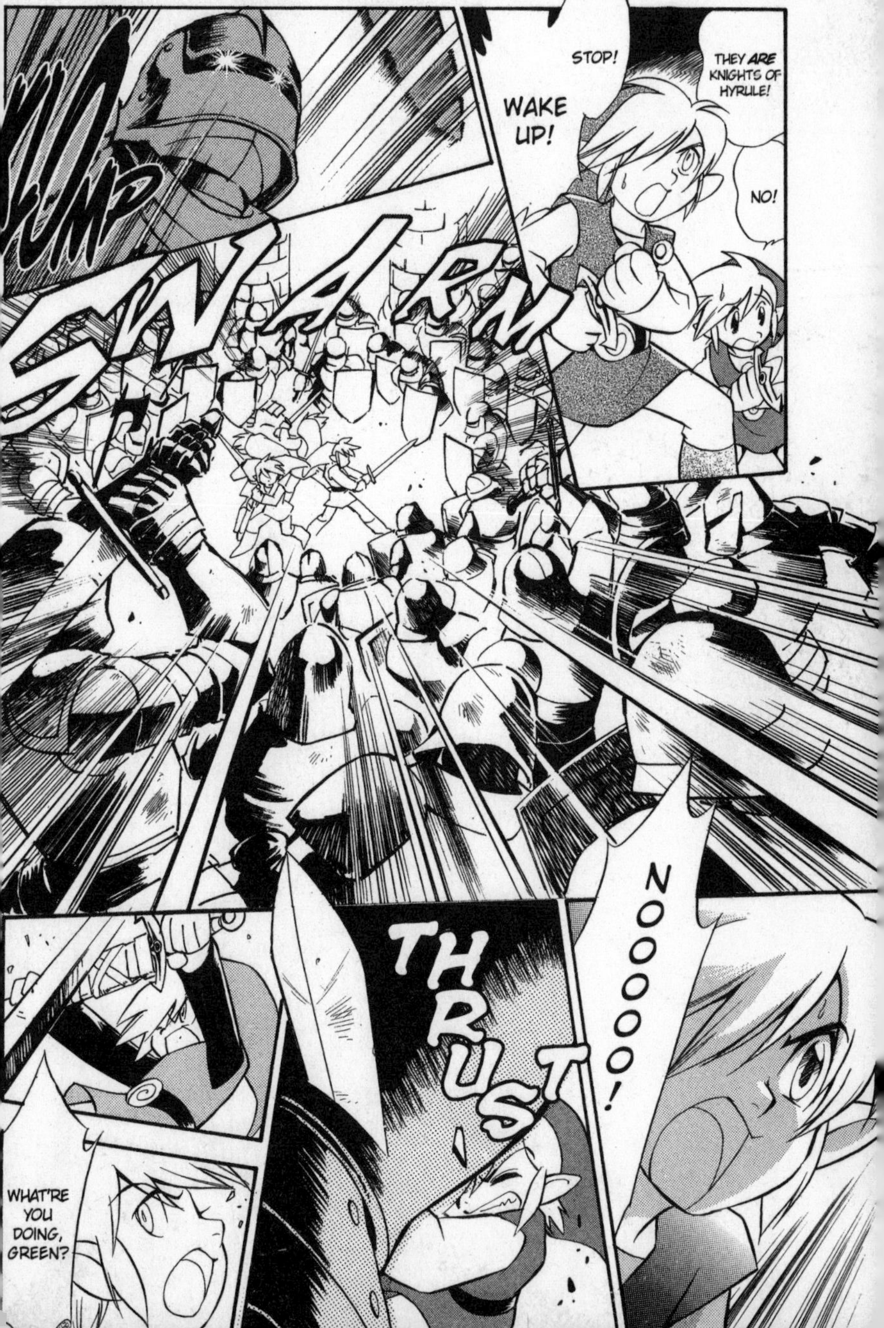
THEY ARE KNIGHTS OF HYRULE!
STOP!
WAKE UP!
NO!
SWARM
NOOOOOO!
THRUST
WHAT'RE YOU DOING, GREEN?

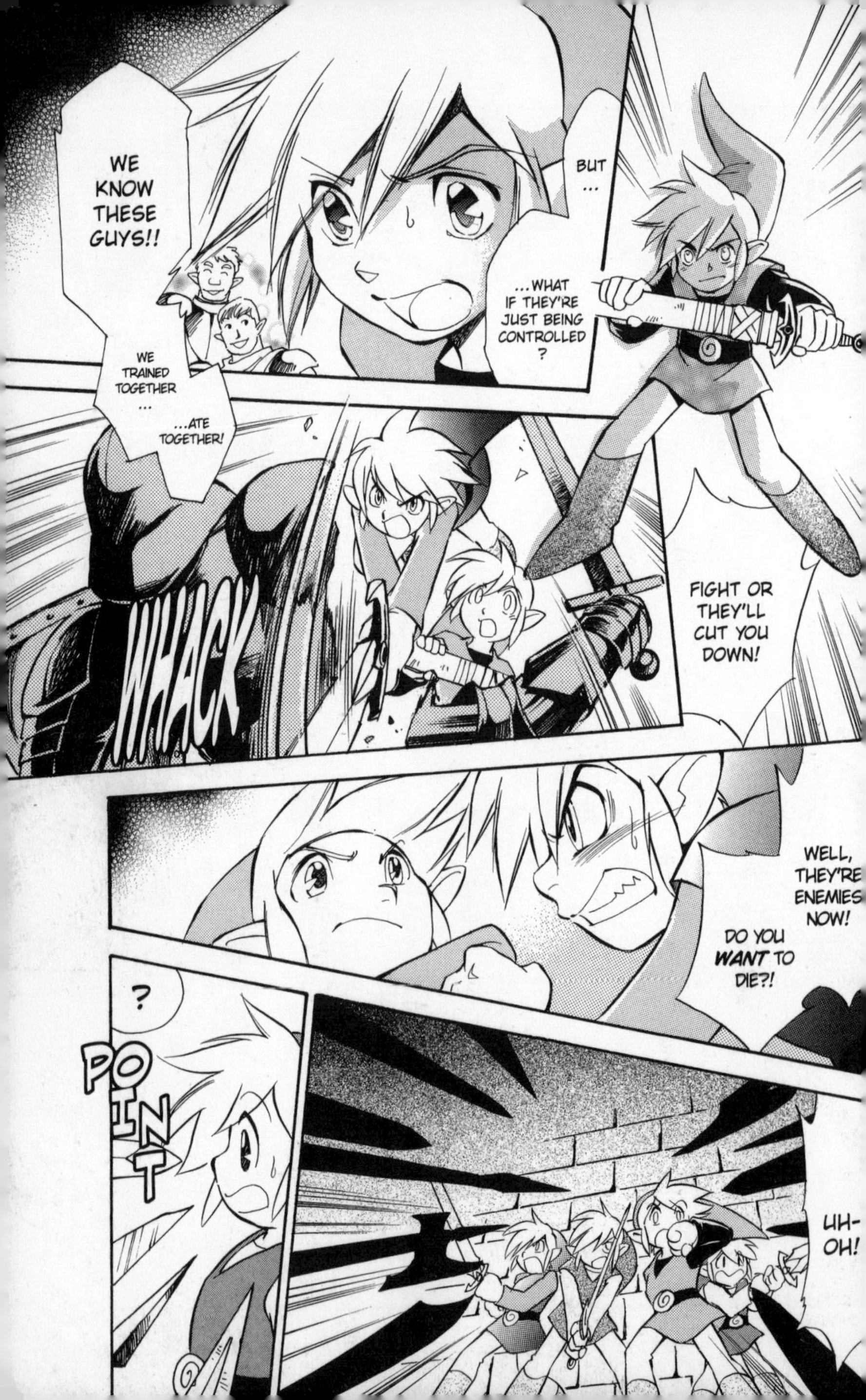
BUT ...
...WHAT IF THEY'RE JUST BEING CONTROLLED?
WE KNOW THESE GUYS!!
WE TRAINED TOGETHER ...
...ATE TOGETHER!
WHACK
FIGHT OR THEY'LL CUT YOU DOWN!
WELL, THEY'RE ENEMIES NOW!
DO YOU *WANT* TO DIE?!
UH-OH!
?
POINT

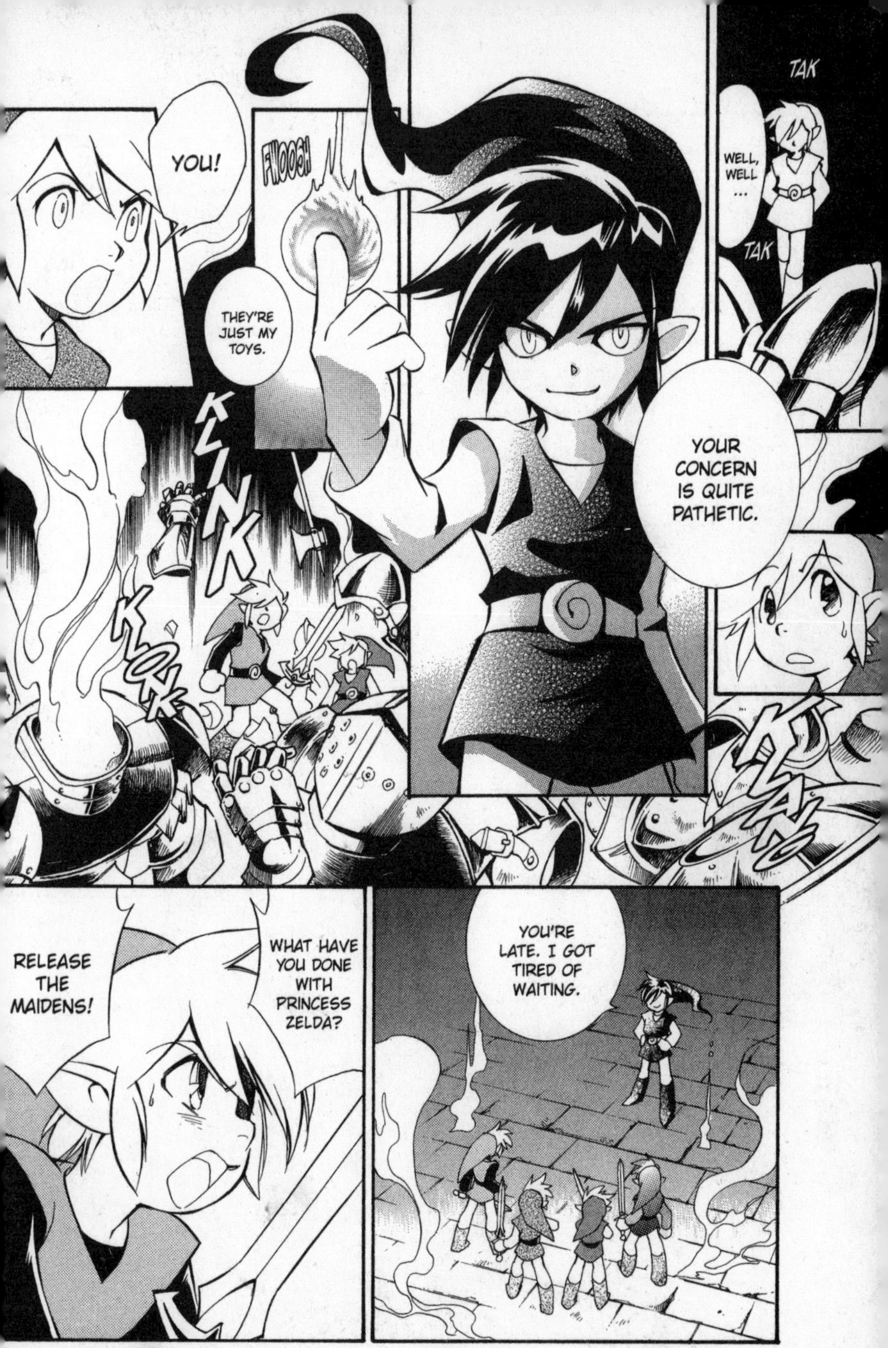
TAK
WELL, WELL ...
TAK
YOUR CONCERN IS QUITE PATHETIC.
FWOOSH
THEY'RE JUST MY TOYS.
YOU!
KLANG
KLINK
KLONK
YOU'RE LATE. I GOT TIRED OF WAITING.
WHAT HAVE YOU DONE WITH PRINCESS ZELDA?
RELEASE THE MAIDENS!

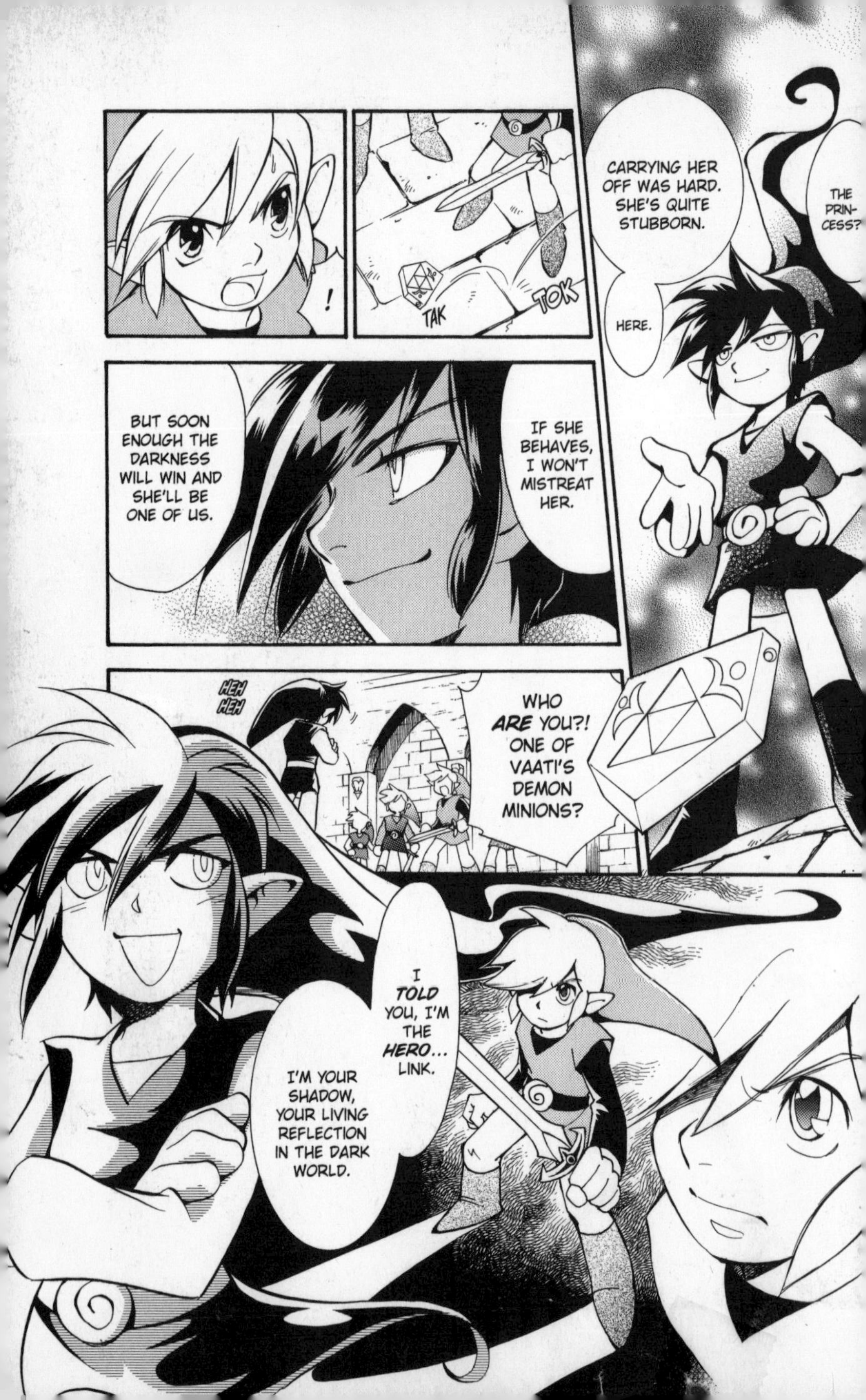
THE PRIN-CESS?
CARRYING HER OFF WAS HARD. SHE'S QUITE STUBBORN.
HERE.
TOK
TAK
!
IF SHE BEHAVES, I WON'T MISTREAT HER.
BUT SOON ENOUGH THE DARKNESS WILL WIN AND SHE'LL BE ONE OF US.
WHO **ARE** YOU?! ONE OF VAATI'S DEMON MINIONS?
HEH HEH
I **TOLD** YOU, I'M THE **HERO**... LINK.
I'M YOUR SHADOW, YOUR LIVING REFLECTION IN THE DARK WORLD.

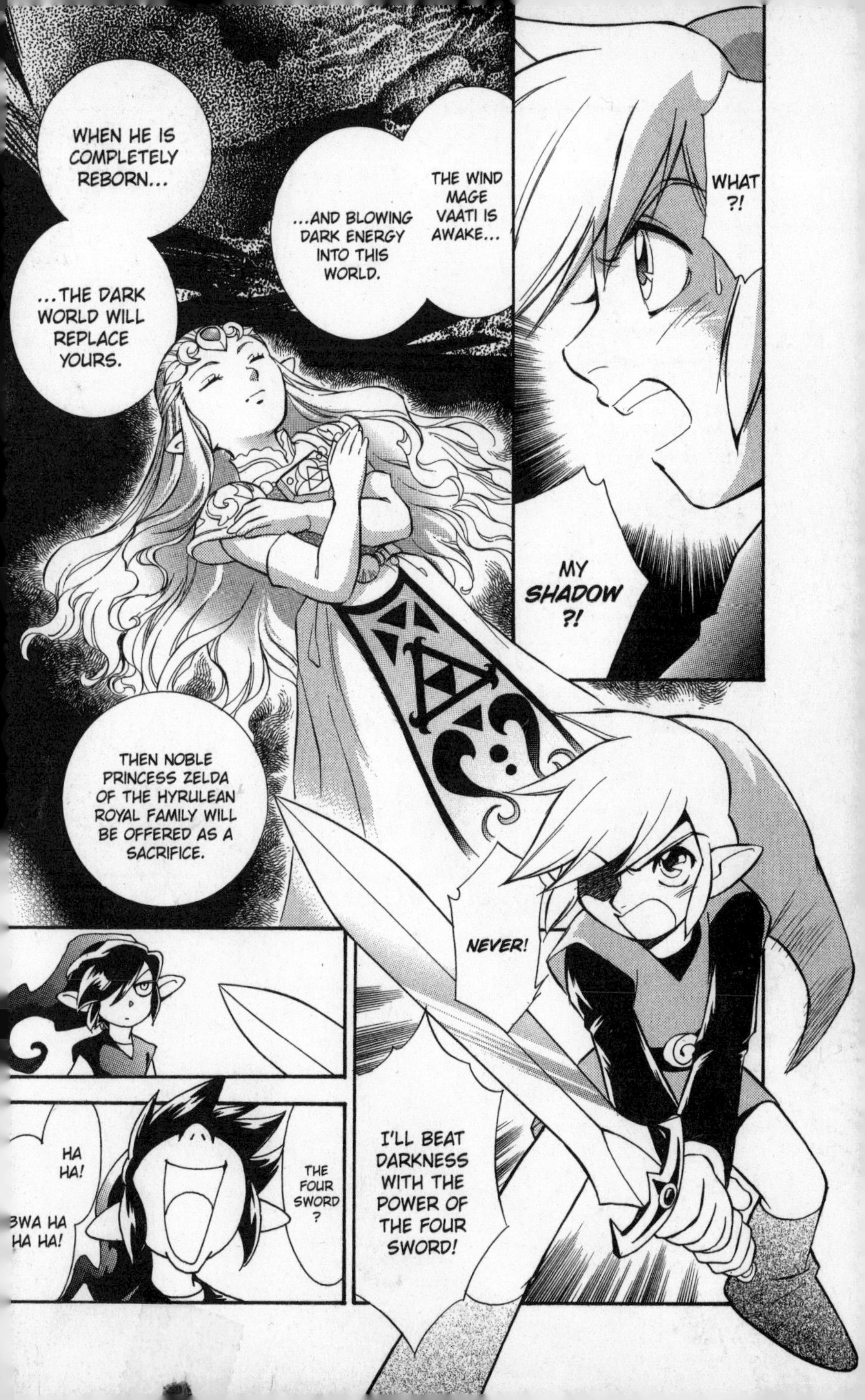
WHAT?!
MY SHADOW?!
THE WIND MAGE VAATI IS AWAKE...
...AND BLOWING DARK ENERGY INTO THIS WORLD.
WHEN HE IS COMPLETELY REBORN...
...THE DARK WORLD WILL REPLACE YOURS.
THEN NOBLE PRINCESS ZELDA OF THE HYRULEAN ROYAL FAMILY WILL BE OFFERED AS A SACRIFICE.
NEVER!
I'LL BEAT DARKNESS WITH THE POWER OF THE FOUR SWORD!
THE FOUR SWORD?
HA HA!
BWA HA HA HA!

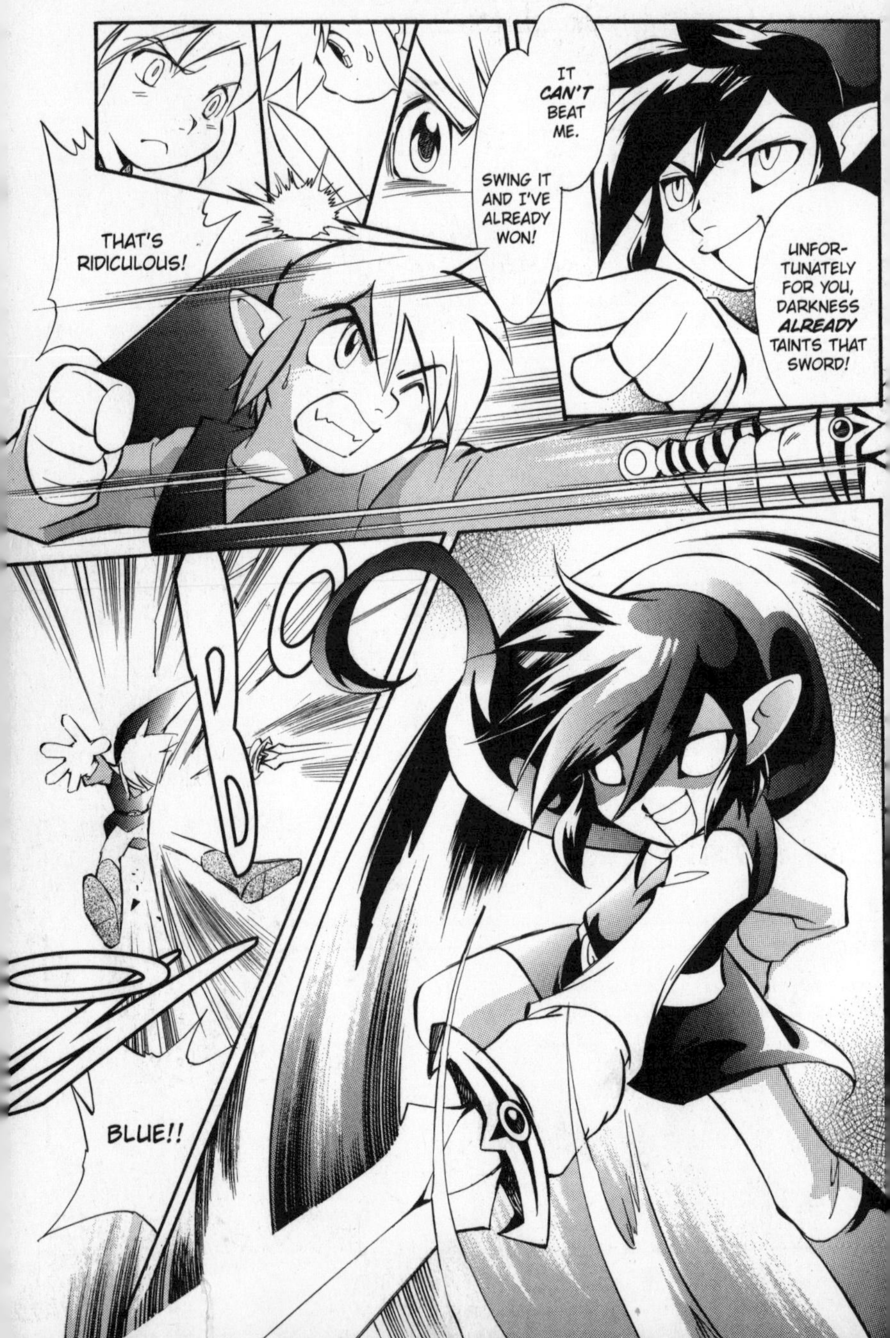
IT **CAN'T** BEAT ME.
SWING IT AND I'VE ALREADY WON!
UNFORTUNATELY FOR YOU, DARKNESS **ALREADY** TAINTS THAT SWORD!
THAT'S RIDICULOUS!
BLUE!!

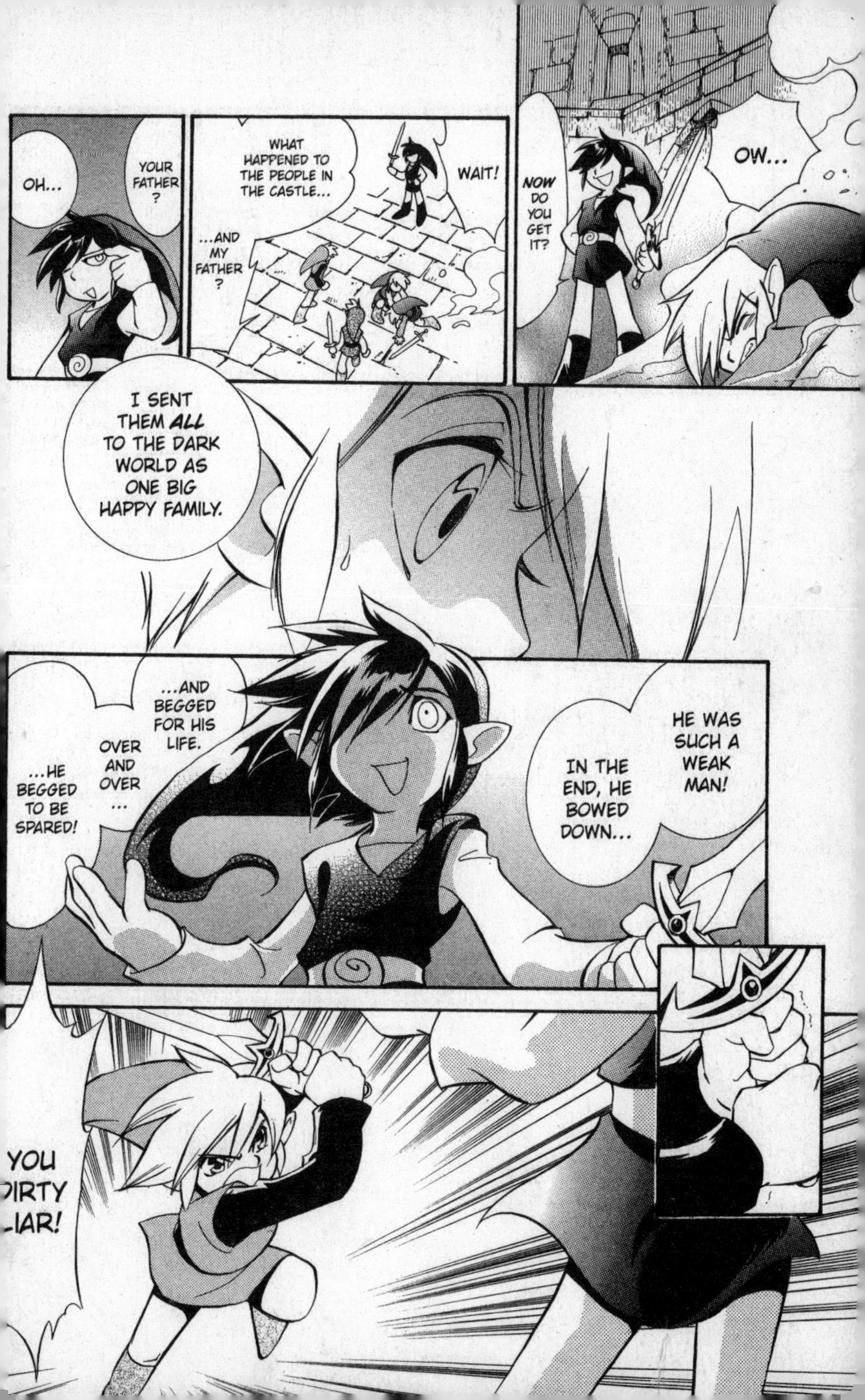
OW...
NOW DO YOU GET IT?
WAIT!
WHAT HAPPENED TO THE PEOPLE IN THE CASTLE...
...AND MY FATHER?
YOUR FATHER?
OH...
I SENT THEM ALL TO THE DARK WORLD AS ONE BIG HAPPY FAMILY.
HE WAS SUCH A WEAK MAN!
IN THE END, HE BOWED DOWN...
...AND BEGGED FOR HIS LIFE.
OVER AND OVER...
...HE BEGGED TO BE SPARED!
YOU IRTY IAR!

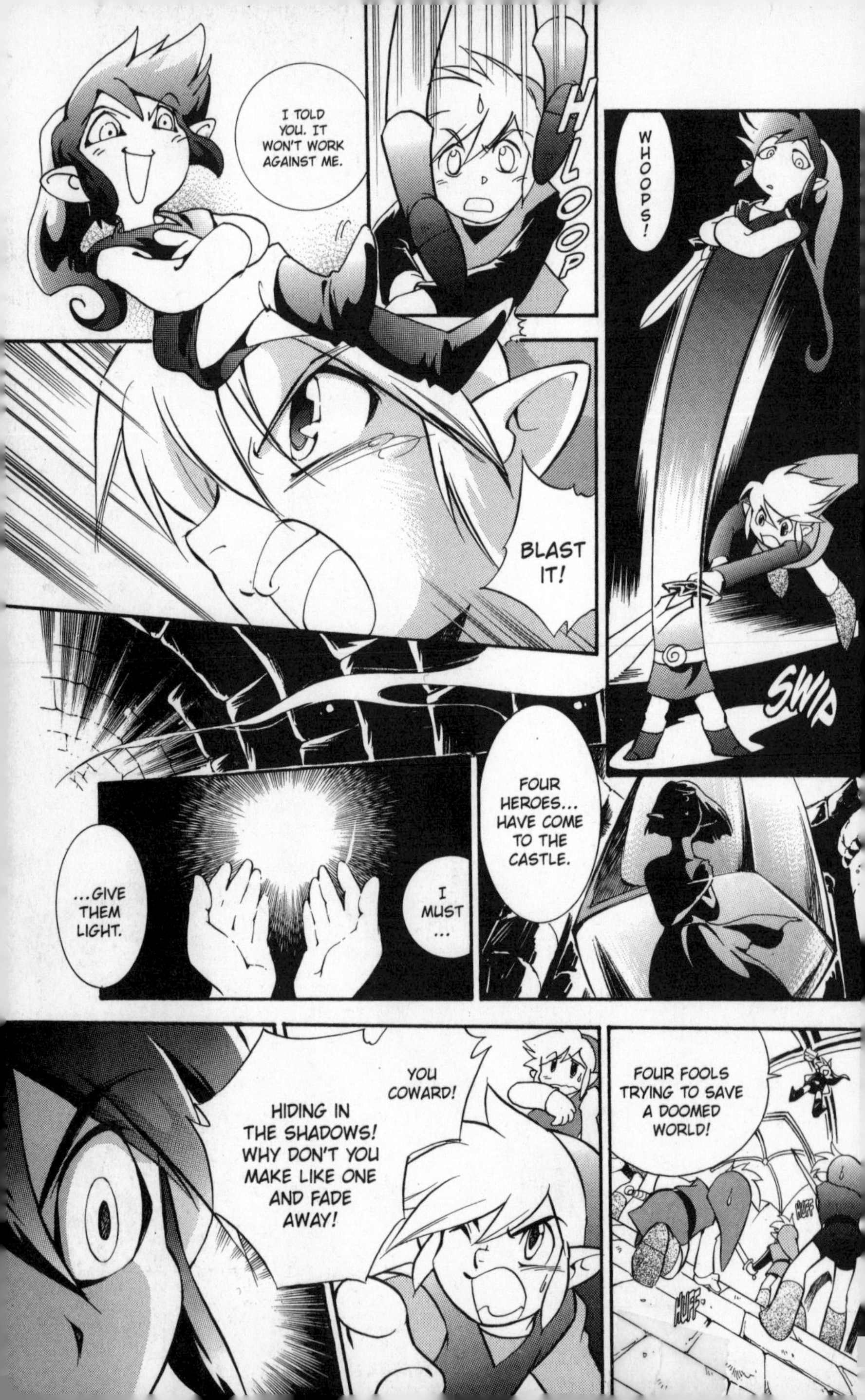
WHOOPS!
SWIP
HLLOOOP
I TOLD YOU. IT WON'T WORK AGAINST ME.
BLAST IT!
FOUR HEROES... HAVE COME TO THE CASTLE.
I MUST...
...GIVE THEM LIGHT.
FOUR FOOLS TRYING TO SAVE A DOOMED WORLD!
HUFF
HUFF
YOU COWARD!
HIDING IN THE SHADOWS! WHY DON'T YOU MAKE LIKE ONE AND FADE AWAY!

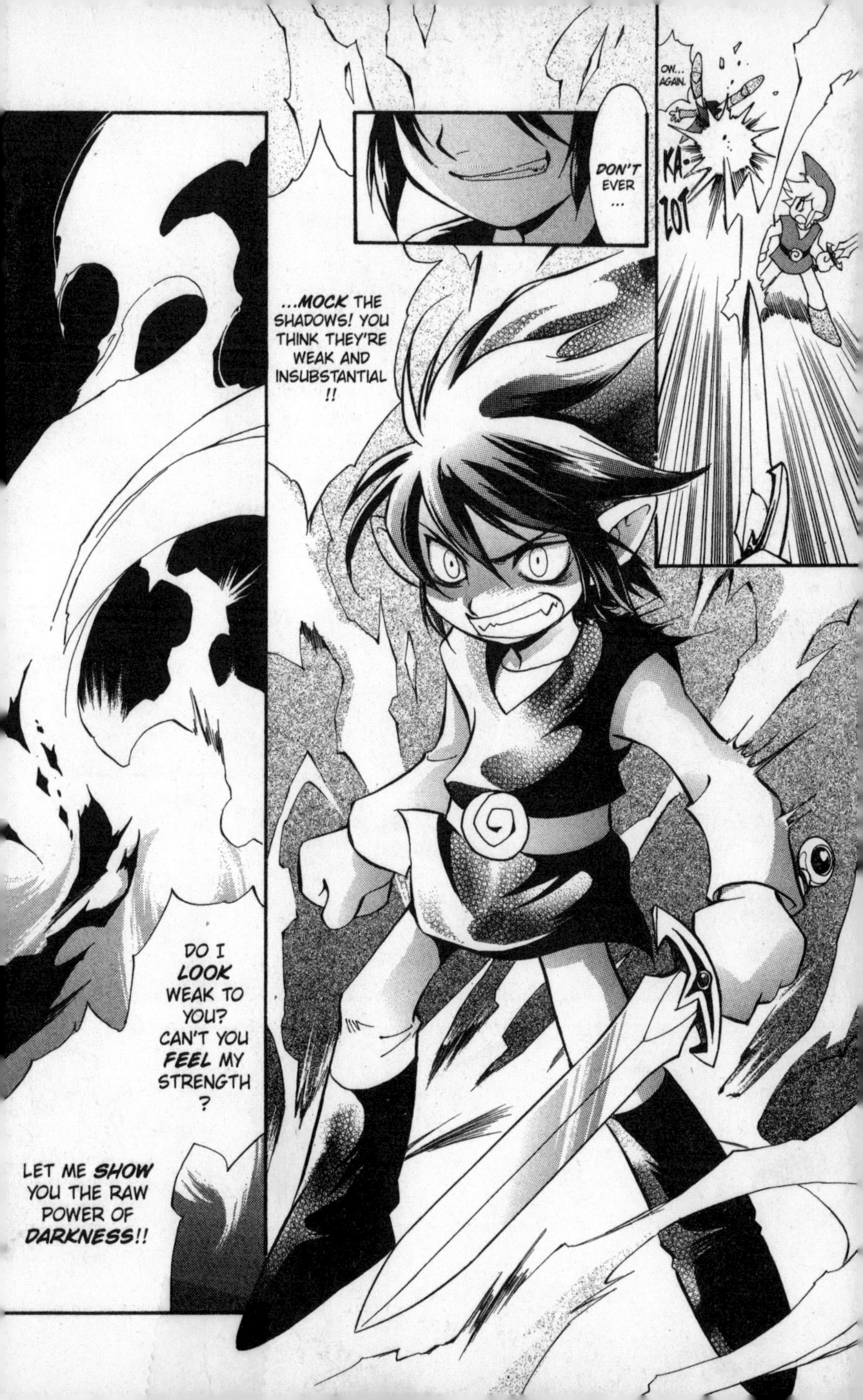
OW... AGAIN.
KA-ZOT
DON'T EVER ...
...MOCK THE SHADOWS! YOU THINK THEY'RE WEAK AND INSUBSTANTIAL !!
DO I LOOK WEAK TO YOU? CAN'T YOU FEEL MY STRENGTH ?
LET ME SHOW YOU THE RAW POWER OF DARKNESS!!

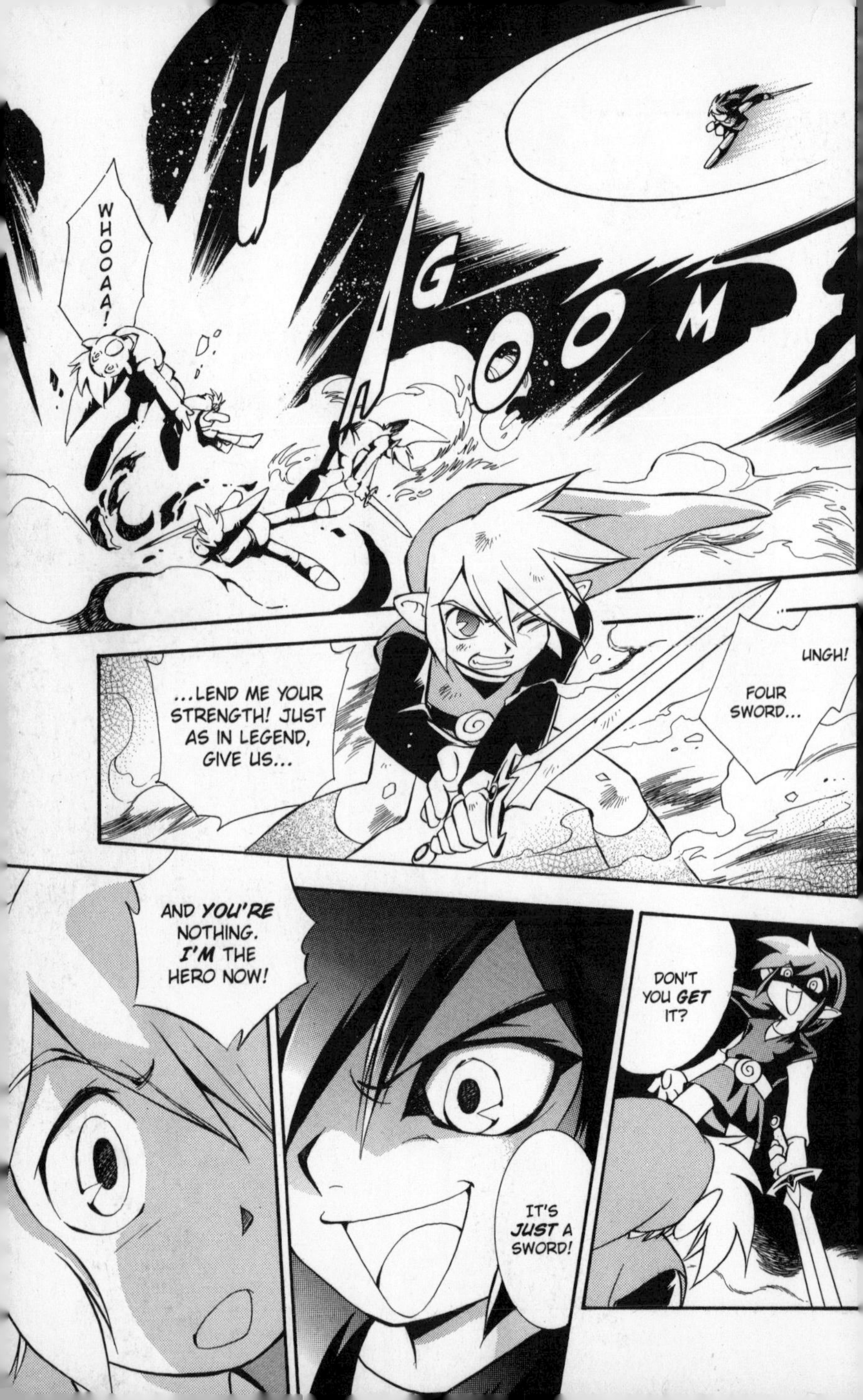
GAGOOM
WHOOOAA!
UNGH!
FOUR SWORD...
...LEND ME YOUR STRENGTH! JUST AS IN LEGEND, GIVE US...
DON'T YOU GET IT?
IT'S JUST A SWORD!
AND YOU'RE NOTHING. I'M THE HERO NOW!

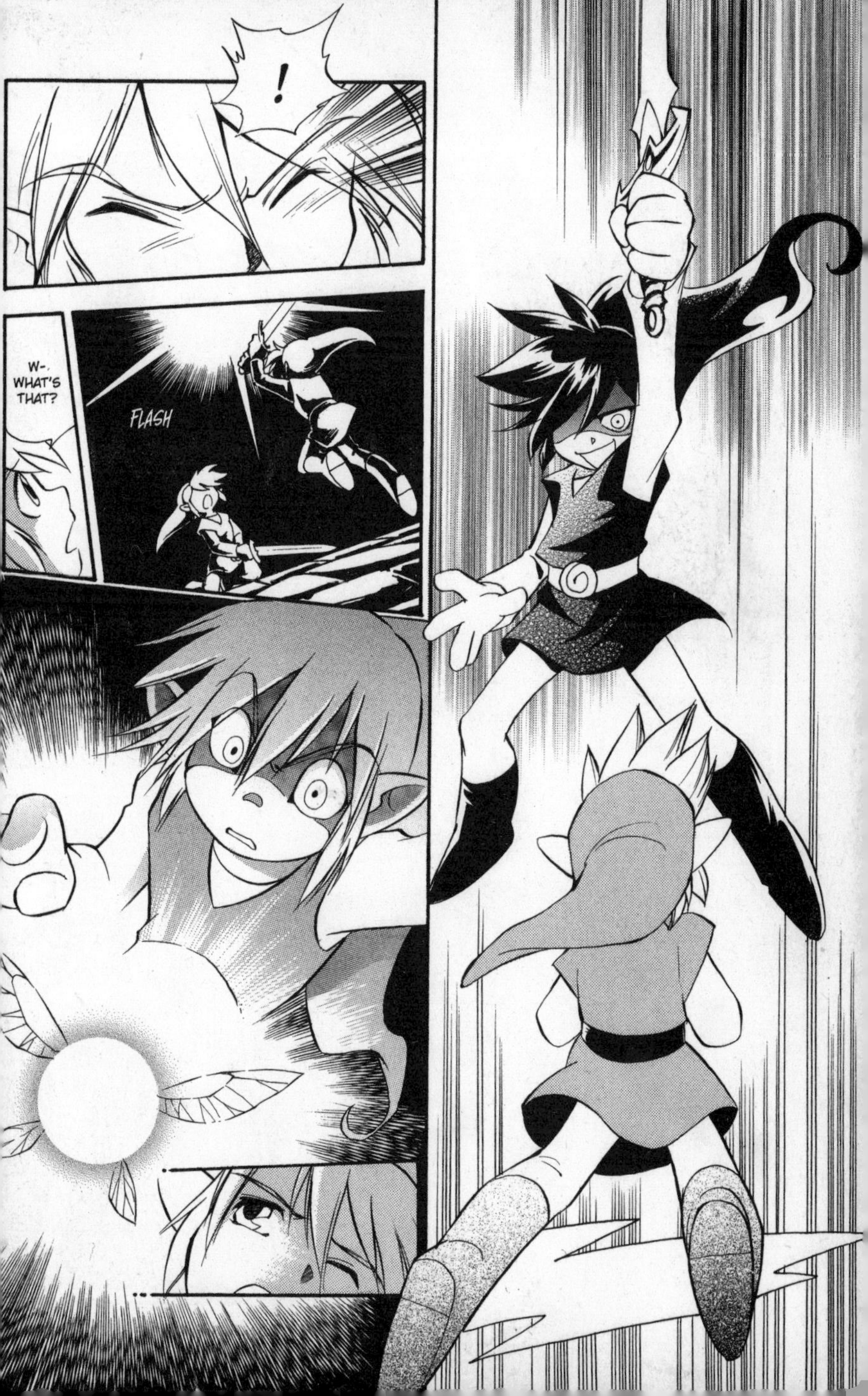
!
W-. WHAT'S THAT?
FLASH

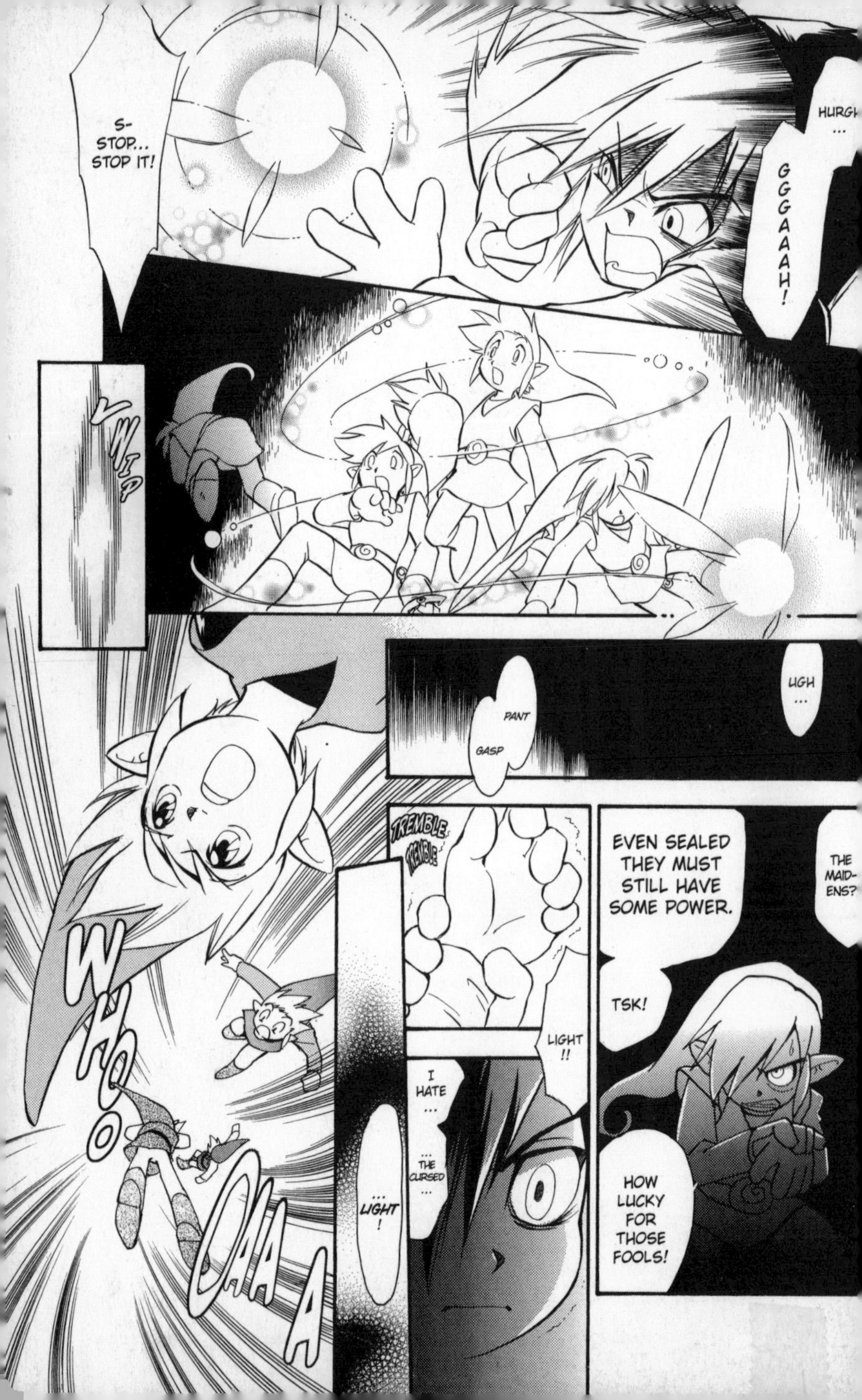
HURGK... GGGAAAH!
S-STOP... STOP IT!
WHIP
UGH...
PANT
GASP
THE MAIDENS?
EVEN SEALED THEY MUST STILL HAVE SOME POWER.
TSK!
HOW LUCKY FOR THOSE FOOLS!
TREMBLE
TREMBLE
LIGHT!!
I HATE...
...THE CURSED...
...LIGHT!
WHOOOAAAA

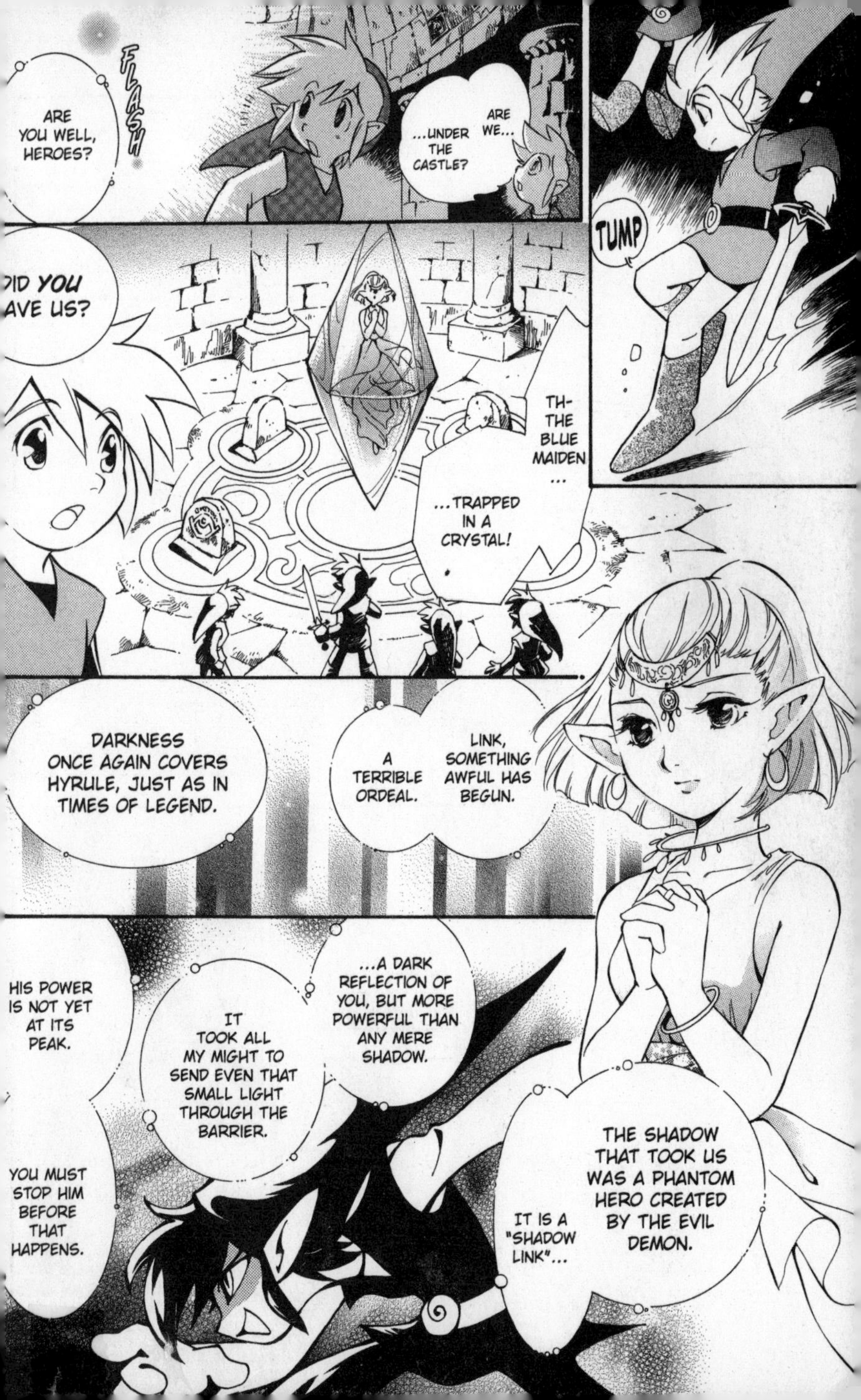
TUMP
ARE WE...
...UNDER THE CASTLE?
FLASH
ARE YOU WELL, HEROES?
TH- THE BLUE MAIDEN ...
...TRAPPED IN A CRYSTAL!
DID *YOU* AVE US?
LINK, SOMETHING AWFUL HAS BEGUN.
A TERRIBLE ORDEAL.
DARKNESS ONCE AGAIN COVERS HYRULE, JUST AS IN TIMES OF LEGEND.
THE SHADOW THAT TOOK US WAS A PHANTOM HERO CREATED BY THE EVIL DEMON.
IT IS A "SHADOW LINK"...
...A DARK REFLECTION OF YOU, BUT MORE POWERFUL THAN ANY MERE SHADOW.
IT TOOK ALL MY MIGHT TO SEND EVEN THAT SMALL LIGHT THROUGH THE BARRIER.
HIS POWER IS NOT YET AT ITS PEAK.
YOU MUST STOP HIM BEFORE THAT HAPPENS.

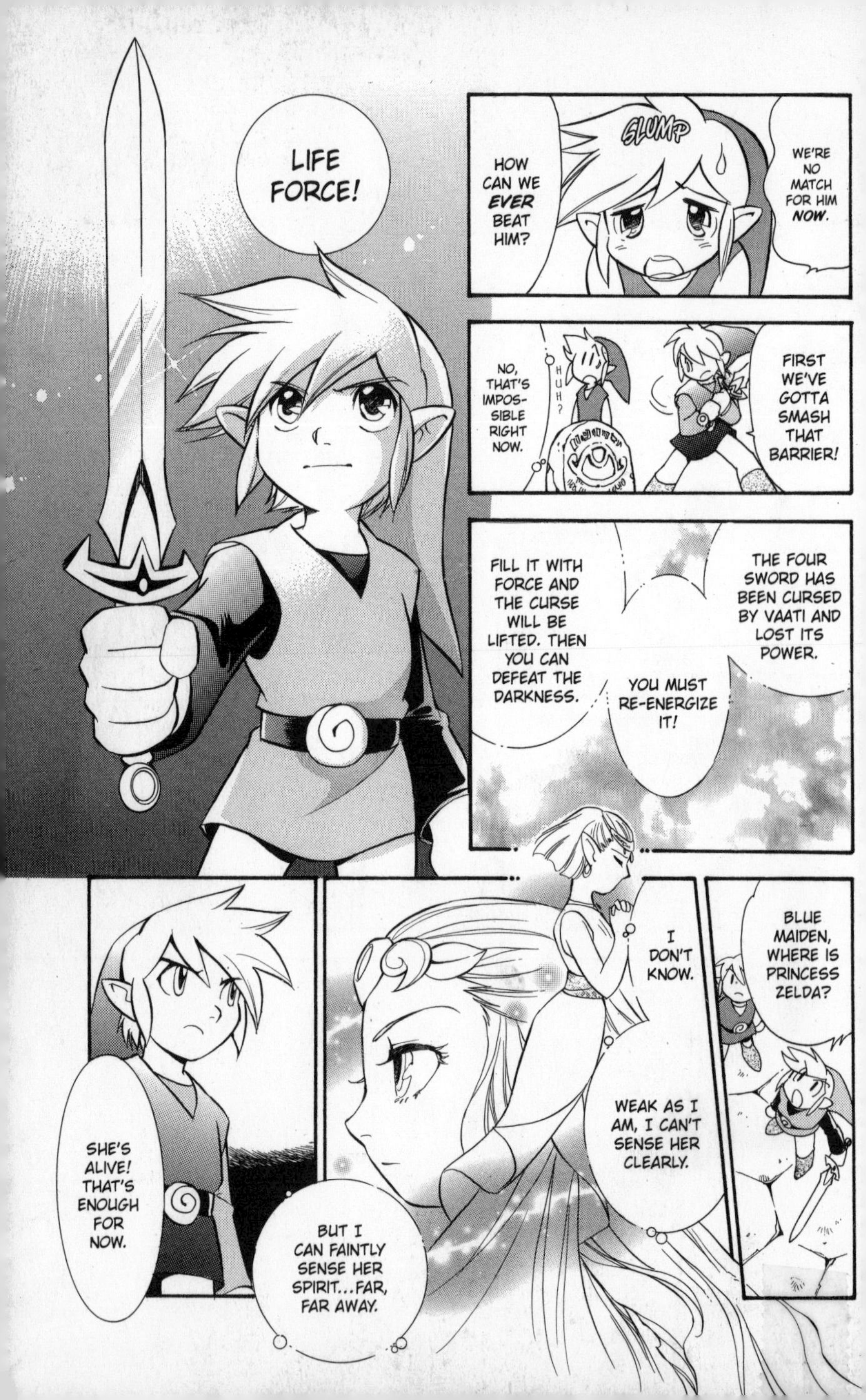
SLUMP
WE'RE NO MATCH FOR HIM **NOW**.
HOW CAN WE **EVER** BEAT HIM?
FIRST WE'VE GOTTA SMASH THAT BARRIER!
HUH?
NO, THAT'S IMPOSSIBLE RIGHT NOW.
THE FOUR SWORD HAS BEEN CURSED BY VAATI AND LOST ITS POWER.
YOU MUST RE-ENERGIZE IT!
FILL IT WITH FORCE AND THE CURSE WILL BE LIFTED. THEN YOU CAN DEFEAT THE DARKNESS.
LIFE FORCE!
BLUE MAIDEN, WHERE IS PRINCESS ZELDA?
I DON'T KNOW.
WEAK AS I AM, I CAN'T SENSE HER CLEARLY.
BUT I CAN FAINTLY SENSE HER SPIRIT...FAR, FAR AWAY.
SHE'S ALIVE! THAT'S ENOUGH FOR NOW.

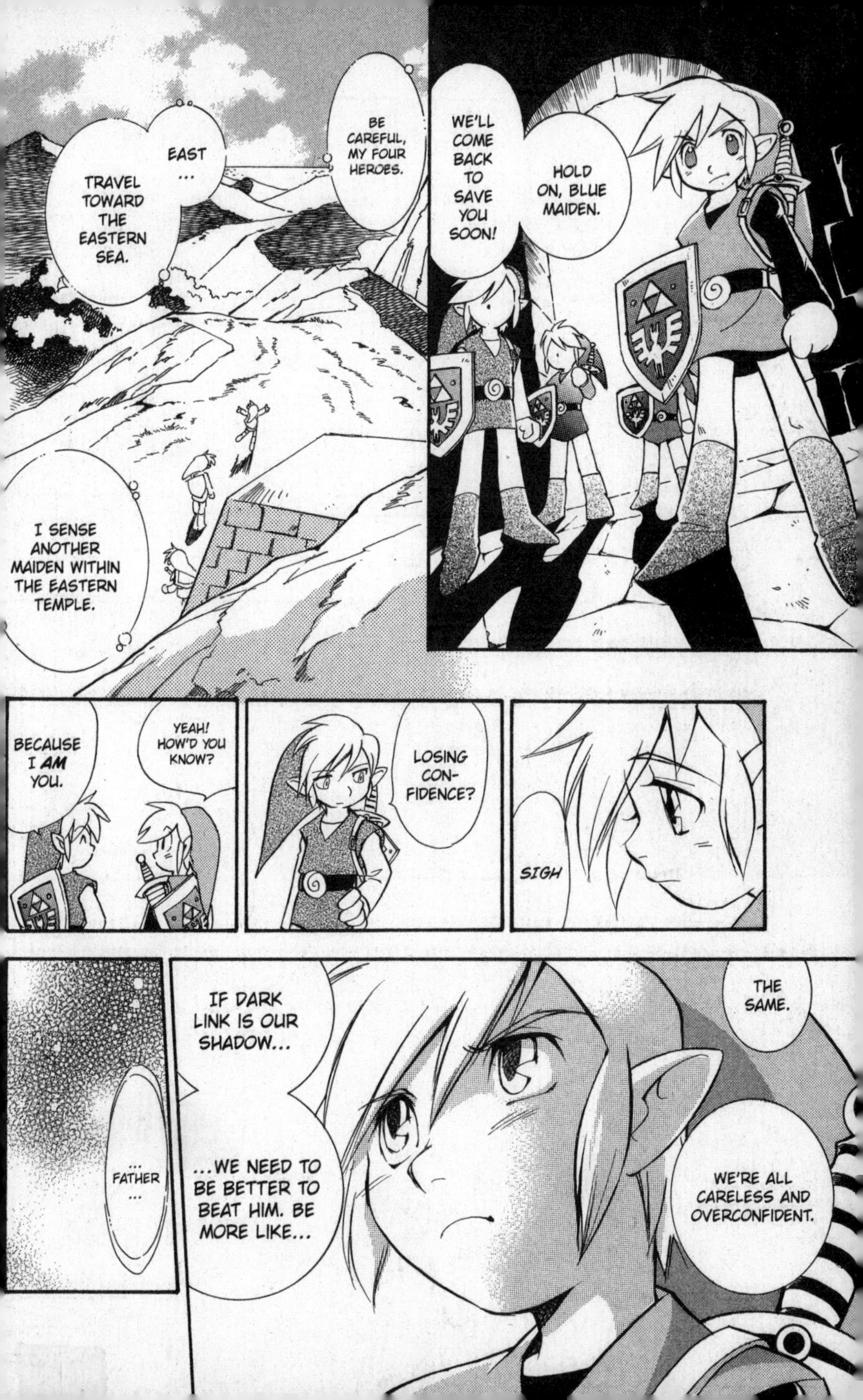
HOLD ON, BLUE MAIDEN.
WE'LL COME BACK TO SAVE YOU SOON!
BE CAREFUL, MY FOUR HEROES.
EAST ...
TRAVEL TOWARD THE EASTERN SEA.
I SENSE ANOTHER MAIDEN WITHIN THE EASTERN TEMPLE.
SIGH
LOSING CON-FIDENCE?
YEAH! HOW'D YOU KNOW?
BECAUSE I *AM* YOU.
THE SAME.
WE'RE ALL CARELESS AND OVERCONFIDENT.
IF DARK LINK IS OUR SHADOW...
...WE NEED TO BE BETTER TO BEAT HIM. BE MORE LIKE...
... FATHER ...

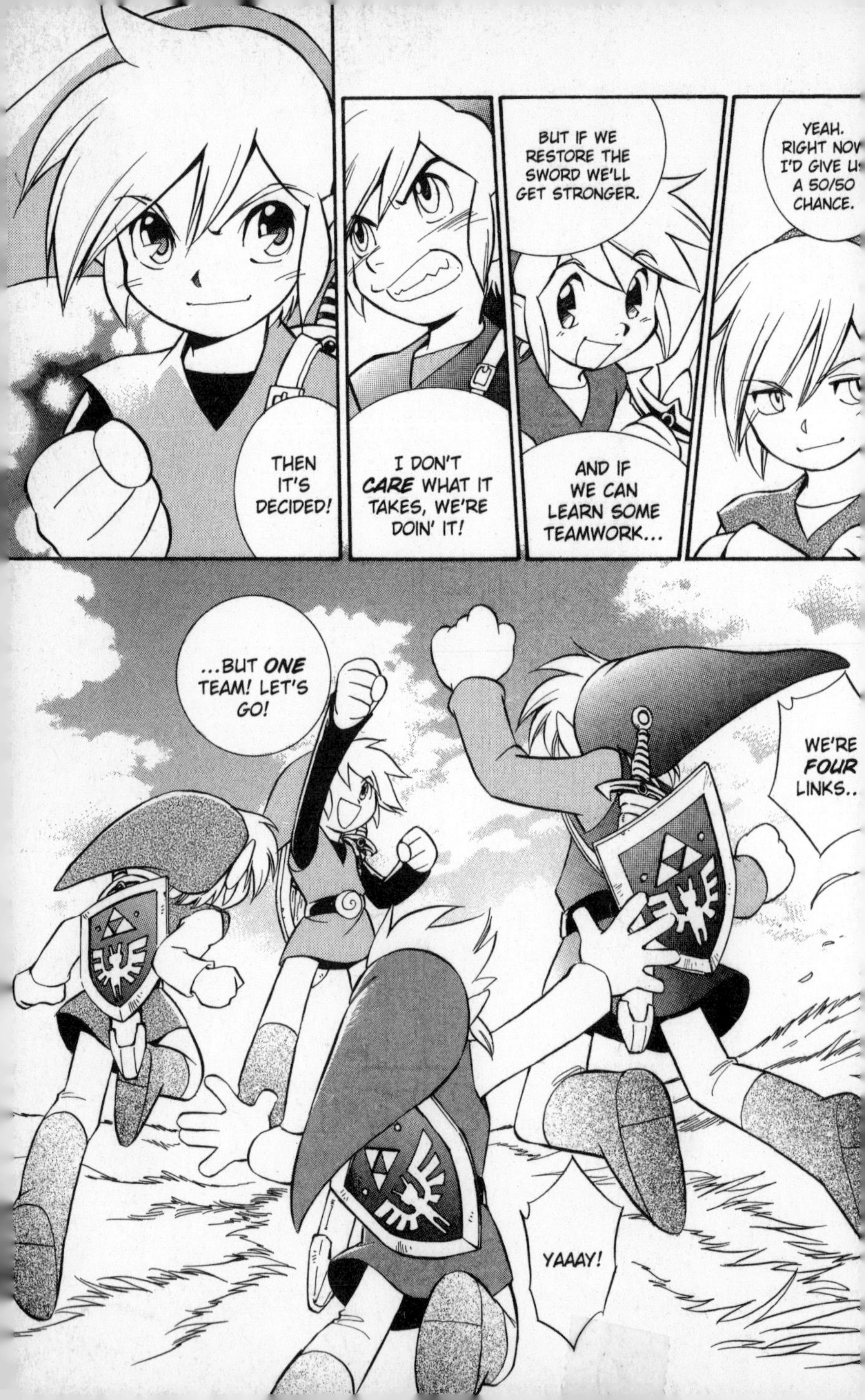
YEAH. RIGHT NOW I'D GIVE US A 50/50 CHANCE.
BUT IF WE RESTORE THE SWORD WE'LL GET STRONGER.
AND IF WE CAN LEARN SOME TEAMWORK...
I DON'T *CARE* WHAT IT TAKES, WE'RE DOIN' IT!
THEN IT'S DECIDED!
WE'RE *FOUR* LINKS...
...BUT *ONE* TEAM! LET'S GO!
YAAAY!

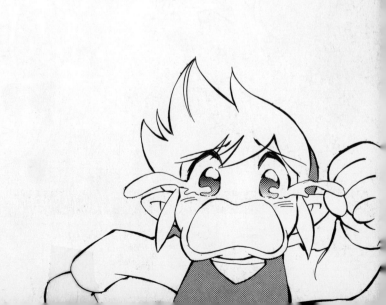

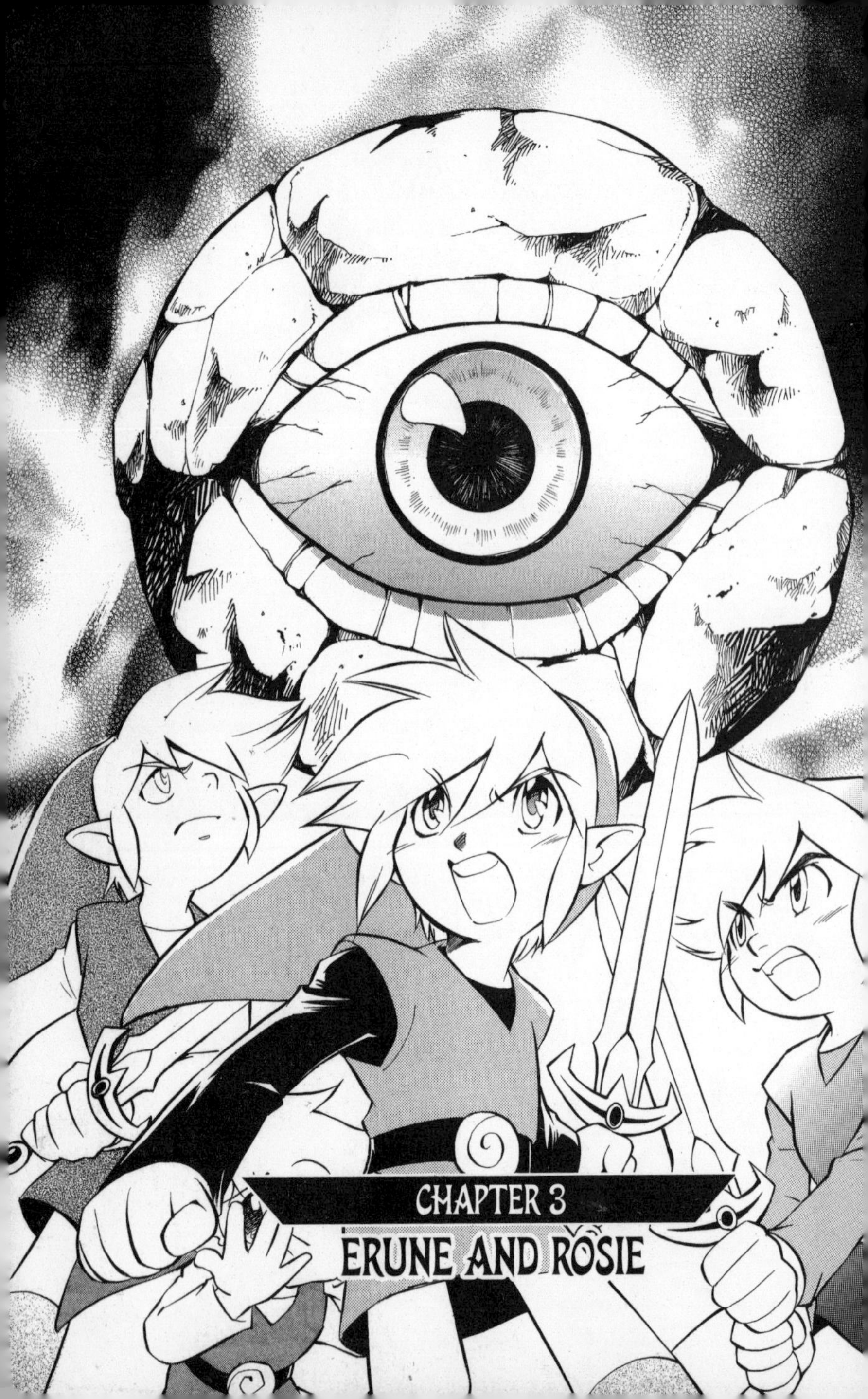
CHAPTER 3
ERUNE AND ROSIE

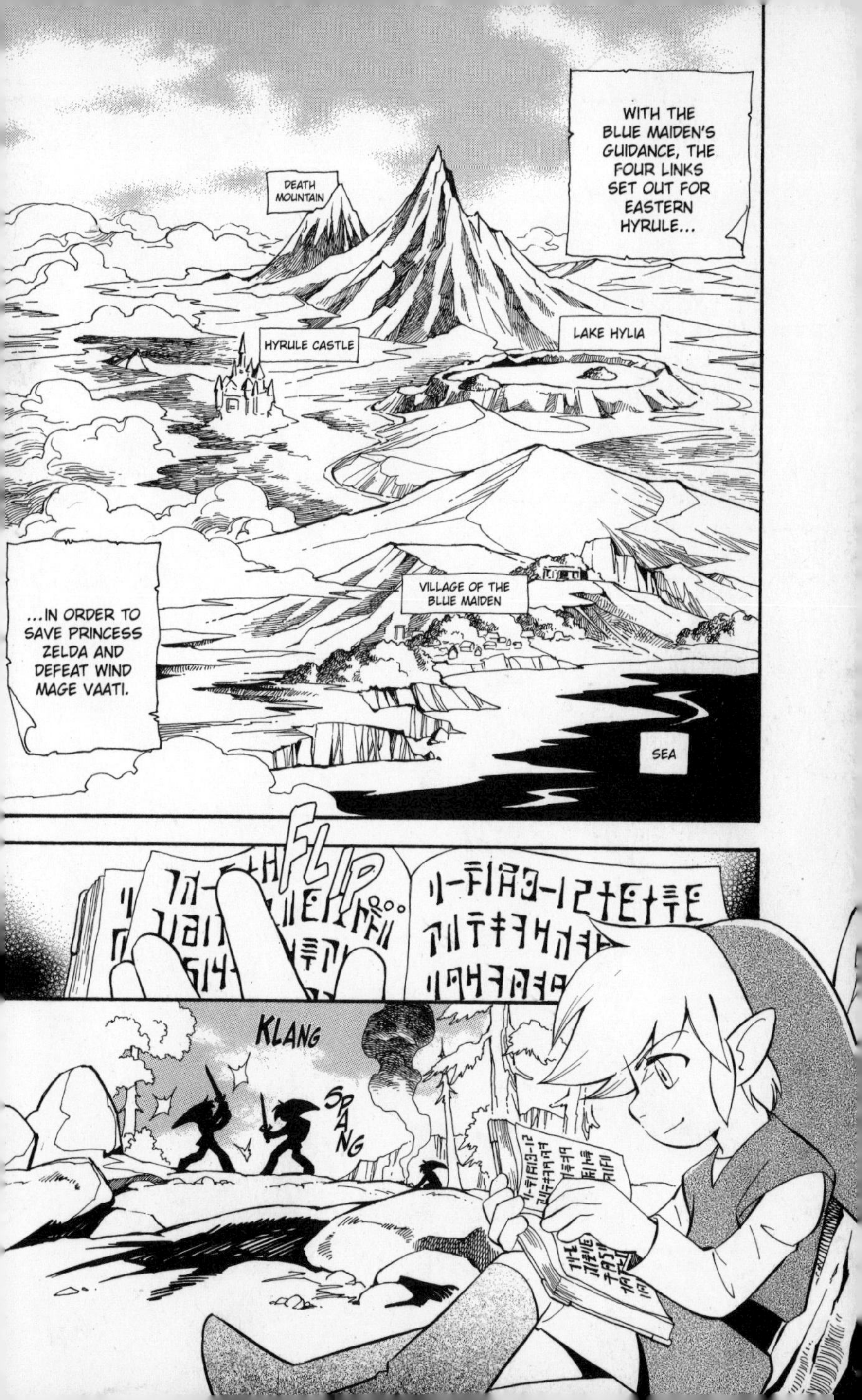
WITH THE BLUE MAIDEN'S GUIDANCE, THE FOUR LINKS SET OUT FOR EASTERN HYRULE...
DEATH MOUNTAIN
LAKE HYLIA
HYRULE CASTLE
VILLAGE OF THE BLUE MAIDEN
SEA
...IN ORDER TO SAVE PRINCESS ZELDA AND DEFEAT WIND MAGE VAATI.
FLIP
KLANG
SPANG

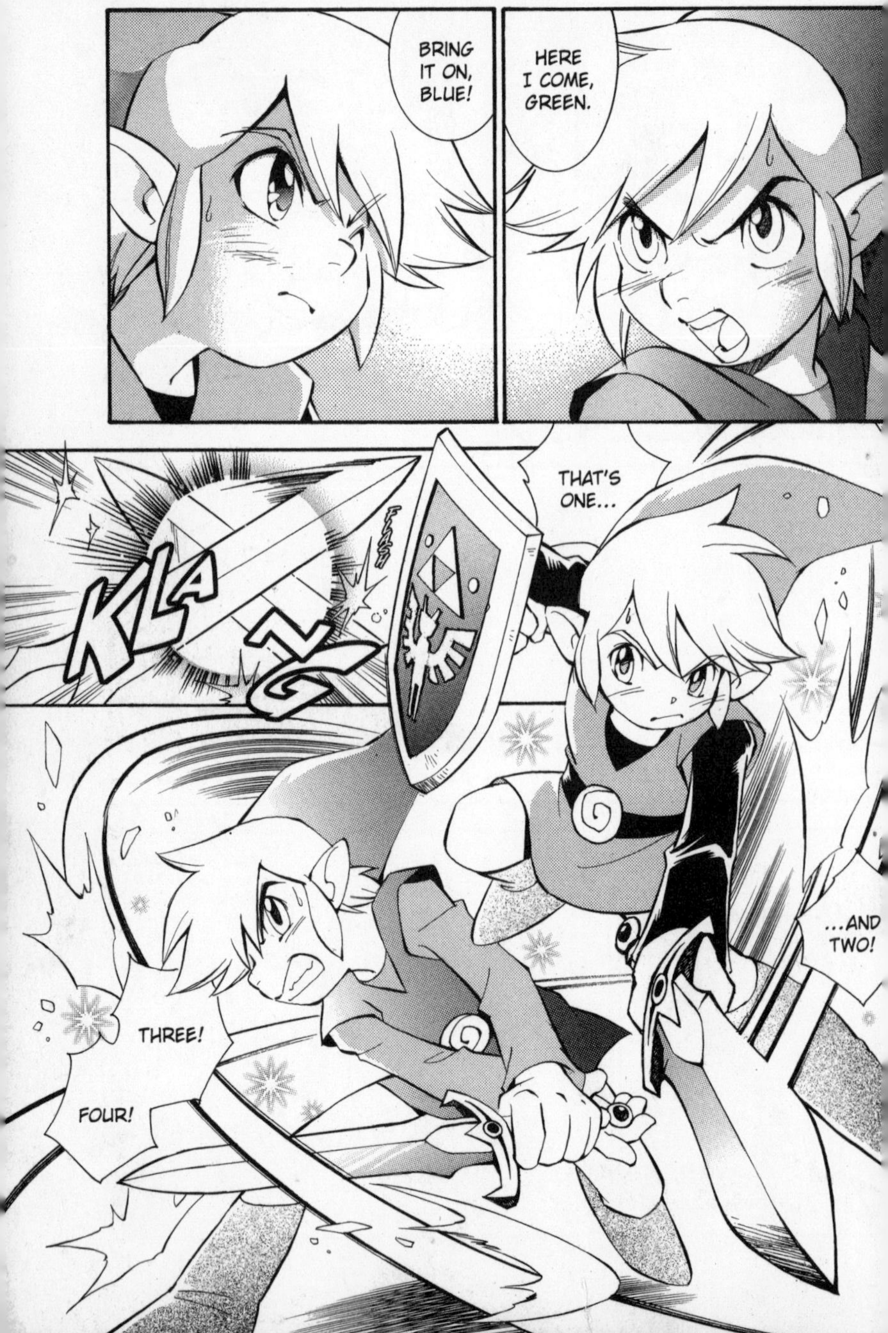
HERE I COME, GREEN.
BRING IT ON, BLUE!
THAT'S ONE...
FLASH
KLANG
...AND TWO!
THREE!
FOUR!

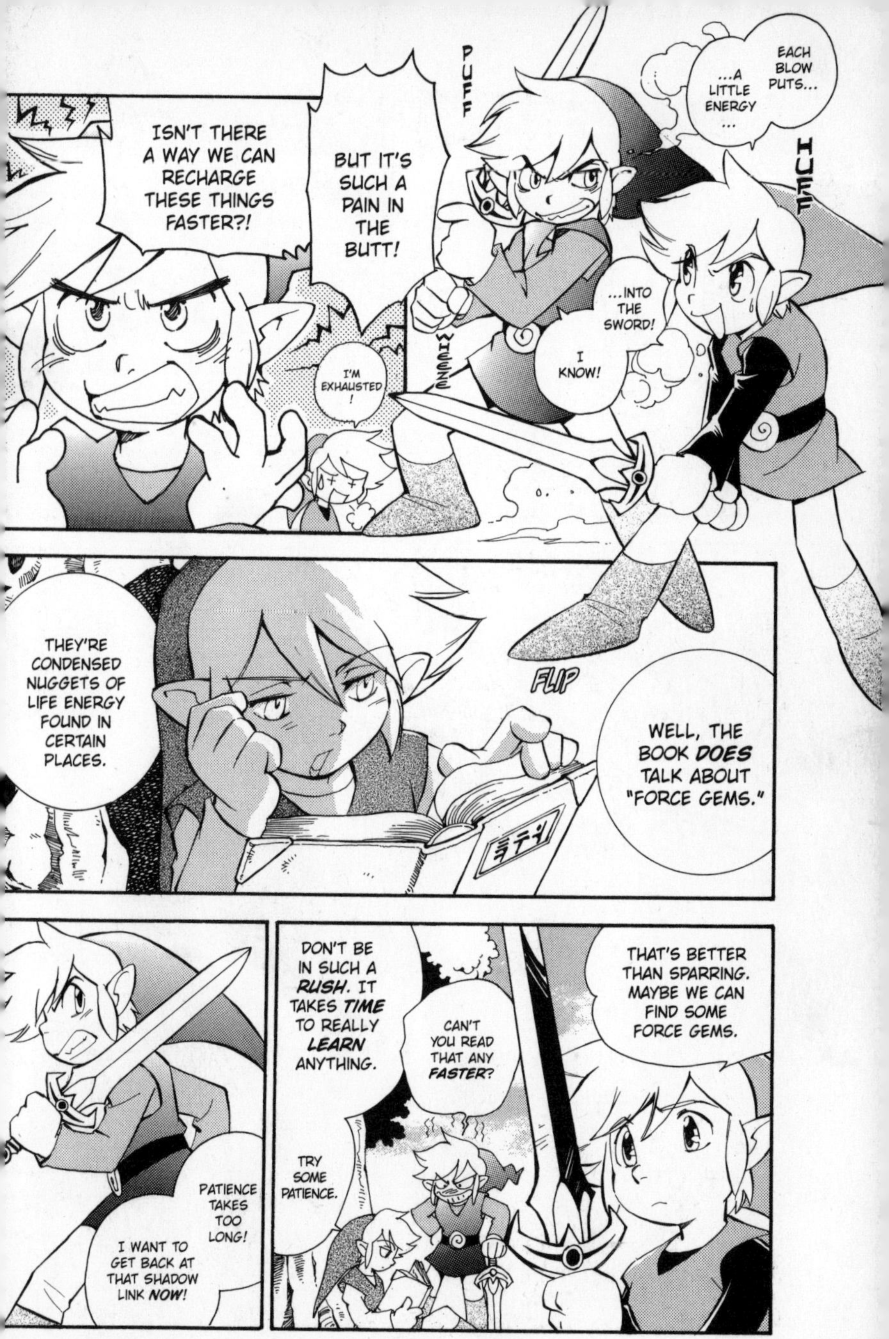
EACH BLOW PUTS...
...A LITTLE ENERGY ...
HUFF
PUFF
...INTO THE SWORD!
I KNOW!
WHEEZE
BUT IT'S SUCH A PAIN IN THE BUTT!
I'M EXHAUSTED!
ISN'T THERE A WAY WE CAN RECHARGE THESE THINGS FASTER?!
WELL, THE BOOK DOES TALK ABOUT "FORCE GEMS."
FLIP
THEY'RE CONDENSED NUGGETS OF LIFE ENERGY FOUND IN CERTAIN PLACES.
THAT'S BETTER THAN SPARRING. MAYBE WE CAN FIND SOME FORCE GEMS.
CAN'T YOU READ THAT ANY FASTER?
DON'T BE IN SUCH A RUSH. IT TAKES TIME TO REALLY LEARN ANYTHING.
TRY SOME PATIENCE.
PATIENCE TAKES TOO LONG!
I WANT TO GET BACK AT THAT SHADOW LINK NOW!

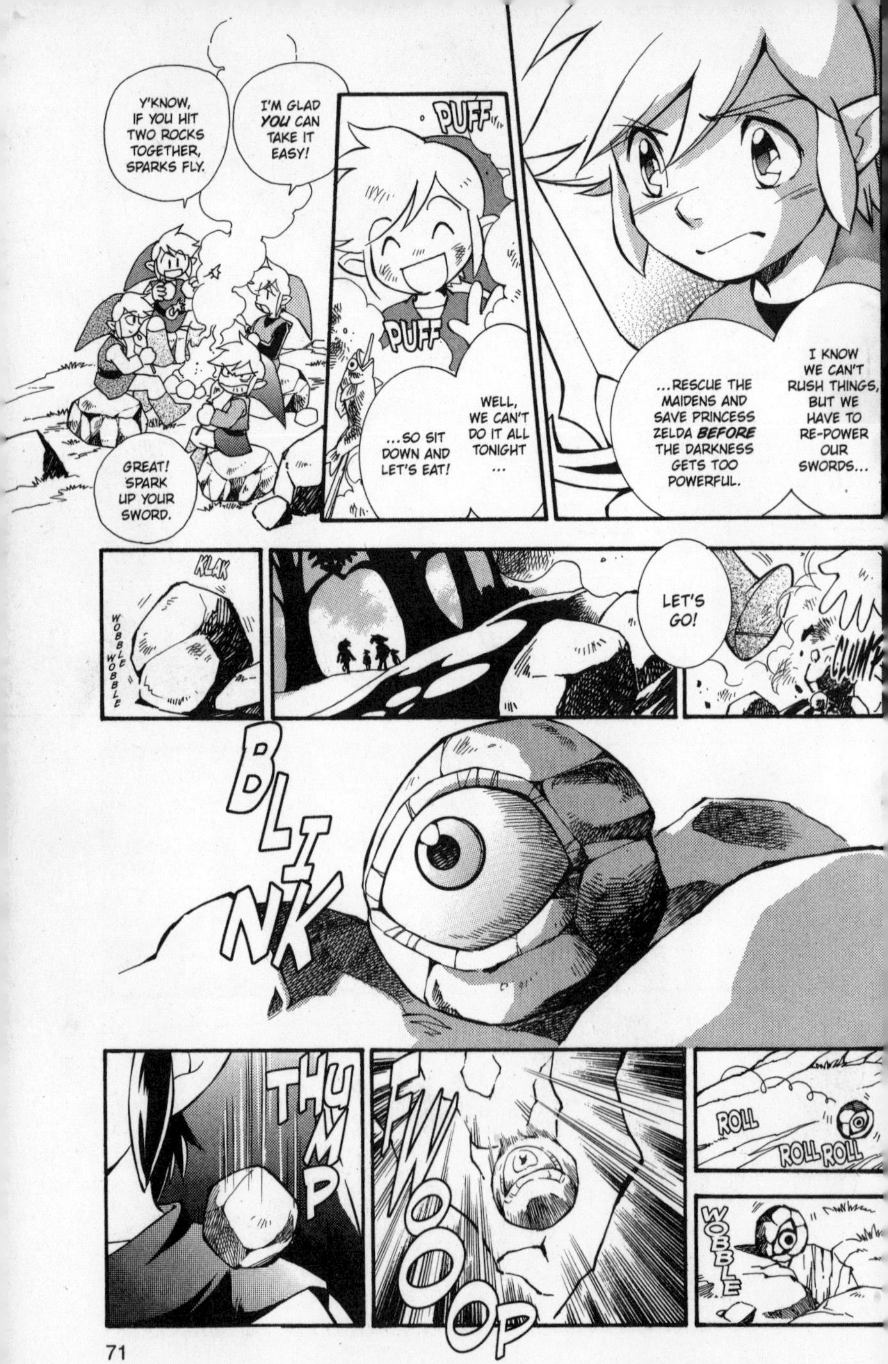
I KNOW WE CAN'T RUSH THINGS, BUT WE HAVE TO RE-POWER OUR SWORDS...
...RESCUE THE MAIDENS AND SAVE PRINCESS ZELDA BEFORE THE DARKNESS GETS TOO POWERFUL.
PUFF
WELL, WE CAN'T DO IT ALL TONIGHT ...
...SO SIT DOWN AND LET'S EAT!
PUFF
I'M GLAD YOU CAN TAKE IT EASY!
Y'KNOW, IF YOU HIT TWO ROCKS TOGETHER, SPARKS FLY.
GREAT! SPARK UP YOUR SWORD.
LET'S GO!
KLAK
WOBBLE WOBBLE
BLINK
ROLL
ROLL ROLL
WOBBLE
FWOOOOP
THUMP

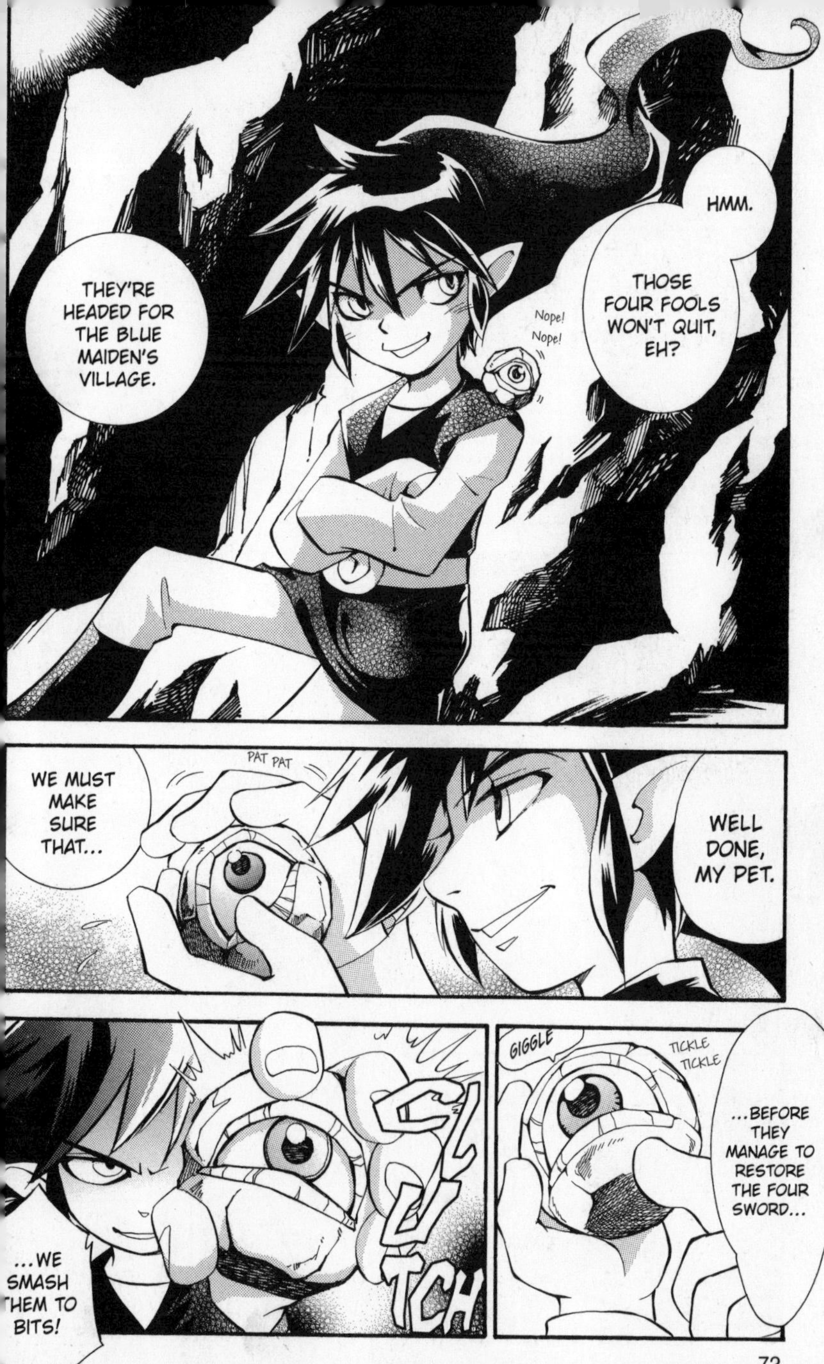
HMM.
THOSE FOUR FOOLS WON'T QUIT, EH?
Nope! Nope!
THEY'RE HEADED FOR THE BLUE MAIDEN'S VILLAGE.
WELL DONE, MY PET.
PAT PAT
WE MUST MAKE SURE THAT...
...BEFORE THEY MANAGE TO RESTORE THE FOUR SWORD...
TICKLE TICKLE
GIGGLE
CLUTCH
...WE SMASH THEM TO BITS!

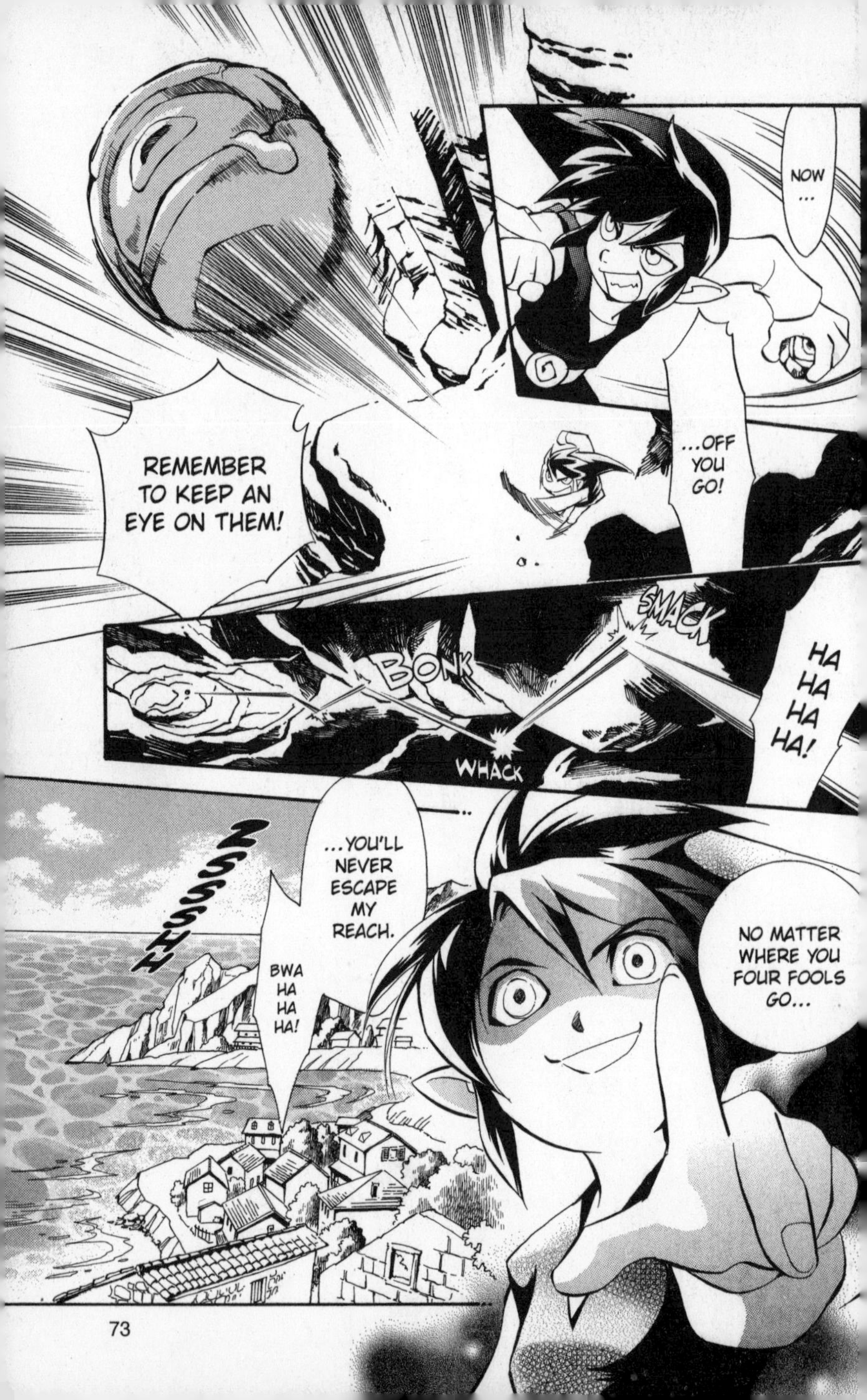
NOW...
...OFF YOU GO!
REMEMBER TO KEEP AN EYE ON THEM!
SMACK
BONK
WHACK
HA HA HA HA!
NO MATTER WHERE YOU FOUR FOOLS GO...
...YOU'LL NEVER ESCAPE MY REACH.
BWA HA HA HA!
ZSSSSHH

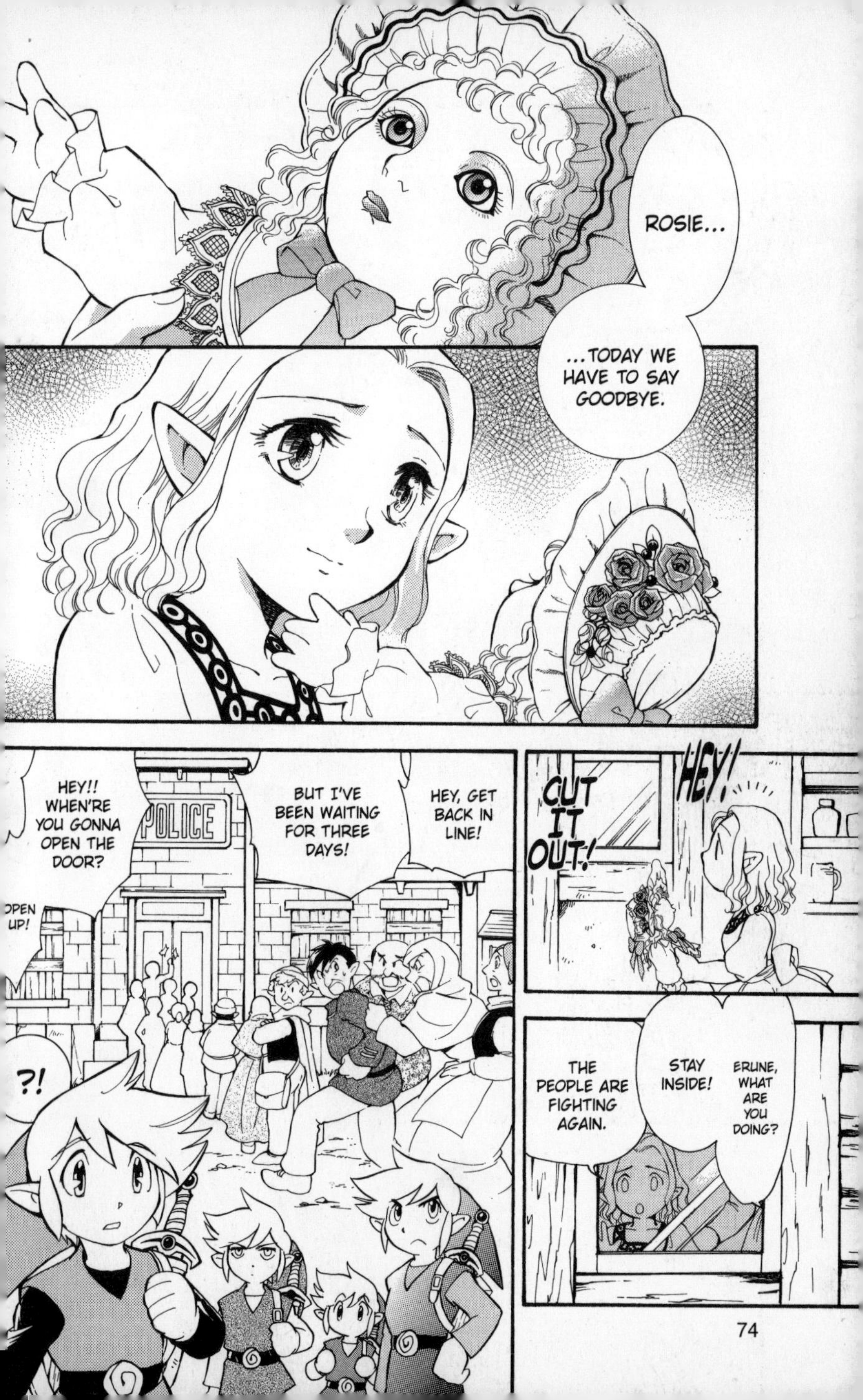
ROSIE...
...TODAY WE HAVE TO SAY GOODBYE.
HEY!
CUT IT OUT!
ERUNE, WHAT ARE YOU DOING?
STAY INSIDE!
THE PEOPLE ARE FIGHTING AGAIN.
HEY, GET BACK IN LINE!
BUT I'VE BEEN WAITING FOR THREE DAYS!
POLICE
HEY!! WHEN'RE YOU GONNA OPEN THE DOOR?
OPEN UP!
?!

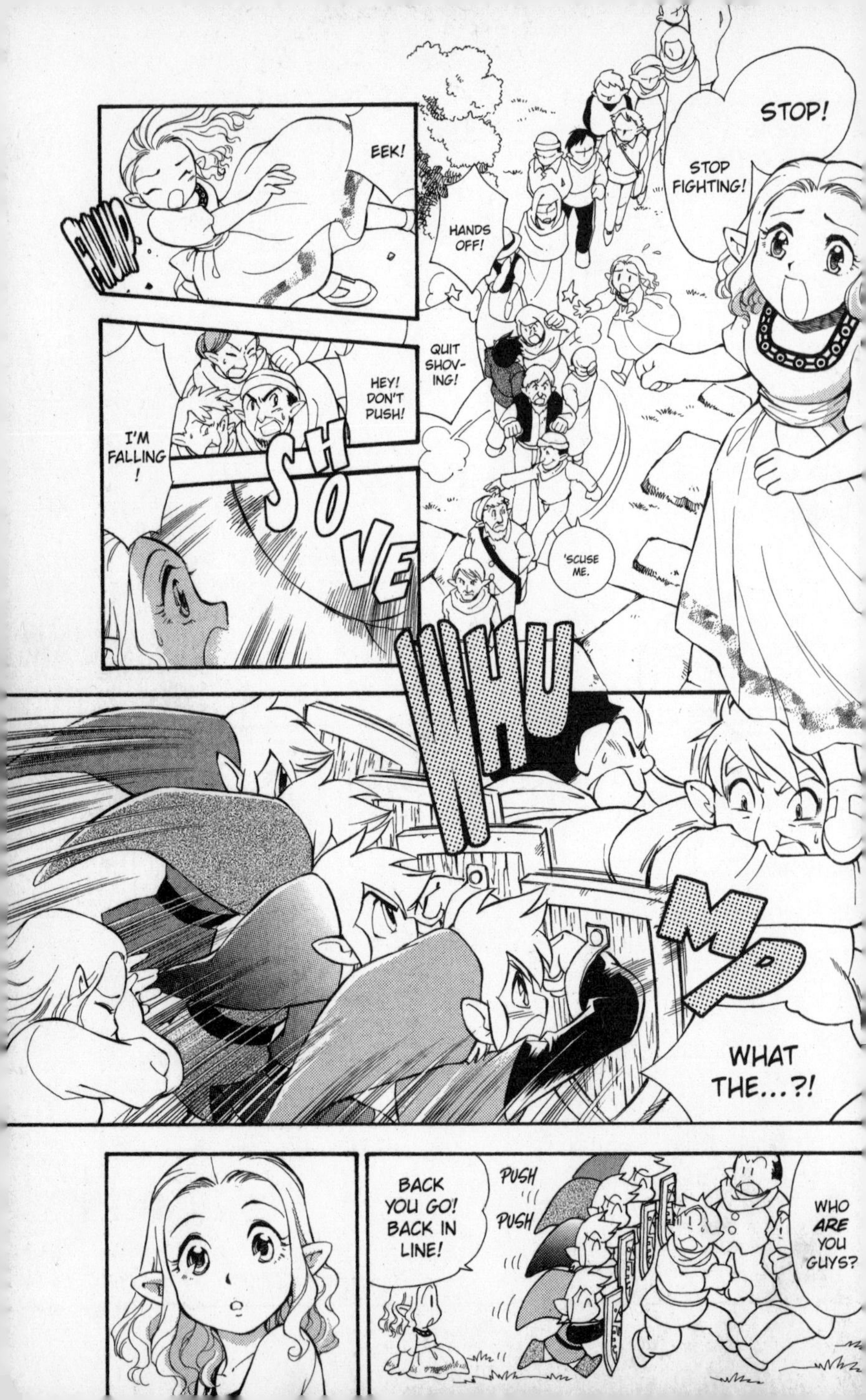
STOP!
STOP FIGHTING!
HANDS OFF!
QUIT SHOVING!
'SCUSE ME.
EEK!
HEY! DON'T PUSH!
I'M FALLING!
SHOVE
WHUMP
WHAT THE...?!
WHO ARE YOU GUYS?
PUSH
PUSH
BACK YOU GO! BACK IN LINE!

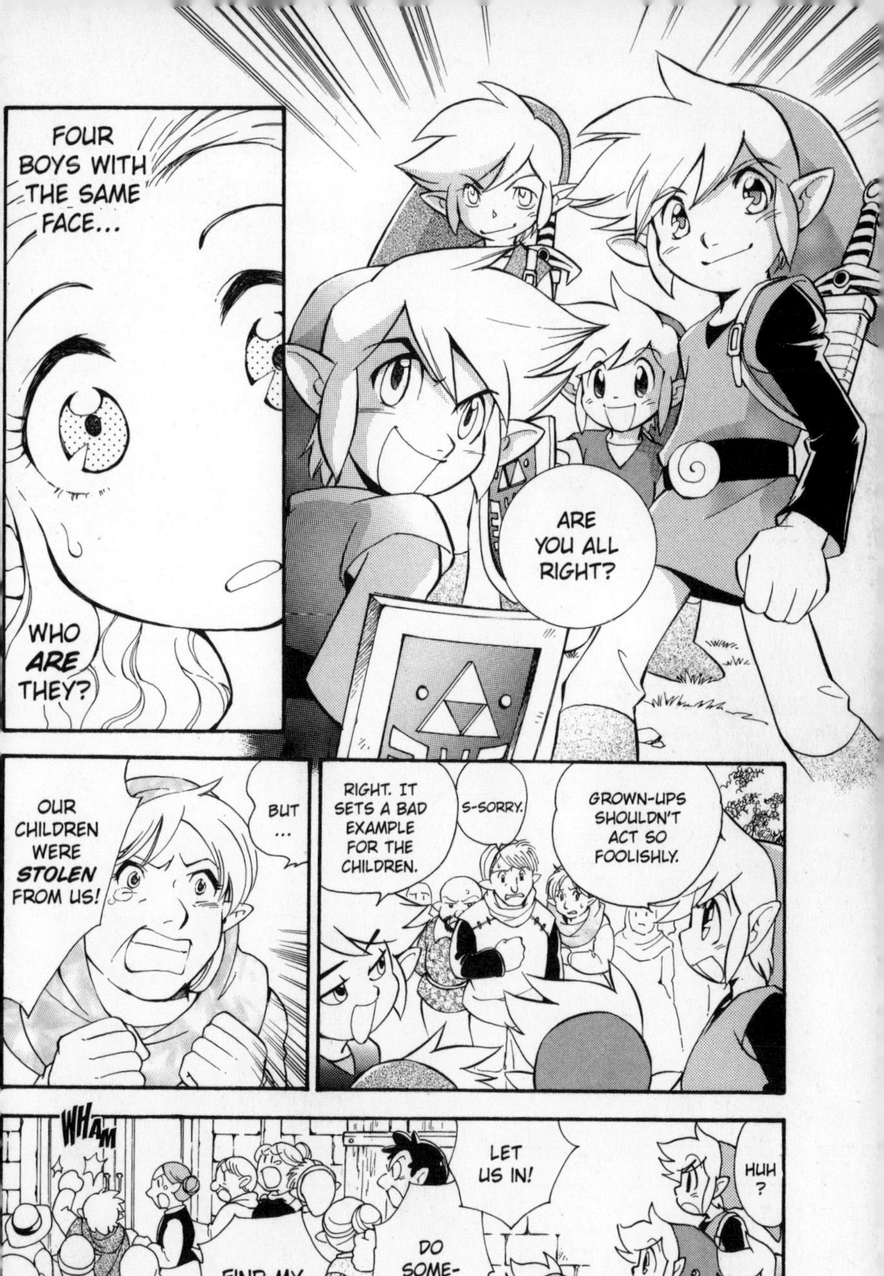
ARE YOU ALL RIGHT?
FOUR BOYS WITH THE SAME FACE...
WHO **ARE** THEY?
GROWN-UPS SHOULDN'T ACT SO FOOLISHLY.
S-SORRY.
RIGHT. IT SETS A BAD EXAMPLE FOR THE CHILDREN.
BUT ...
OUR CHILDREN WERE **STOLEN** FROM US!
HUH ?
LET US IN!
DO SOME-THING!
FIND MY BOY!
WHAM

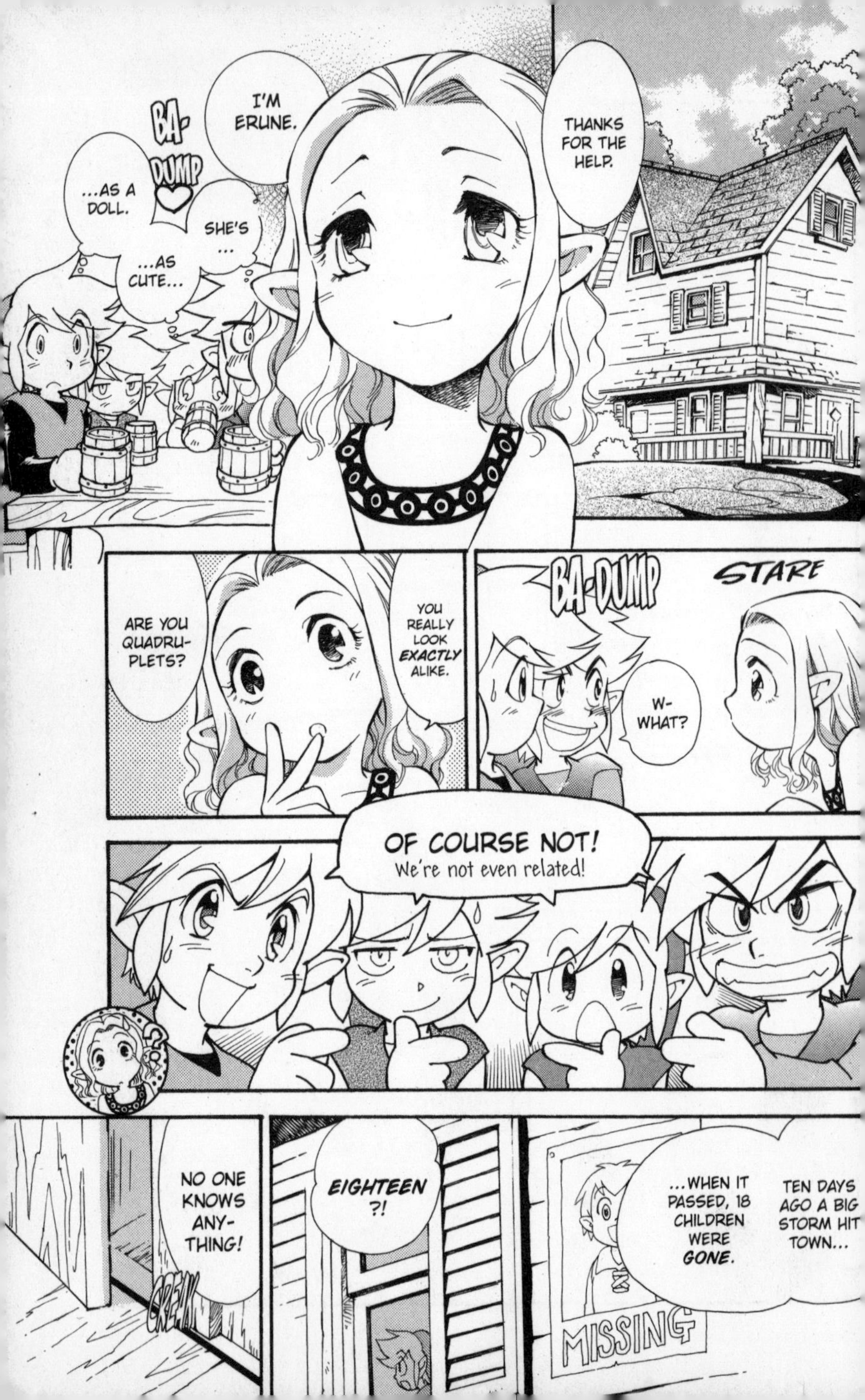
THANKS FOR THE HELP.
I'M ERUNE.
BA-DUMP
SHE'S...
...AS CUTE...
...AS A DOLL.
STARE
BA-DUMP
W-WHAT?
YOU REALLY LOOK EXACTLY ALIKE.
ARE YOU QUADRUPLETS?
OF COURSE NOT!
We're not even related!
TEN DAYS AGO A BIG STORM HIT TOWN...
...WHEN IT PASSED, 18 CHILDREN WERE GONE.
MISSING
EIGHTEEN?!
NO ONE KNOWS ANYTHING!
CREAK

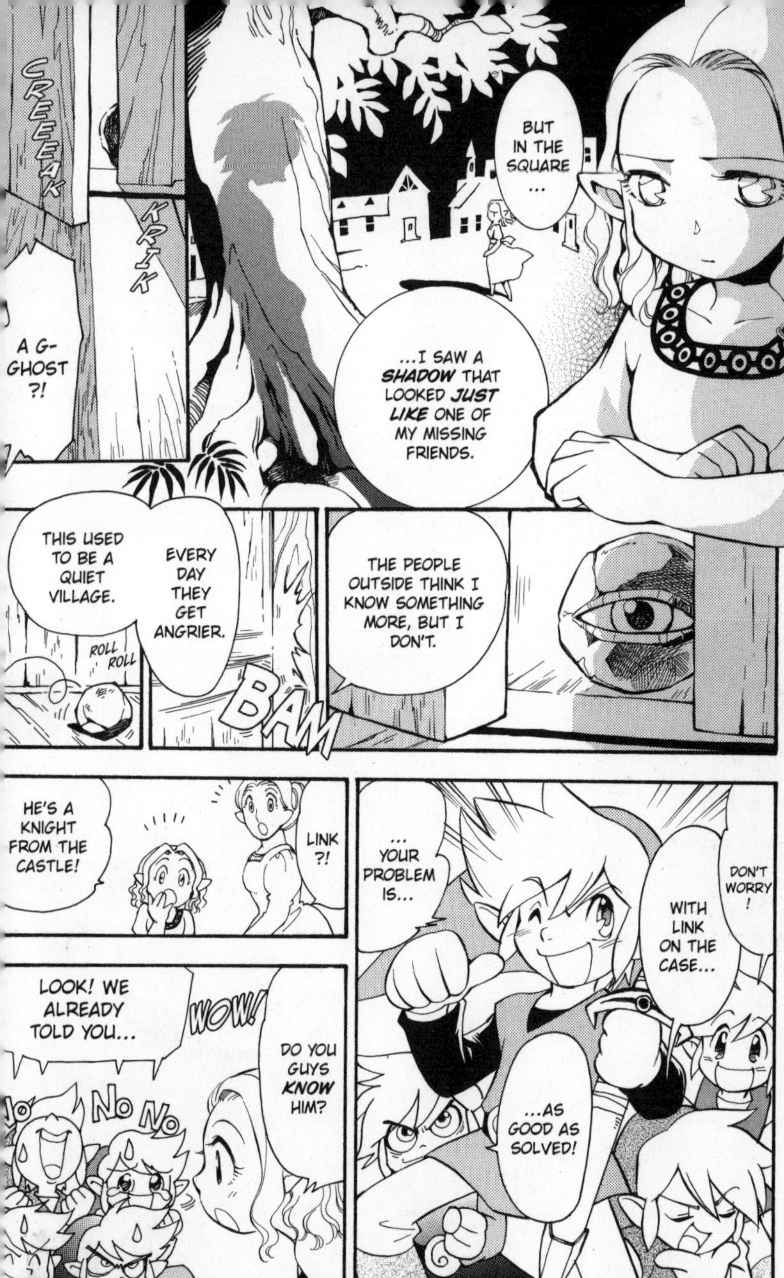
BUT IN THE SQUARE...
...I SAW A **SHADOW** THAT LOOKED **JUST LIKE** ONE OF MY MISSING FRIENDS.
CREEEAK
KRIK
A G-GHOST ?!
THE PEOPLE OUTSIDE THINK I KNOW SOMETHING MORE, BUT I DON'T.
BAM
THIS USED TO BE A QUIET VILLAGE.
EVERY DAY THEY GET ANGRIER.
ROLL ROLL
DON'T WORRY!
WITH LINK ON THE CASE...
... YOUR PROBLEM IS...
...AS GOOD AS SOLVED!
LINK ?!
HE'S A KNIGHT FROM THE CASTLE!
DO YOU GUYS **KNOW** HIM?
WOW!
LOOK! WE ALREADY TOLD YOU...
No No No

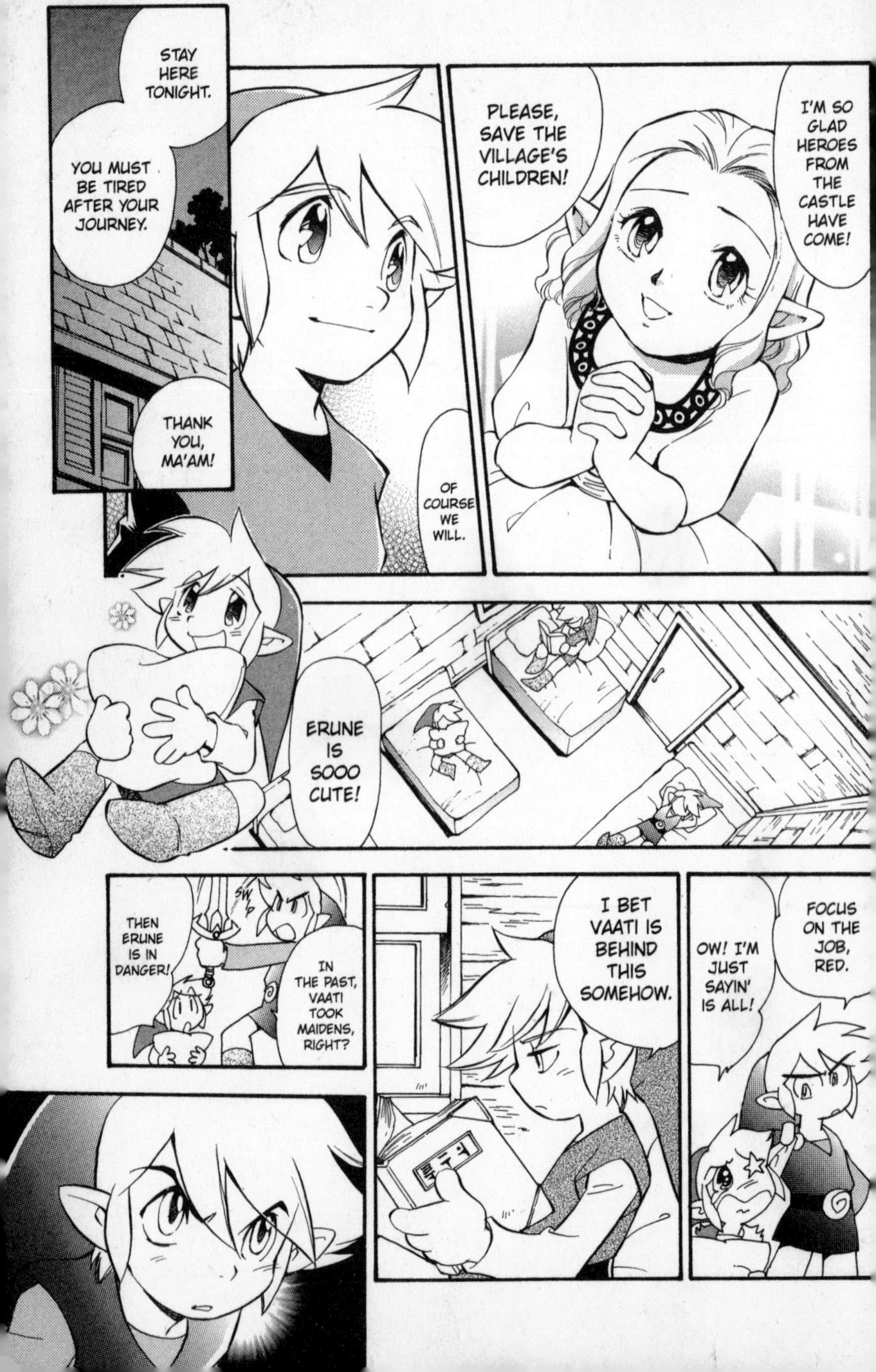

I'M SO GLAD HEROES FROM THE CASTLE HAVE COME!
PLEASE, SAVE THE VILLAGE'S CHILDREN!
OF COURSE WE WILL.
STAY HERE TONIGHT.
YOU MUST BE TIRED AFTER YOUR JOURNEY.
THANK YOU, MA'AM!
ERUNE IS SOOO CUTE!
FOCUS ON THE JOB, RED.
OW! I'M JUST SAYIN' IS ALL!
I BET VAATI IS BEHIND THIS SOMEHOW.
IN THE PAST, VAATI TOOK MAIDENS, RIGHT?
THEN ERUNE IS IN DANGER!

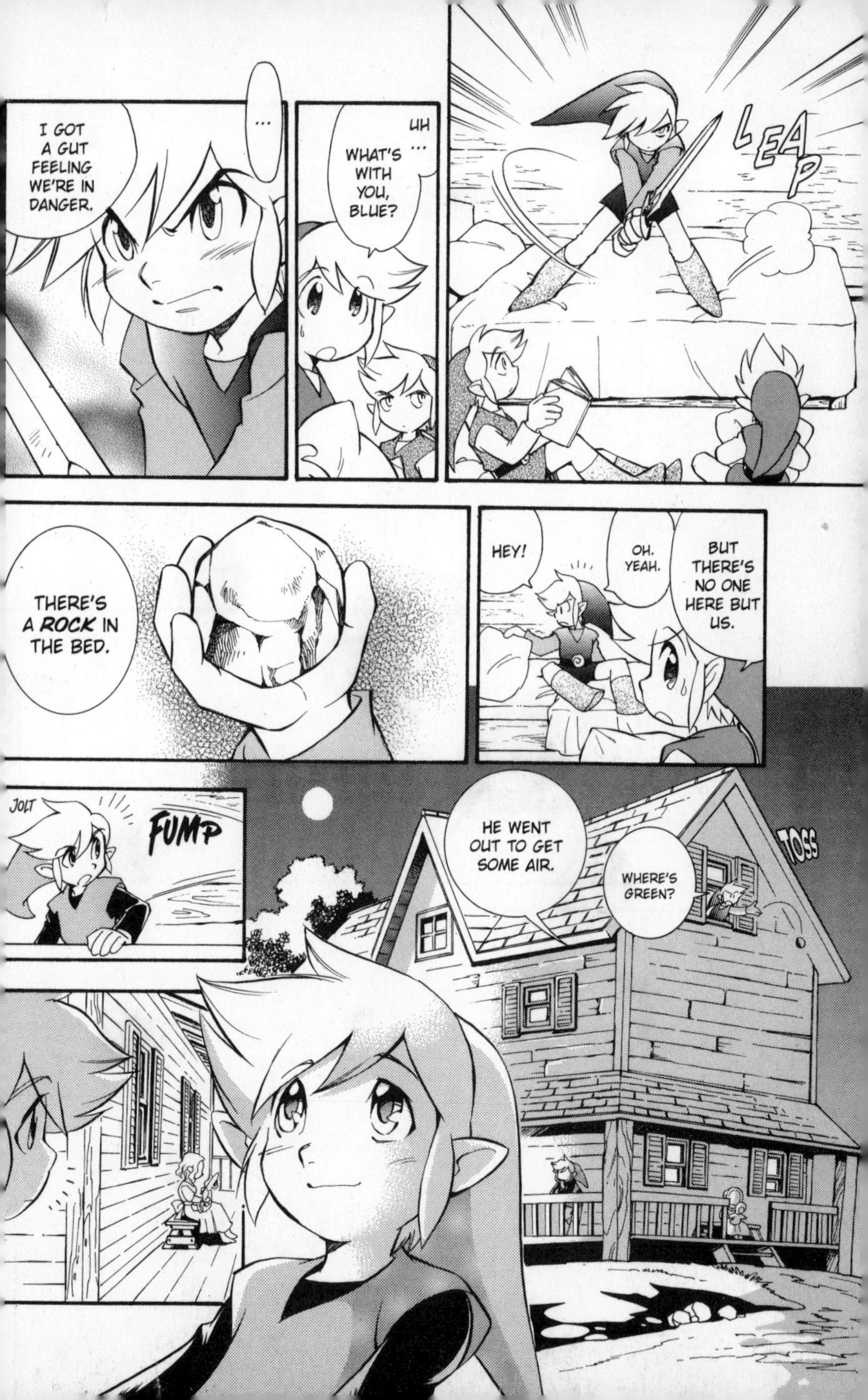
LEAP
UH ...
WHAT'S WITH YOU, BLUE?
...
I GOT A GUT FEELING WE'RE IN DANGER.
BUT THERE'S NO ONE HERE BUT US.
OH. YEAH.
HEY!
THERE'S A **ROCK** IN THE BED.
TOSS
WHERE'S GREEN?
HE WENT OUT TO GET SOME AIR.
FUMP
JOLT

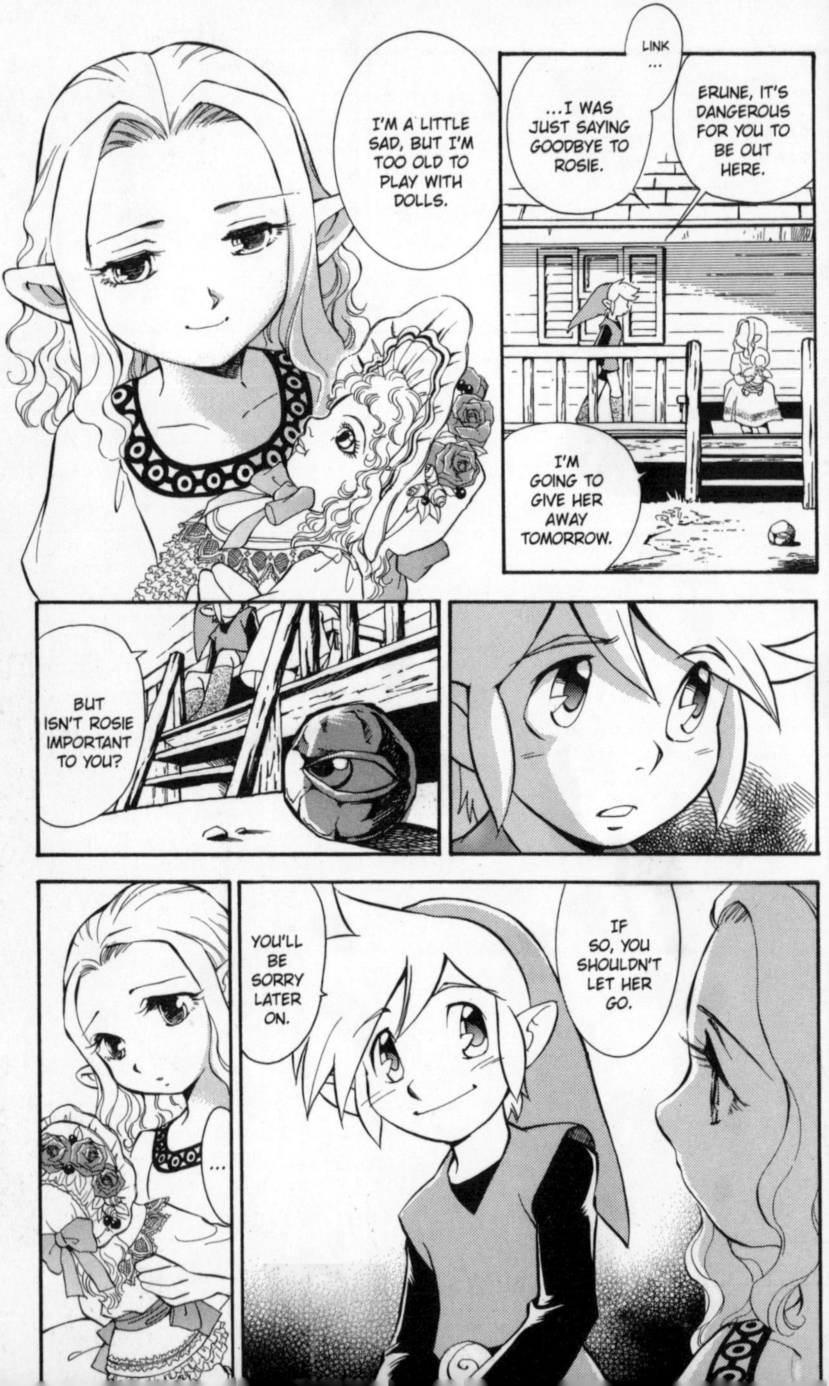
ERUNE, IT'S DANGEROUS FOR YOU TO BE OUT HERE.
LINK ...
...I WAS JUST SAYING GOODBYE TO ROSIE.
I'M GOING TO GIVE HER AWAY TOMORROW.
I'M A LITTLE SAD, BUT I'M TOO OLD TO PLAY WITH DOLLS.
BUT ISN'T ROSIE IMPORTANT TO YOU?
IF SO, YOU SHOULDN'T LET HER GO.
YOU'LL BE SORRY LATER ON.
...

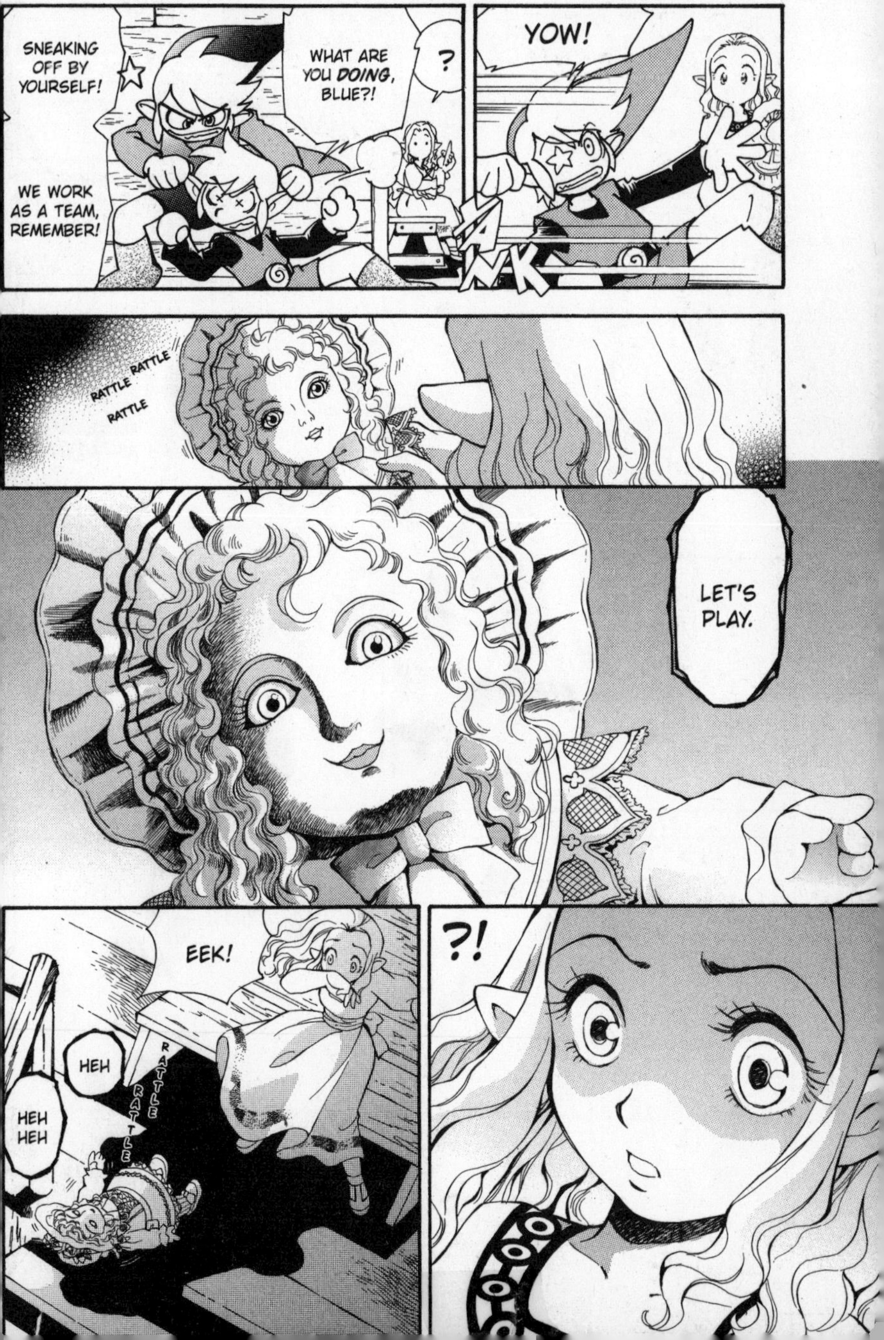
YOW!
YANK
?
WHAT ARE YOU DOING, BLUE?!
SNEAKING OFF BY YOURSELF!
WE WORK AS A TEAM, REMEMBER!
RATTLE RATTLE
RATTLE
LET'S PLAY.
?!
EEK!
RATTLE
RATTLE
HEH
HEH HEH

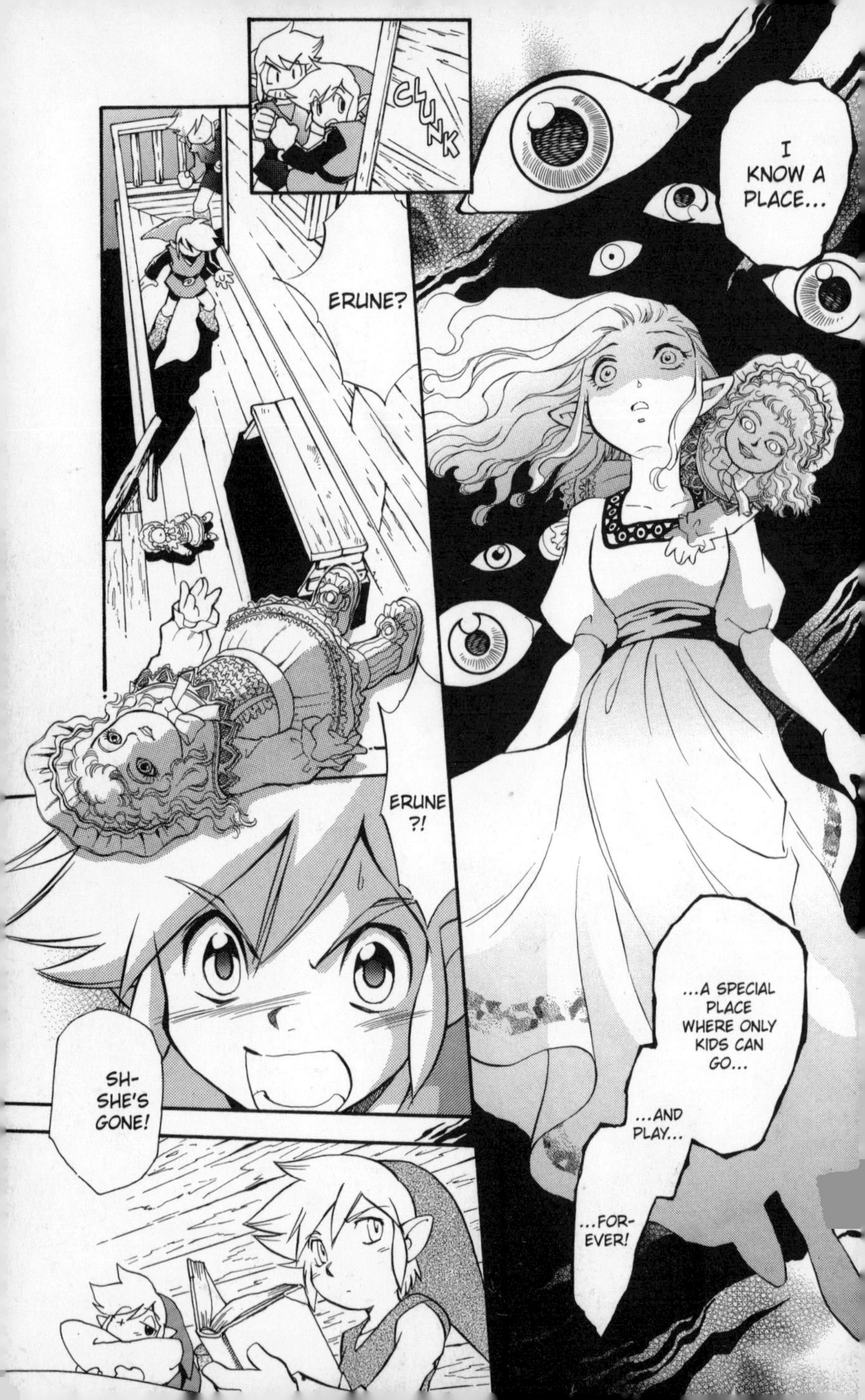
I KNOW A PLACE...
...A SPECIAL PLACE WHERE ONLY KIDS CAN GO...
...AND PLAY...
...FOR-EVER!
CLUNK
ERUNE?
ERUNE ?!
SH- SHE'S GONE!

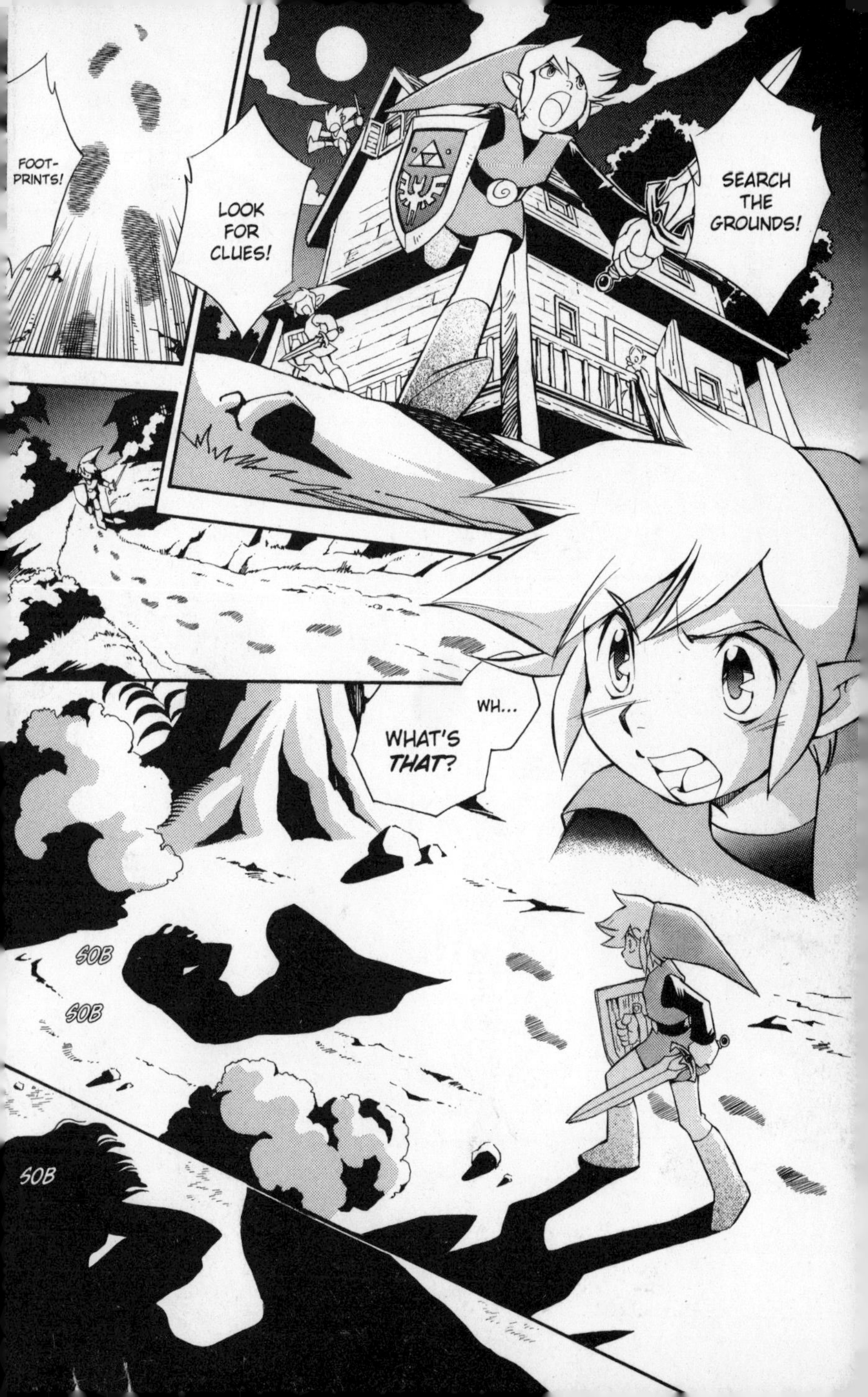
SEARCH THE GROUNDS!
LOOK FOR CLUES!
FOOT-PRINTS!
WH...
WHAT'S *THAT*?
SOB
SOB
SOB

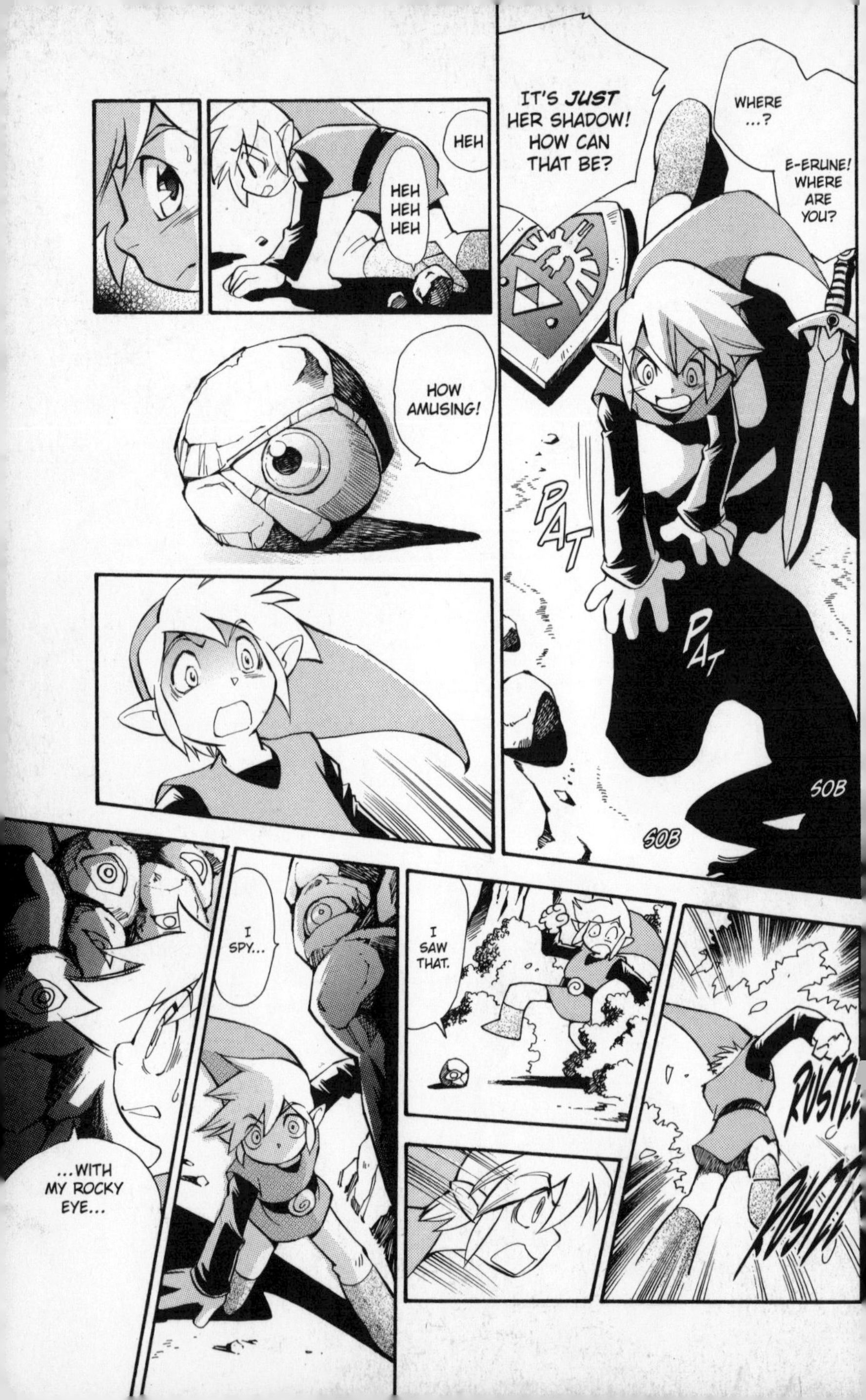
WHERE ...?
E-ERUNE! WHERE ARE YOU?
IT'S *JUST* HER SHADOW! HOW CAN THAT BE?
PAT
PAT
SOB
SOB
HEH
HEH HEH HEH
HOW AMUSING!
RUSTL
RUSTL
I SAW THAT.
I SPY...
...WITH MY ROCKY EYE...

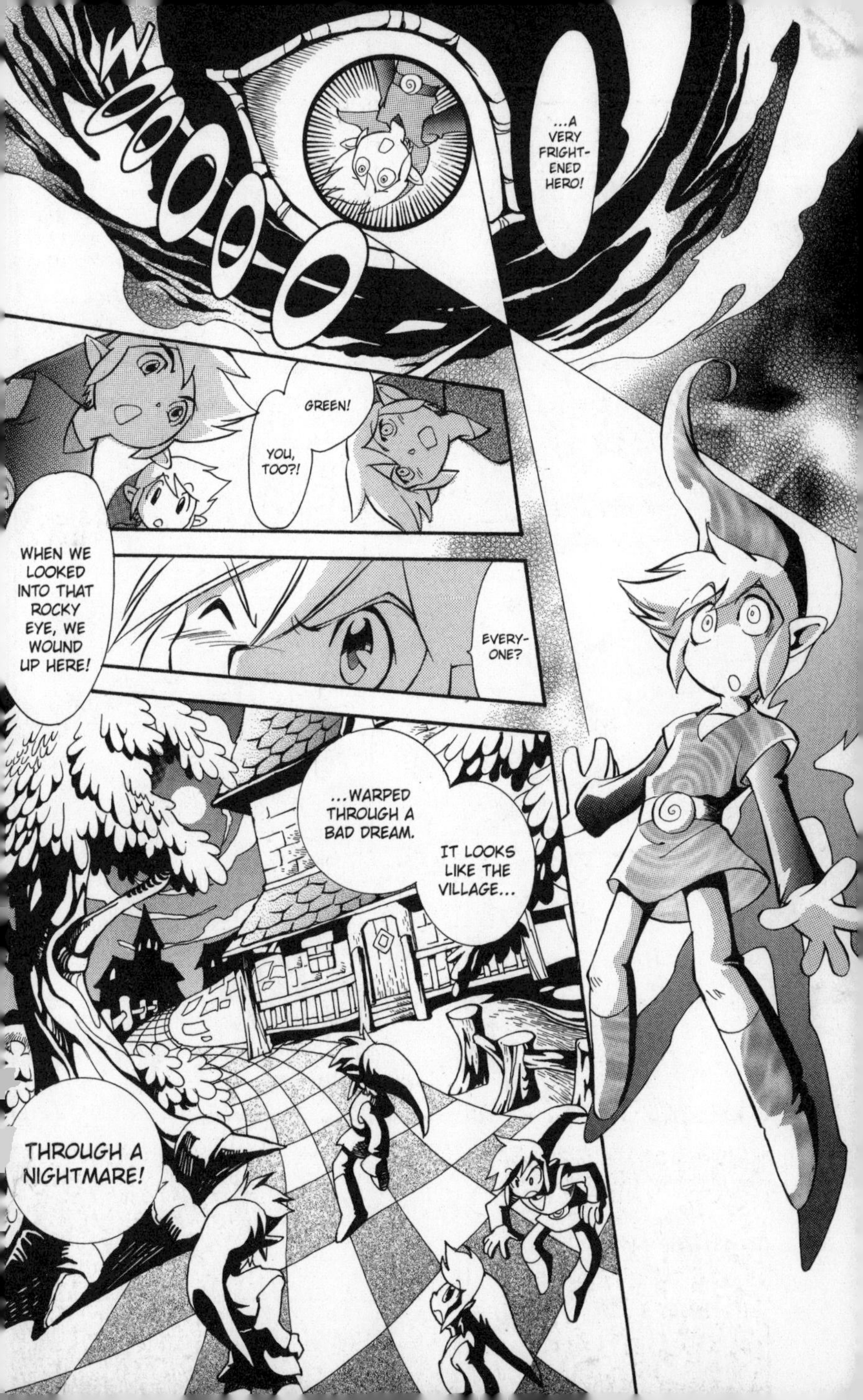
...A VERY FRIGHT-ENED HERO!
WOOOOOOO
GREEN!
YOU, TOO?!
EVERY-ONE?
WHEN WE LOOKED INTO THAT ROCKY EYE, WE WOUND UP HERE!
IT LOOKS LIKE THE VILLAGE...
...WARPED THROUGH A BAD DREAM.
THROUGH A NIGHTMARE!

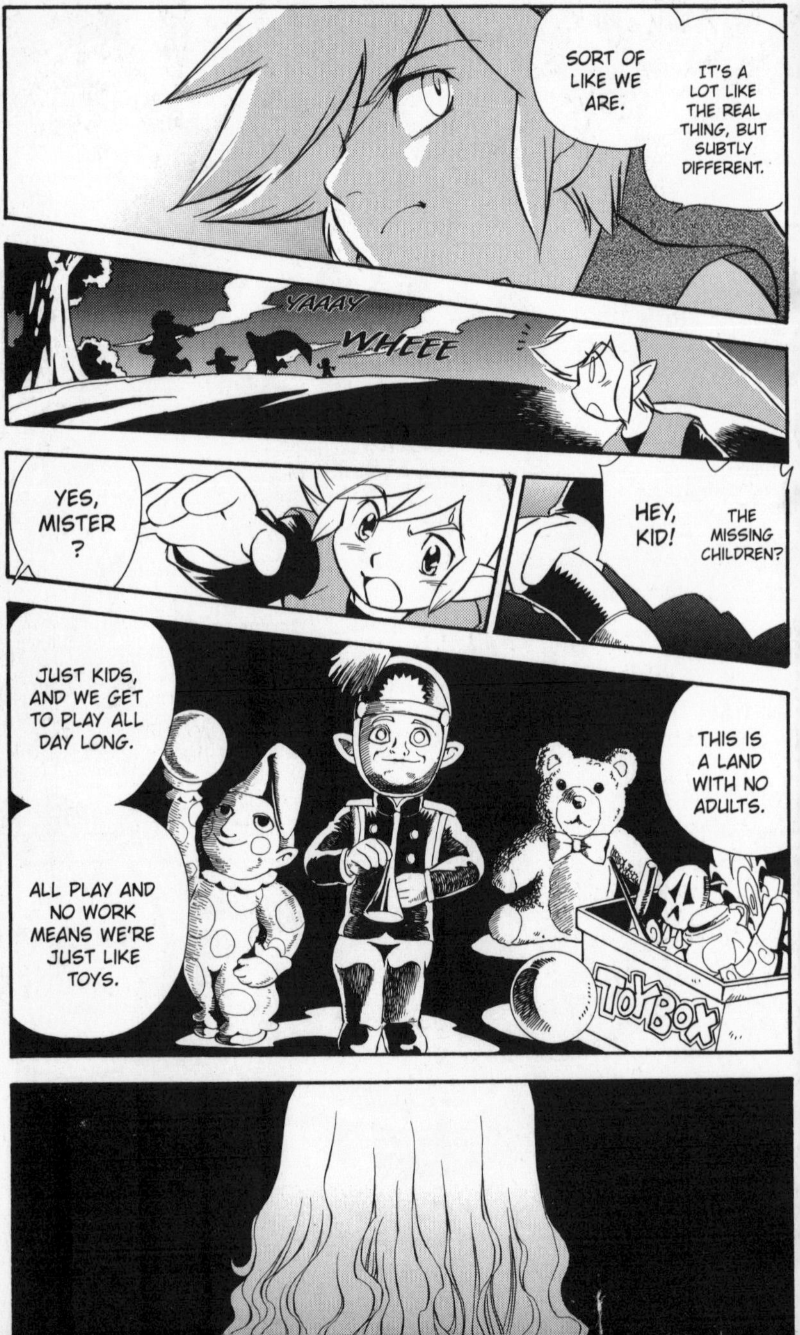
IT'S A LOT LIKE THE REAL THING, BUT SUBTLY DIFFERENT.
SORT OF LIKE WE ARE.
YAAAY
WHEEE
THE MISSING CHILDREN?
HEY, KID!
YES, MISTER?
THIS IS A LAND WITH NO ADULTS.
JUST KIDS, AND WE GET TO PLAY ALL DAY LONG.
ALL PLAY AND NO WORK MEANS WE'RE JUST LIKE TOYS.
TOYBOX

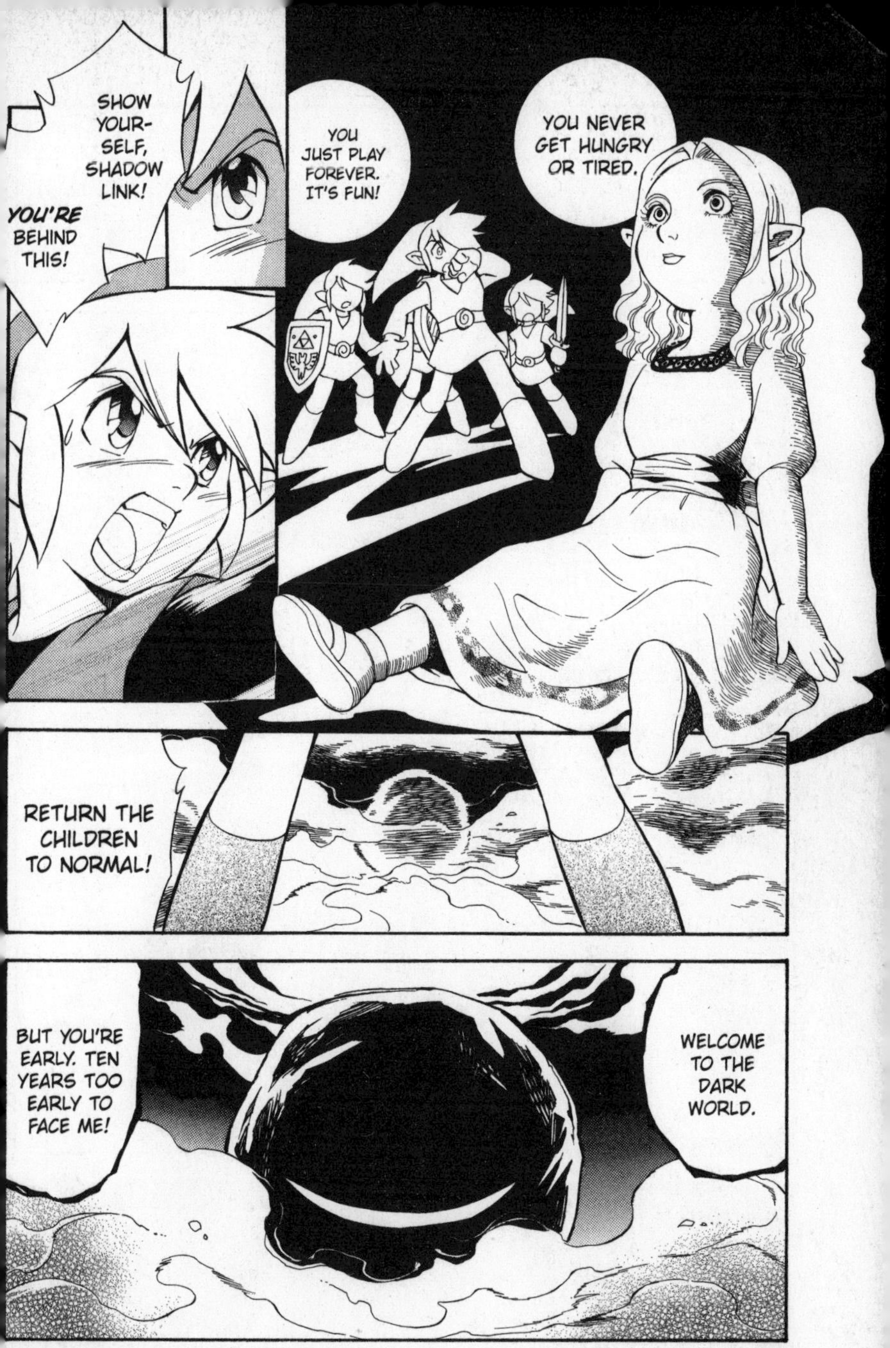
YOU NEVER GET HUNGRY OR TIRED.
YOU JUST PLAY FOREVER. IT'S FUN!
SHOW YOURSELF, SHADOW LINK!
YOU'RE BEHIND THIS!
RETURN THE CHILDREN TO NORMAL!
WELCOME TO THE DARK WORLD.
BUT YOU'RE EARLY. TEN YEARS TOO EARLY TO FACE ME!

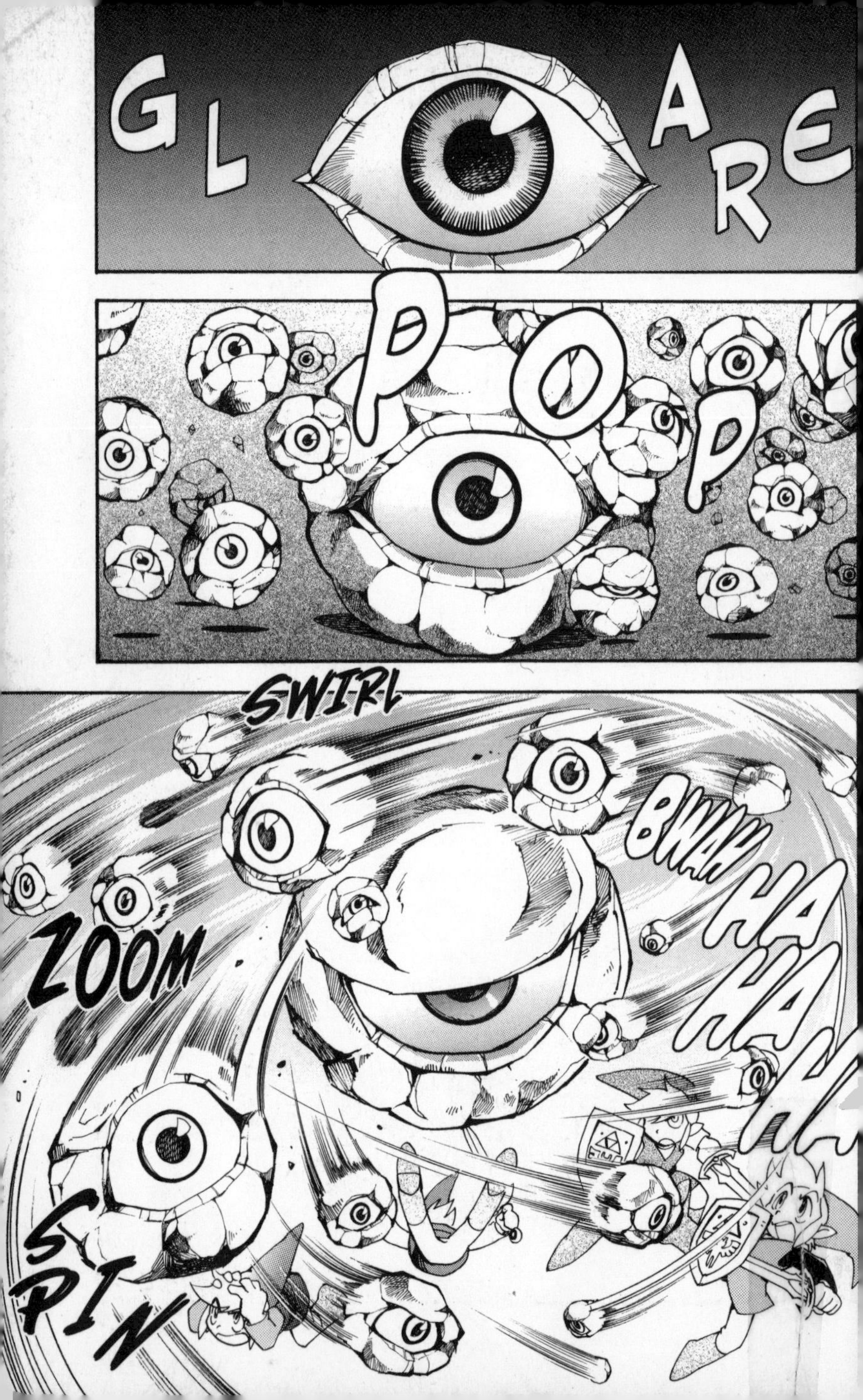
GLARE
POP
SWIRL
BWAH HA HA HA HA
ZOOM
SPIN

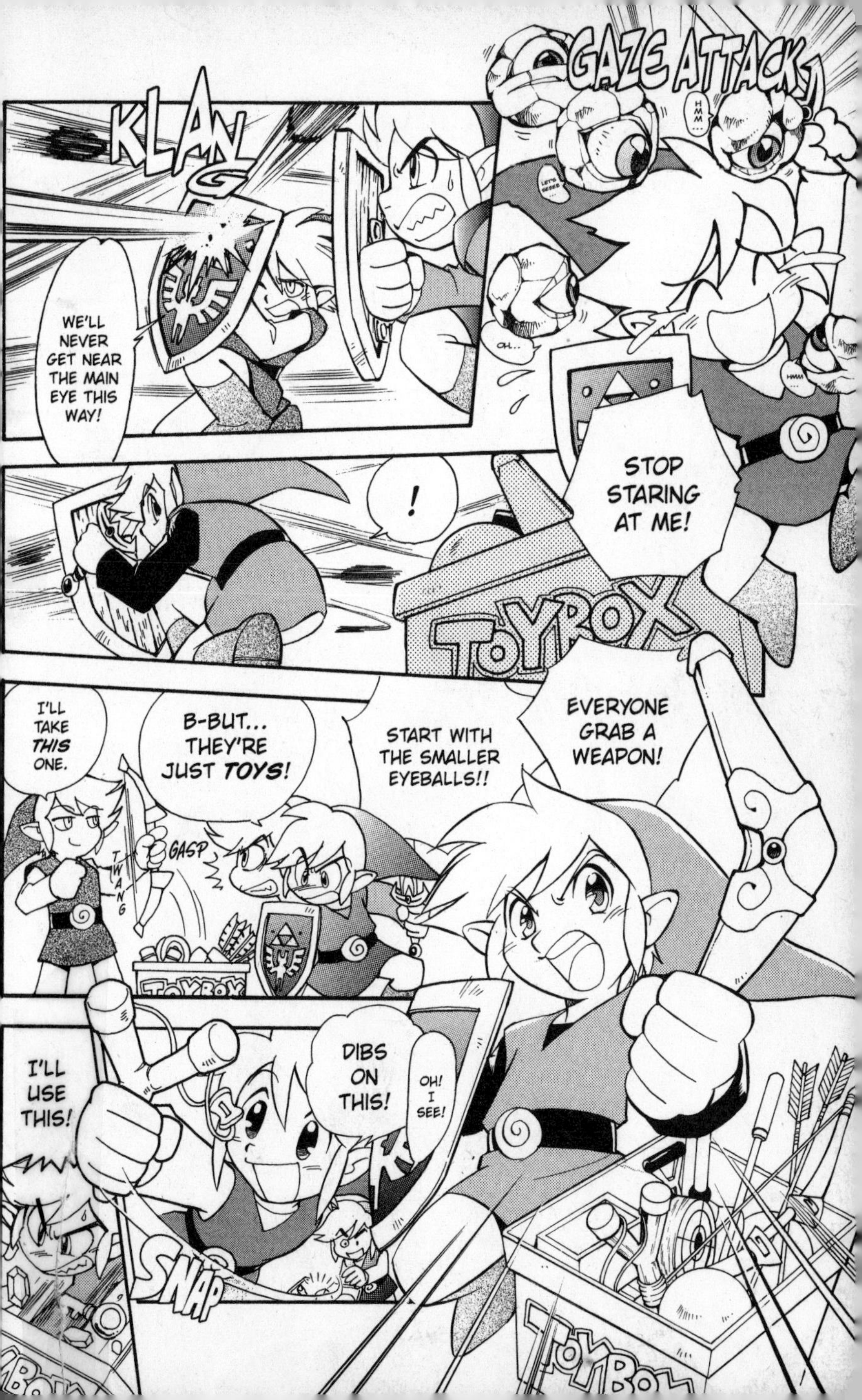
GAZE ATTACK
HMM...
LET'S SEEE...
OH...
HMM
STOP STARING AT ME!
KLANG
WE'LL NEVER GET NEAR THE MAIN EYE THIS WAY!
!
EVERYONE GRAB A WEAPON!
START WITH THE SMALLER EYEBALLS!!
B-BUT... THEY'RE JUST *TOYS*!
GASP
I'LL TAKE *THIS* ONE.
TWANG
TOYBOX
OH! I SEE!
DIBS ON THIS!
I'LL USE THIS!
SNAP

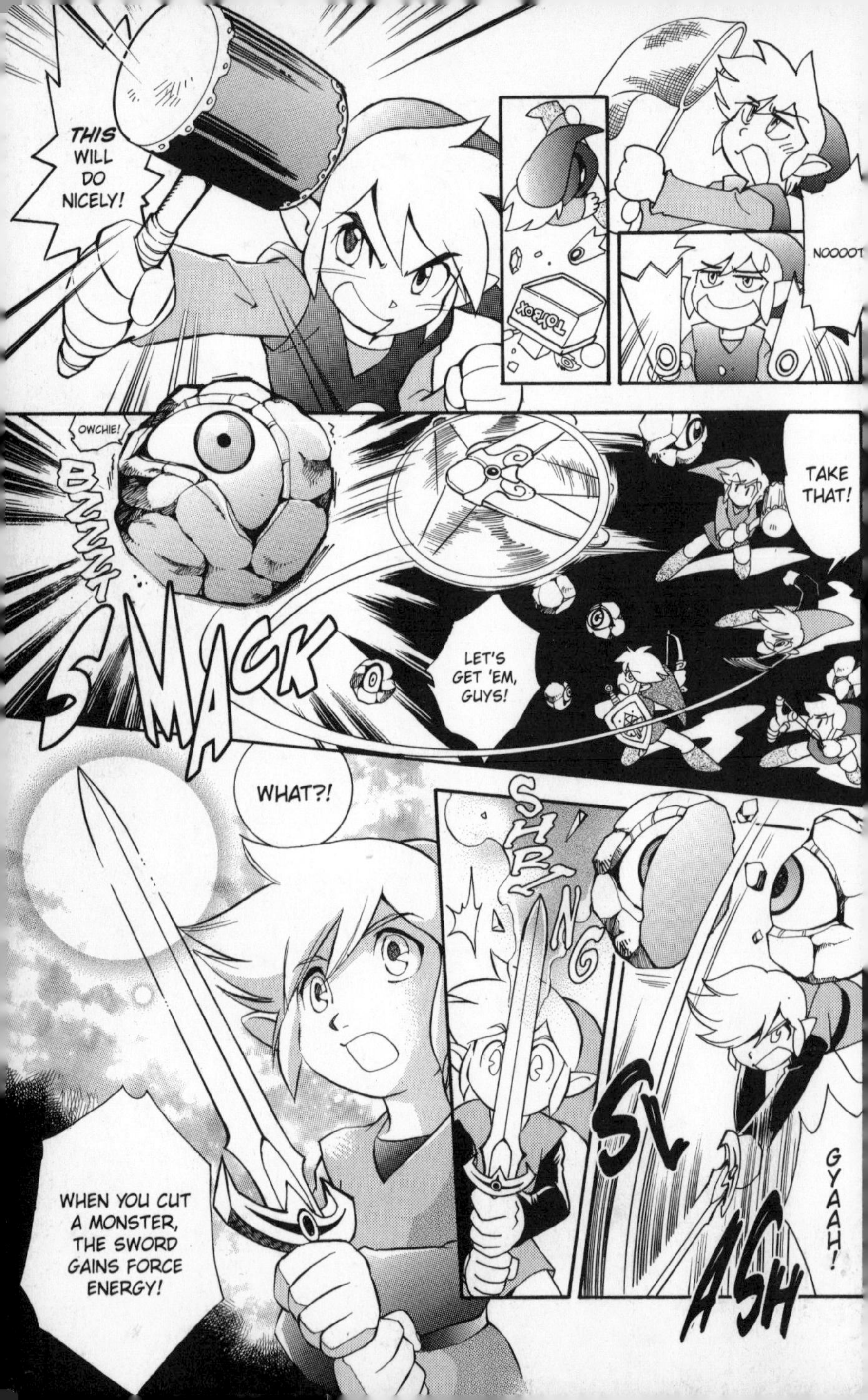
NOOOOT
TOYBOX
THIS WILL DO NICELY!
TAKE THAT!
LET'S GET 'EM, GUYS!
OWCHIE!
BZZZT
SMACK
SHRING
GYAAH!
SLASH
WHAT?!
WHEN YOU CUT A MONSTER, THE SWORD GAINS FORCE ENERGY!

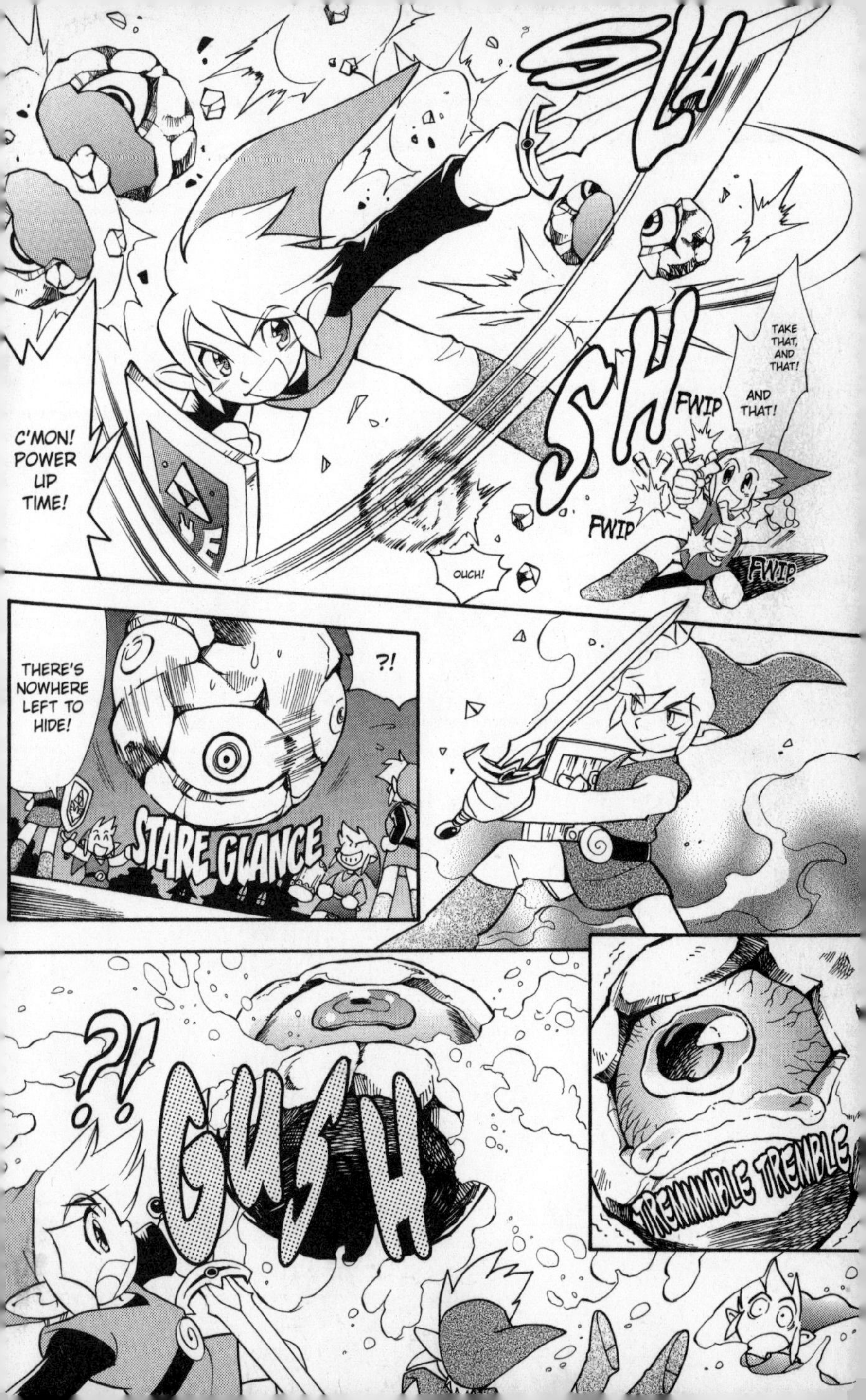
SLA
TAKE THAT, AND THAT!
AND THAT!
SH
FWIP
FWIP
FWIP
OUCH!
C'MON! POWER UP TIME!
?!
THERE'S NOWHERE LEFT TO HIDE!
STARE GLANCE
TREMMMBLE TREMBLE
?!
GUSH

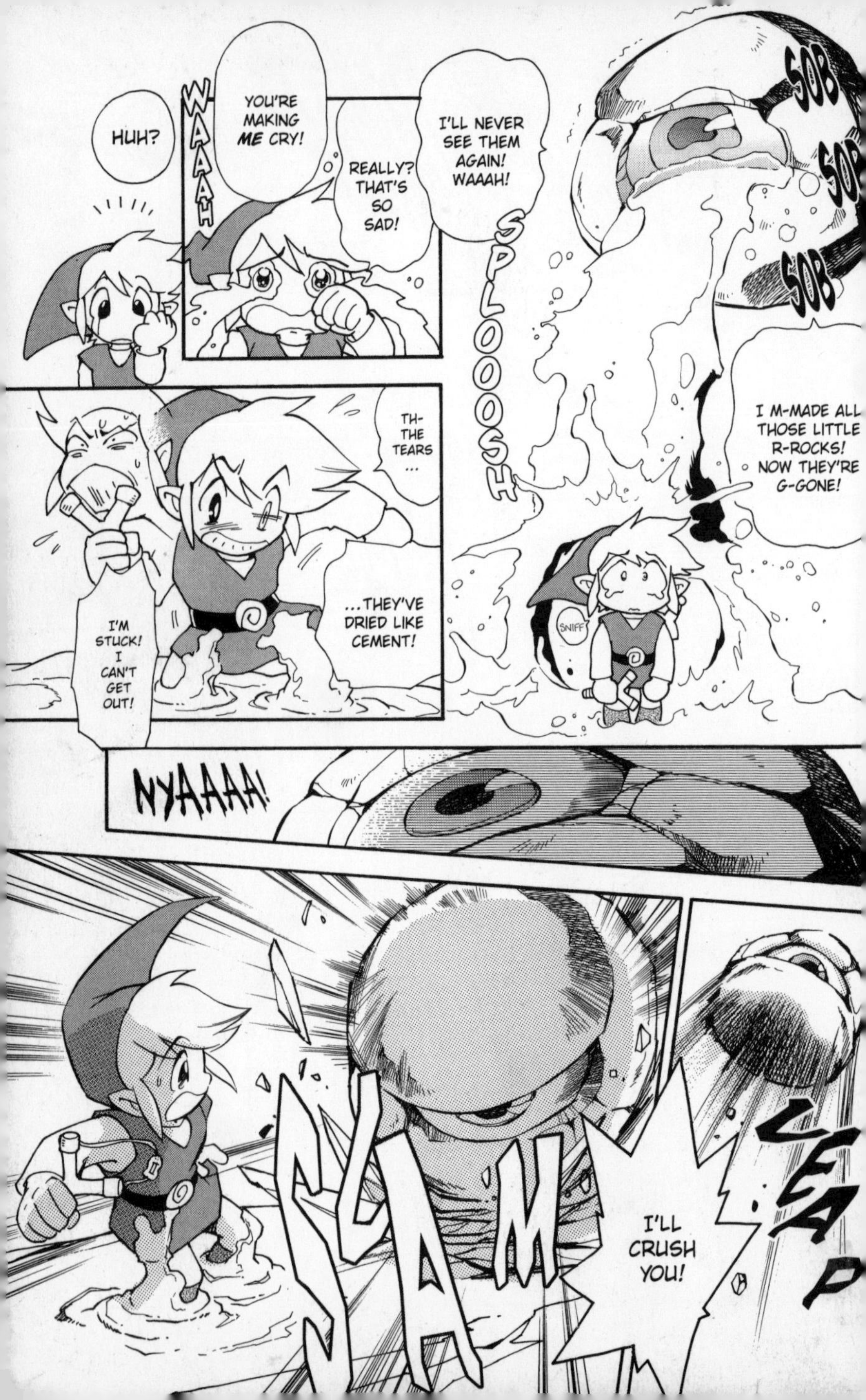
SOB
SOB
SOB
SPLOOOSH
I M-MADE ALL THOSE LITTLE R-ROCKS! NOW THEY'RE G-GONE!
SNIFF
I'LL NEVER SEE THEM AGAIN! WAAAH!
REALLY? THAT'S SO SAD!
YOU'RE MAKING *ME* CRY!
WAAAAH
HUH?
TH- THE TEARS...
...THEY'VE DRIED LIKE CEMENT!
I'M STUCK! I CAN'T GET OUT!
NYAAAA!
LEAP
I'LL CRUSH YOU!
SLAM

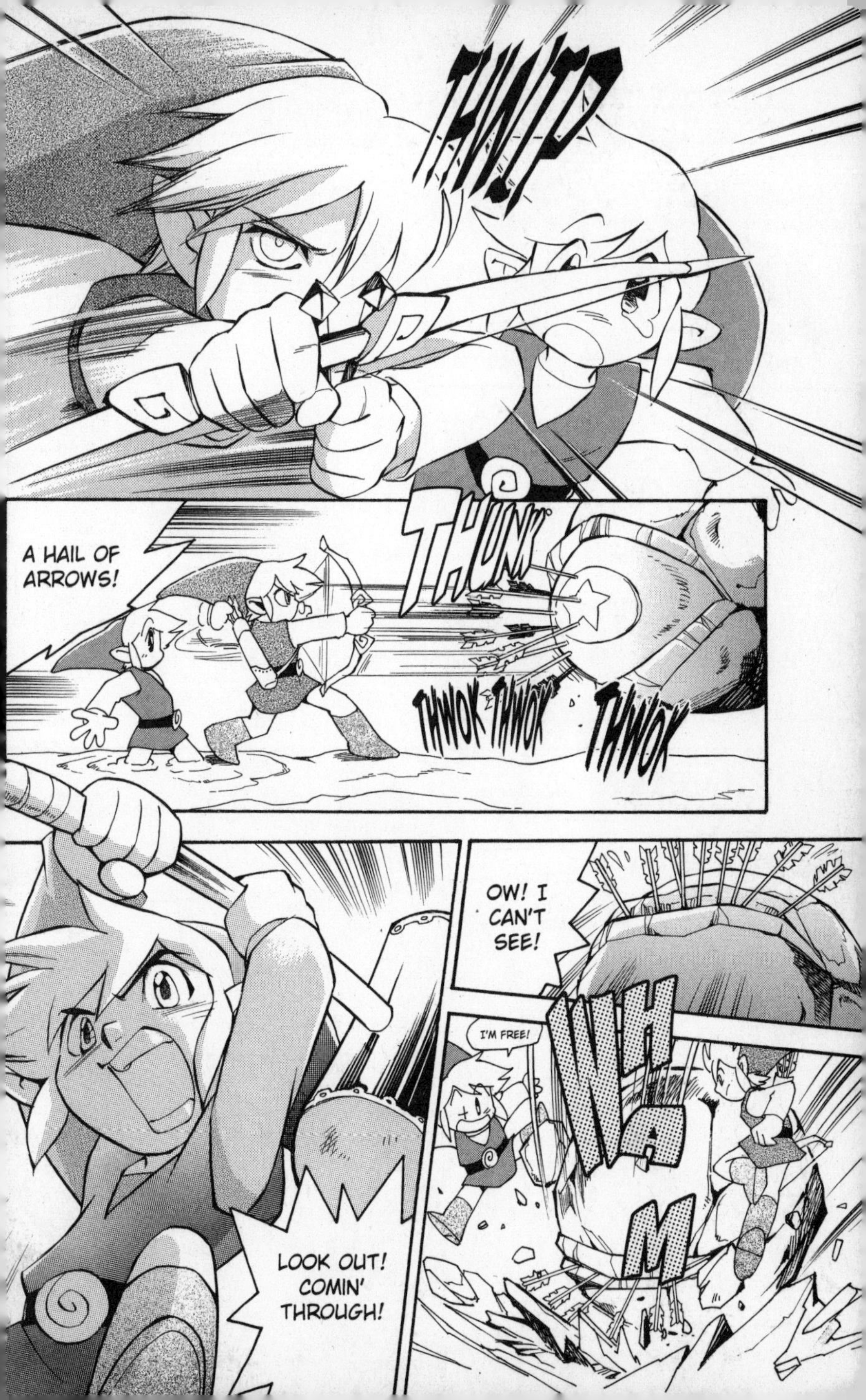
THWIP
THUNK
A HAIL OF ARROWS!
THWOK THWOK THWOK
OW! I CAN'T SEE!
I'M FREE!
WHAM
LOOK OUT! COMIN' THROUGH!

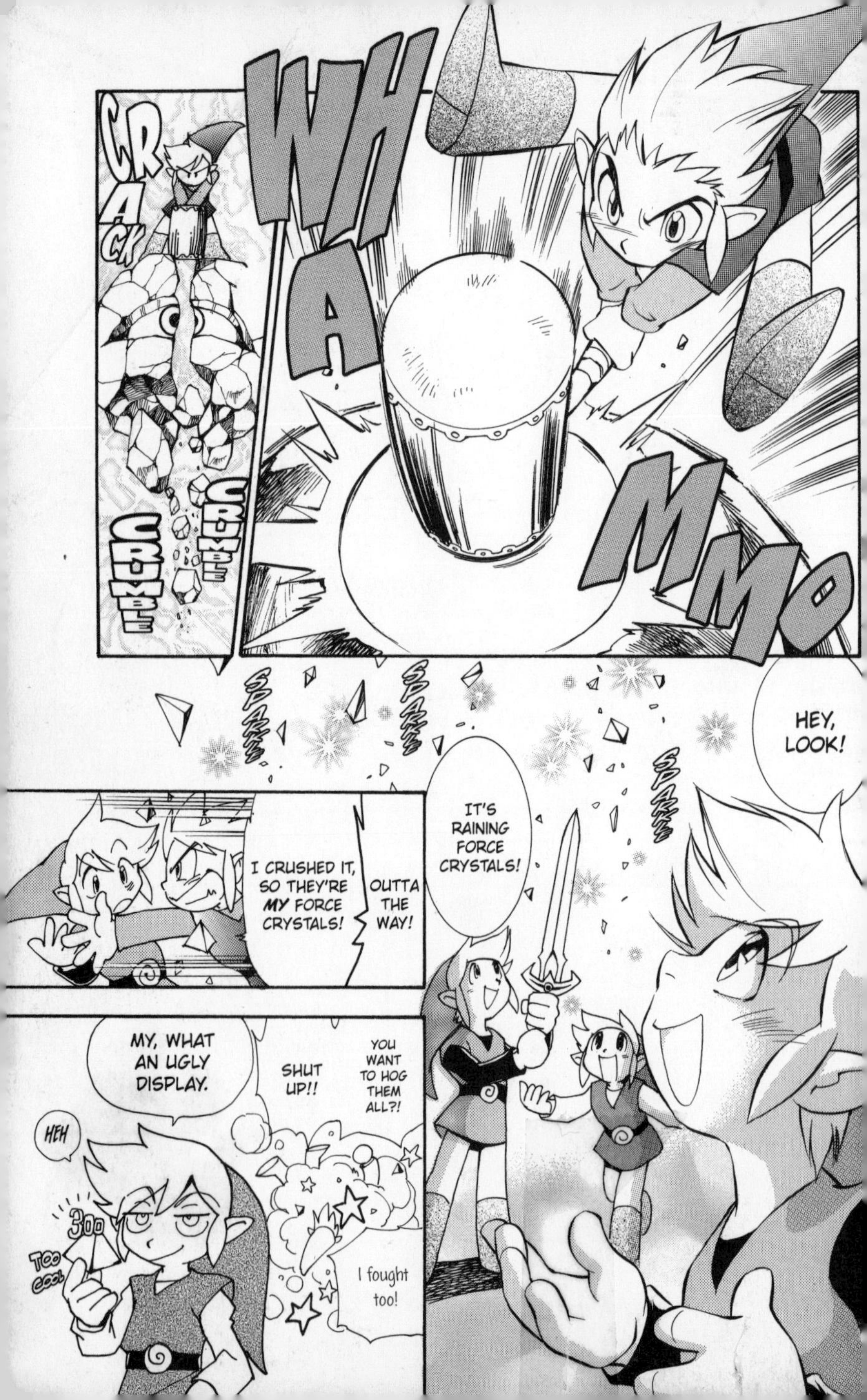
WHAMMO
CRACK
CRUMBLE
CRUMBLE
SPARK
SPARK
SPARK
SPARK
HEY, LOOK!
IT'S RAINING FORCE CRYSTALS!
OUTTA THE WAY!
I CRUSHED IT, SO THEY'RE *MY* FORCE CRYSTALS!
YOU WANT TO HOG THEM ALL?!
SHUT UP!!
MY, WHAT AN UGLY DISPLAY.
HEH
300
TOO COOL
I fought too!

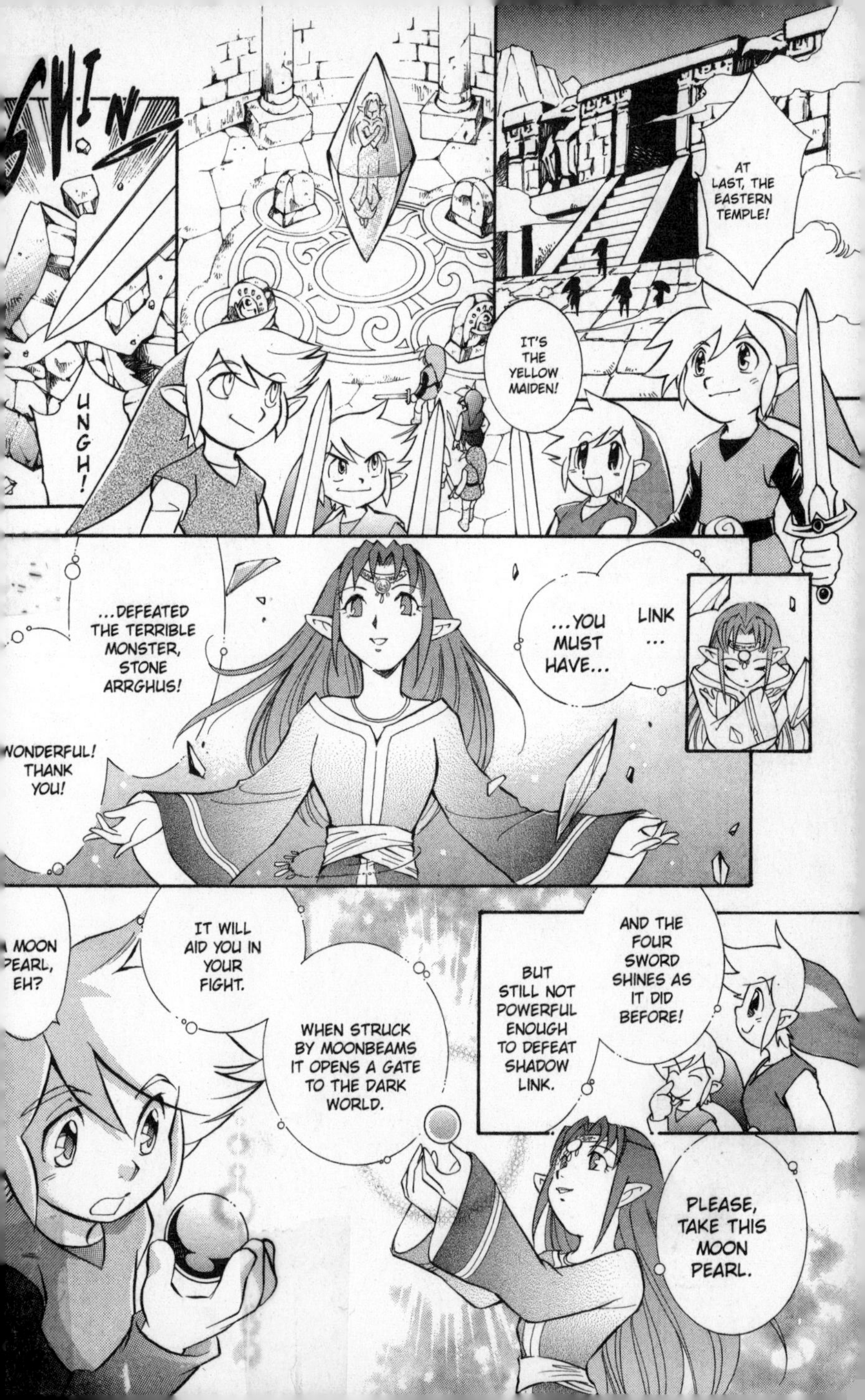
AT LAST, THE EASTERN TEMPLE!
IT'S THE YELLOW MAIDEN!
SHIN
UNGH!
LINK ...
...YOU MUST HAVE...
...DEFEATED THE TERRIBLE MONSTER, STONE ARRGHUS!
WONDERFUL! THANK YOU!
AND THE FOUR SWORD SHINES AS IT DID BEFORE!
BUT STILL NOT POWERFUL ENOUGH TO DEFEAT SHADOW LINK.
PLEASE, TAKE THIS MOON PEARL.
WHEN STRUCK BY MOONBEAMS IT OPENS A GATE TO THE DARK WORLD.
IT WILL AID YOU IN YOUR FIGHT.
A MOON PEARL, EH?

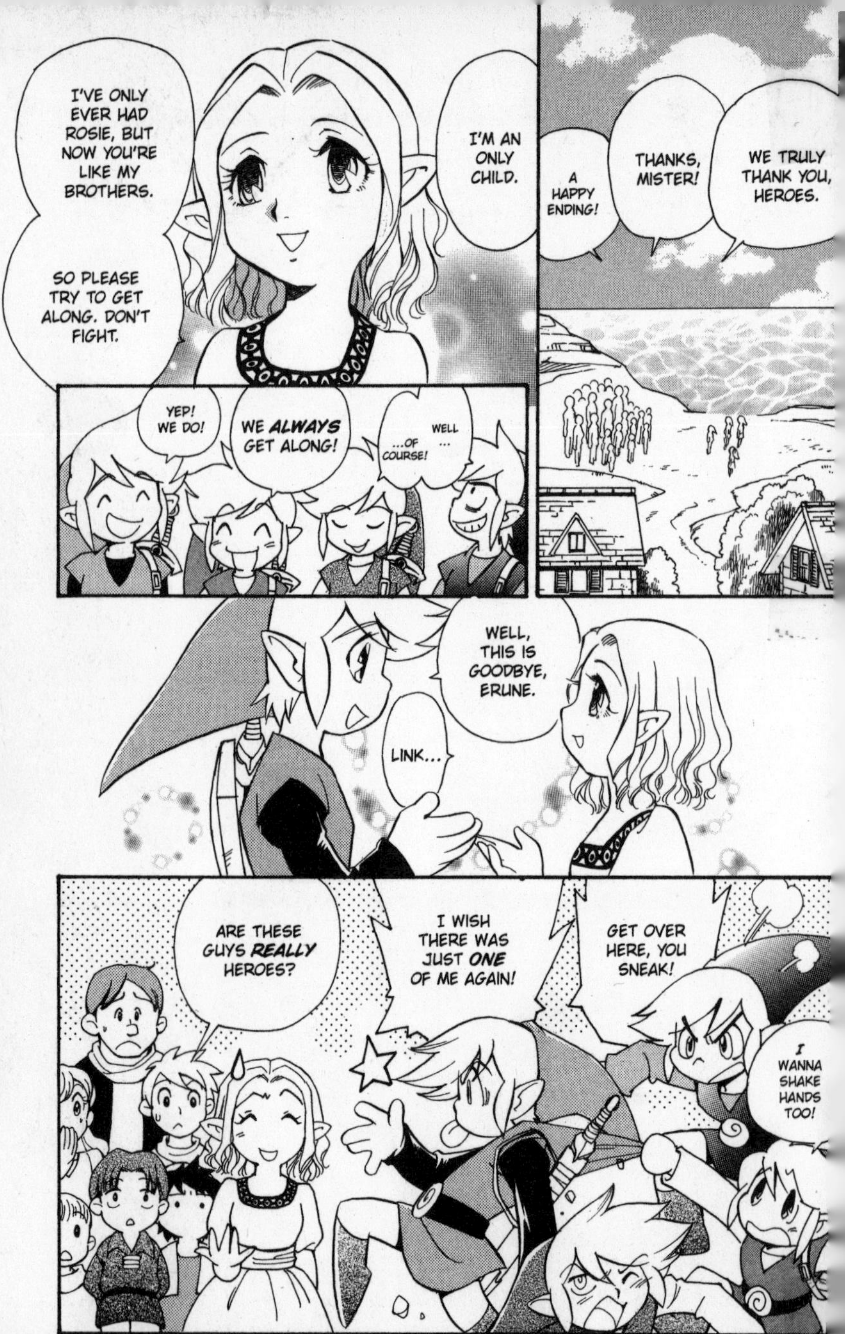
WE TRULY THANK YOU, HEROES.
THANKS, MISTER!
A HAPPY ENDING!
I'M AN ONLY CHILD.
I'VE ONLY EVER HAD ROSIE, BUT NOW YOU'RE LIKE MY BROTHERS.
SO PLEASE TRY TO GET ALONG. DON'T FIGHT.
WELL...
...OF COURSE!
WE ALWAYS GET ALONG!
YEP! WE DO!
WELL, THIS IS GOODBYE, ERUNE.
LINK...
I WANNA SHAKE HANDS TOO!
GET OVER HERE, YOU SNEAK!
I WISH THERE WAS JUST ONE OF ME AGAIN!
ARE THESE GUYS REALLY HEROES?

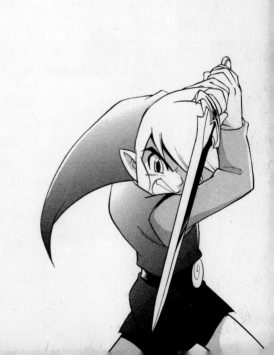

CHAPTER 4 LINKS TORN APART

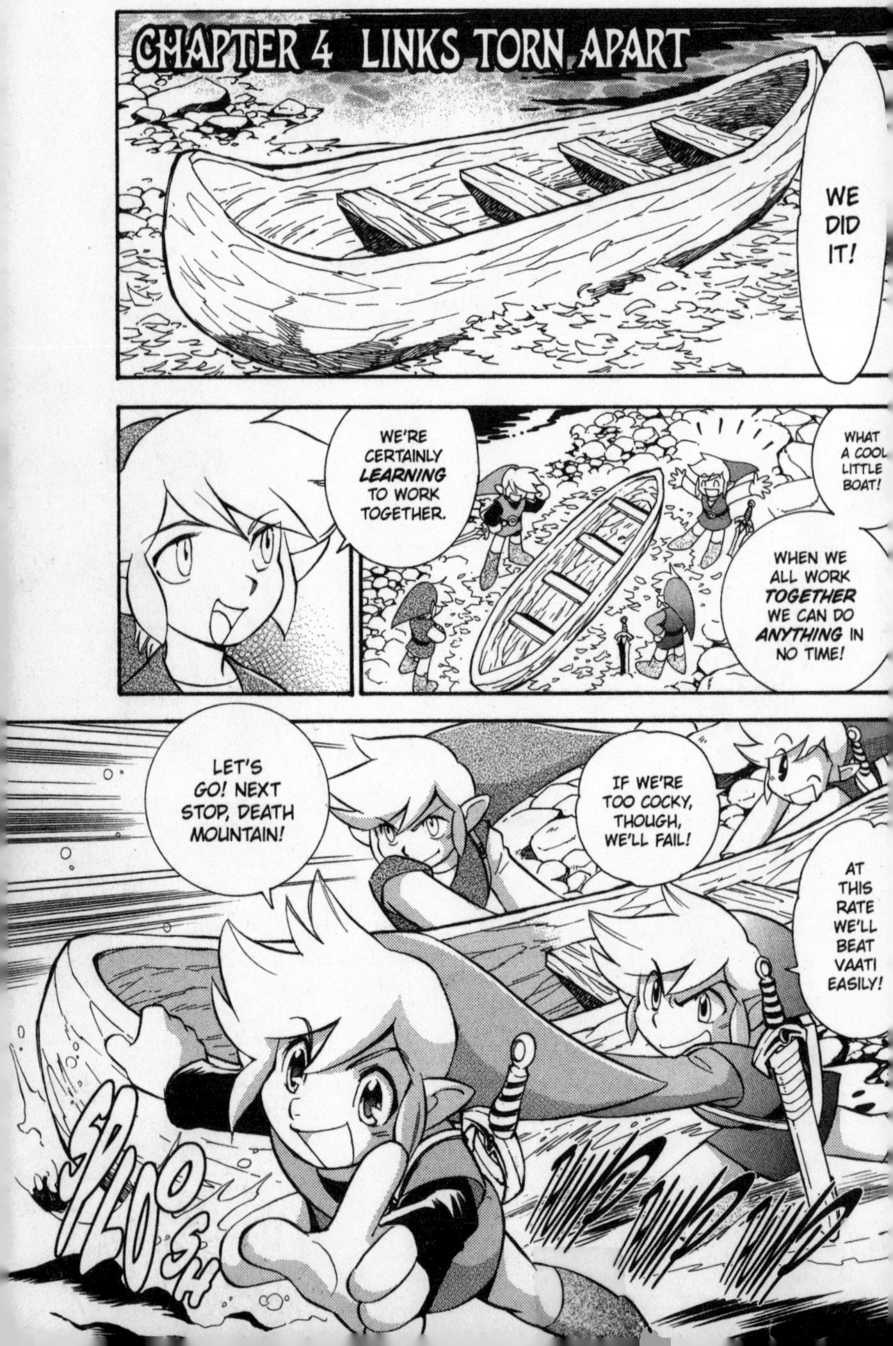
WE DID IT!
WHAT A COOL LITTLE BOAT!
WHEN WE ALL WORK TOGETHER WE CAN DO ANYTHING IN NO TIME!
WE'RE CERTAINLY LEARNING TO WORK TOGETHER.
AT THIS RATE WE'LL BEAT VAATI EASILY!
IF WE'RE TOO COCKY, THOUGH, WE'LL FAIL!
LET'S GO! NEXT STOP, DEATH MOUNTAIN!
SPLOOSH

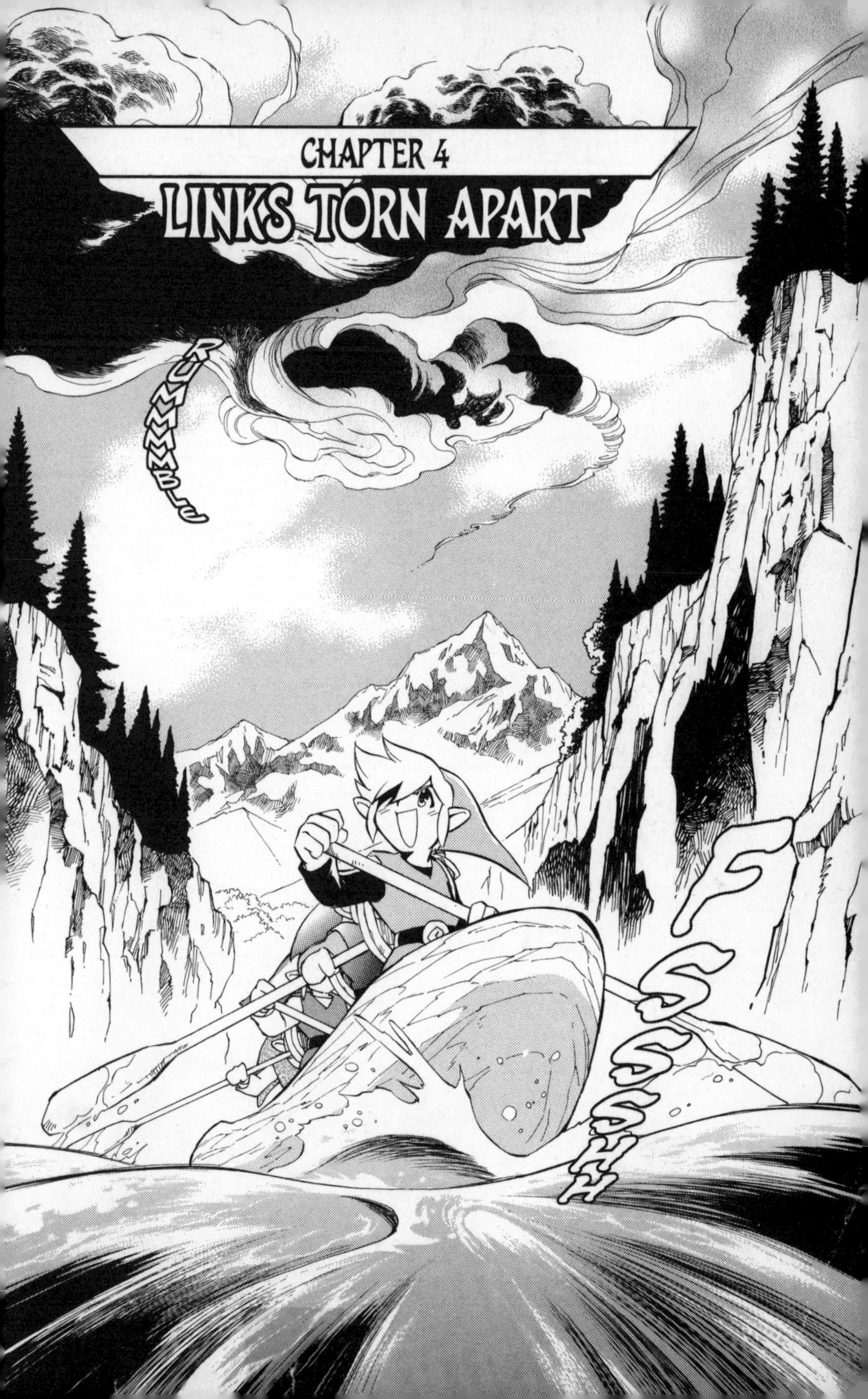
CHAPTER 4
LINKS TORN APART
RUMMMMBLE
FSSSSHH

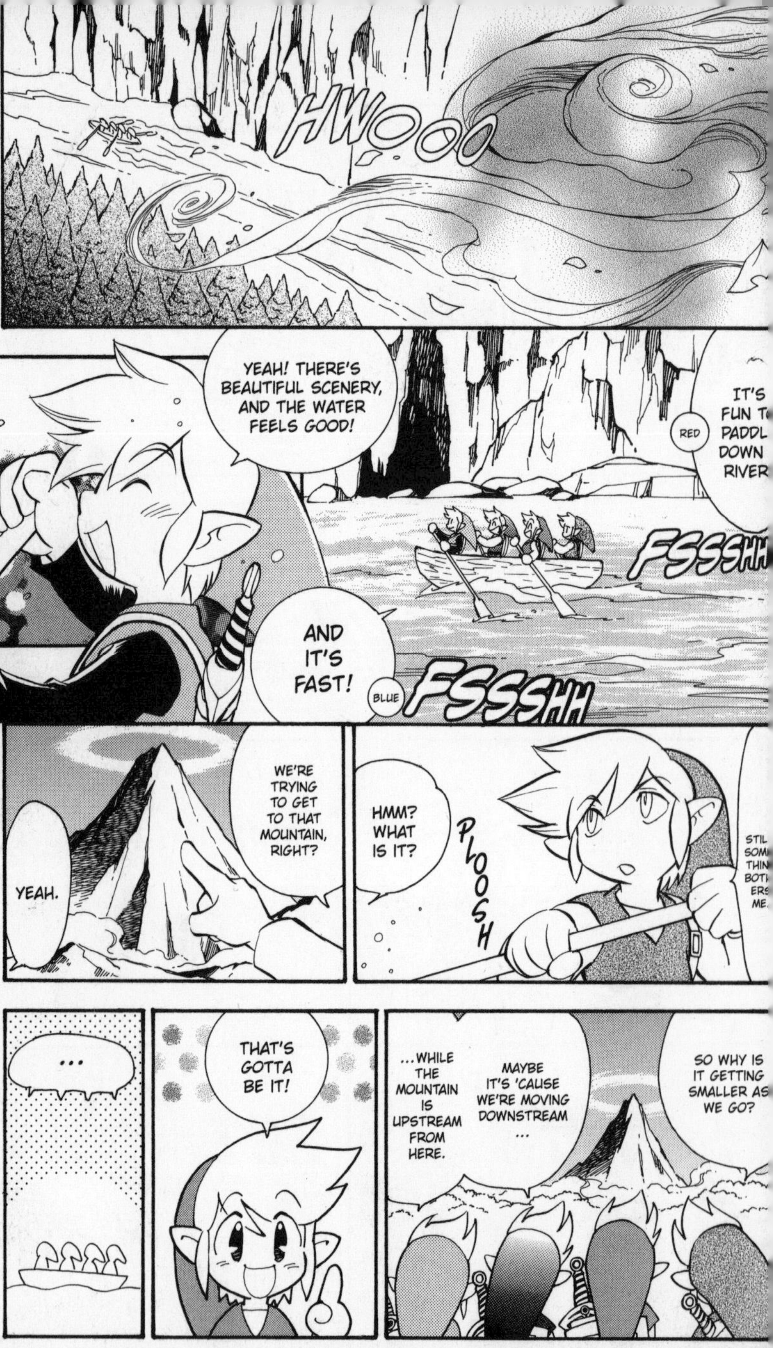
HWOOO
IT'S FUN T PADDL DOWN RIVER
RED
FSSSHH
YEAH! THERE'S BEAUTIFUL SCENERY, AND THE WATER FEELS GOOD!
AND IT'S FAST!
BLUE
FSSSHH
STIL SOM THIN BOTH ERS ME.
HMM? WHAT IS IT?
PLOOSH
WE'RE TRYING TO GET TO THAT MOUNTAIN, RIGHT?
YEAH.
SO WHY IS IT GETTING SMALLER AS WE GO?
MAYBE IT'S 'CAUSE WE'RE MOVING DOWNSTREAM ...
...WHILE THE MOUNTAIN IS UPSTREAM FROM HERE.
THAT'S GOTTA BE IT!
...

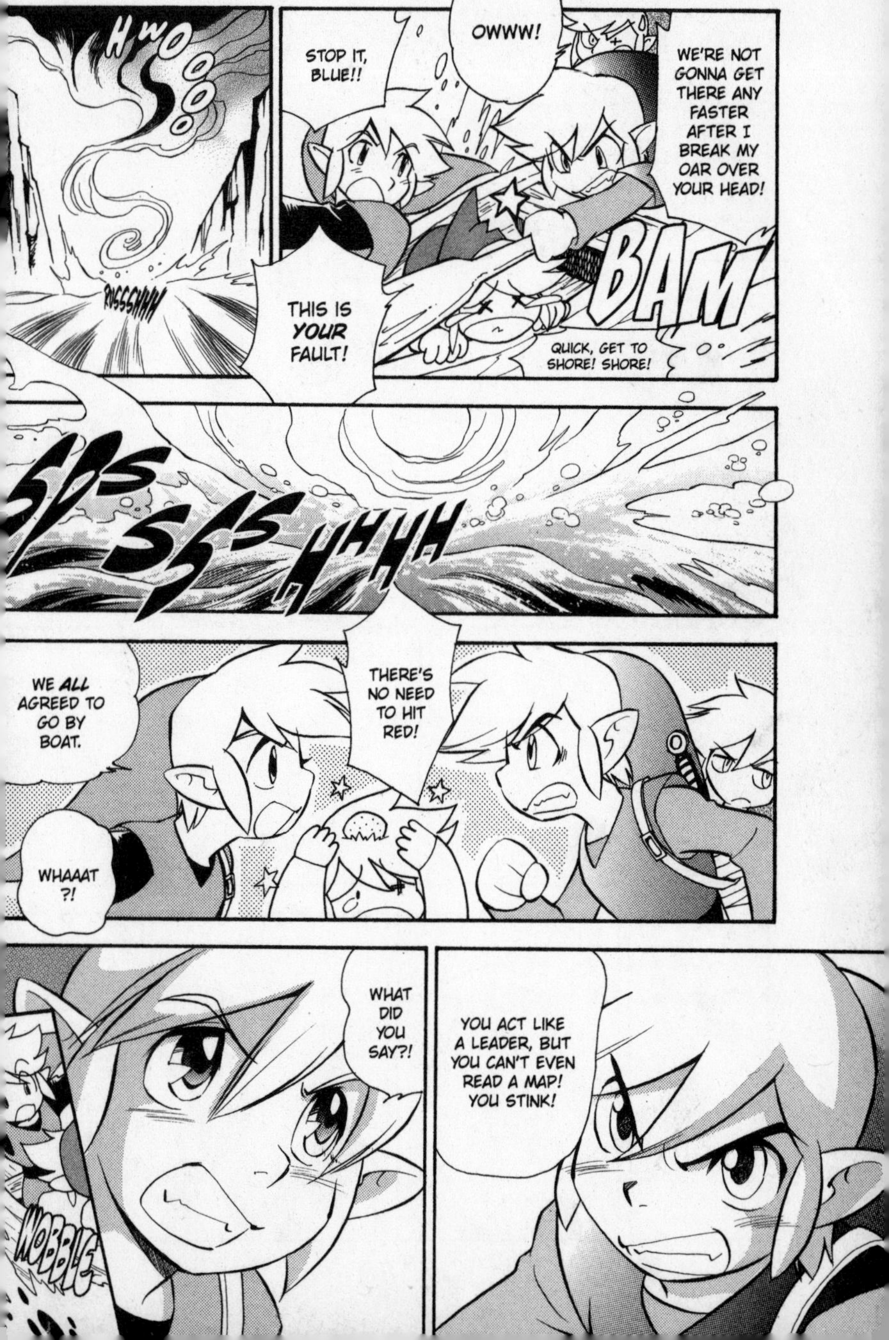
OWWW!
WE'RE NOT GONNA GET THERE ANY FASTER AFTER I BREAK MY OAR OVER YOUR HEAD!
STOP IT, BLUE!!
BAM
QUICK, GET TO SHORE! SHORE!
THIS IS YOUR FAULT!
HWOOOOO
RUSSSHHH
THERE'S NO NEED TO HIT RED!
WE ALL AGREED TO GO BY BOAT.
WHAAAT?!
YOU ACT LIKE A LEADER, BUT YOU CAN'T EVEN READ A MAP! YOU STINK!
WHAT DID YOU SAY?!
WOBBLE

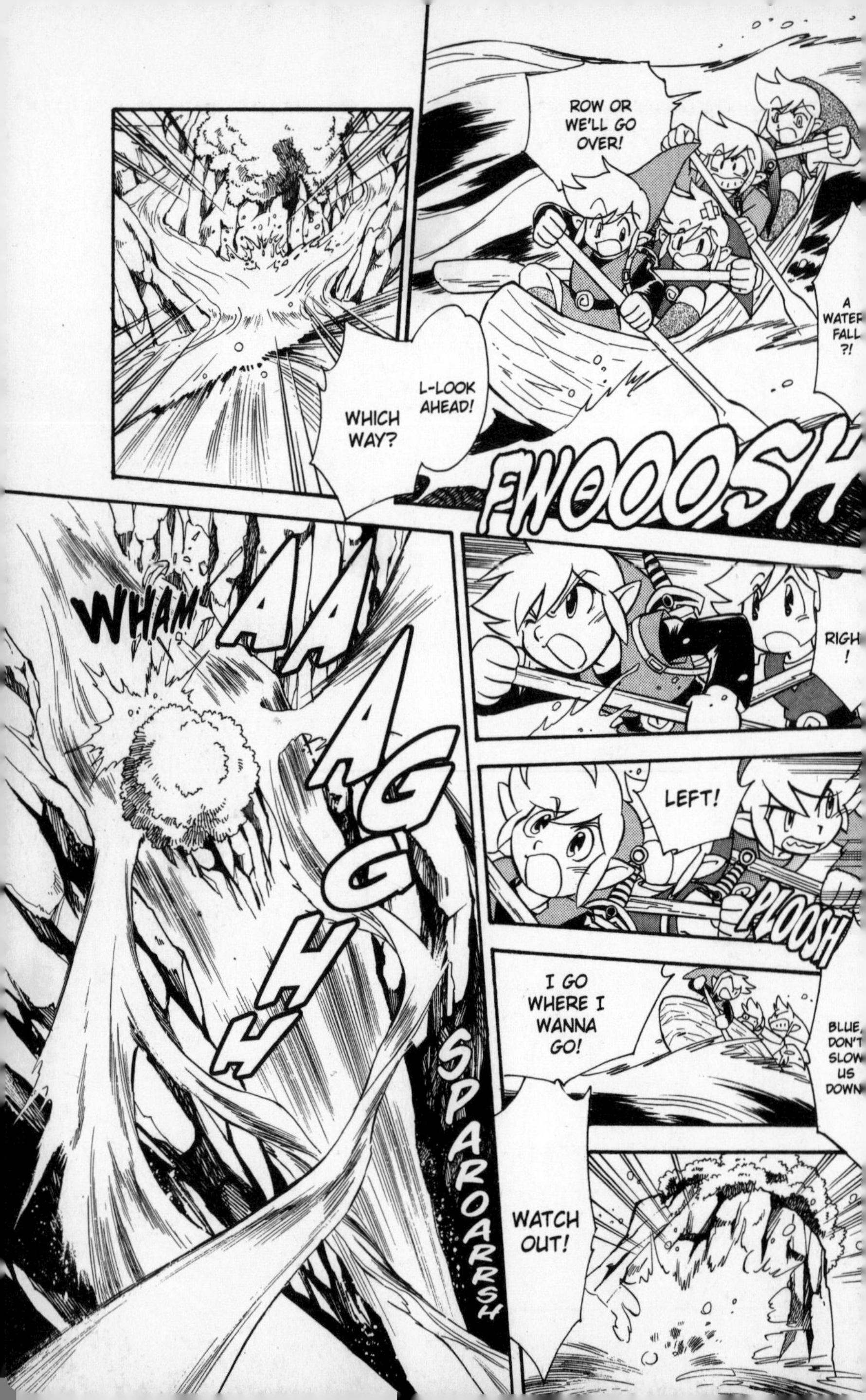
ROW OR WE'LL GO OVER!
A WATER FALL ?!
FWOOOSH
L-LOOK AHEAD!
WHICH WAY?
RIGH !
LEFT!
PLOOSH
BLUE, DON'T SLOW US DOWN
I GO WHERE I WANNA GO!
WATCH OUT!
WHAM
AAAAGGHHH
SPAROARRSH

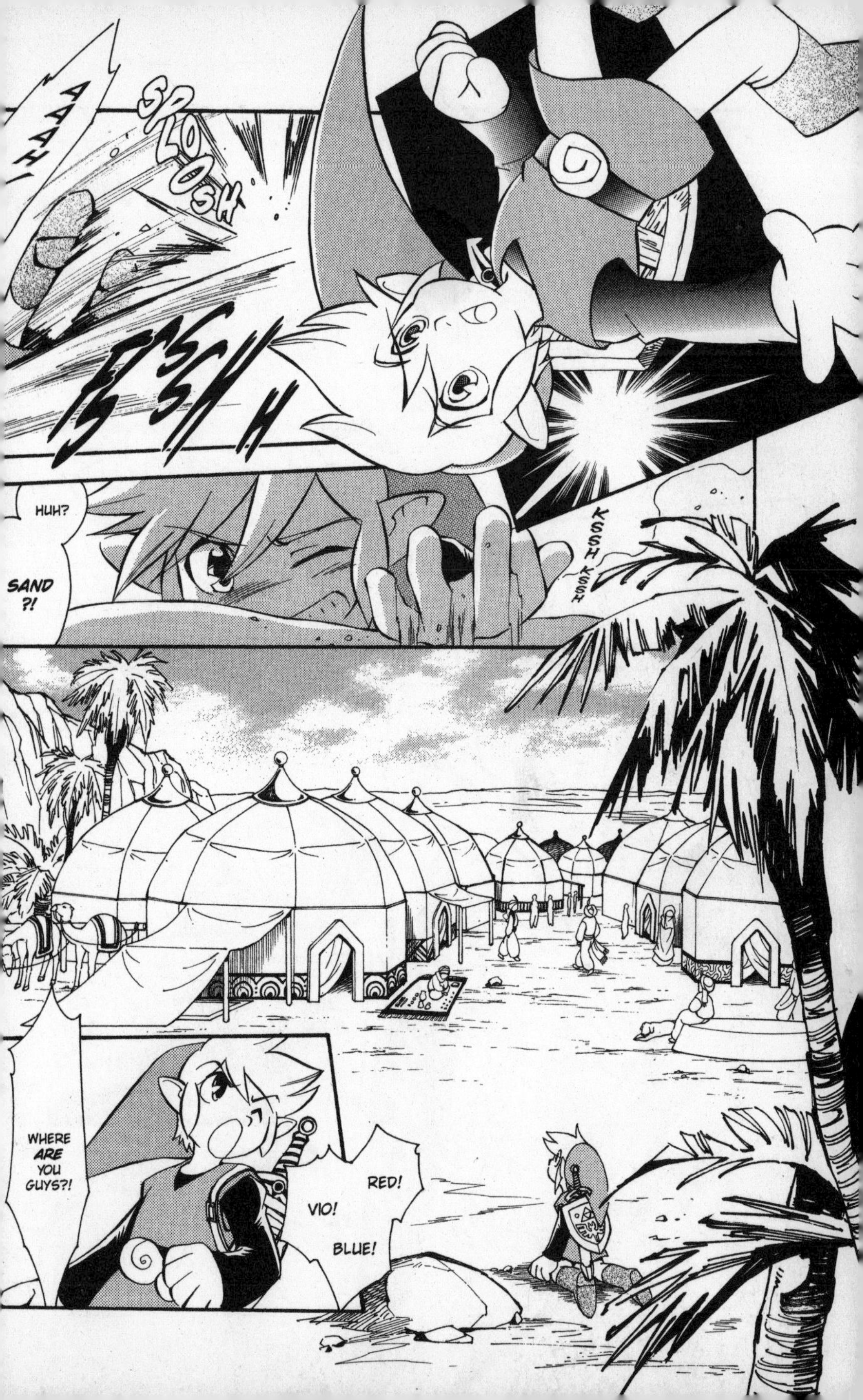
SPLOOSH
AAAAH!
FSSSHH
KSSH KSSH
HUH?
SAND?!
RED!
VIO!
BLUE!
WHERE ARE YOU GUYS?!

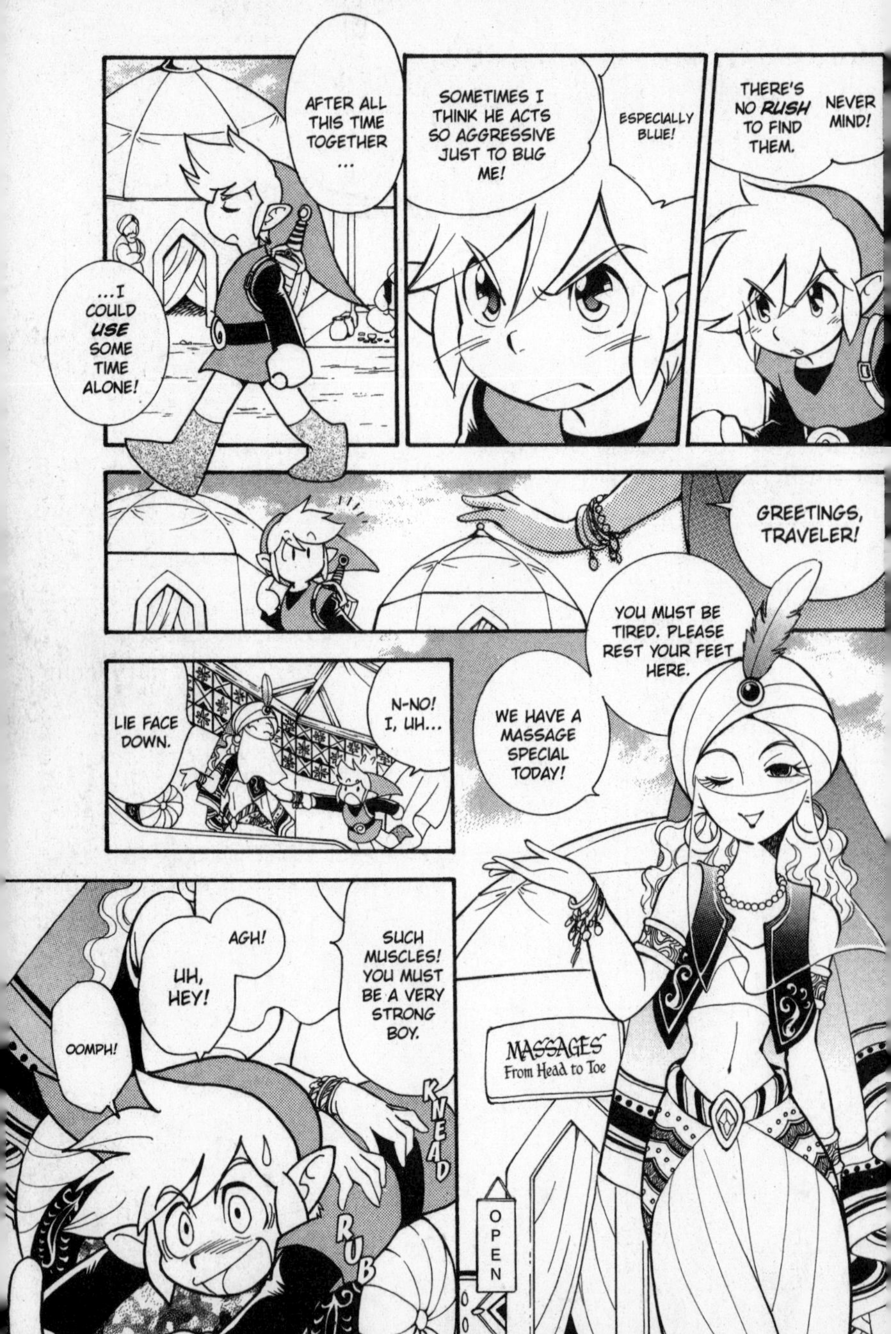
NEVER MIND!
THERE'S NO **RUSH** TO FIND THEM.
ESPECIALLY BLUE!
SOMETIMES I THINK HE ACTS SO AGGRESSIVE JUST TO BUG ME!
AFTER ALL THIS TIME TOGETHER ...
...I COULD **USE** SOME TIME ALONE!
GREETINGS, TRAVELER!
YOU MUST BE TIRED. PLEASE REST YOUR FEET HERE.
WE HAVE A MASSAGE SPECIAL TODAY!
MASSAGES
From Head to Toe
OPEN
N-NO! I, UH...
LIE FACE DOWN.
SUCH MUSCLES! YOU MUST BE A VERY STRONG BOY.
KNEAD
RUB
AGH!
UH, HEY!
OOMPH!

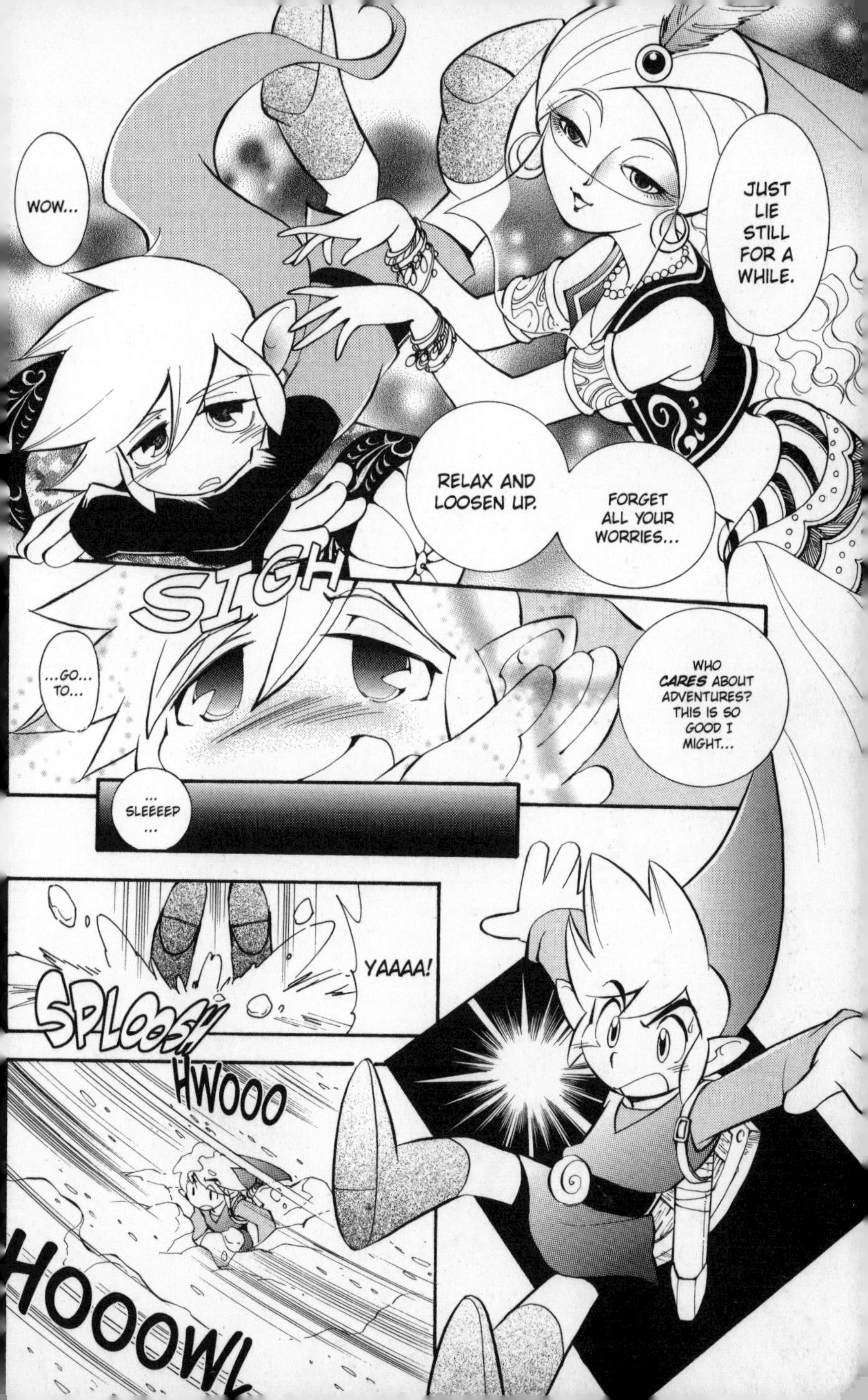
JUST LIE STILL FOR A WHILE.
WOW...
FORGET ALL YOUR WORRIES...
RELAX AND LOOSEN UP.
SIGH
WHO CARES ABOUT ADVENTURES? THIS IS SO GOOD I MIGHT...
...GO... TO...
... SLEEEEP ...
YAAAA!
SPLOOSH
HWOOO
HOOOWL

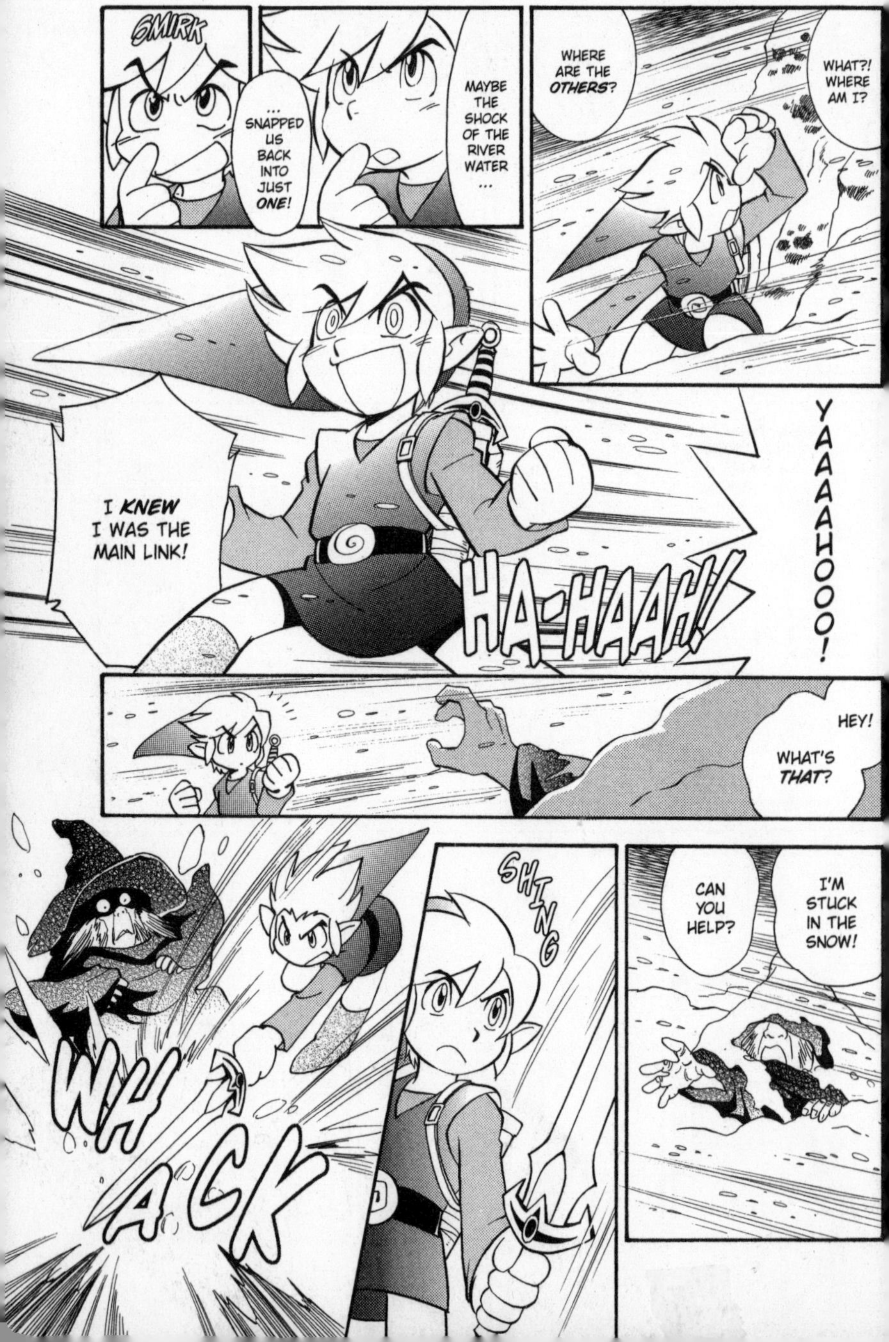
WHAT?! WHERE AM I?
WHERE ARE THE *OTHERS*?
MAYBE THE SHOCK OF THE RIVER WATER...
SMIRK
...SNAPPED US BACK INTO JUST *ONE*!
YAAAAAHOOOO!
HA-HAAAH!
I *KNEW* I WAS THE MAIN LINK!
HEY!
WHAT'S *THAT*?
I'M STUCK IN THE SNOW!
CAN YOU HELP?
SHING
WHACK

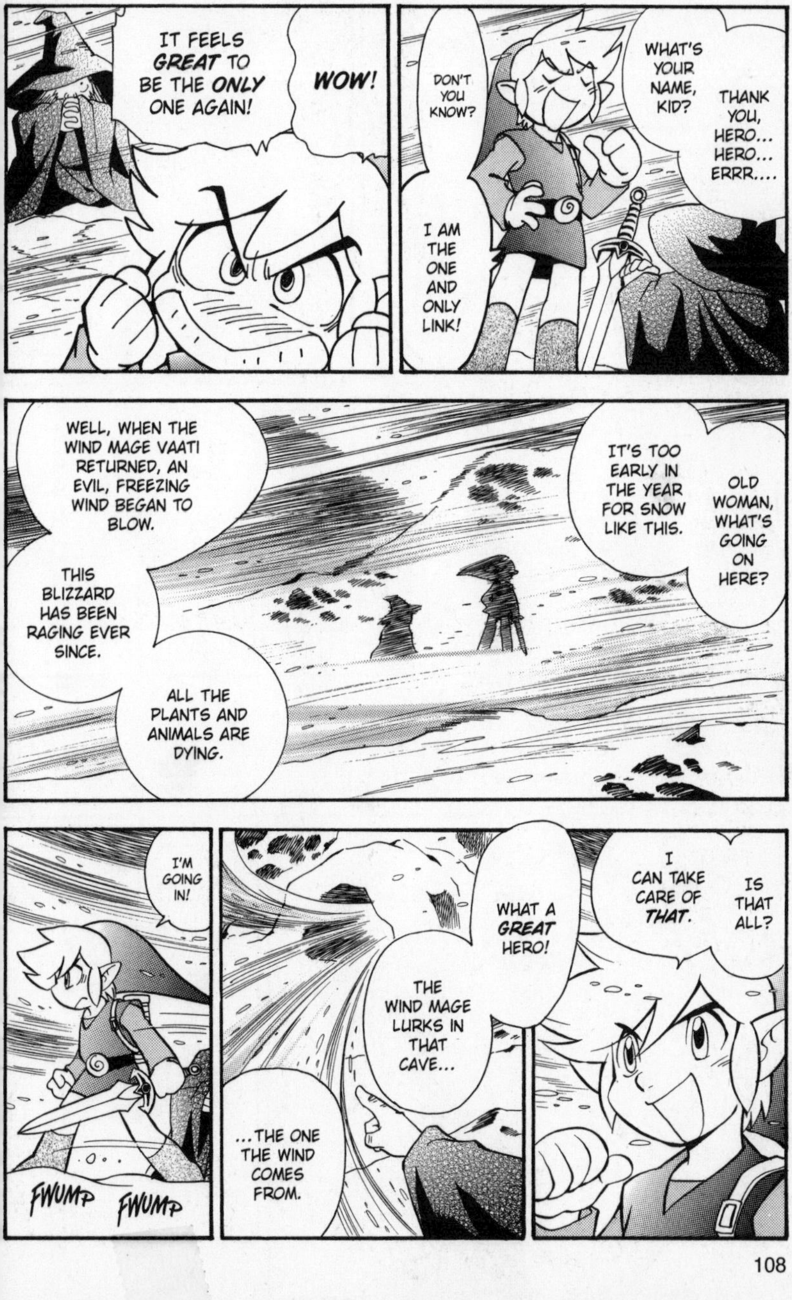
THANK YOU, HERO... HERO... ERRR....
WHAT'S YOUR NAME, KID?
DON'T YOU KNOW?
I AM THE ONE AND ONLY LINK!
WOW!
IT FEELS GREAT TO BE THE ONLY ONE AGAIN!
OLD WOMAN, WHAT'S GOING ON HERE?
IT'S TOO EARLY IN THE YEAR FOR SNOW LIKE THIS.
WELL, WHEN THE WIND MAGE VAATI RETURNED, AN EVIL, FREEZING WIND BEGAN TO BLOW.
THIS BLIZZARD HAS BEEN RAGING EVER SINCE.
ALL THE PLANTS AND ANIMALS ARE DYING.
IS THAT ALL?
I CAN TAKE CARE OF THAT.
WHAT A GREAT HERO!
THE WIND MAGE LURKS IN THAT CAVE...
...THE ONE THE WIND COMES FROM.
I'M GOING IN!
FWUMP
FWUMP

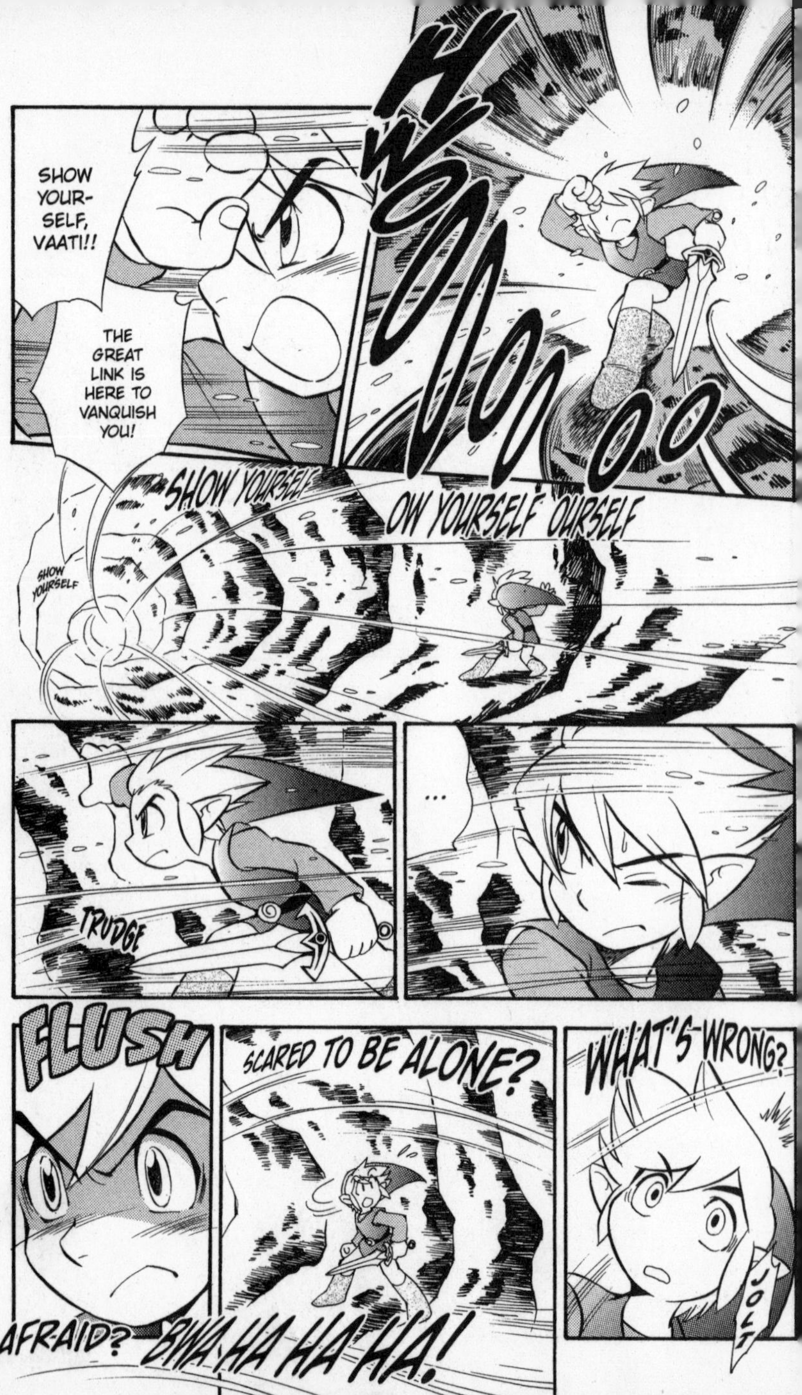
WHOOOOOOOO
SHOW YOURSELF, VAATI!!
THE GREAT LINK IS HERE TO VANQUISH YOU!
OW YOURSELF OURSELF
SHOW YOURSELF
SHOW YOURSELF
...
TRUDGE
WHAT'S WRONG?
JOLT
SCARED TO BE ALONE?
FLUSH
AFRAID? BWA-HA HA HA HA!

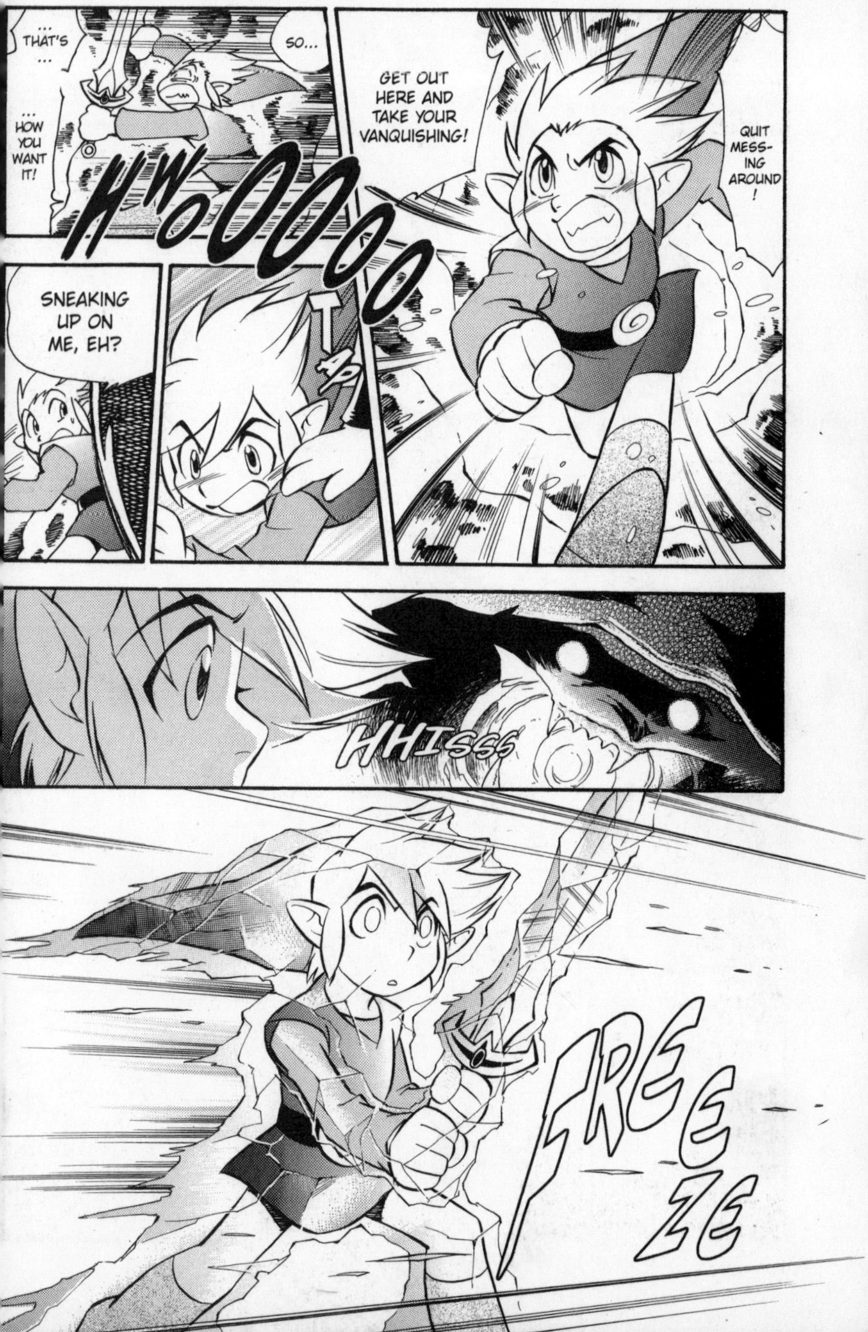
GET OUT HERE AND TAKE YOUR VANQUISHING!
QUIT MESS-ING AROUND!
HWOOOOOO
SO...
... THAT'S ...
... HOW YOU WANT IT!
TAP!
SNEAKING UP ON ME, EH?
HHISSS
FREEZE

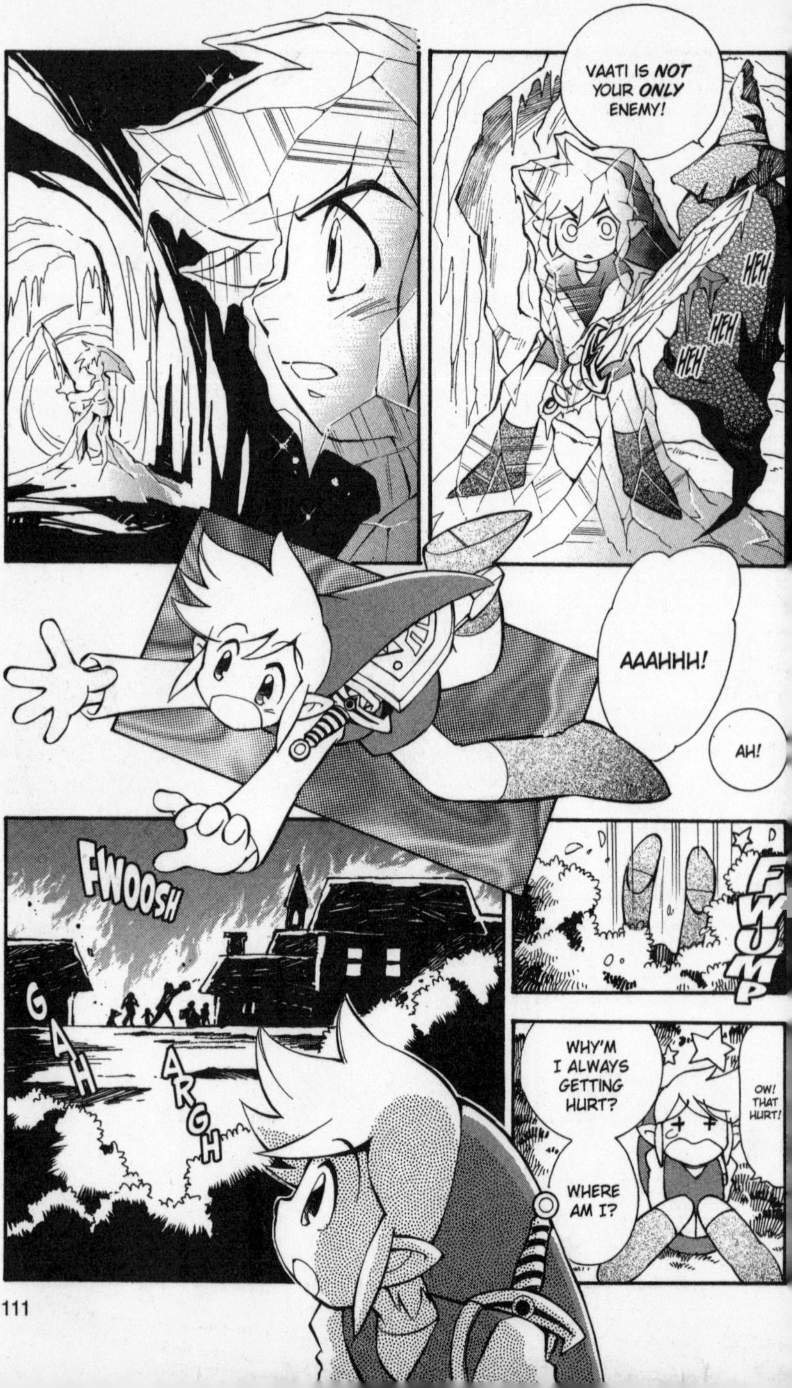
VAATI IS NOT YOUR ONLY ENEMY!
HEH
HEH
HEH
AAAHHH!
AH!
FWUMP
OW! THAT HURT!
WHY'M I ALWAYS GETTING HURT?
WHERE AM I?
FWOOSH
GAAH
ARGH

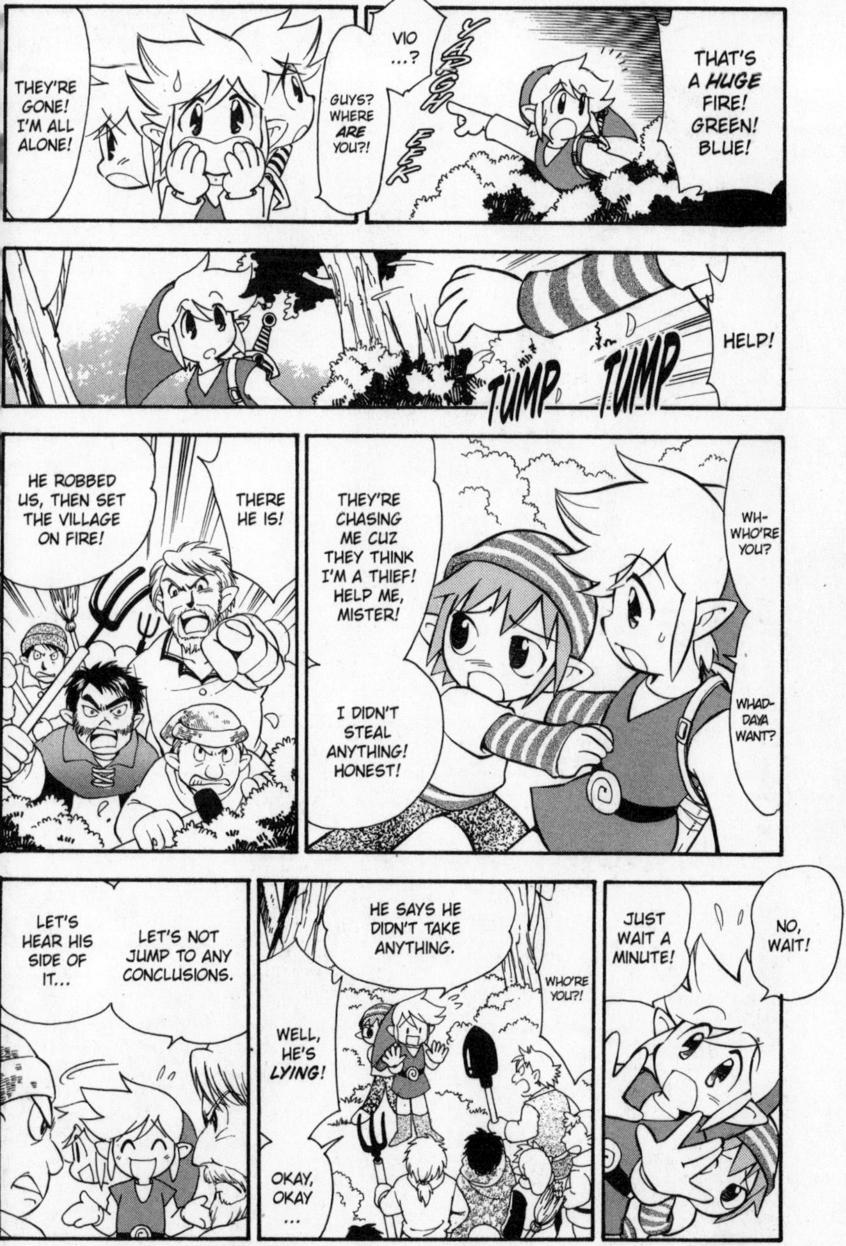
THAT'S A **HUGE** FIRE! GREEN! BLUE!
VIO ...?
GUYS? WHERE **ARE** YOU?!
THEY'RE GONE! I'M ALL ALONE!
HELP!
TUMP TUMP
WH-WHO'RE YOU?
THEY'RE CHASING ME CUZ THEY THINK I'M A THIEF! HELP ME, MISTER!
WHAD-DAYA WANT?
I DIDN'T STEAL ANYTHING! HONEST!
THERE HE IS!
HE ROBBED US, THEN SET THE VILLAGE ON FIRE!
NO, WAIT!
JUST WAIT A MINUTE!
WHO'RE YOU?!
HE SAYS HE DIDN'T TAKE ANYTHING.
WELL, HE'S **LYING**!
OKAY, OKAY ...
LET'S NOT JUMP TO ANY CONCLUSIONS.
LET'S HEAR HIS SIDE OF IT...

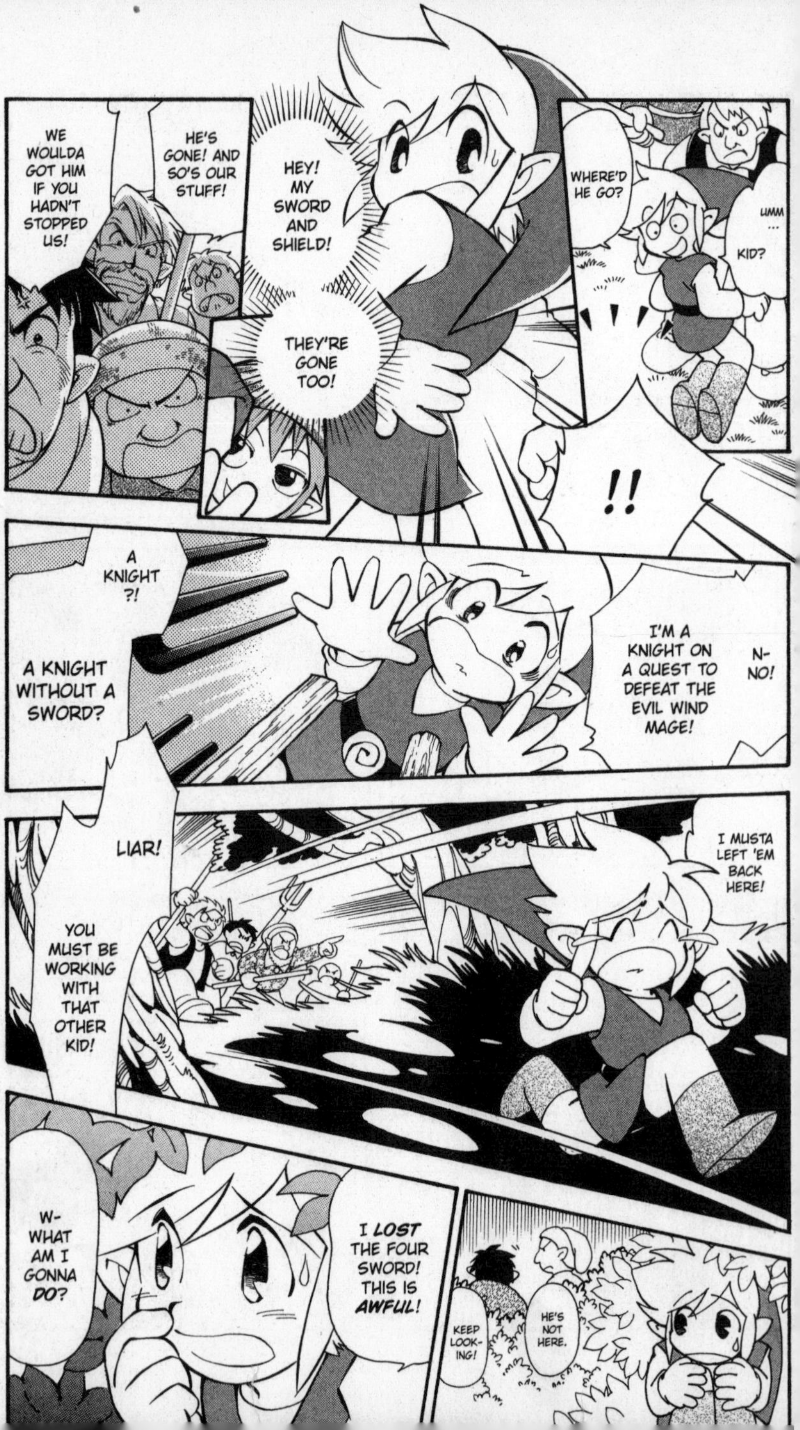
WHERE'D HE GO?
UMM ... KID?
HEY! MY SWORD AND SHIELD!
THEY'RE GONE TOO!
!!
HE'S GONE! AND SO'S OUR STUFF!
WE WOULDA GOT HIM IF YOU HADN'T STOPPED US!
N-NO!
I'M A KNIGHT ON A QUEST TO DEFEAT THE EVIL WIND MAGE!
A KNIGHT ?!
A KNIGHT WITHOUT A SWORD?
I MUSTA LEFT 'EM BACK HERE!
LIAR!
YOU MUST BE WORKING WITH THAT OTHER KID!
HE'S NOT HERE.
KEEP LOOK-ING!
I *LOST* THE FOUR SWORD! THIS IS ***AWFUL!***
W-WHAT AM I GONNA *DO*?

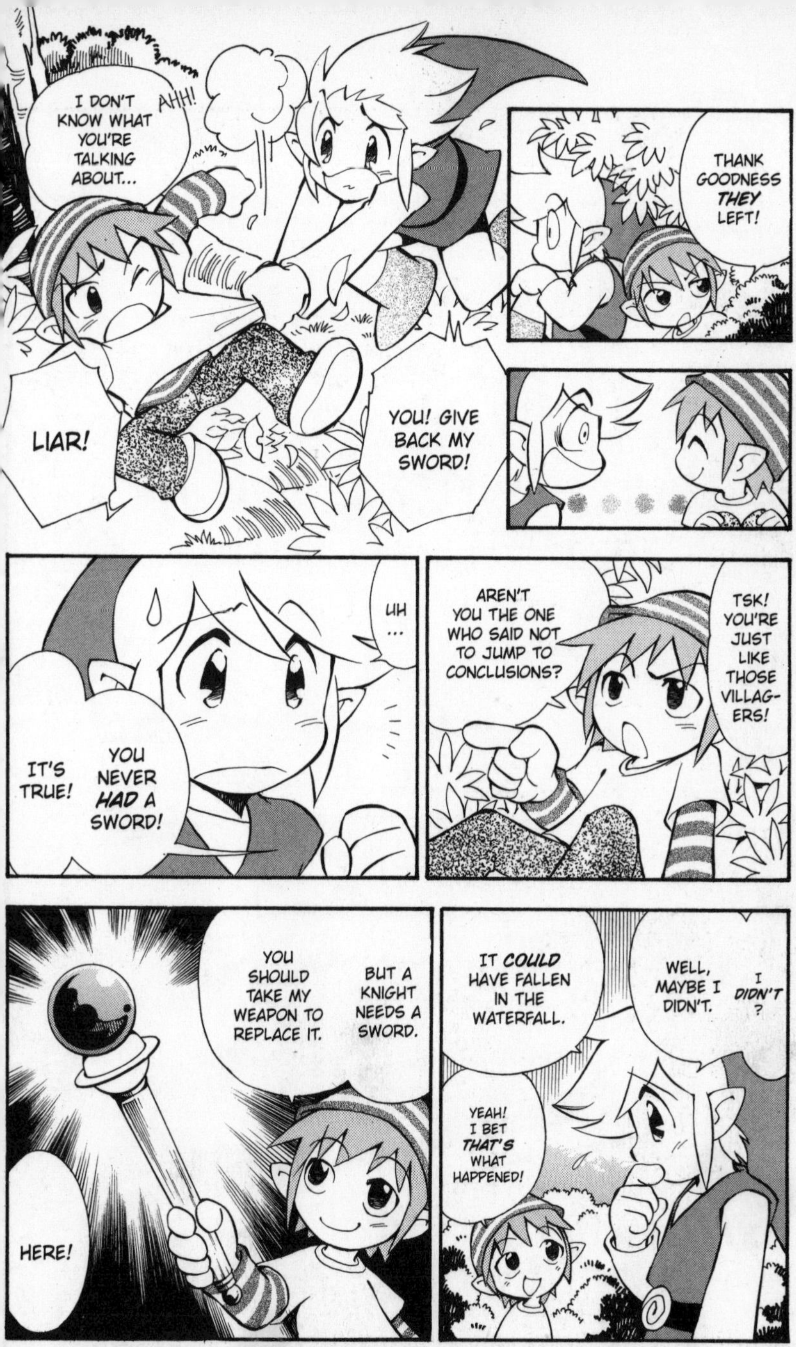
THANK GOODNESS THEY LEFT!
YOU! GIVE BACK MY SWORD!
I DON'T KNOW WHAT YOU'RE TALKING ABOUT...
AHH!
LIAR!
TSK! YOU'RE JUST LIKE THOSE VILLAGERS!
AREN'T YOU THE ONE WHO SAID NOT TO JUMP TO CONCLUSIONS?
UH ...
YOU NEVER HAD A SWORD!
IT'S TRUE!
I DIDN'T ?
WELL, MAYBE I DIDN'T.
IT COULD HAVE FALLEN IN THE WATERFALL.
YEAH! I BET THAT'S WHAT HAPPENED!
BUT A KNIGHT NEEDS A SWORD.
YOU SHOULD TAKE MY WEAPON TO REPLACE IT.
HERE!

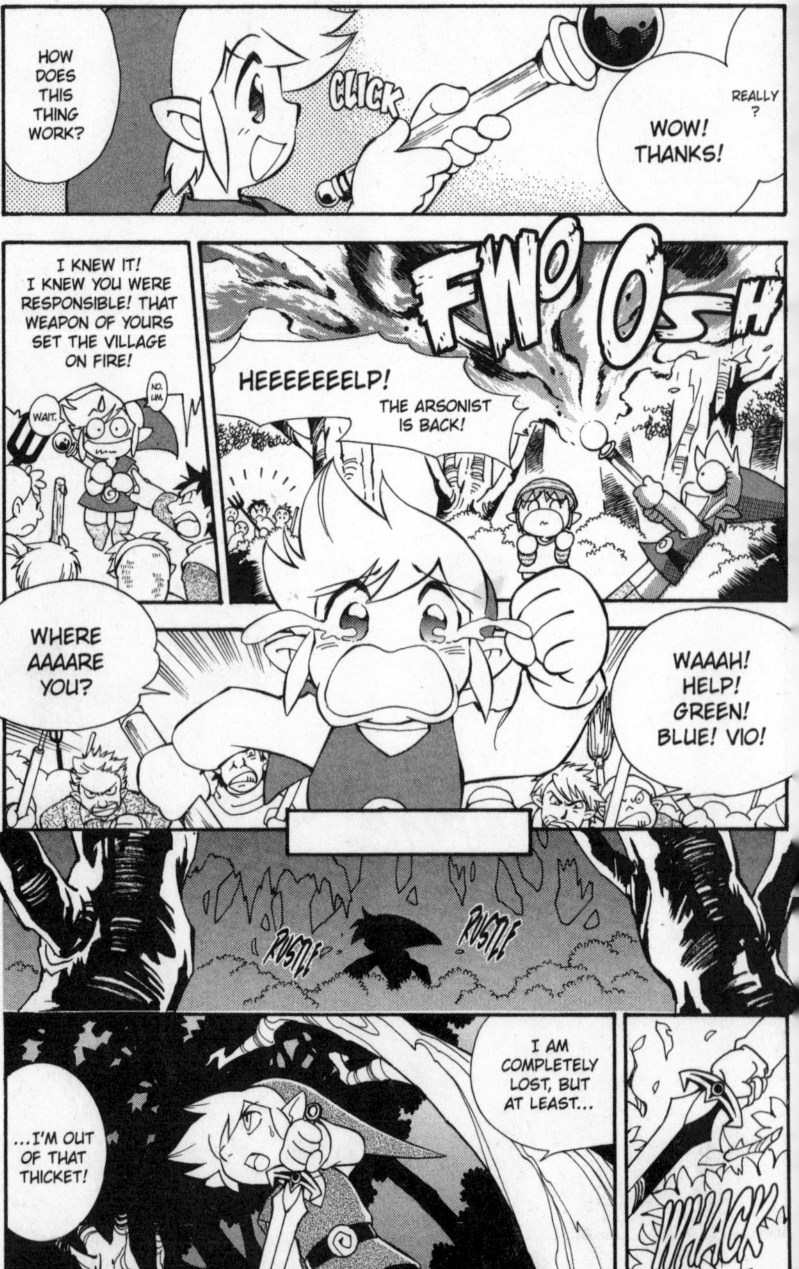
REALLY ?
WOW! THANKS!
CLICK
HOW DOES THIS THING WORK?
FWOOOSH
HEEEEEEELP!
THE ARSONIST IS BACK!
I KNEW IT! I KNEW YOU WERE RESPONSIBLE! THAT WEAPON OF YOURS SET THE VILLAGE ON FIRE!
NO. UM.
WAIT.
WAAAH! HELP! GREEN! BLUE! VIO!
WHERE AAAARE YOU?
RUSTLE
RUSTLE
WHACK
I AM COMPLETELY LOST, BUT AT LEAST...
...I'M OUT OF THAT THICKET!

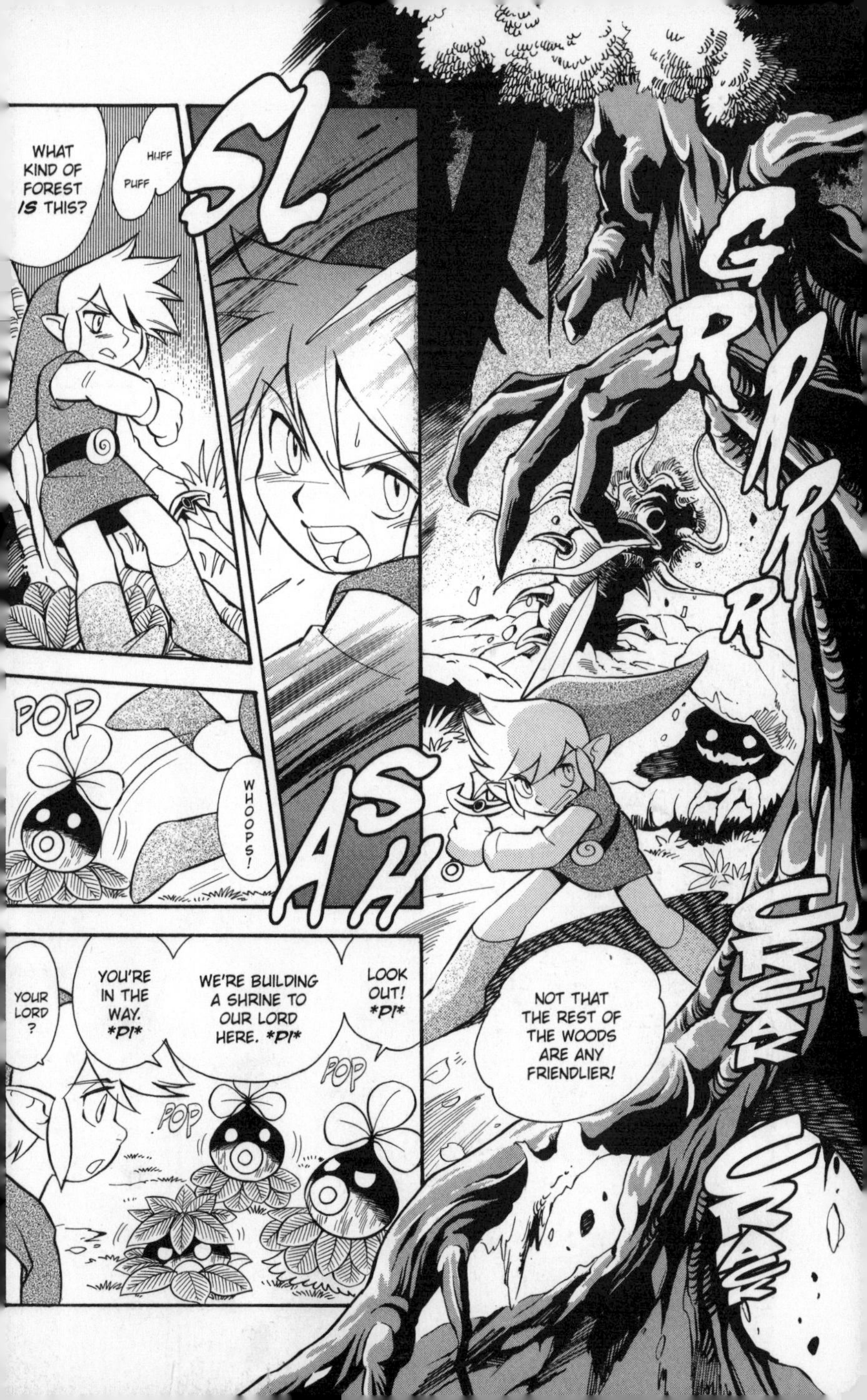
GRRRRR
NOT THAT THE REST OF THE WOODS ARE ANY FRIENDLIER!
SL
HUFF
PUFF
WHAT KIND OF FOREST *IS* THIS?
ASH
WHOOPS!
POP
LOOK OUT! *PI*
WE'RE BUILDING A SHRINE TO OUR LORD HERE. *PI*
YOU'RE IN THE WAY. *PI*
POP
POP
YOUR LORD?

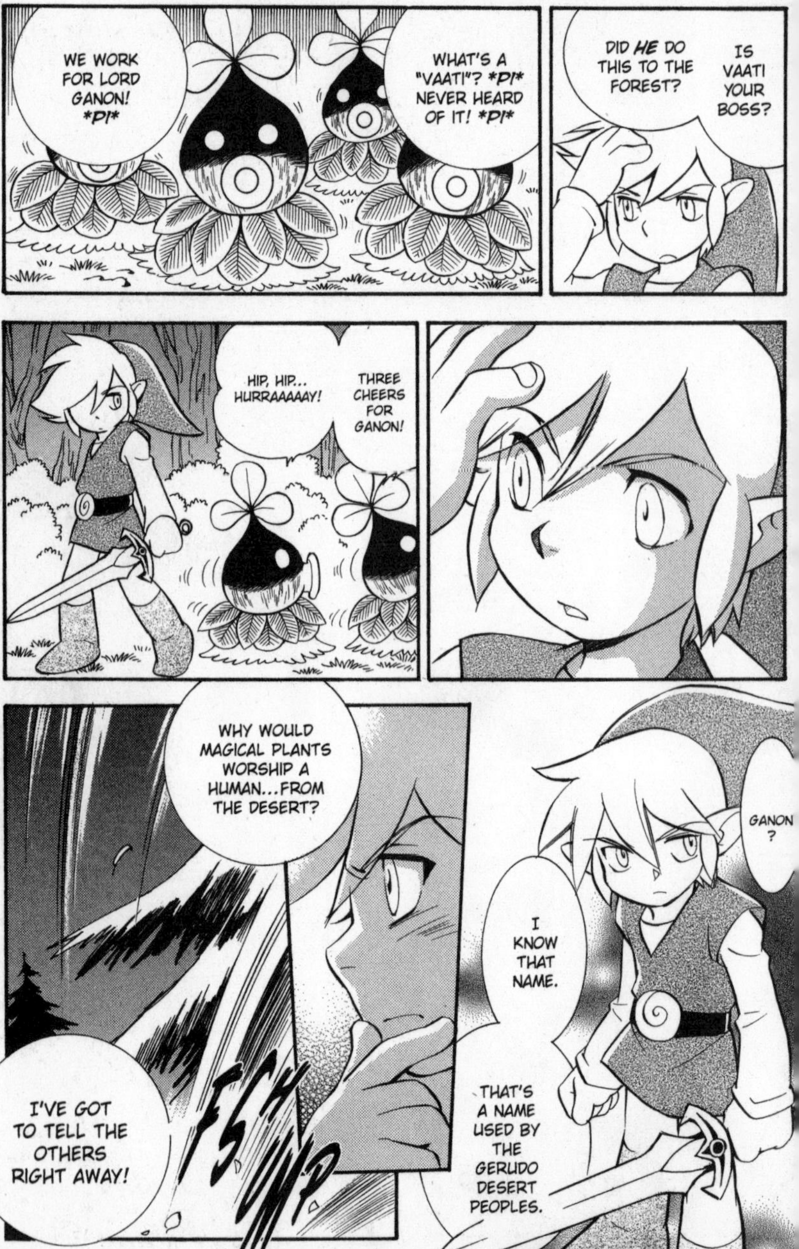
IS VAATI YOUR BOSS?
DID HE DO THIS TO THE FOREST?
WHAT'S A "VAATI"? *PI* NEVER HEARD OF IT! *PI*
WE WORK FOR LORD GANON! *PI*
THREE CHEERS FOR GANON!
HIP, HIP... HURRAAAAAY!
GANON?
I KNOW THAT NAME.
THAT'S A NAME USED BY THE GERUDO DESERT PEOPLES.
WHY WOULD MAGICAL PLANTS WORSHIP A HUMAN...FROM THE DESERT?
I'VE GOT TO TELL THE OTHERS RIGHT AWAY!

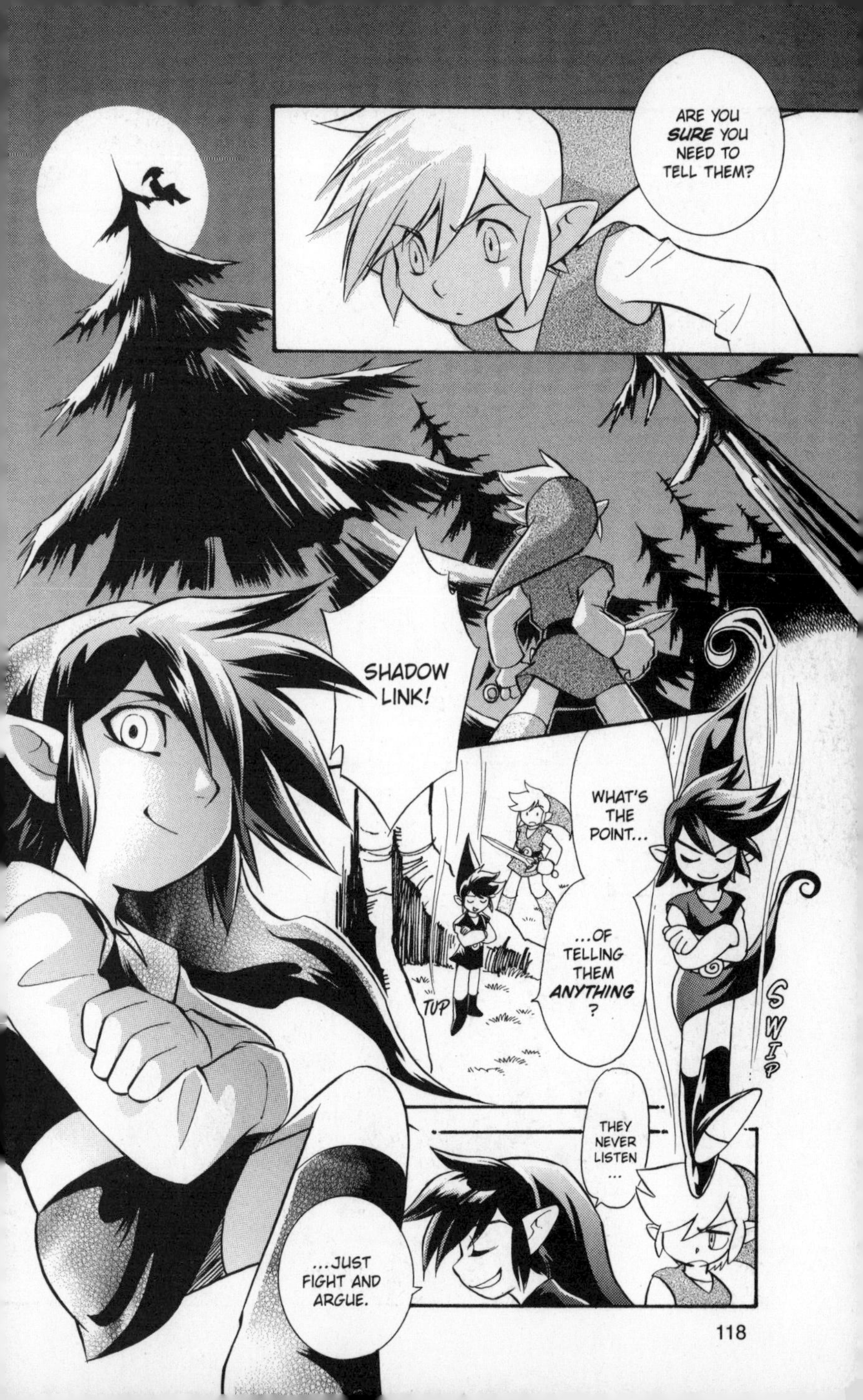

ARE YOU SURE YOU NEED TO TELL THEM?
SHADOW LINK!
SWIP
WHAT'S THE POINT...
...OF TELLING THEM ANYTHING?
TUP
THEY NEVER LISTEN...
...JUST FIGHT AND ARGUE.

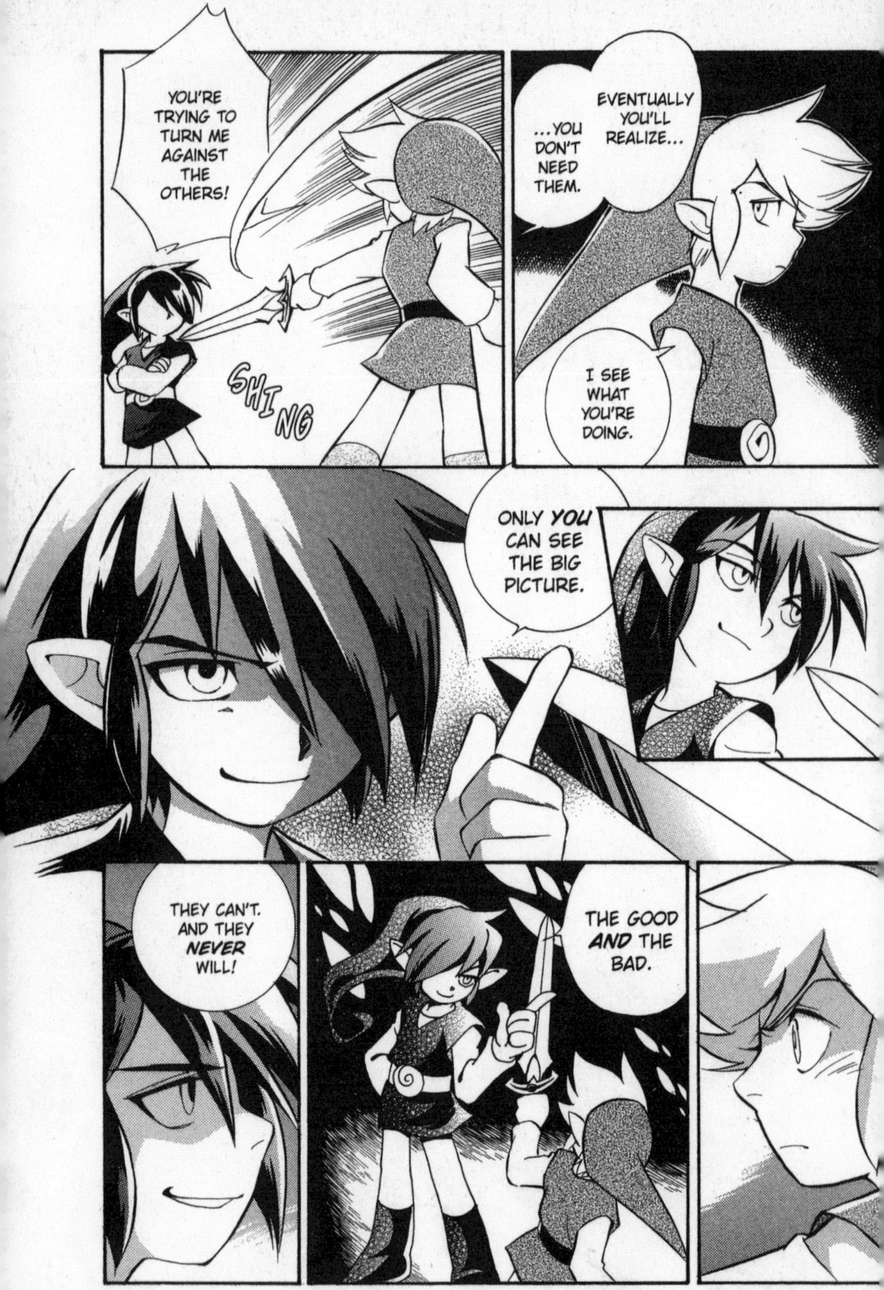
EVENTUALLY YOU'LL REALIZE...
...YOU DON'T NEED THEM.
I SEE WHAT YOU'RE DOING.
YOU'RE TRYING TO TURN ME AGAINST THE OTHERS!
SHING
ONLY *YOU* CAN SEE THE BIG PICTURE.
THE GOOD *AND* THE BAD.
THEY CAN'T. AND THEY *NEVER* WILL!

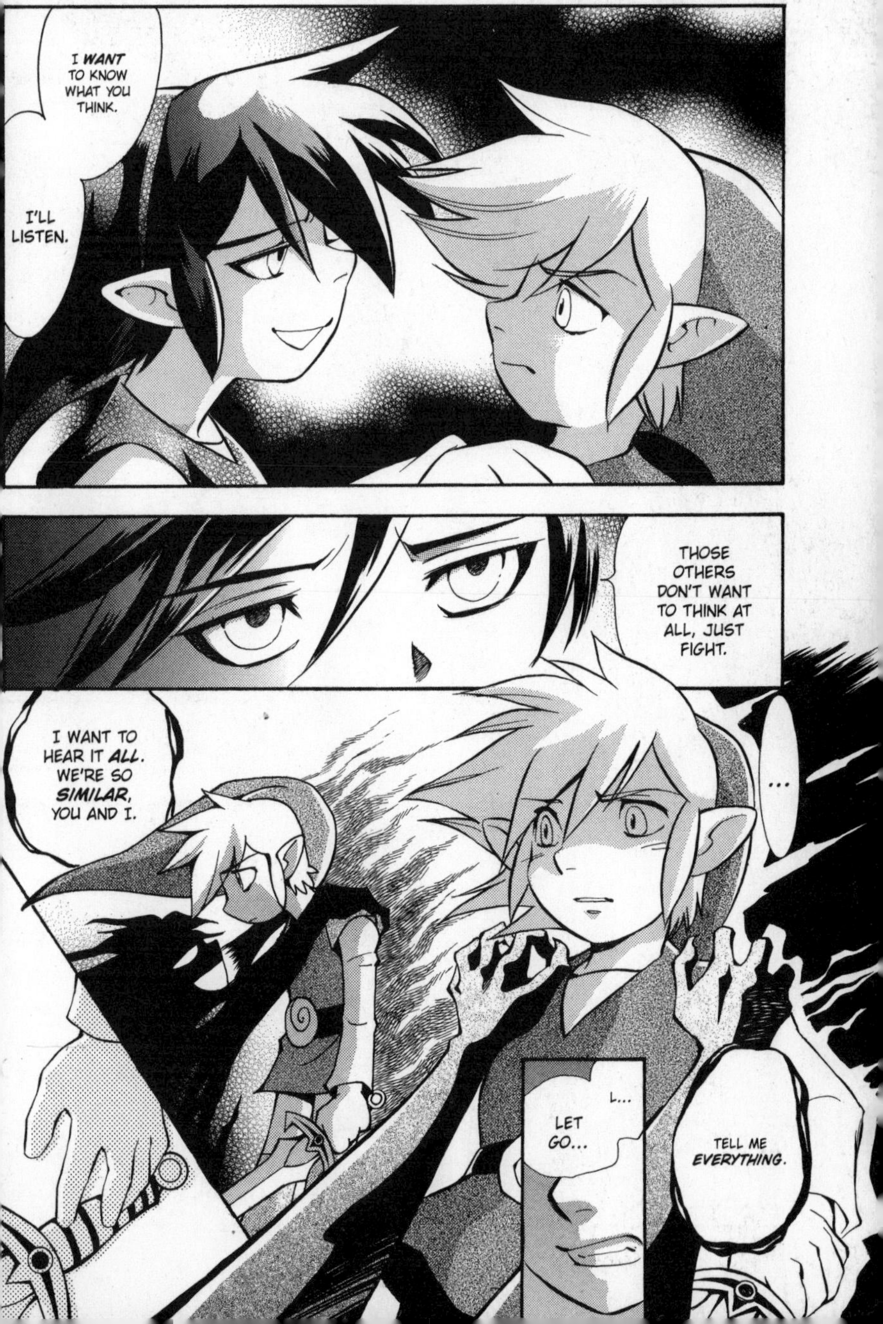
I *WANT* TO KNOW WHAT YOU THINK.
I'LL LISTEN.
THOSE OTHERS DON'T WANT TO THINK AT ALL, JUST FIGHT.
...
I WANT TO HEAR IT *ALL*. WE'RE SO *SIMILAR*, YOU AND I.
TELL ME *EVERYTHING*.
L... LET GO...

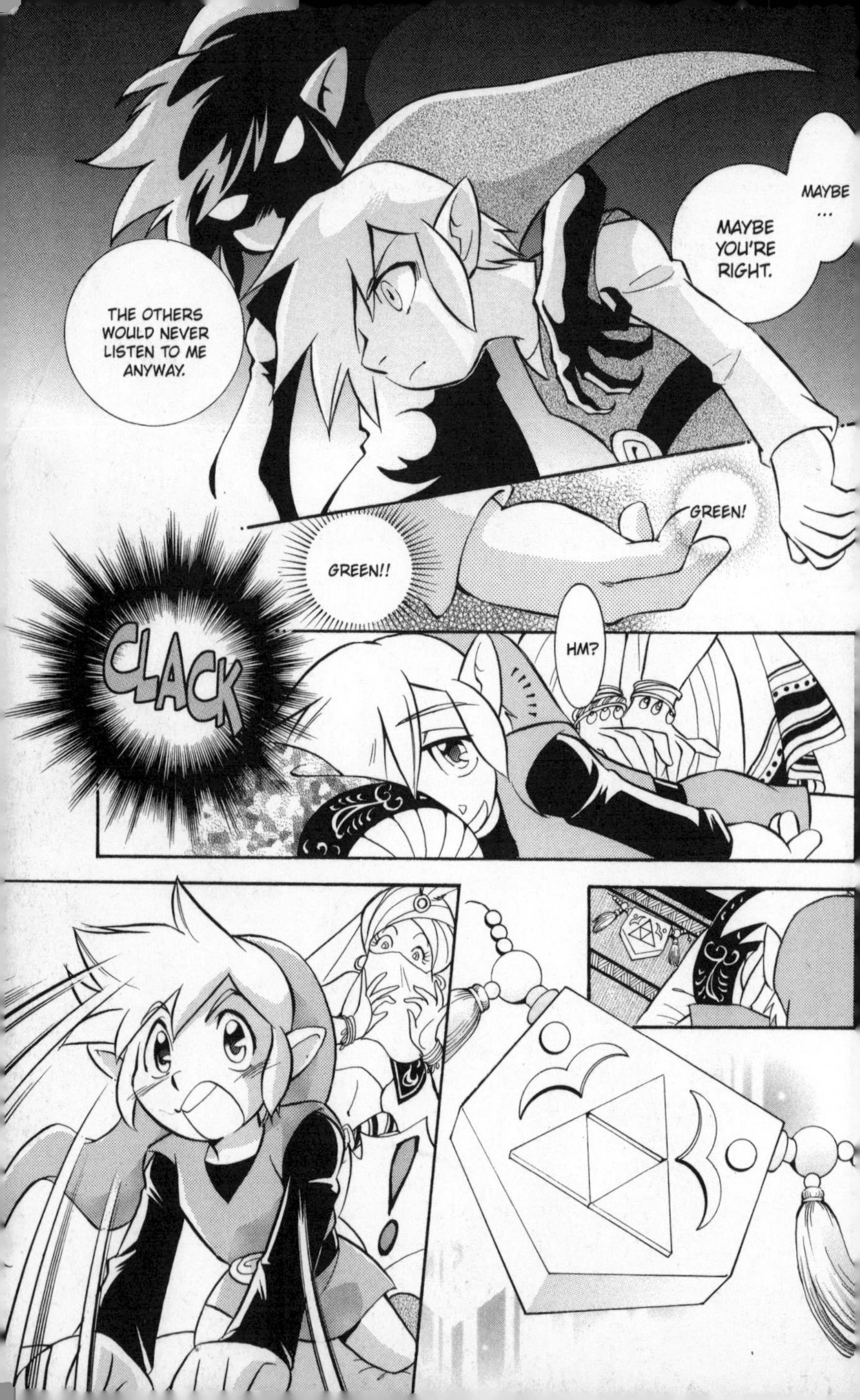
MAYBE ...
MAYBE YOU'RE RIGHT.
THE OTHERS WOULD NEVER LISTEN TO ME ANYWAY.
GREEN!
GREEN!!
HM?
CLACK

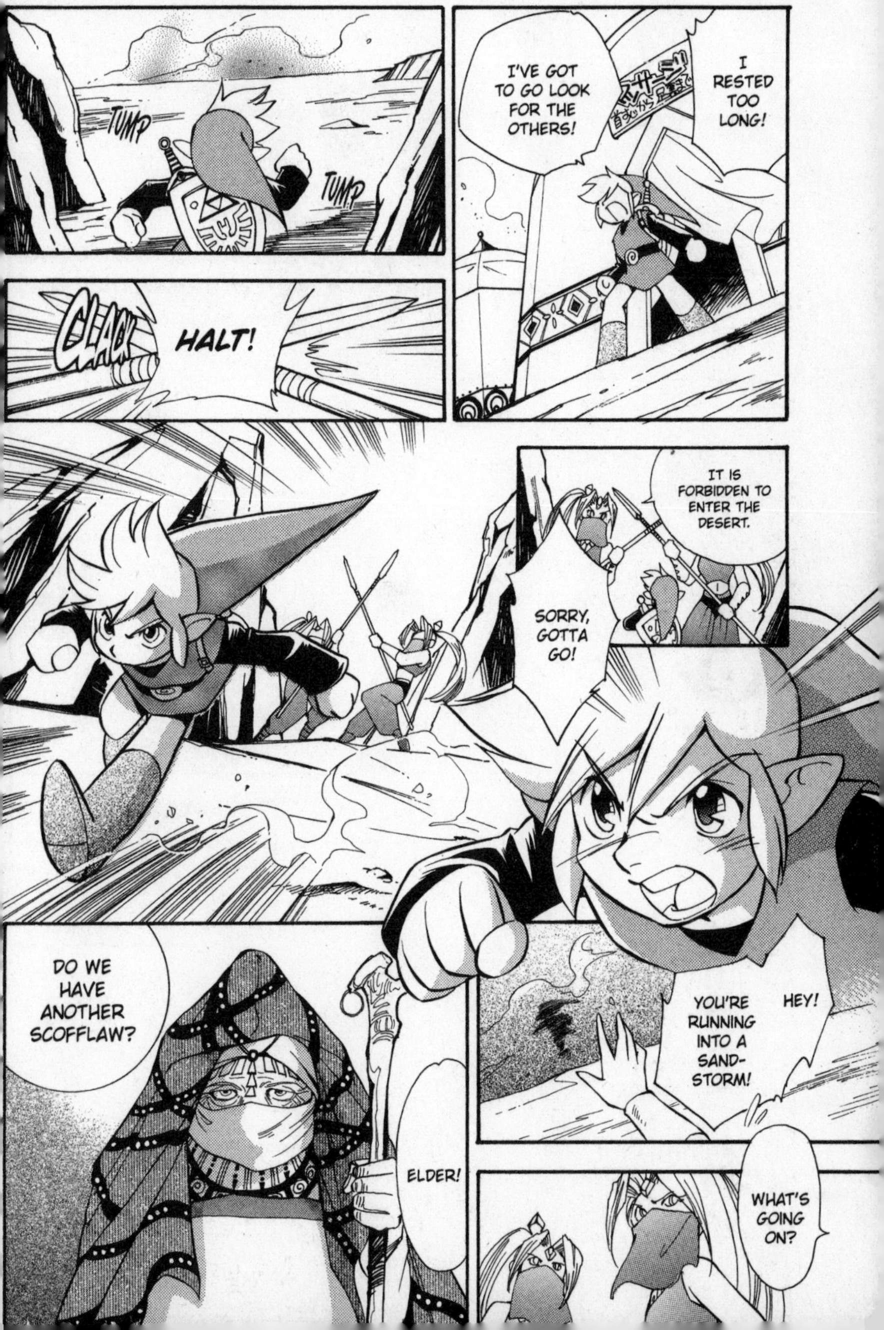
I RESTED TOO LONG!
I'VE GOT TO GO LOOK FOR THE OTHERS!
TUMP
TUMP
HALT!
CLACK
IT IS FORBIDDEN TO ENTER THE DESERT.
SORRY, GOTTA GO!
HEY!
YOU'RE RUNNING INTO A SAND-STORM!
WHAT'S GOING ON?
ELDER!
DO WE HAVE ANOTHER SCOFFLAW?

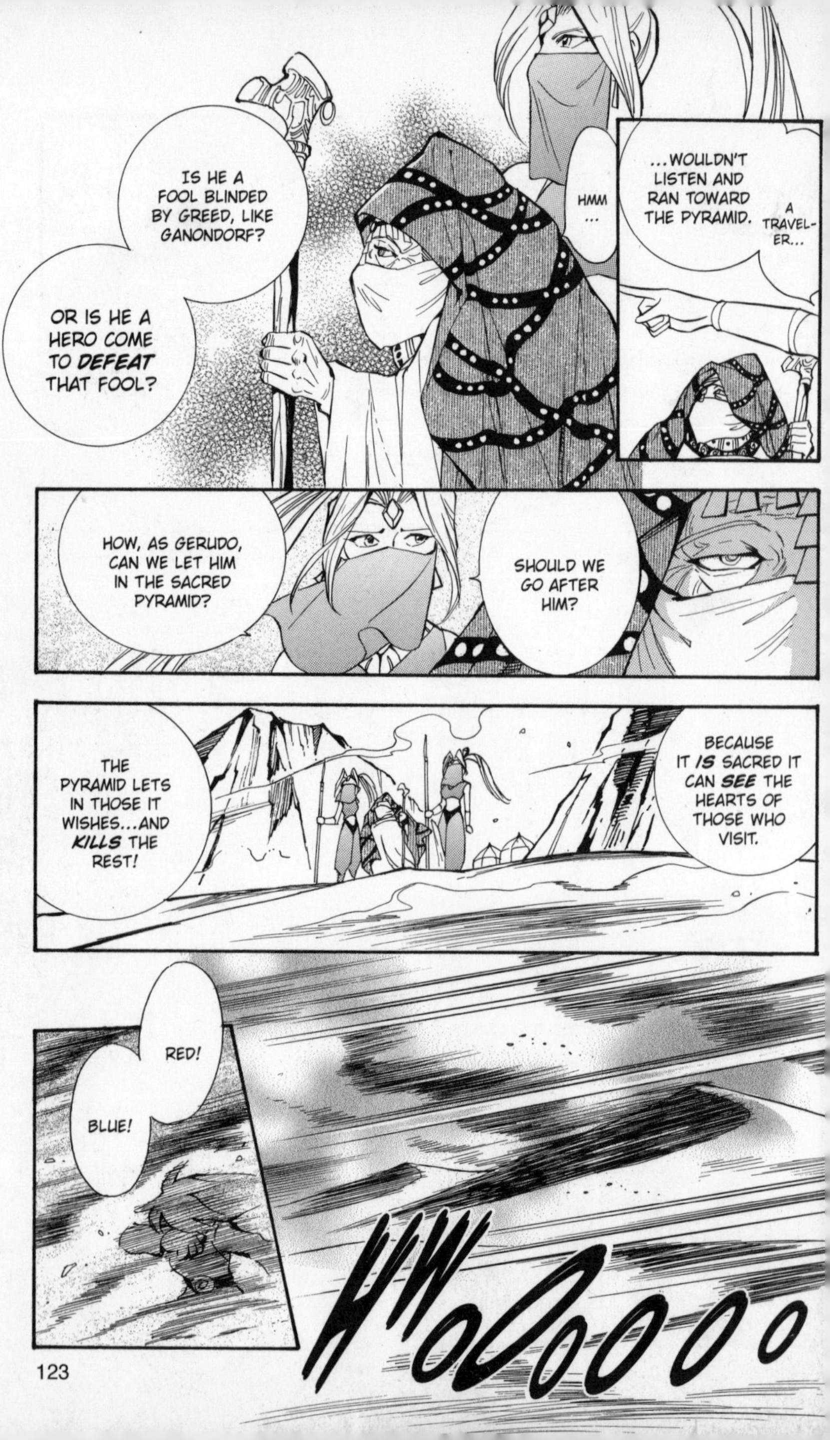
A TRAVELER...
...WOULDN'T LISTEN AND RAN TOWARD THE PYRAMID.
HMM...
IS HE A FOOL BLINDED BY GREED, LIKE GANONDORF?
OR IS HE A HERO COME TO *DEFEAT* THAT FOOL?
SHOULD WE GO AFTER HIM?
HOW, AS GERUDO, CAN WE LET HIM IN THE SACRED PYRAMID?
BECAUSE IT *IS* SACRED IT CAN *SEE* THE HEARTS OF THOSE WHO VISIT.
THE PYRAMID LETS IN THOSE IT WISHES...AND *KILLS* THE REST!
RED!
BLUE!
HWOOOOOOO

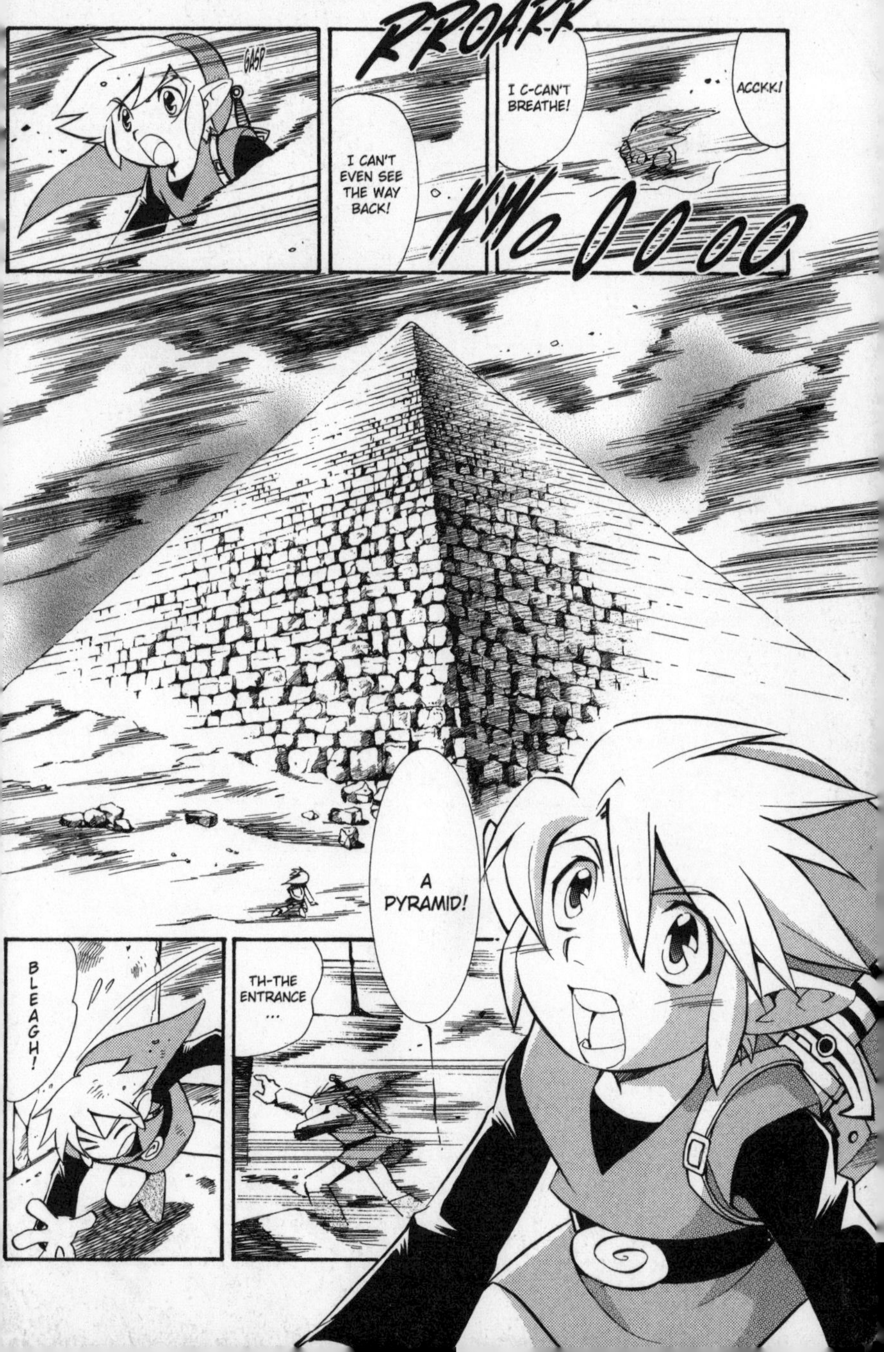
ACCKK!
I C-CAN'T BREATHE!
HWOOOOO
RROARR
I CAN'T EVEN SEE THE WAY BACK!
GASP
A PYRAMID!
TH-THE ENTRANCE ...
BLEAGH!

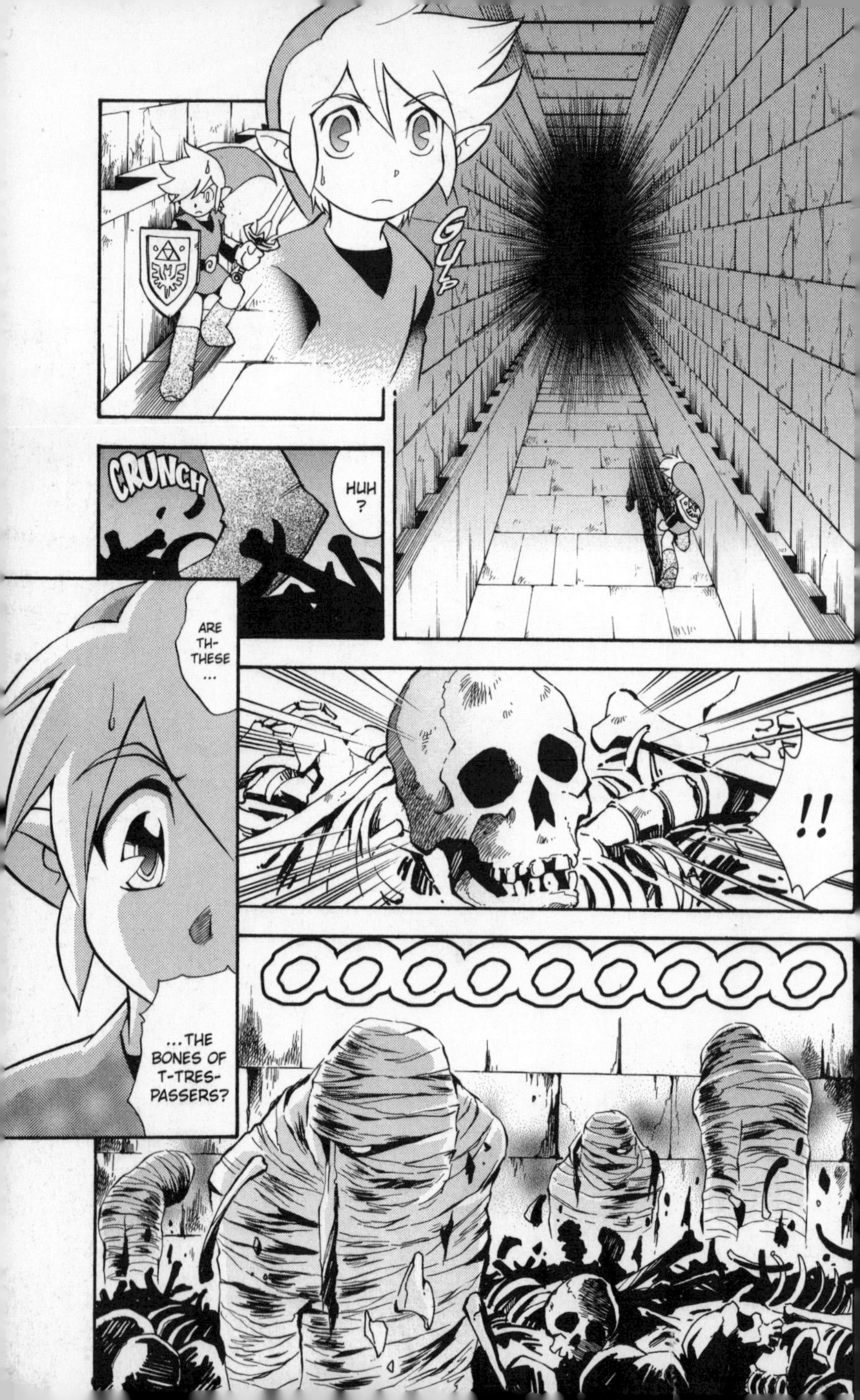
GULP
CRUNCH
HUH?
!!
OOOOOOOOOO
ARE TH- THESE ...
...THE BONES OF T-TRESPASSERS?

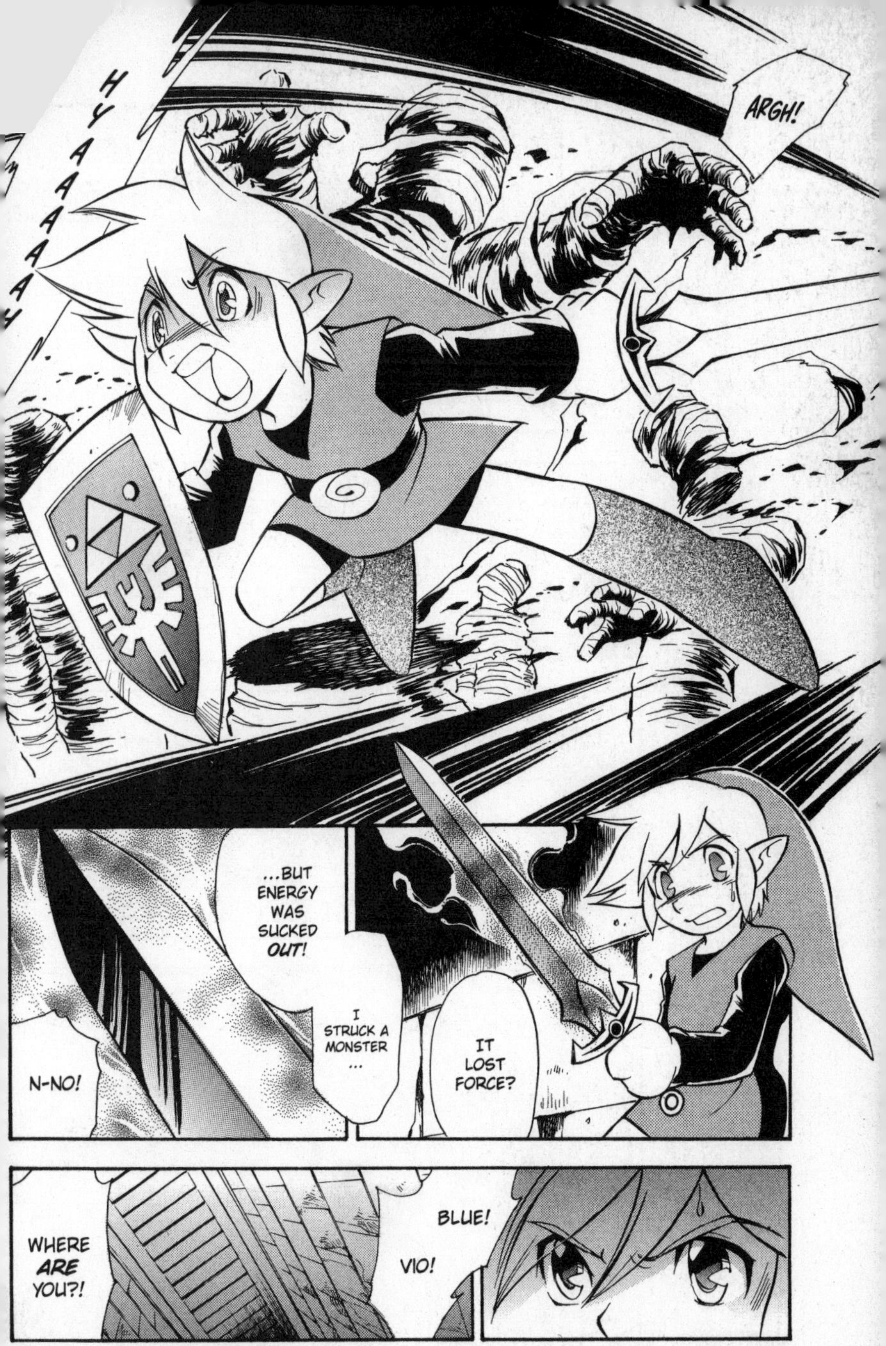
ARGH!
HYAAAAAAAH
IT LOST FORCE?
I STRUCK A MONSTER...
...BUT ENERGY WAS SUCKED OUT!
N-NO!
BLUE!
VIO!
WHERE ARE YOU?!

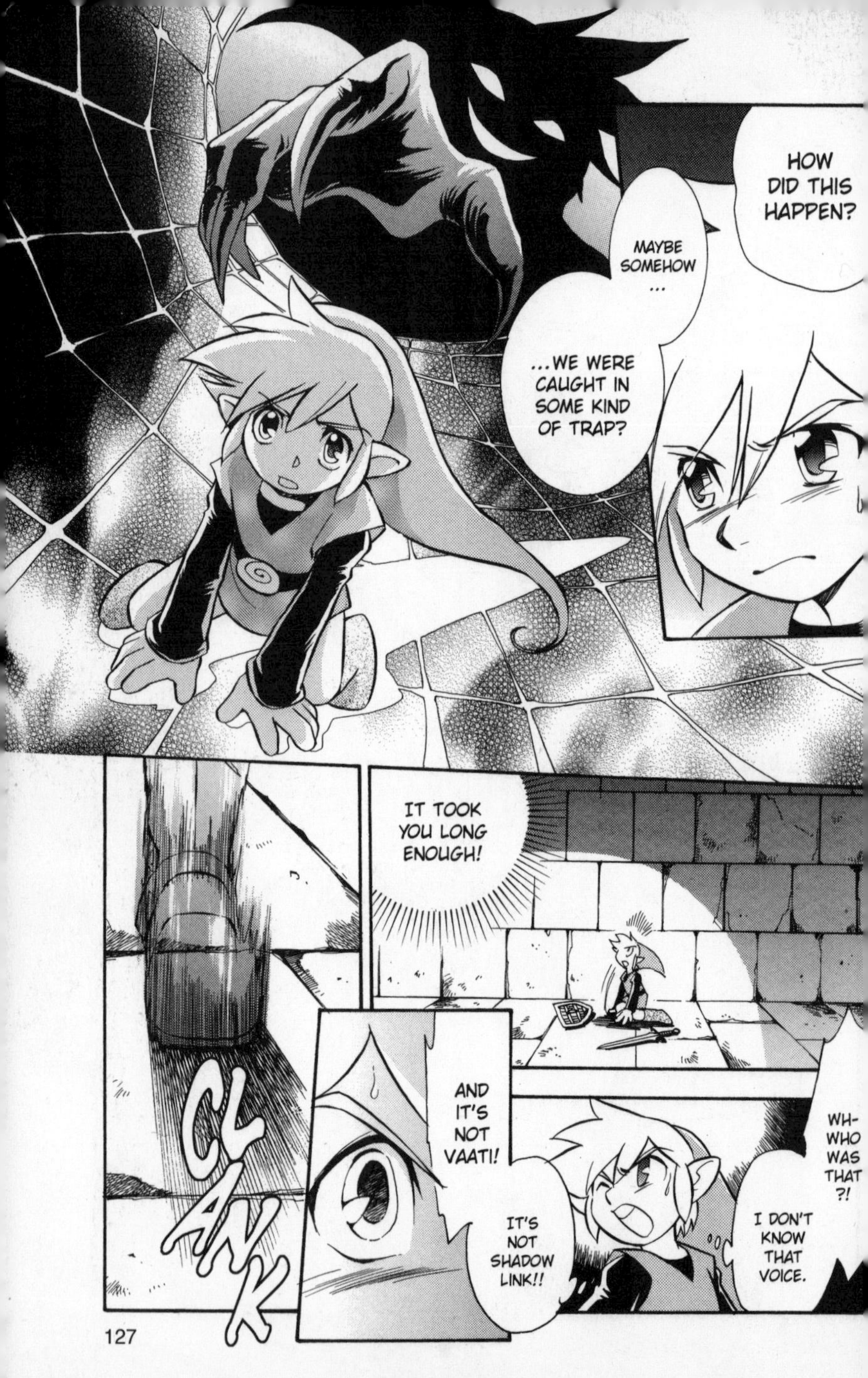
HOW DID THIS HAPPEN?
MAYBE SOMEHOW ...
...WE WERE CAUGHT IN SOME KIND OF TRAP?
IT TOOK YOU LONG ENOUGH!
WH-WHO WAS THAT?!
I DON'T KNOW THAT VOICE.
IT'S NOT SHADOW LINK!!
AND IT'S NOT VAATI!
CLANK

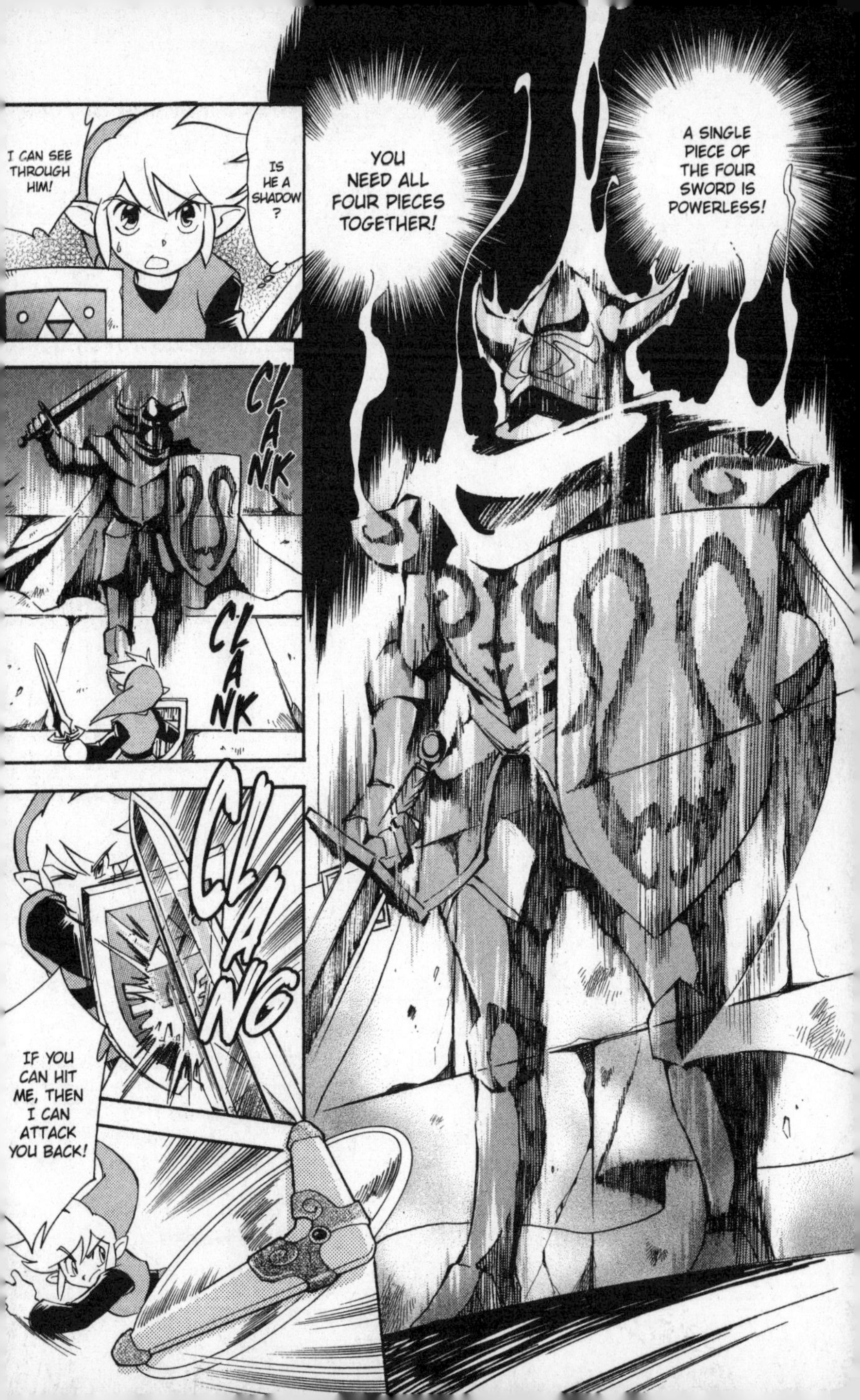

A SINGLE PIECE OF THE FOUR SWORD IS POWERLESS!
YOU NEED ALL FOUR PIECES TOGETHER!
IS HE A SHADOW?
I CAN SEE THROUGH HIM!
CLANK
CLANK
CLANG
IF YOU CAN HIT ME, THEN I CAN ATTACK YOU BACK!

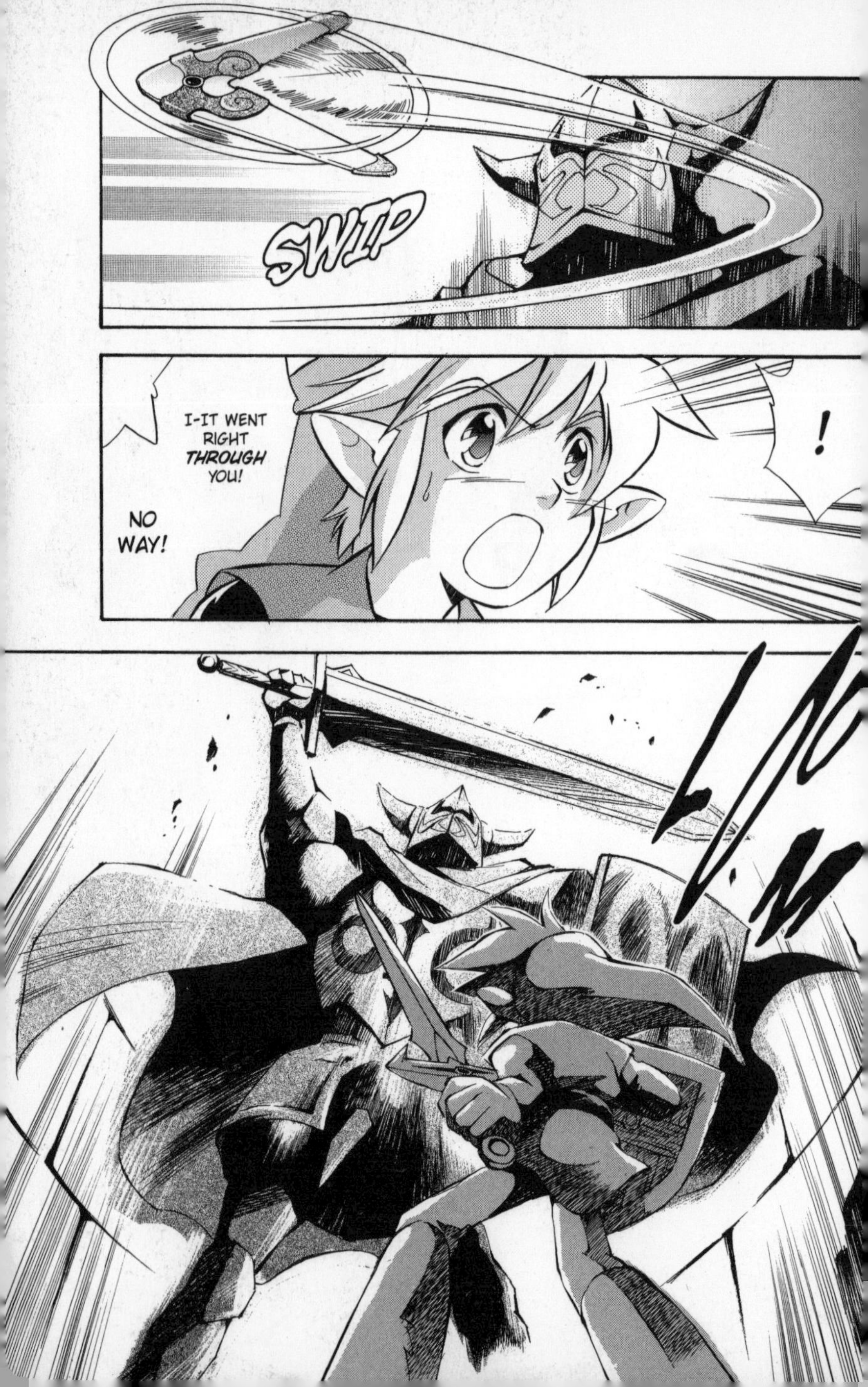
SWIP
!
I-IT WENT RIGHT ***THROUGH*** YOU!
NO WAY!

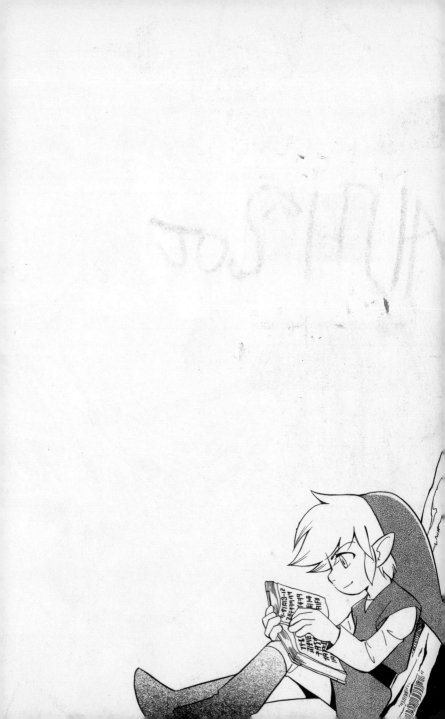

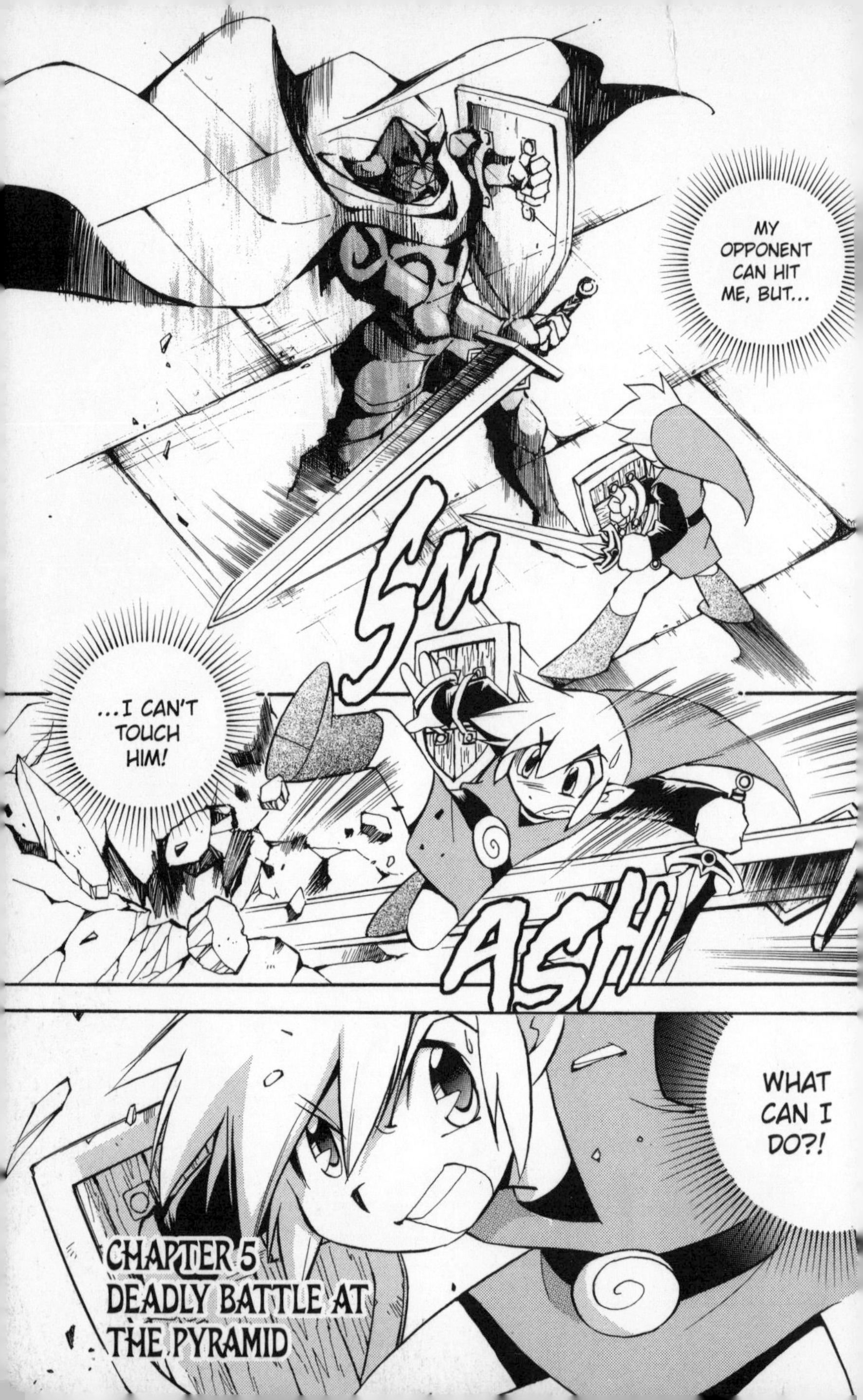
MY OPPONENT CAN HIT ME, BUT...
SMASH
...I CAN'T TOUCH HIM!
WHAT CAN I DO?!
CHAPTER 5
DEADLY BATTLE AT THE PYRAMID

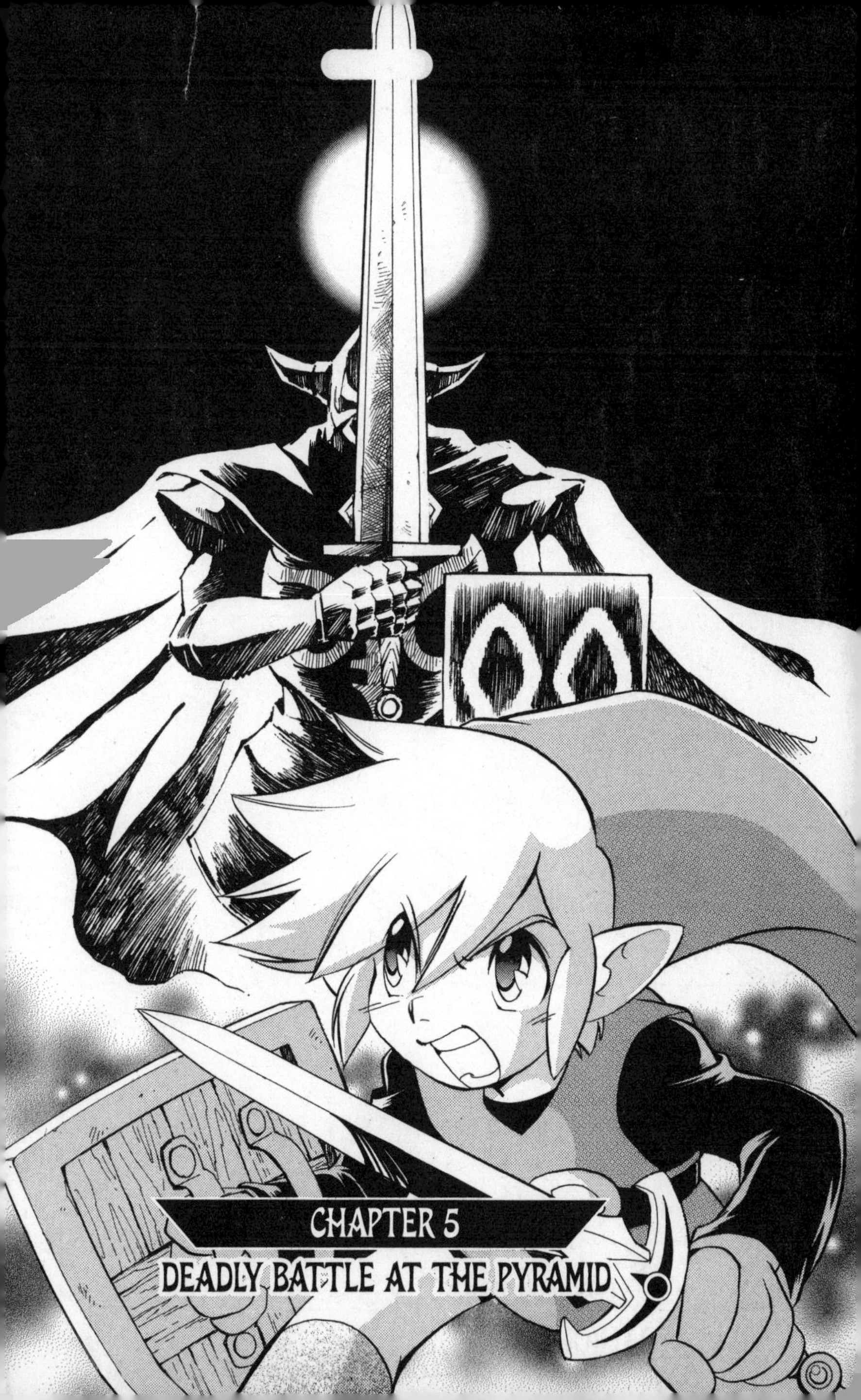
CHAPTER 5
DEADLY BATTLE AT THE PYRAMID

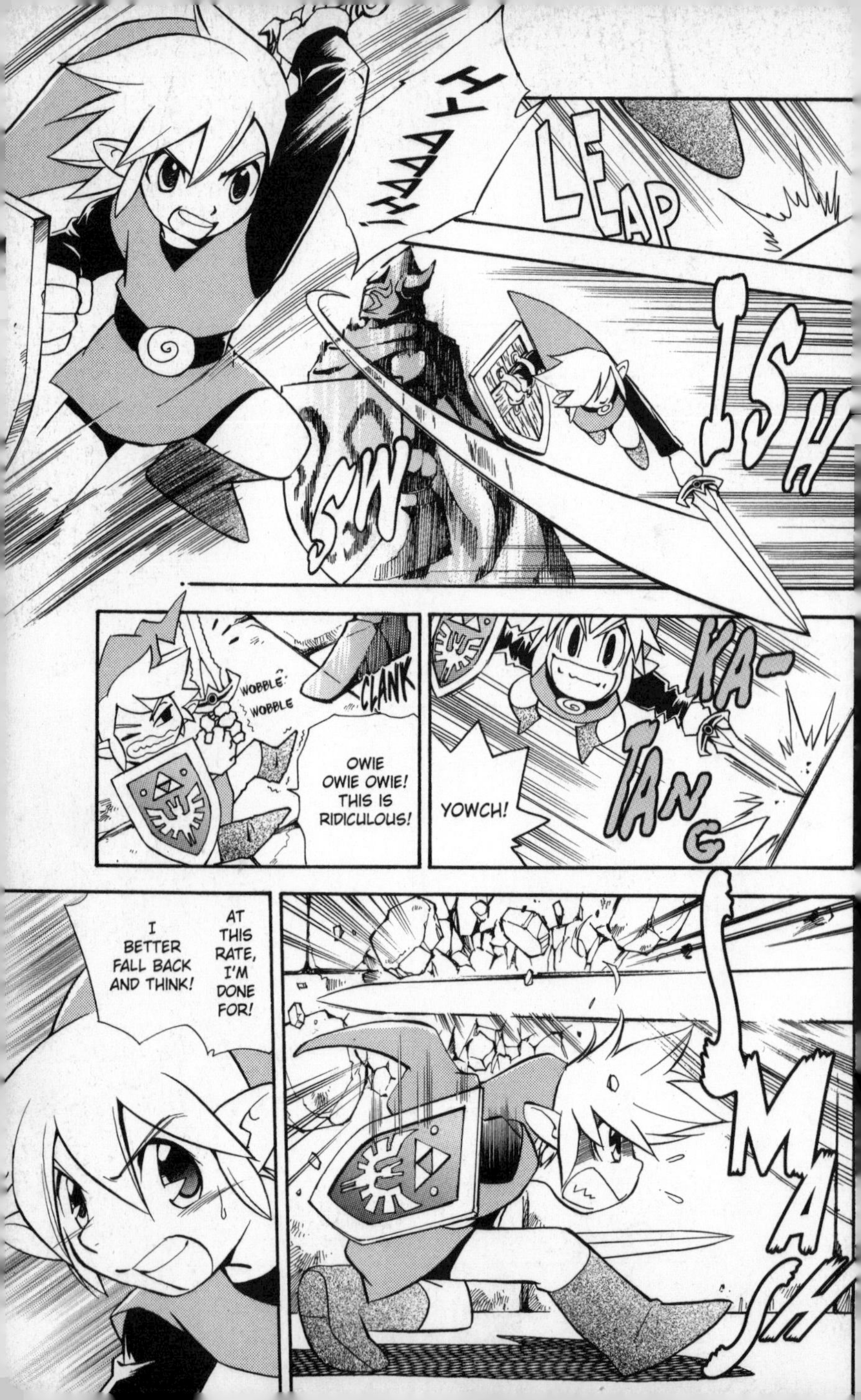

LEAP
HYAAAAH!
SWISH
KA-TANG
YOWCH!
CLANK
WOBBLE WOBBLE
OWIE OWIE OWIE! THIS IS RIDICULOUS!
SMASH
AT THIS RATE, I'M DONE FOR!
I BETTER FALL BACK AND THINK!

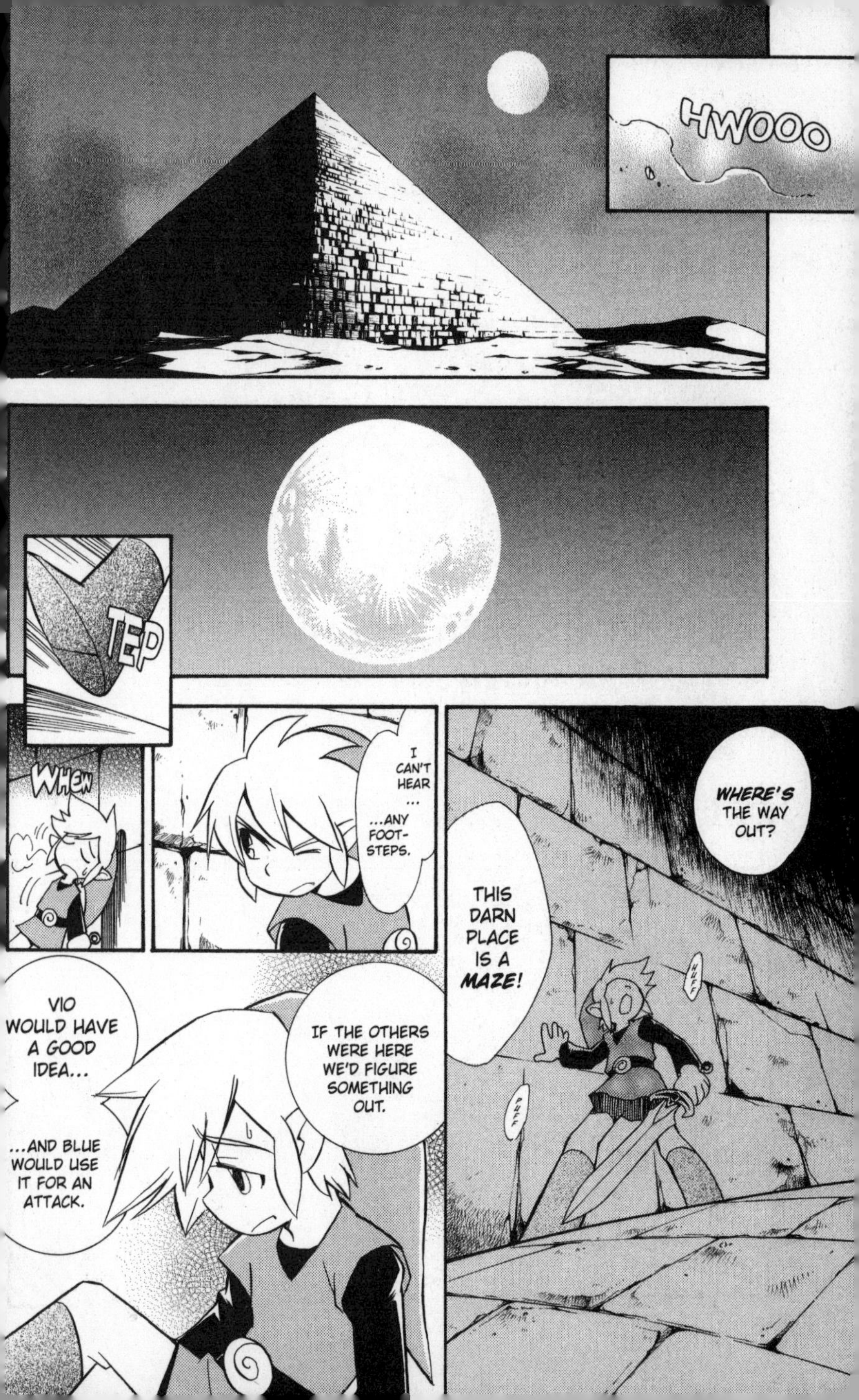
HWOOO
TEP
WHERE'S THE WAY OUT?
THIS DARN PLACE IS A MAZE!
HUFF
PUFF
I CAN'T HEAR...
...ANY FOOT-STEPS.
WHEW
IF THE OTHERS WERE HERE WE'D FIGURE SOMETHING OUT.
VIO WOULD HAVE A GOOD IDEA...
...AND BLUE WOULD USE IT FOR AN ATTACK.

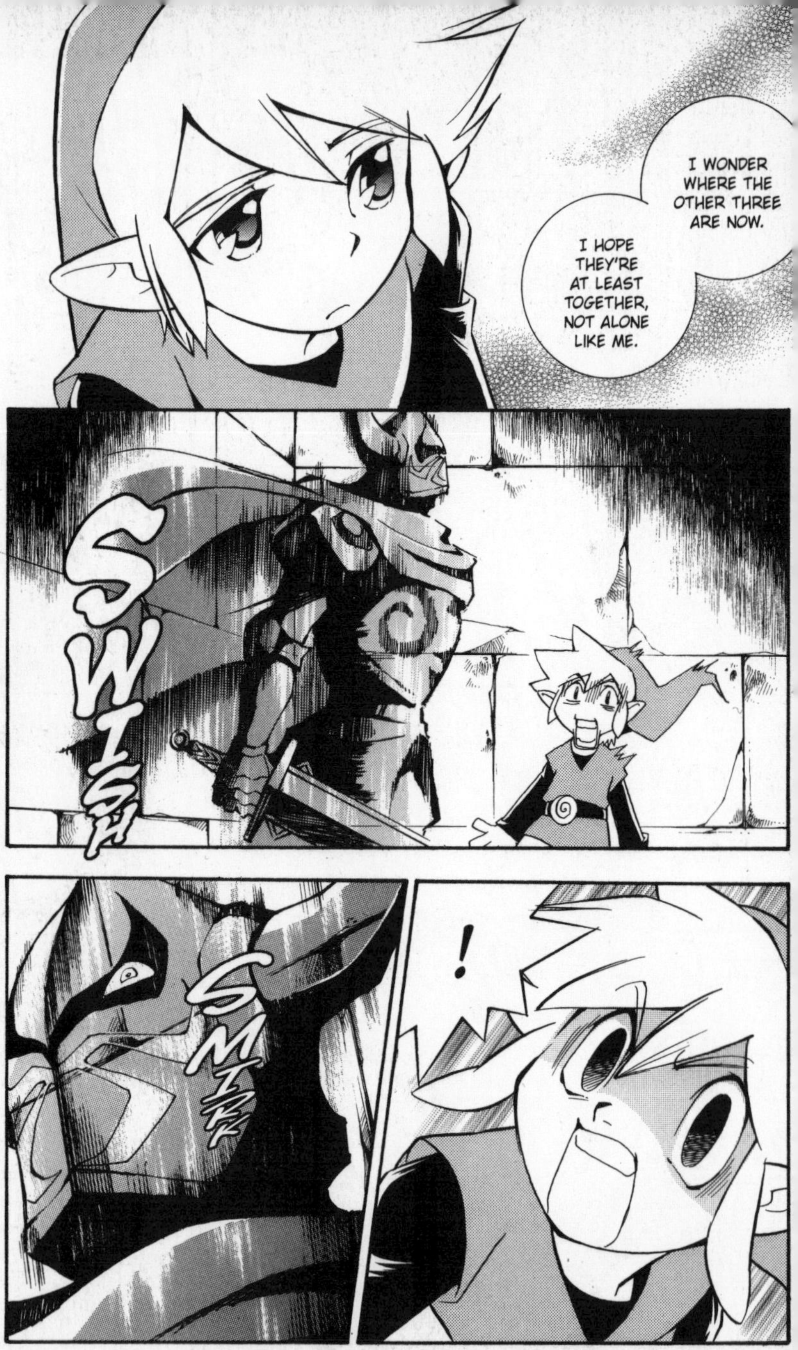
I WONDER WHERE THE OTHER THREE ARE NOW.
I HOPE THEY'RE AT LEAST TOGETHER, NOT ALONE LIKE ME.
SWISH
!
SMIRK

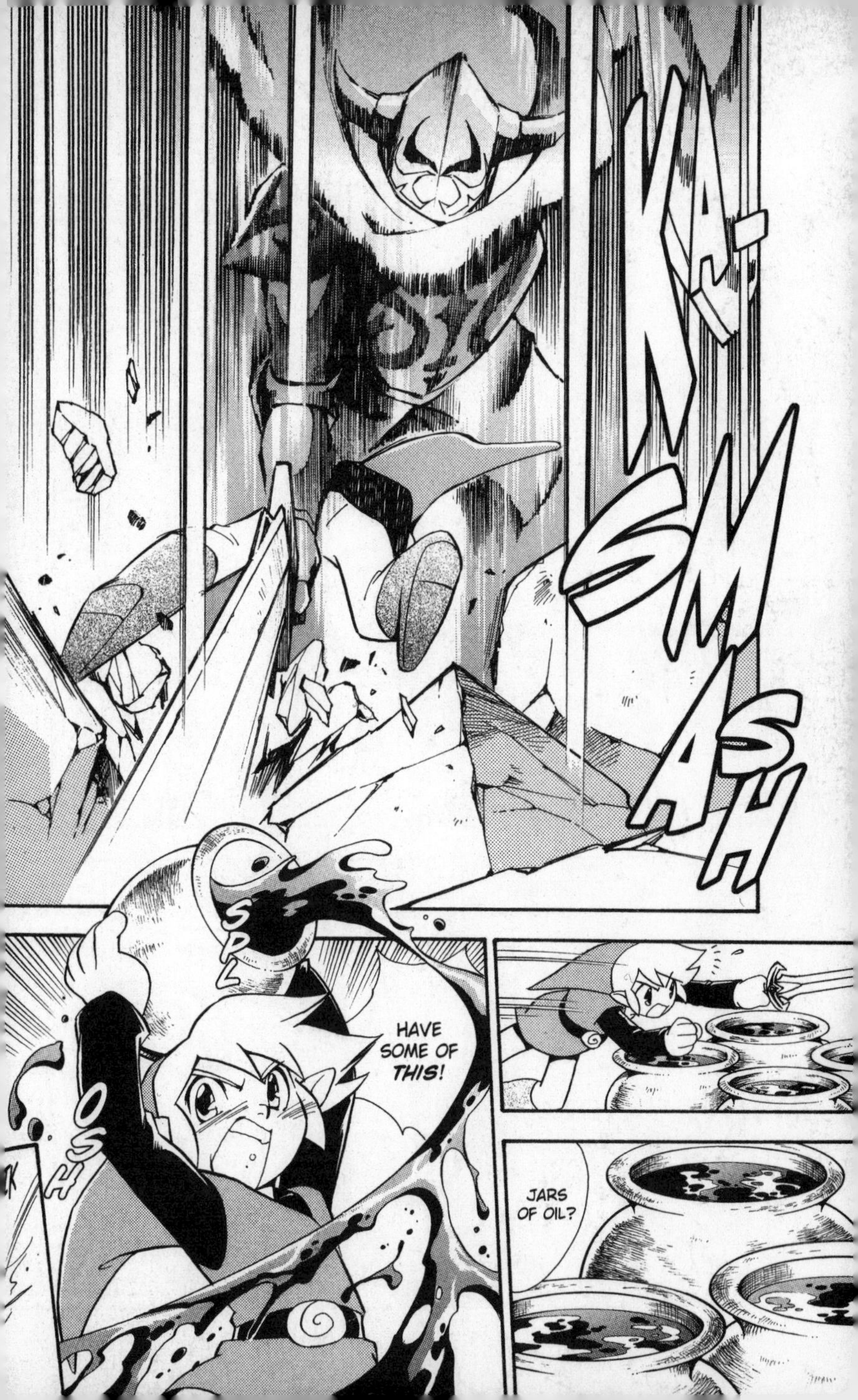
KA-SMASH
JARS OF OIL?
HAVE SOME OF THIS!
SPL
OOSH

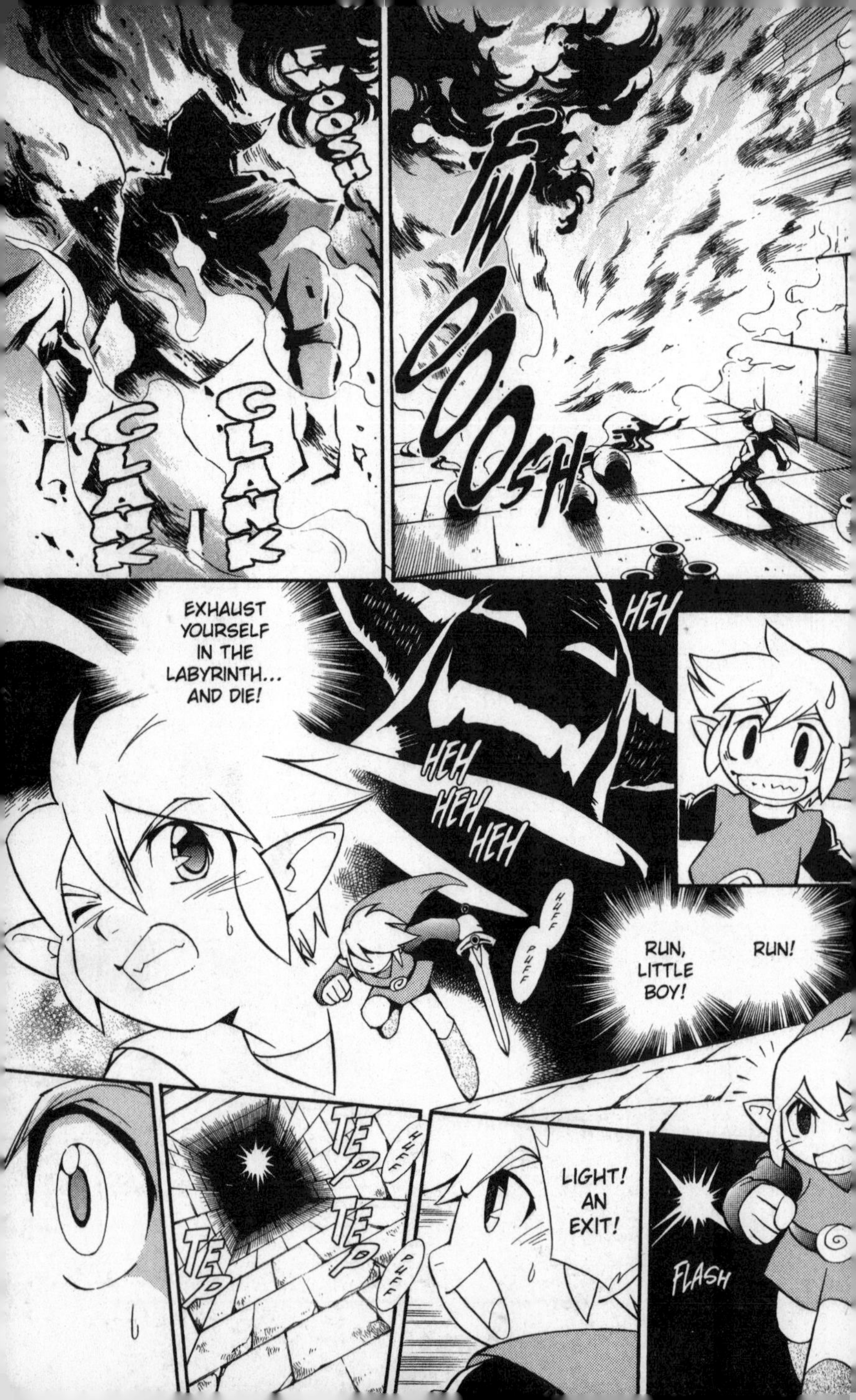
FWOOOSH
FWOOSH
CLANK
CLANK
HEH
EXHAUST YOURSELF IN THE LABYRINTH... AND DIE!
HEH HEH HEH
HUFF PUFF
RUN, LITTLE BOY!
RUN!
FLASH
LIGHT! AN EXIT!
PUFF
HUFF
TEP TEP TEP

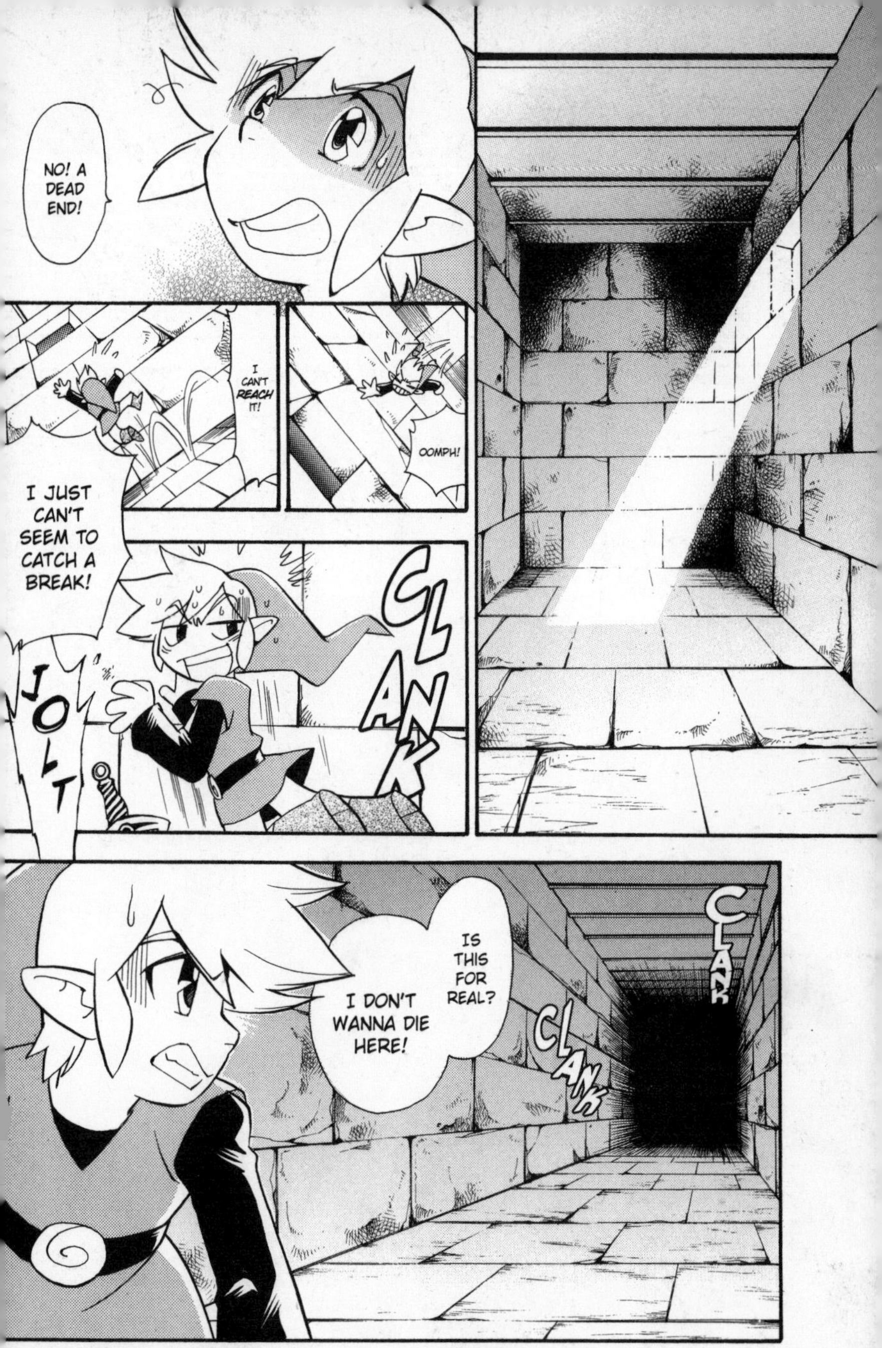
NO! A DEAD END!
OOMPH!
I CAN'T REACH IT!
I JUST CAN'T SEEM TO CATCH A BREAK!
CLANK
JOLT
CLANK
CLANK
IS THIS FOR REAL?
I DON'T WANNA DIE HERE!

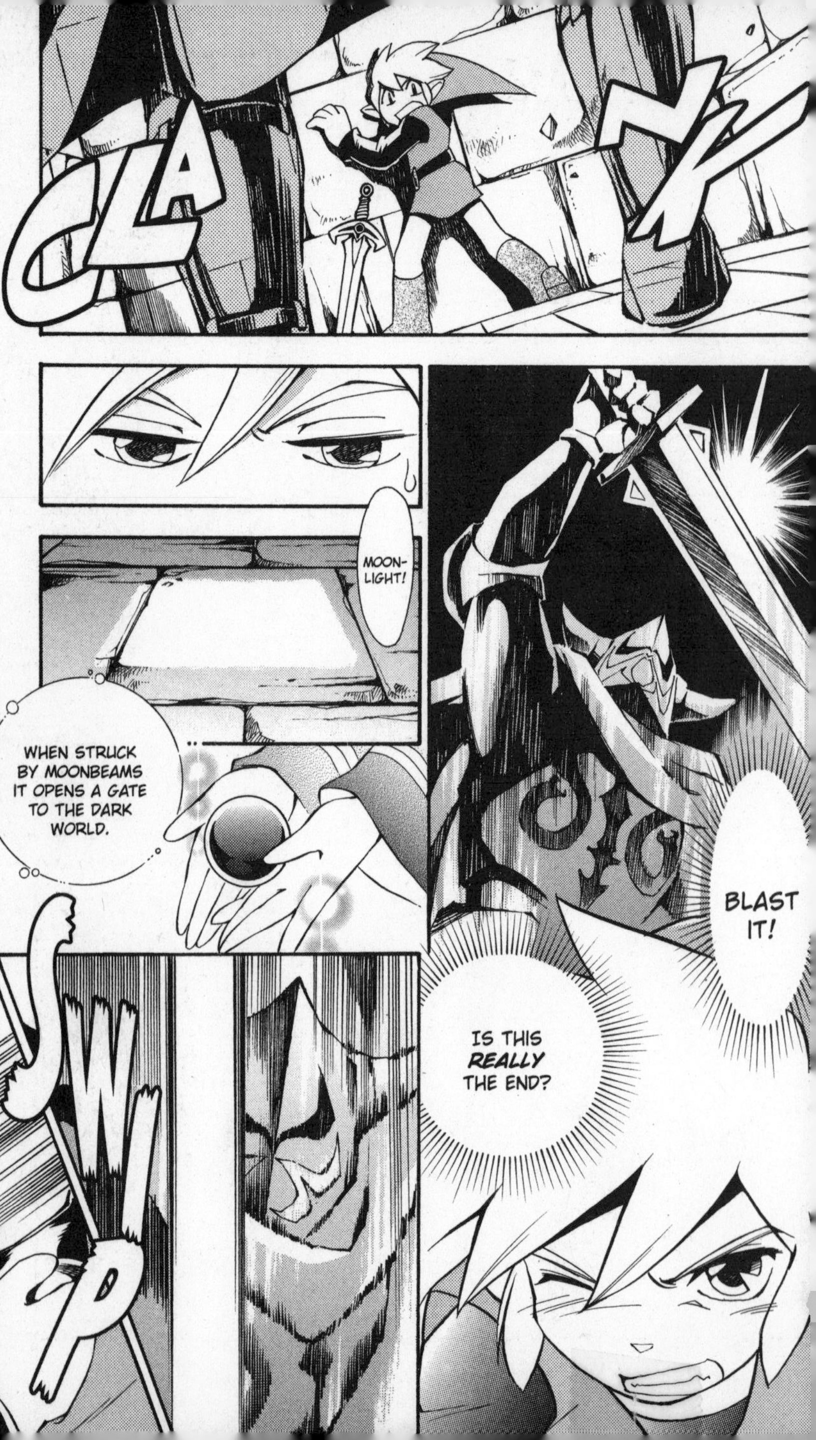
CLANK
MOON-LIGHT!
WHEN STRUCK BY MOONBEAMS IT OPENS A GATE TO THE DARK WORLD.
BLAST IT!
IS THIS *REALLY* THE END?
SWP

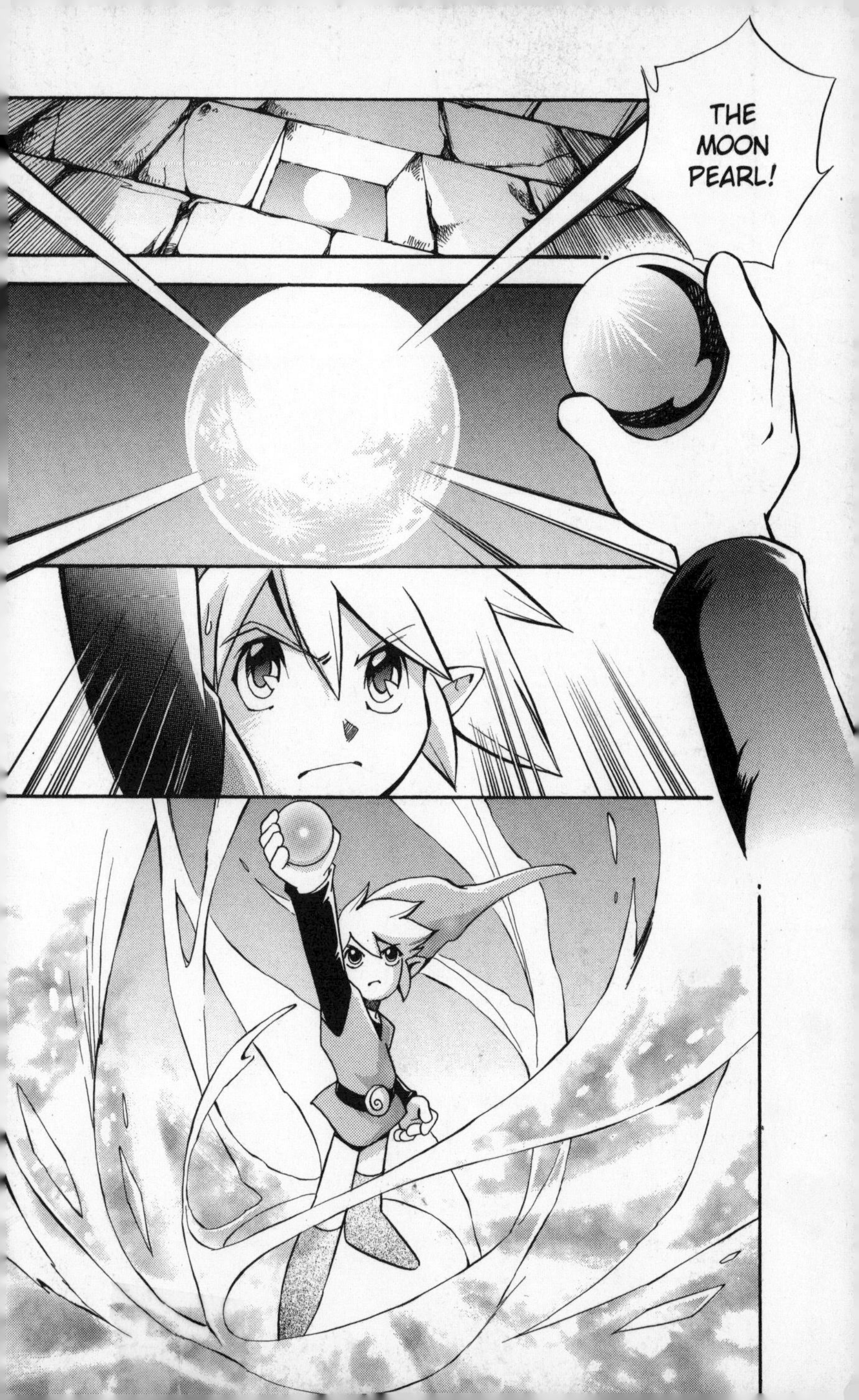
THE MOON PEARL!

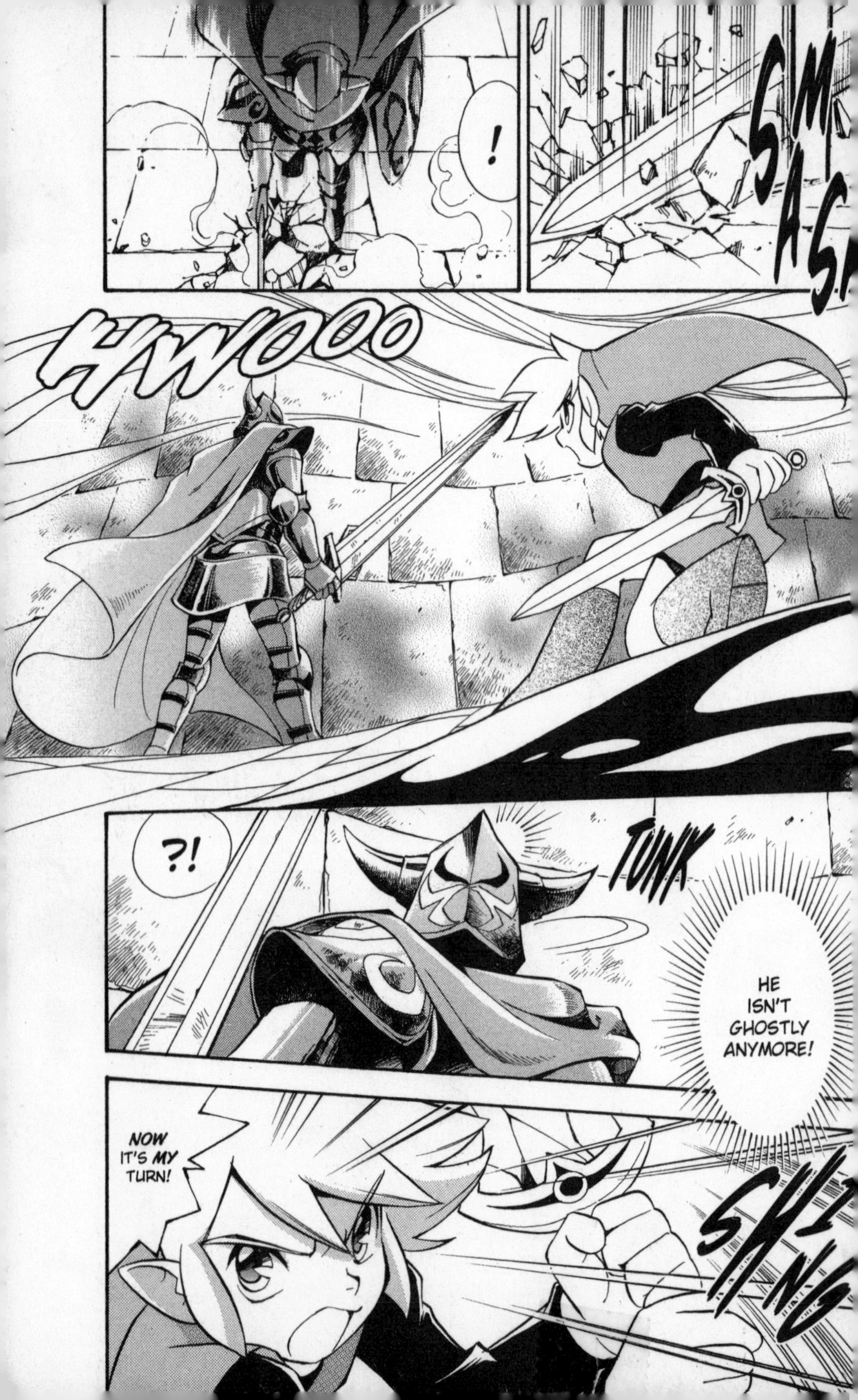
!
HWOOO
?!
TUNK
HE ISN'T GHOSTLY ANYMORE!
NOW IT'S MY TURN!
SHING

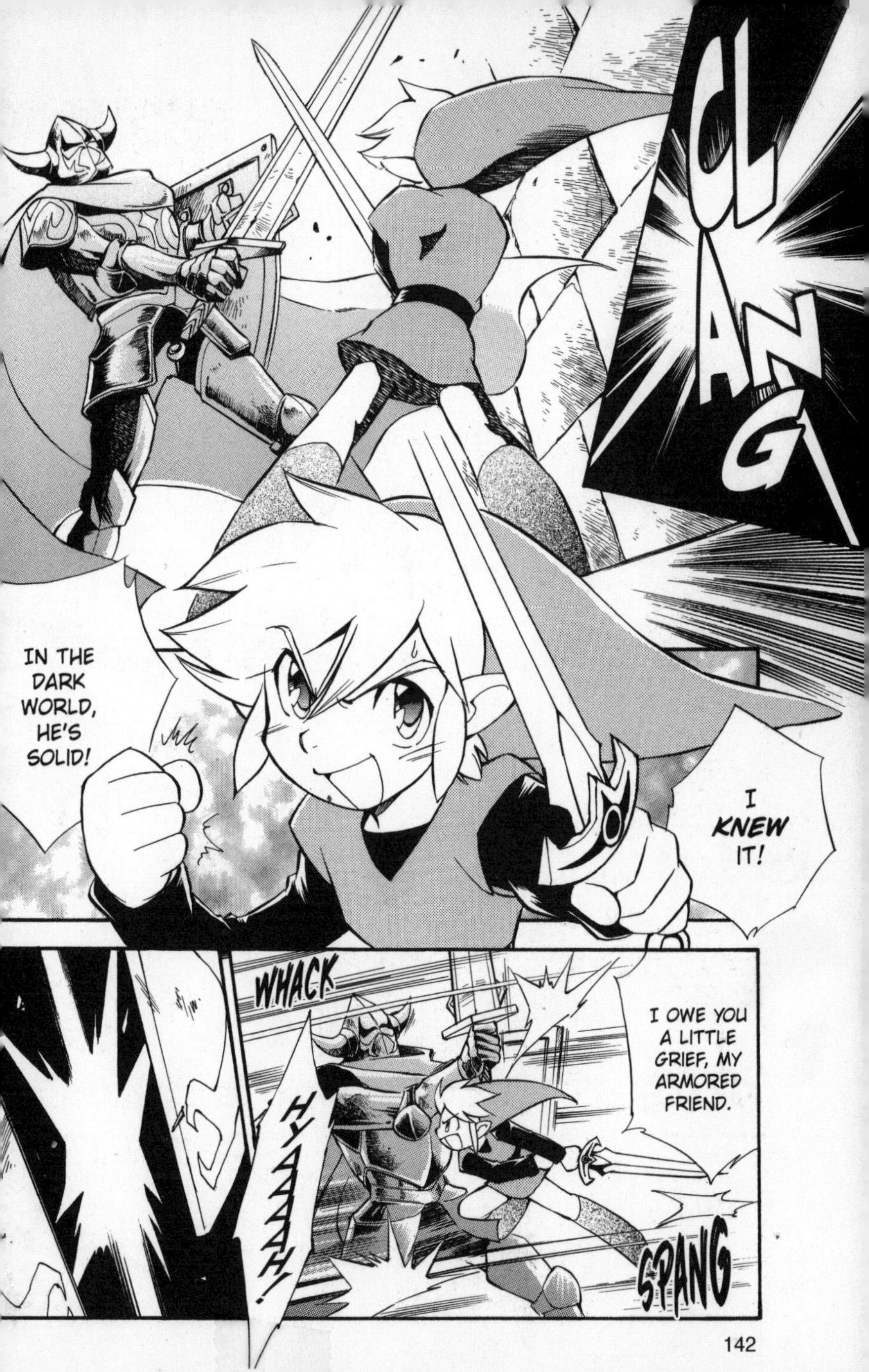
CLANG
I KNEW IT!
IN THE DARK WORLD, HE'S SOLID!
I OWE YOU A LITTLE GRIEF, MY ARMORED FRIEND.
WHACK
SPANG
HYAAAAH!

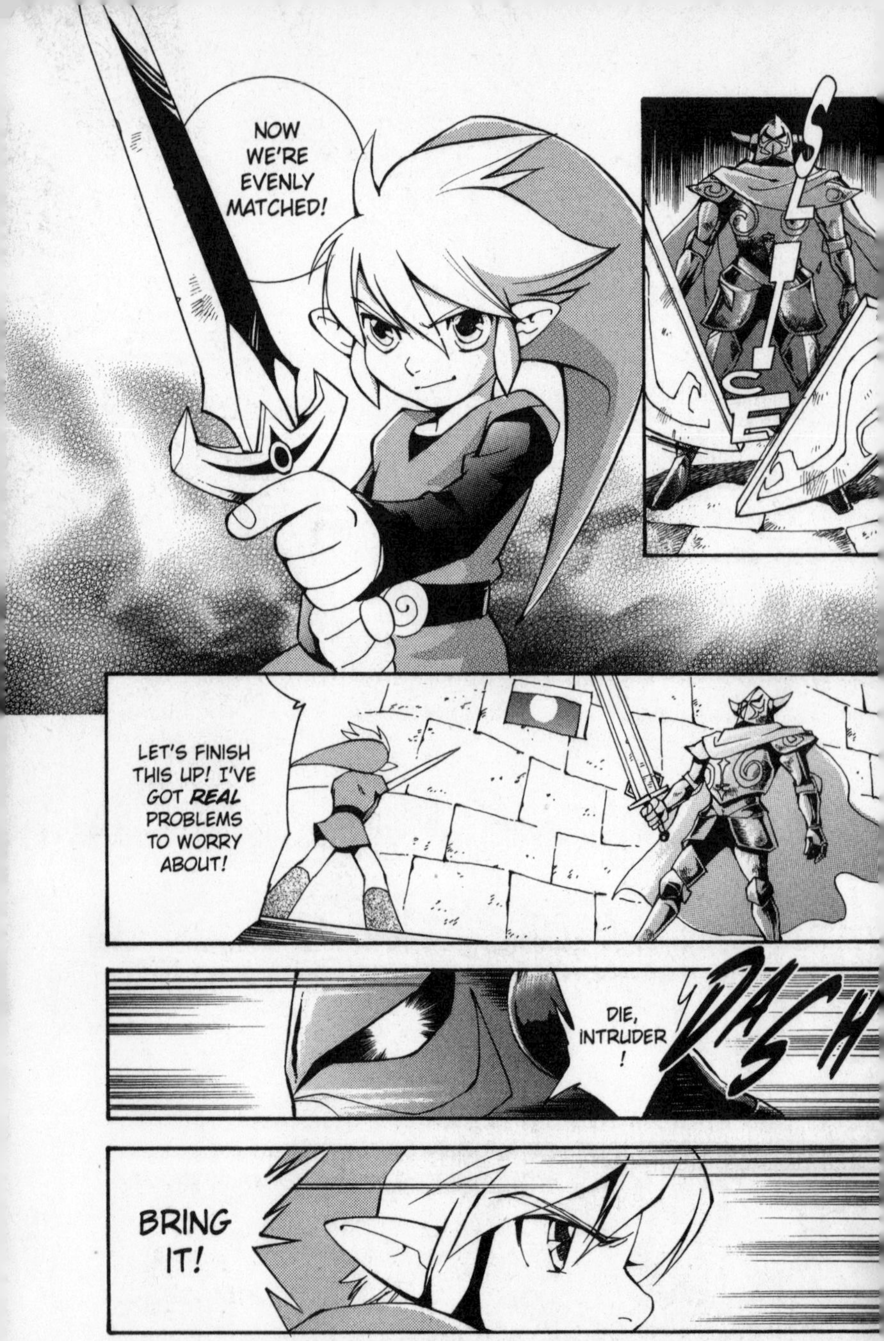
SLICE
NOW WE'RE EVENLY MATCHED!
LET'S FINISH THIS UP! I'VE GOT REAL PROBLEMS TO WORRY ABOUT!
DASH
DIE, INTRUDER!
BRING IT!

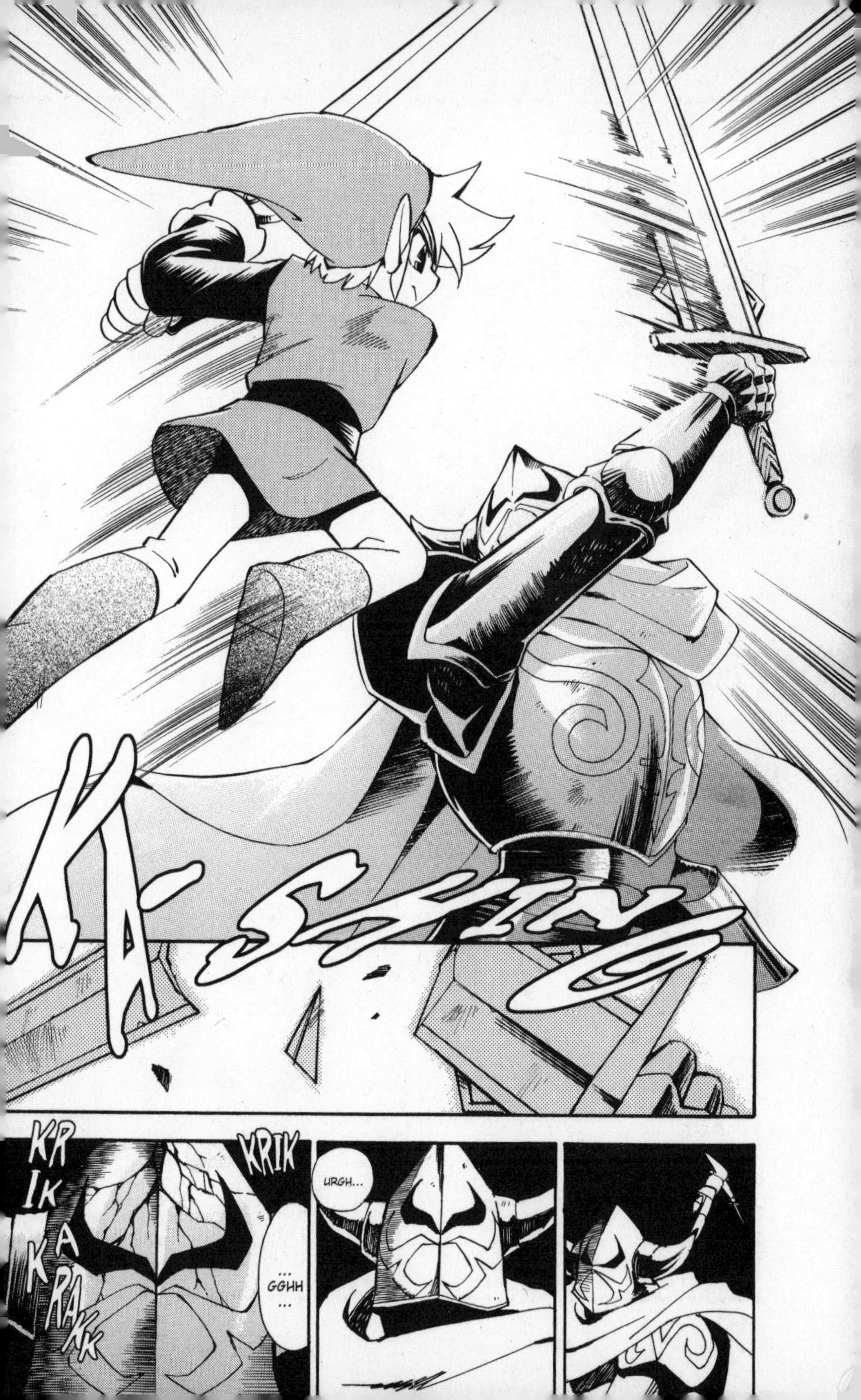
KA-SHING
URGH...
KRIK
KRIKAKRAKK
...GGHH...

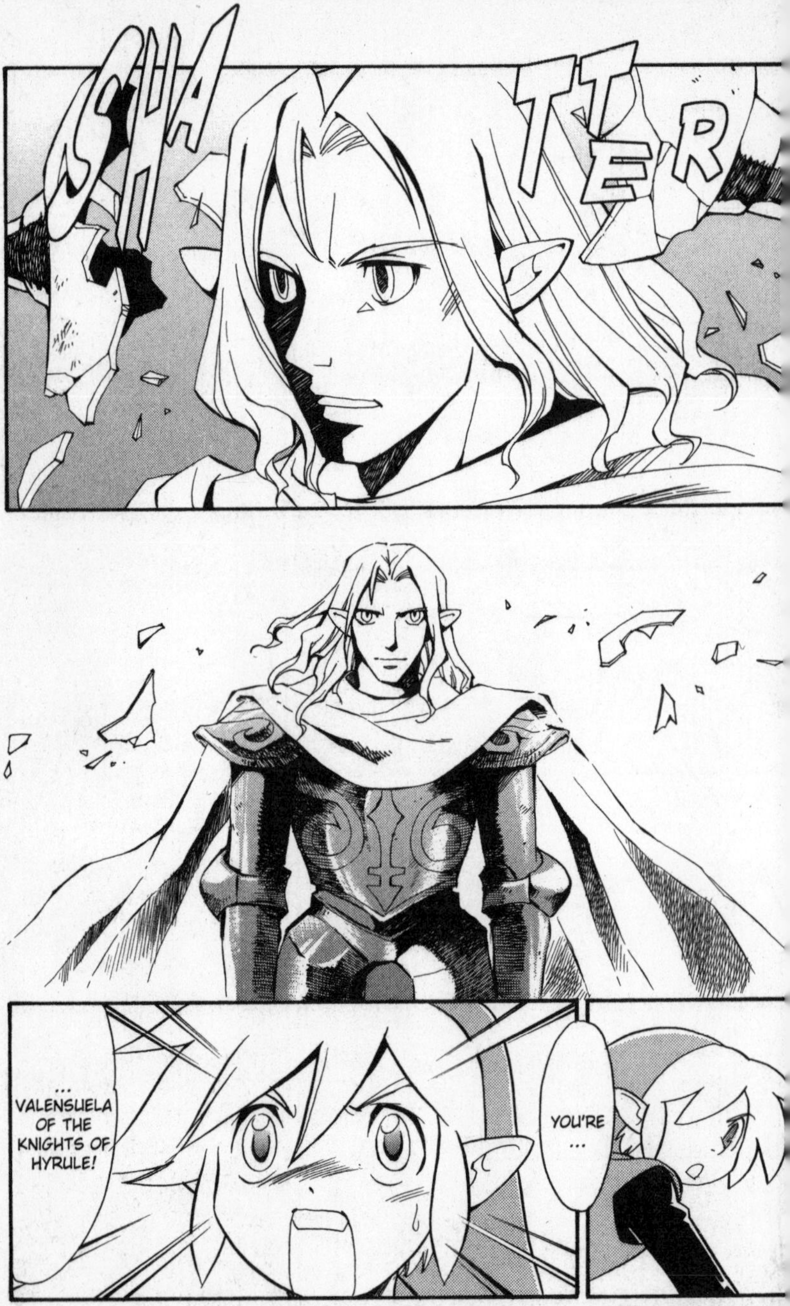
SHATTER
YOU'RE ...
... VALENSUELA OF THE KNIGHTS OF HYRULE!

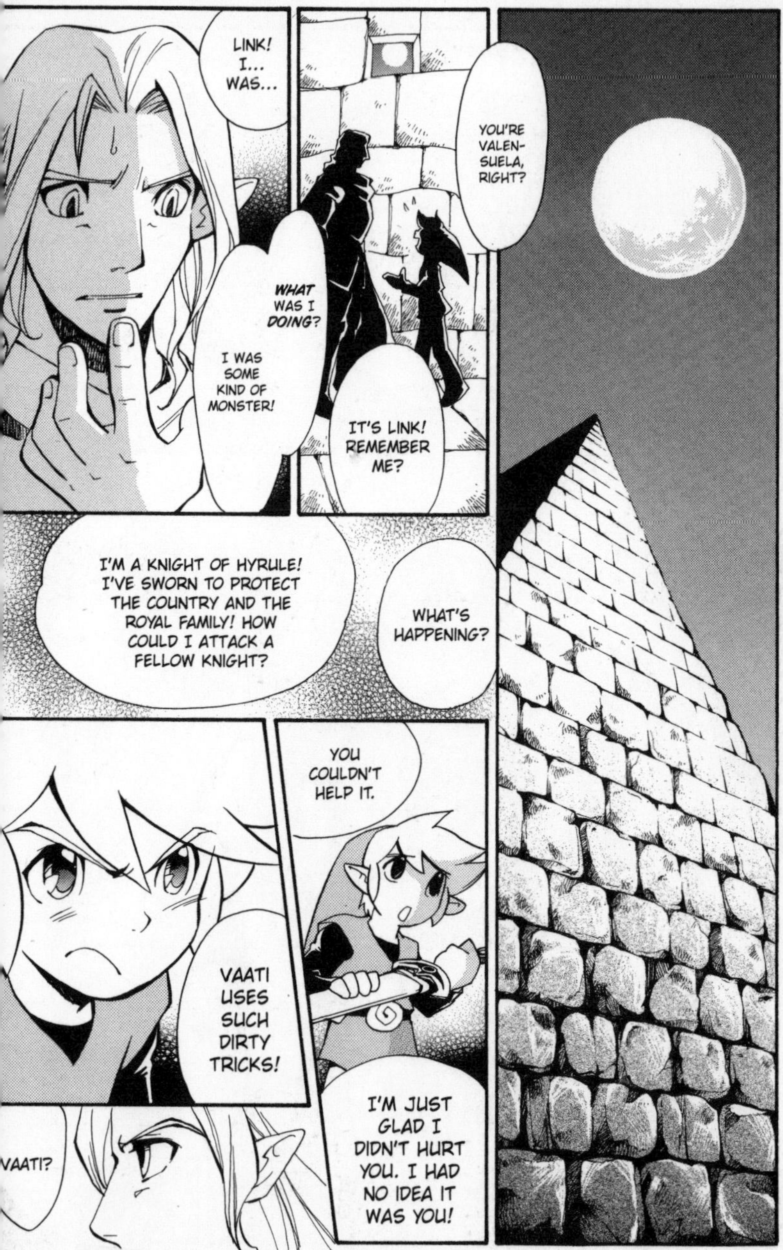
YOU'RE VALEN-SUELA, RIGHT?
IT'S LINK! REMEMBER ME?
LINK! I... WAS...
WHAT WAS I *DOING*?
I WAS SOME KIND OF MONSTER!
WHAT'S HAPPENING?
I'M A KNIGHT OF HYRULE! I'VE SWORN TO PROTECT THE COUNTRY AND THE ROYAL FAMILY! HOW COULD I ATTACK A FELLOW KNIGHT?
YOU COULDN'T HELP IT.
I'M JUST GLAD I DIDN'T HURT YOU. I HAD NO IDEA IT WAS YOU!
VAATI USES SUCH DIRTY TRICKS!
VAATI?

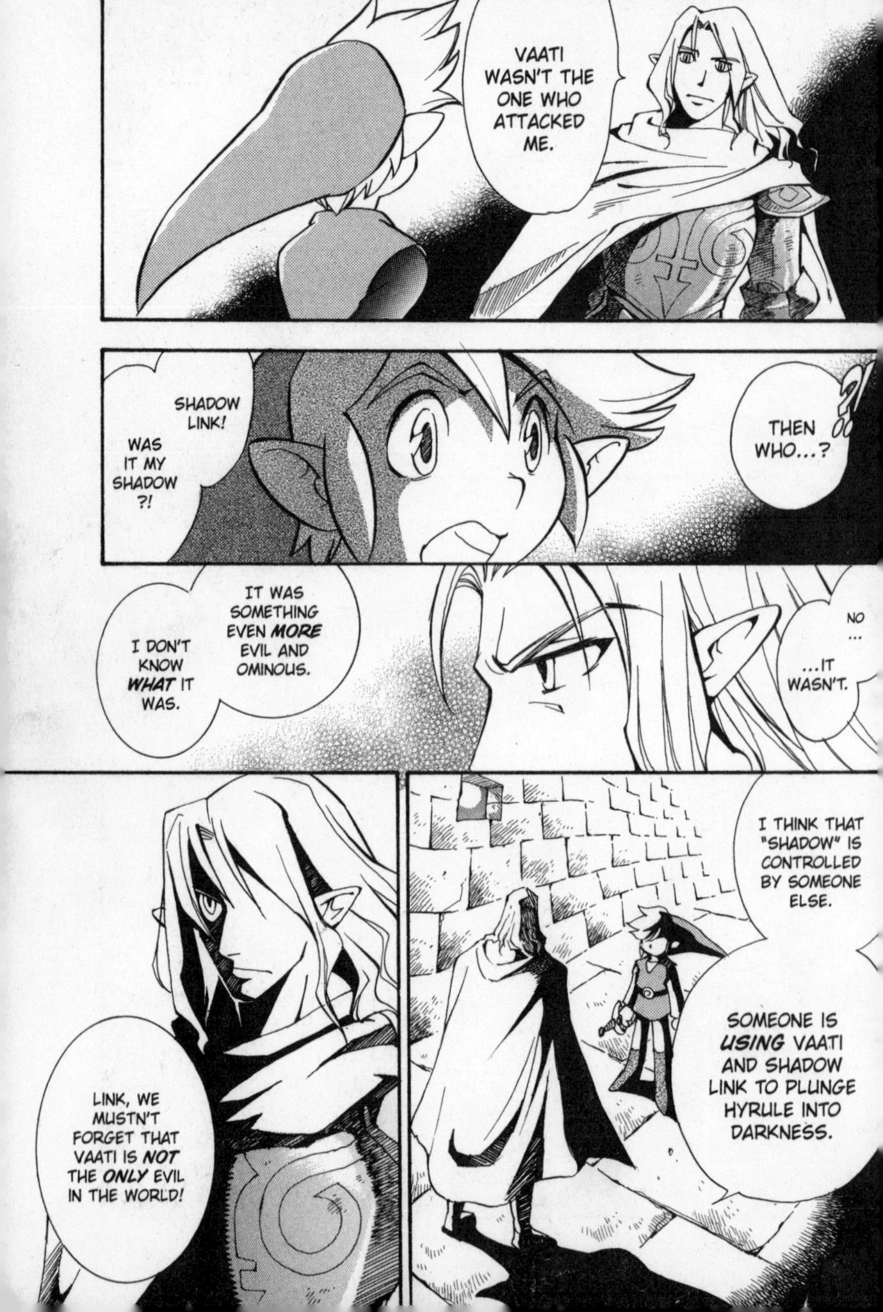

VAATI WASN'T THE ONE WHO ATTACKED ME.
THEN WHO...?
SHADOW LINK!
WAS IT MY SHADOW ?!
NO ...
...IT WASN'T.
IT WAS SOMETHING EVEN MORE EVIL AND OMINOUS.
I DON'T KNOW WHAT IT WAS.
I THINK THAT "SHADOW" IS CONTROLLED BY SOMEONE ELSE.
SOMEONE IS USING VAATI AND SHADOW LINK TO PLUNGE HYRULE INTO DARKNESS.
LINK, WE MUSTN'T FORGET THAT VAATI IS NOT THE ONLY EVIL IN THE WORLD!

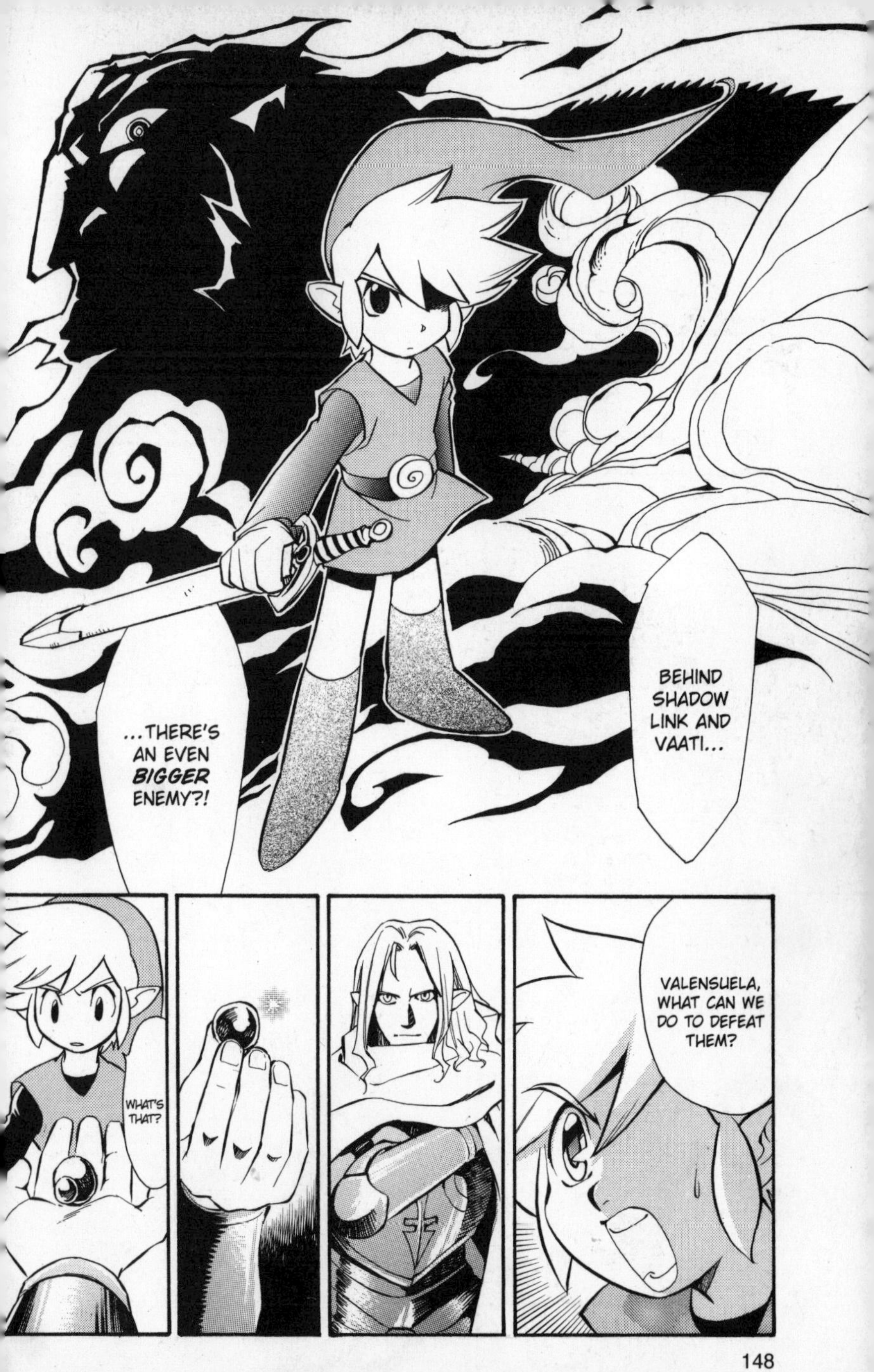
BEHIND SHADOW LINK AND VAATI...
...THERE'S AN EVEN *BIGGER* ENEMY?!
VALENSUELA, WHAT CAN WE DO TO DEFEAT THEM?
WHAT'S THAT?

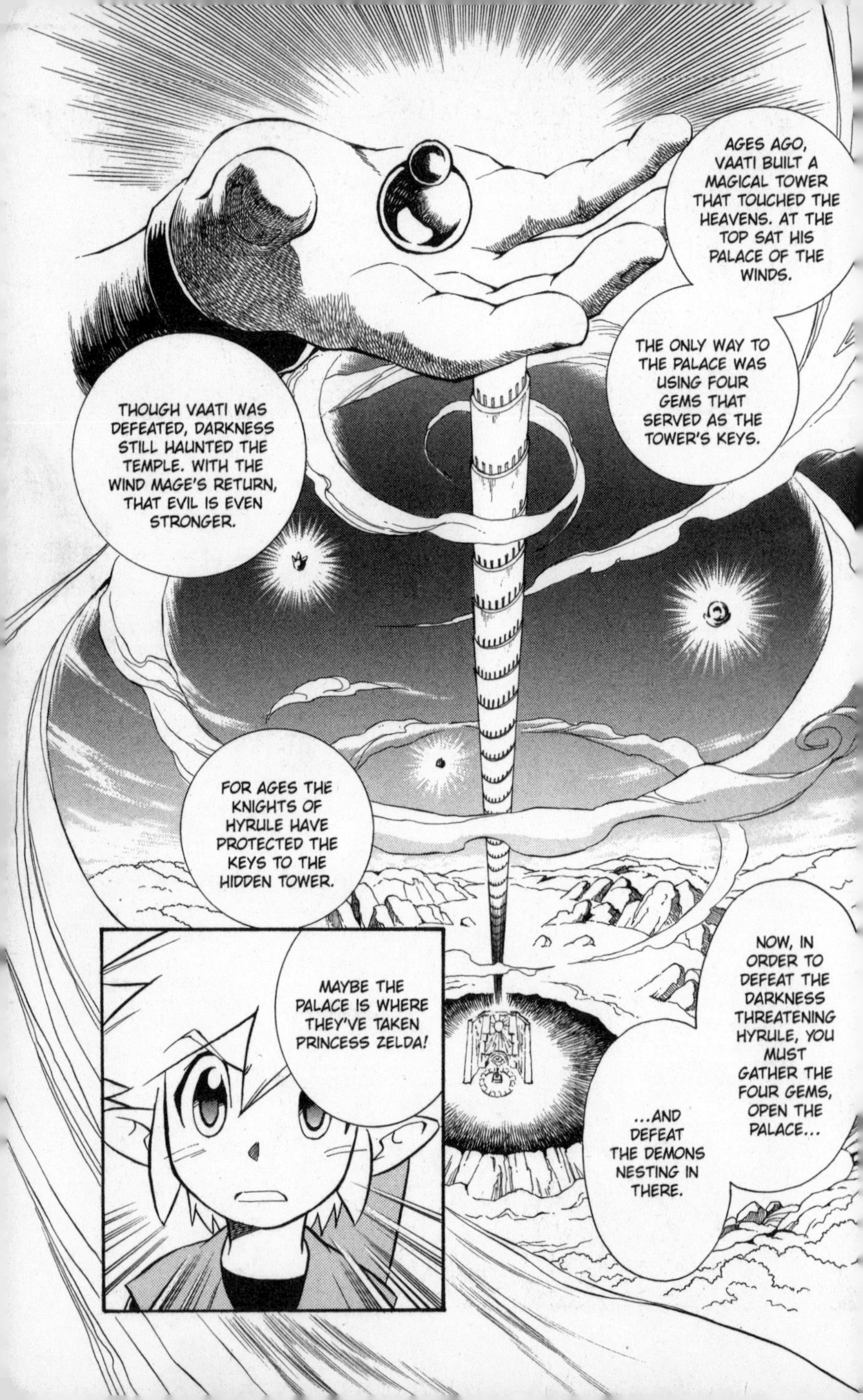
AGES AGO, VAATI BUILT A MAGICAL TOWER THAT TOUCHED THE HEAVENS. AT THE TOP SAT HIS PALACE OF THE WINDS.
THE ONLY WAY TO THE PALACE WAS USING FOUR GEMS THAT SERVED AS THE TOWER'S KEYS.
THOUGH VAATI WAS DEFEATED, DARKNESS STILL HAUNTED THE TEMPLE. WITH THE WIND MAGE'S RETURN, THAT EVIL IS EVEN STRONGER.
FOR AGES THE KNIGHTS OF HYRULE HAVE PROTECTED THE KEYS TO THE HIDDEN TOWER.
NOW, IN ORDER TO DEFEAT THE DARKNESS THREATENING HYRULE, YOU MUST GATHER THE FOUR GEMS, OPEN THE PALACE...
...AND DEFEAT THE DEMONS NESTING IN THERE.
MAYBE THE PALACE IS WHERE THEY'VE TAKEN PRINCESS ZELDA!

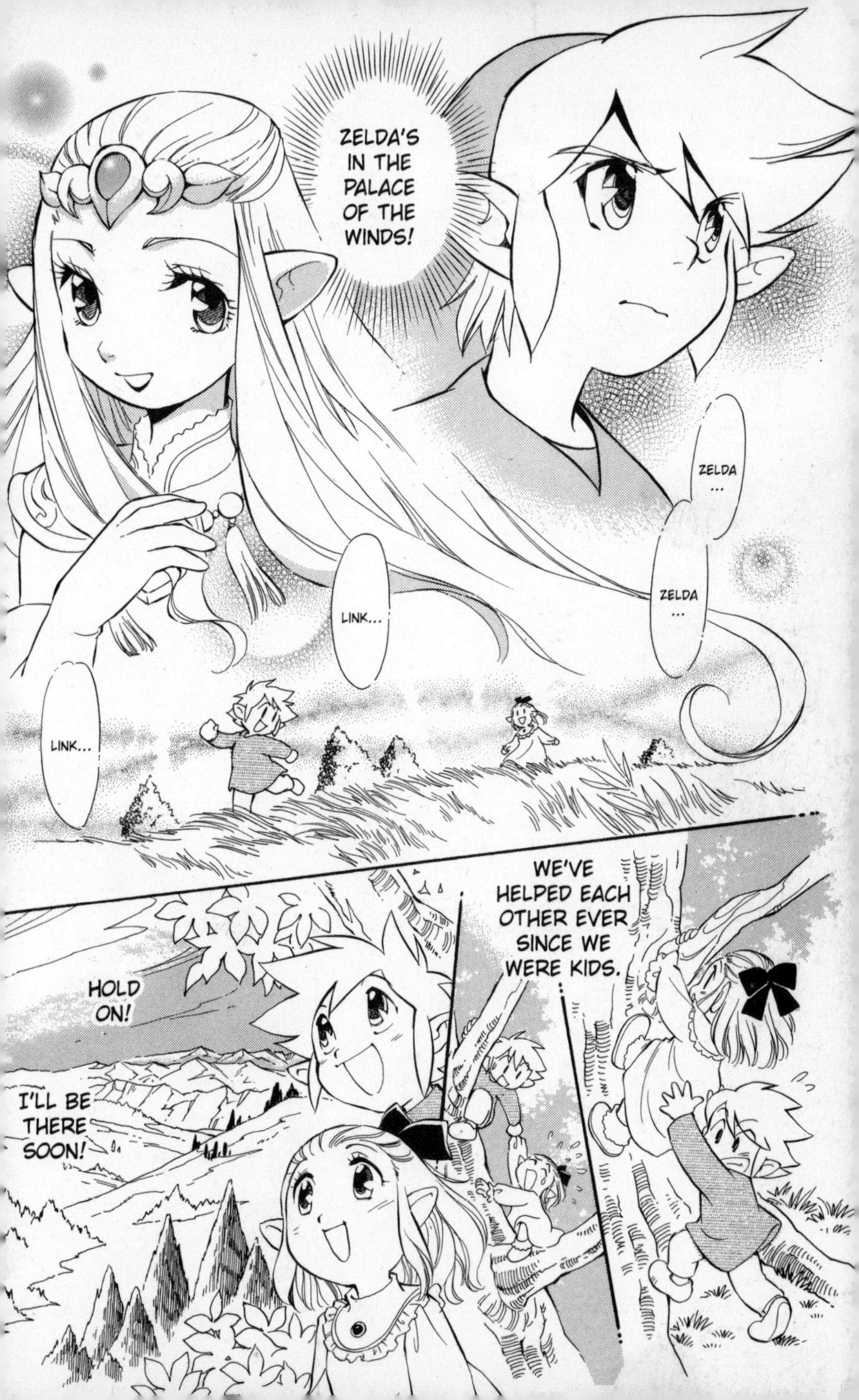
ZELDA'S IN THE PALACE OF THE WINDS!
ZELDA...
ZELDA...
LINK...
LINK...
WE'VE HELPED EACH OTHER EVER SINCE WE WERE KIDS.
HOLD ON!
I'LL BE THERE SOON!

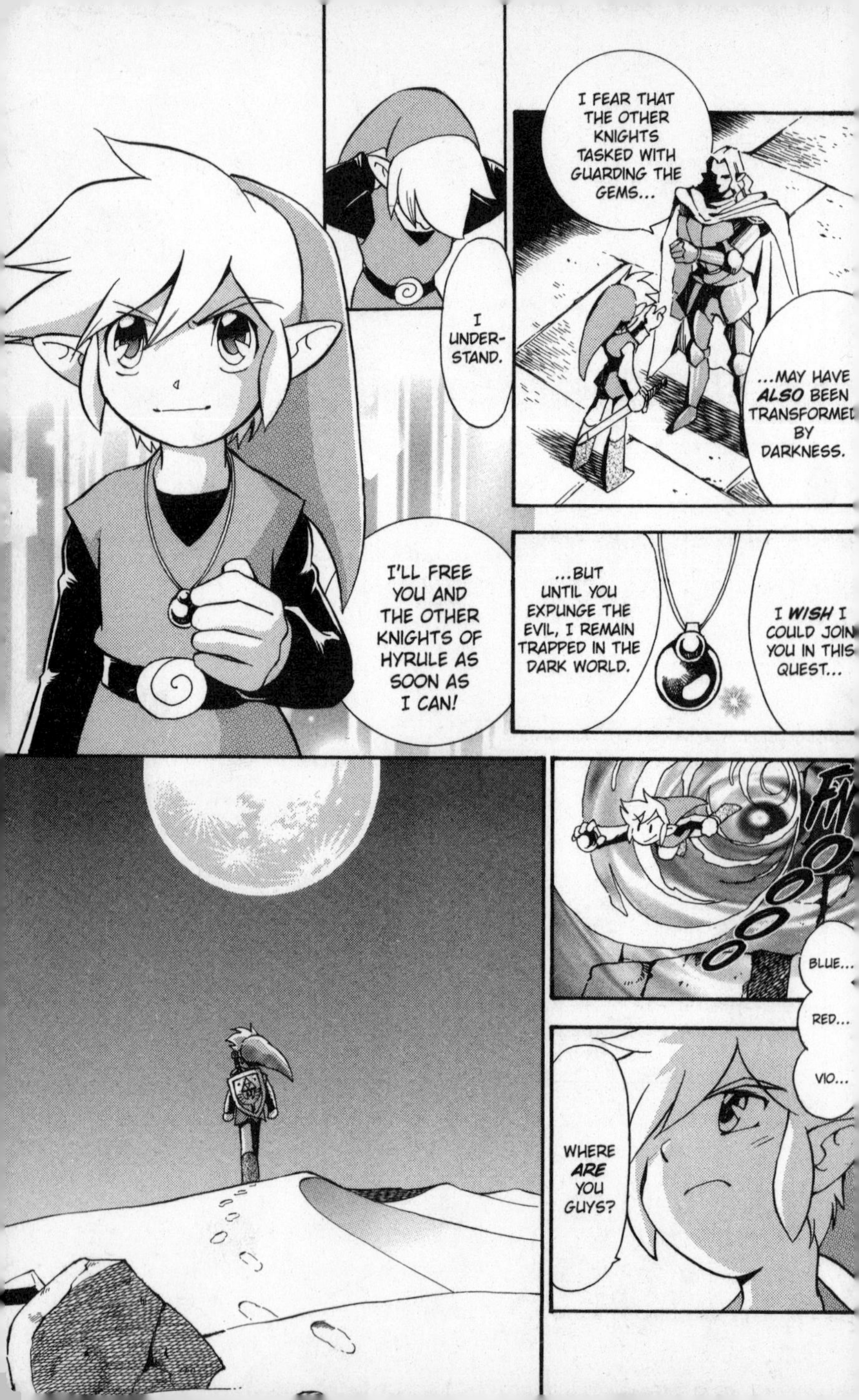

I FEAR THAT THE OTHER KNIGHTS TASKED WITH GUARDING THE GEMS...
...MAY HAVE *ALSO* BEEN TRANSFORMED BY DARKNESS.
I UNDER-STAND.
I *WISH* I COULD JOIN YOU IN THIS QUEST...
...BUT UNTIL YOU EXPUNGE THE EVIL, I REMAIN TRAPPED IN THE DARK WORLD.
I'LL FREE YOU AND THE OTHER KNIGHTS OF HYRULE AS SOON AS I CAN!
FWOOOOOOO
BLUE...
RED...
VIO...
WHERE *ARE* YOU GUYS?

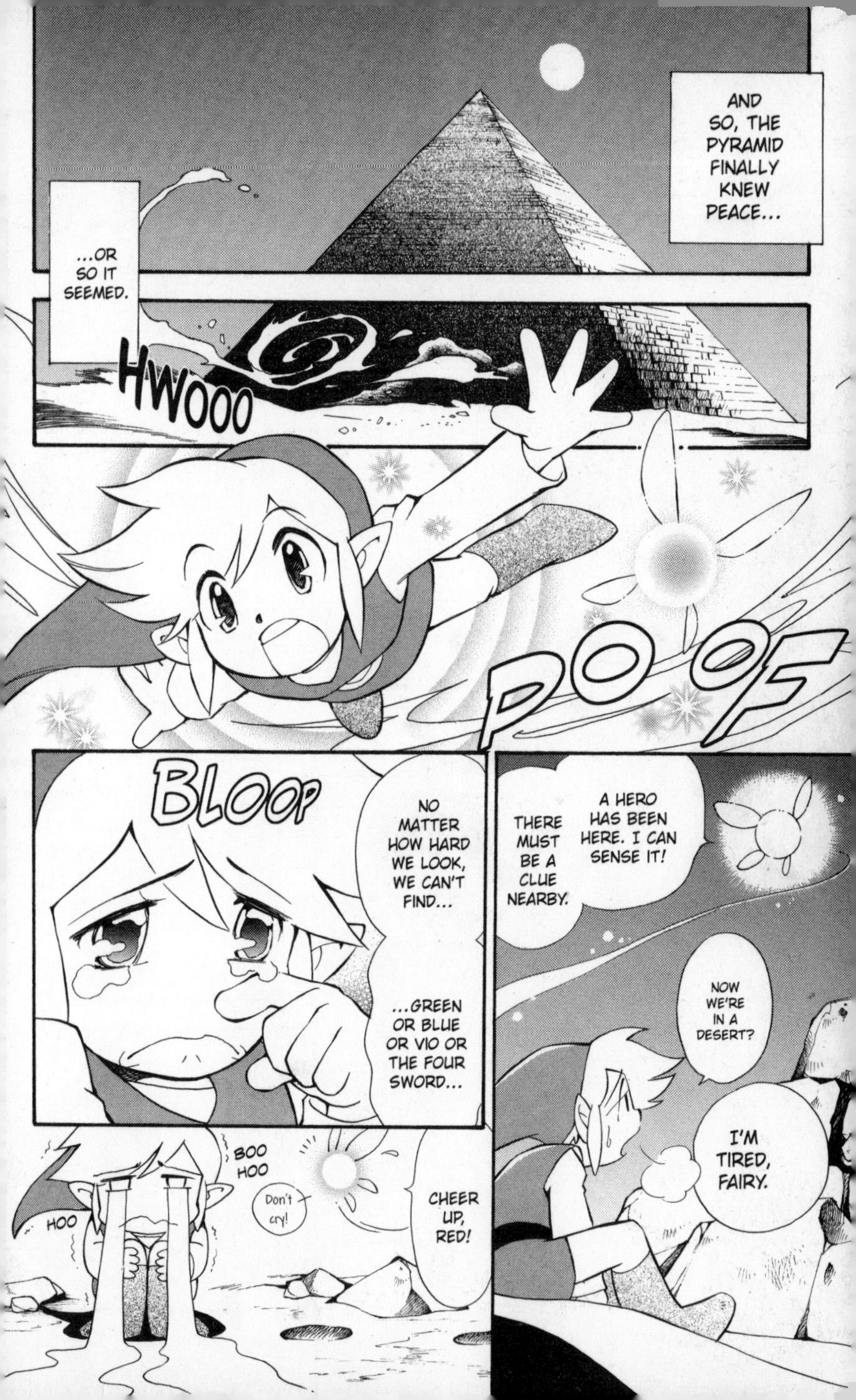
AND SO, THE PYRAMID FINALLY KNEW PEACE...
...OR SO IT SEEMED.
HWOOO
POOF
A HERO HAS BEEN HERE. I CAN SENSE IT!
THERE MUST BE A CLUE NEARBY.
NOW WE'RE IN A DESERT?
I'M TIRED, FAIRY.
BLOOP
NO MATTER HOW HARD WE LOOK, WE CAN'T FIND...
...GREEN OR BLUE OR VIO OR THE FOUR SWORD...
CHEER UP, RED!
Don't cry!
BOO HOO
HOO

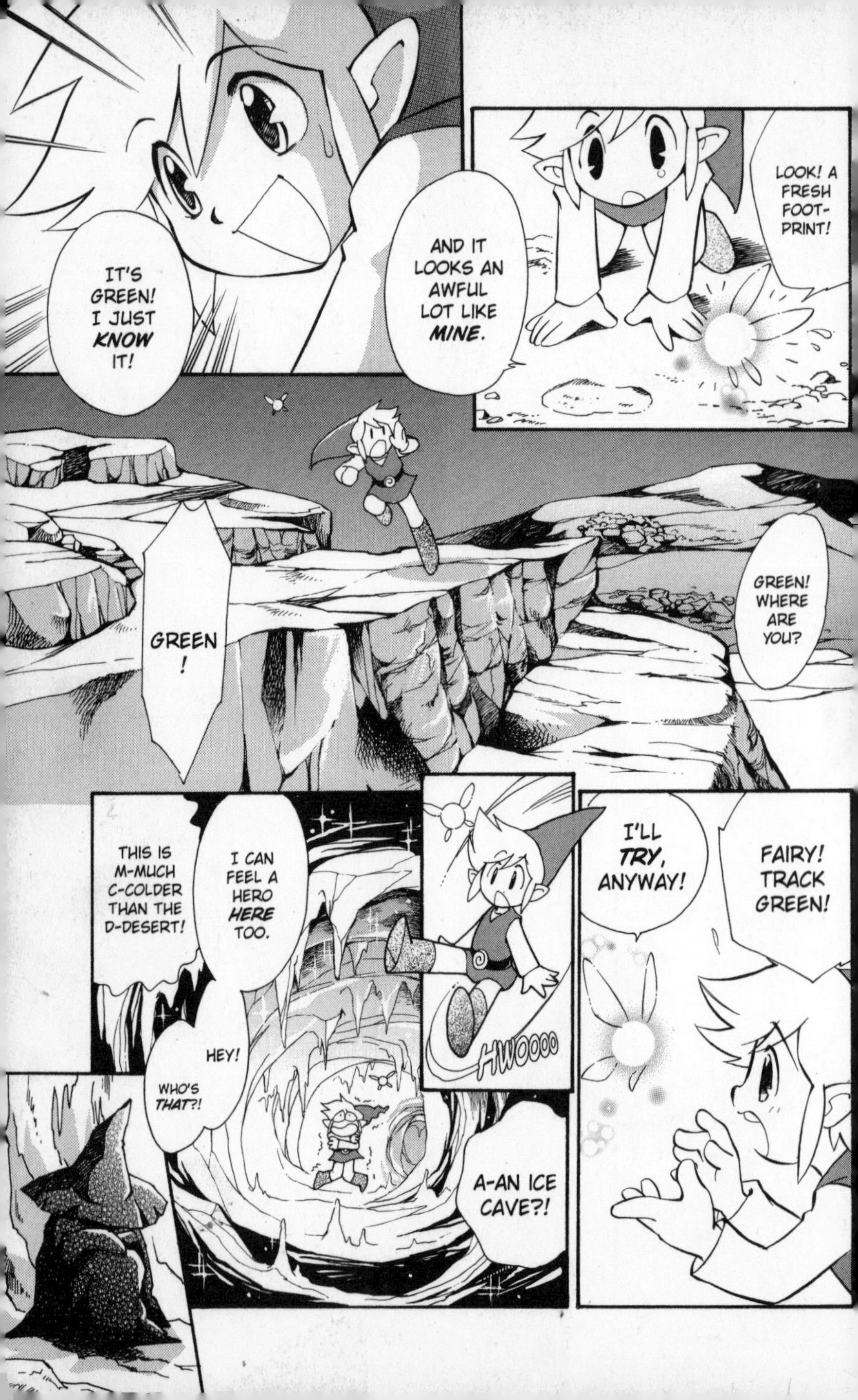
LOOK! A FRESH FOOT-PRINT!
AND IT LOOKS AN AWFUL LOT LIKE **MINE**.
IT'S GREEN! I JUST **KNOW** IT!
GREEN! WHERE ARE YOU?
GREEN!
FAIRY! TRACK GREEN!
I'LL **TRY**, ANYWAY!
HWOOOO
A-AN ICE CAVE?!
I CAN FEEL A HERO **HERE** TOO.
THIS IS M-MUCH C-COLDER THAN THE D-DESERT!
HEY!
WHO'S **THAT**?!

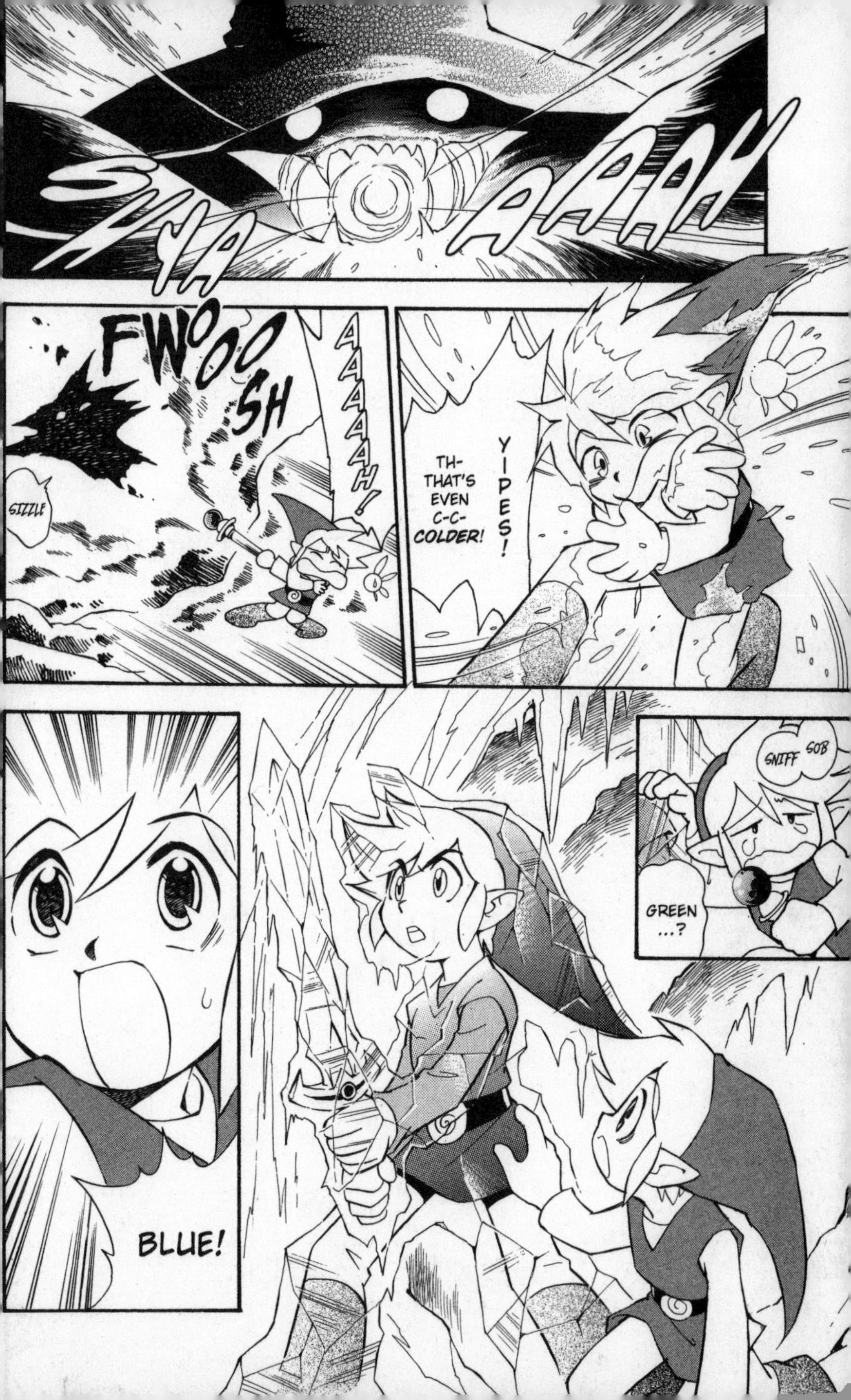
SHHAAAAAH
YIPES!
TH-THAT'S EVEN C-C-COLDER!
AAAAAAH!
FWOOOSH
SIZZLE
SNIFF
SOB
GREEN ...?
BLUE!

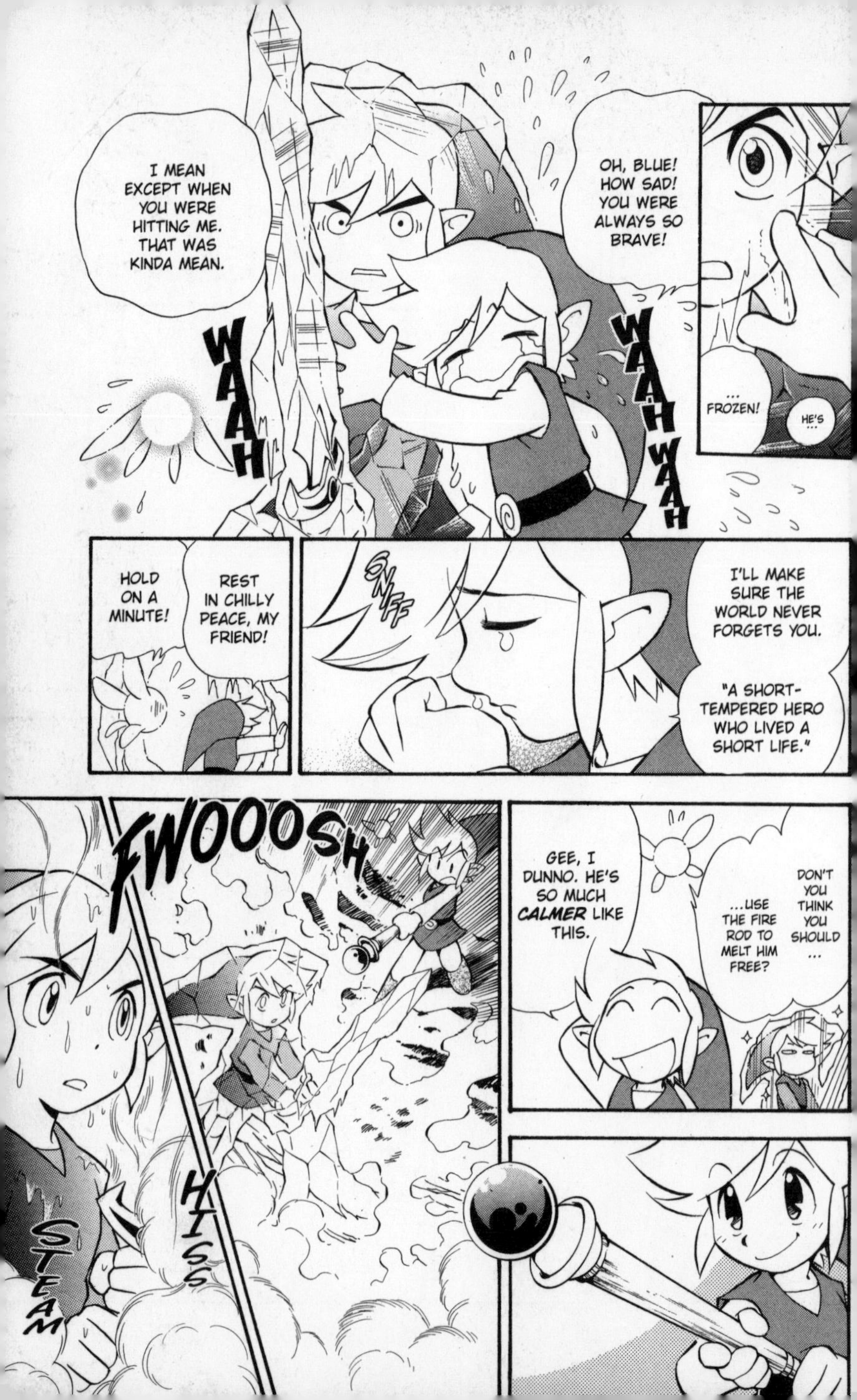
HE'S ...
... FROZEN!
OH, BLUE! HOW SAD! YOU WERE ALWAYS SO BRAVE!
WAAH WAAH
I MEAN EXCEPT WHEN YOU WERE HITTING ME. THAT WAS KINDA MEAN.
WAAH
SNIFF
I'LL MAKE SURE THE WORLD NEVER FORGETS YOU.
"A SHORT-TEMPERED HERO WHO LIVED A SHORT LIFE."
REST IN CHILLY PEACE, MY FRIEND!
HOLD ON A MINUTE!
DON'T YOU THINK YOU SHOULD ...
...USE THE FIRE ROD TO MELT HIM FREE?
GEE, I DUNNO. HE'S SO MUCH CALMER LIKE THIS.
FWOOOSH
HISS
STEAM

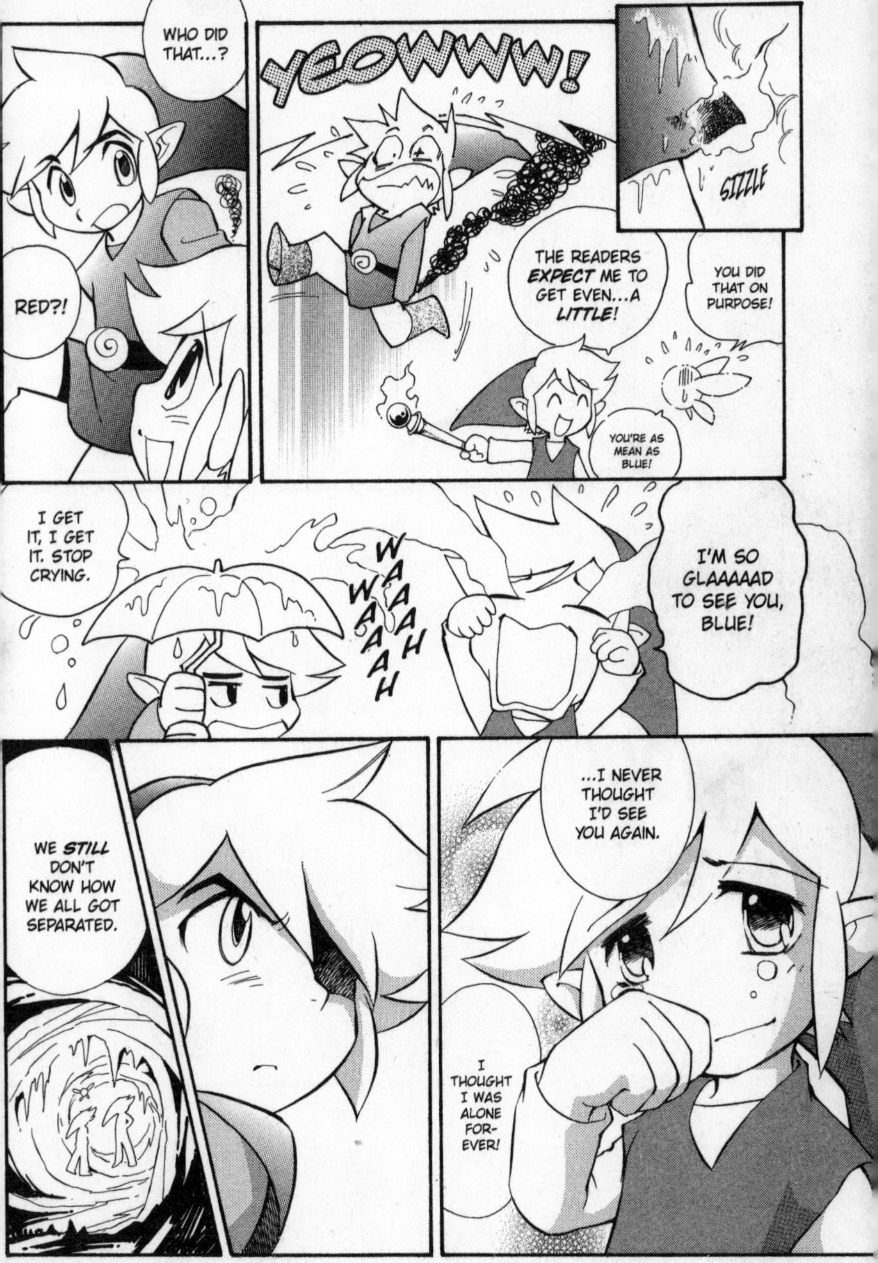
SIZZLE
YCOWWWW!
YOU DID THAT ON PURPOSE!
THE READERS *EXPECT* ME TO GET EVEN...A *LITTLE*!
YOU'RE AS MEAN AS BLUE!
WHO DID THAT...?
RED?!
I'M SO GLAAAAAD TO SEE YOU, BLUE!
WAAAAH
WAAAAH
I GET IT, I GET IT. STOP CRYING.
...I NEVER THOUGHT I'D SEE YOU AGAIN.
I THOUGHT I WAS ALONE FOR-EVER!
WE *STILL* DON'T KNOW HOW WE ALL GOT SEPARATED.

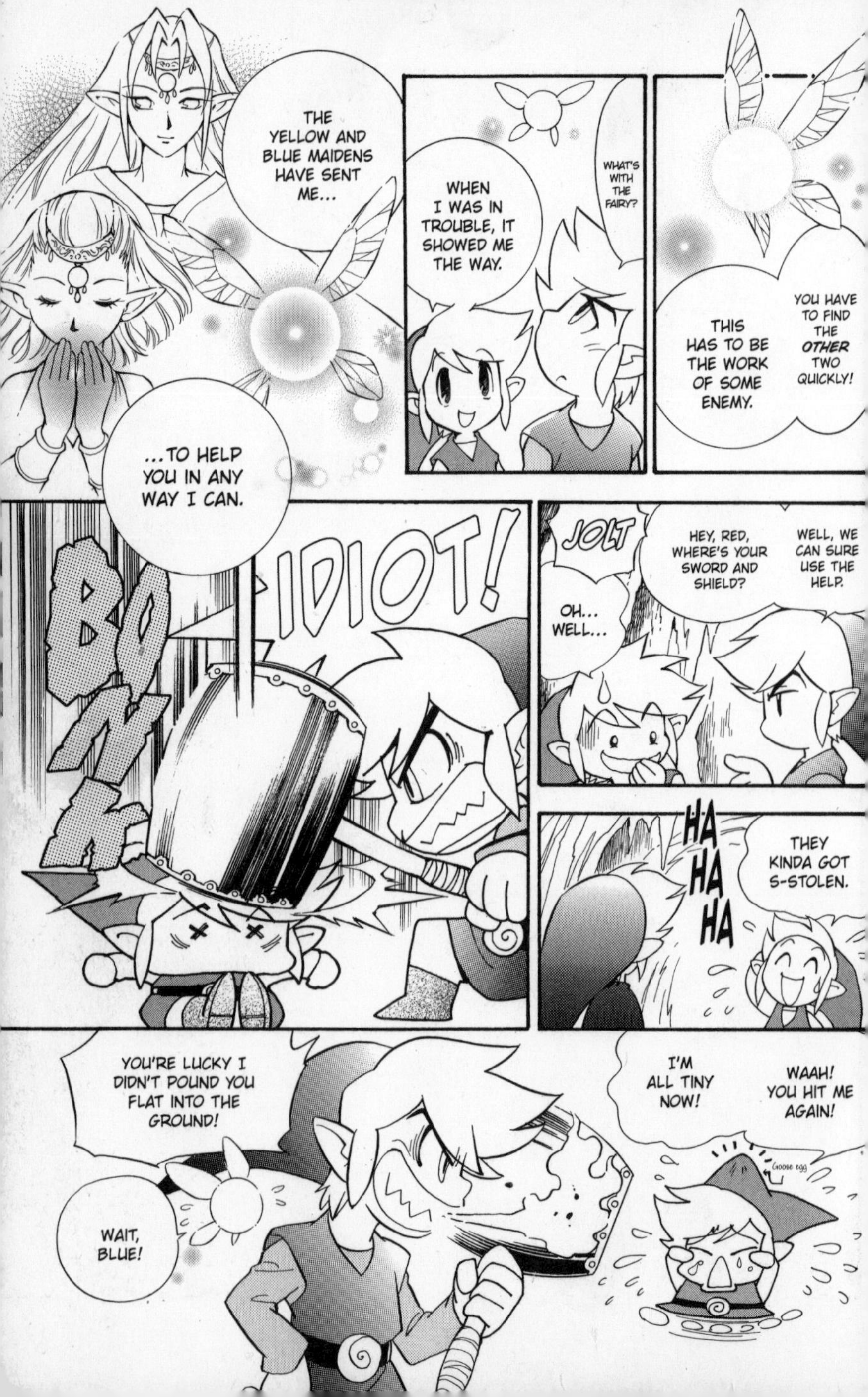

YOU HAVE TO FIND THE *OTHER* TWO QUICKLY!
THIS HAS TO BE THE WORK OF SOME ENEMY.
WHAT'S WITH THE FAIRY?
WHEN I WAS IN TROUBLE, IT SHOWED ME THE WAY.
THE YELLOW AND BLUE MAIDENS HAVE SENT ME...
...TO HELP YOU IN ANY WAY I CAN.
WELL, WE CAN SURE USE THE HELP.
HEY, RED, WHERE'S YOUR SWORD AND SHIELD?
JOLT
OH... WELL...
THEY KINDA GOT S-STOLEN.
HA HA HA HA
IDIOT!
BONK
WAAH! YOU HIT ME AGAIN!
Goose egg
I'M ALL TINY NOW!
YOU'RE LUCKY I DIDN'T POUND YOU FLAT INTO THE GROUND!
WAIT, BLUE!

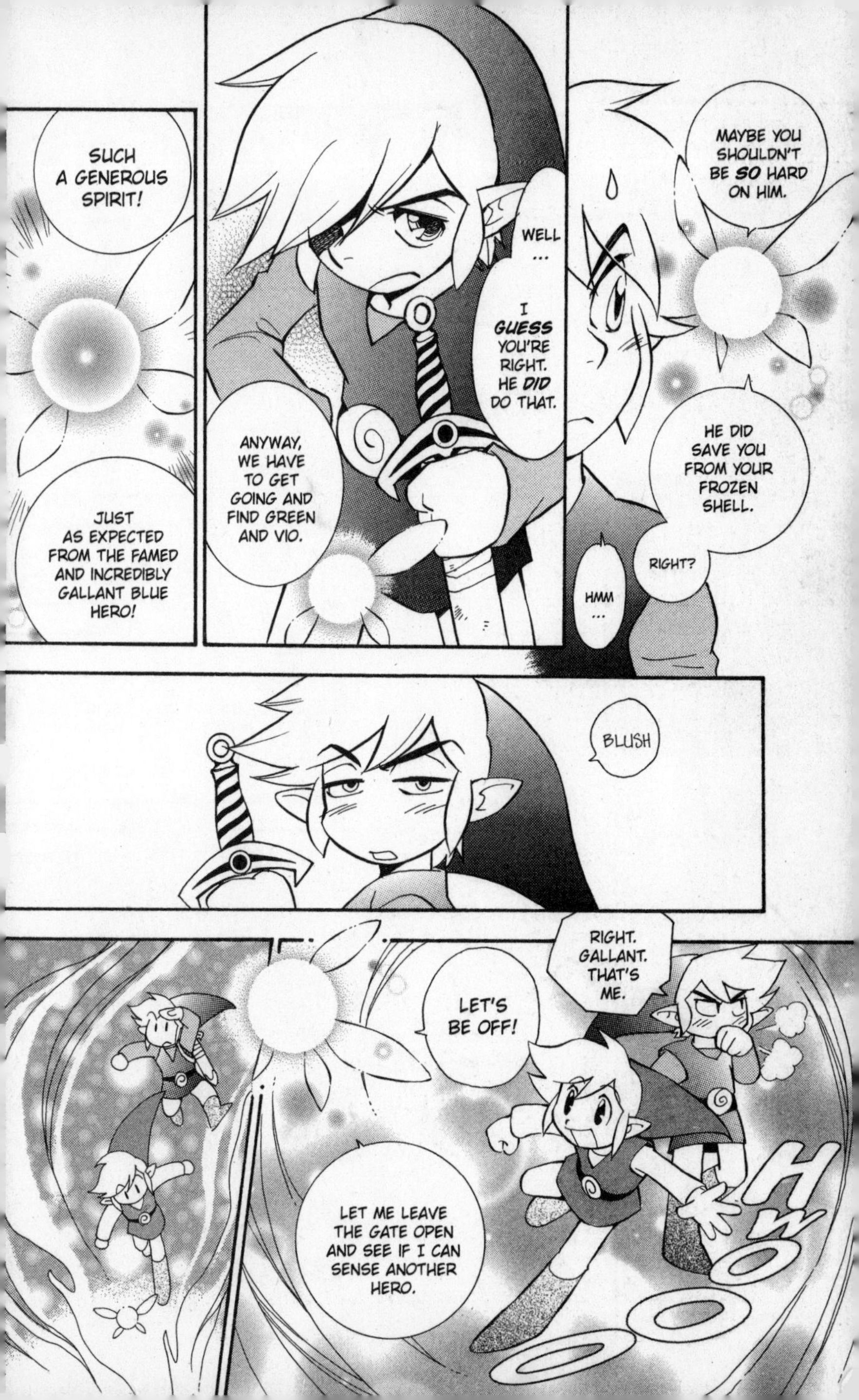
MAYBE YOU SHOULDN'T BE **SO** HARD ON HIM.
HE DID SAVE YOU FROM YOUR FROZEN SHELL.
RIGHT?
HMM ...
WELL ...
I ***GUESS*** YOU'RE RIGHT. HE ***DID*** DO THAT.
ANYWAY, WE HAVE TO GET GOING AND FIND GREEN AND VIO.
SUCH A GENEROUS SPIRIT!
JUST AS EXPECTED FROM THE FAMED AND INCREDIBLY GALLANT BLUE HERO!
BLUSH
RIGHT. GALLANT. THAT'S ME.
LET'S BE OFF!
LET ME LEAVE THE GATE OPEN AND SEE IF I CAN SENSE ANOTHER HERO.
HWOOO

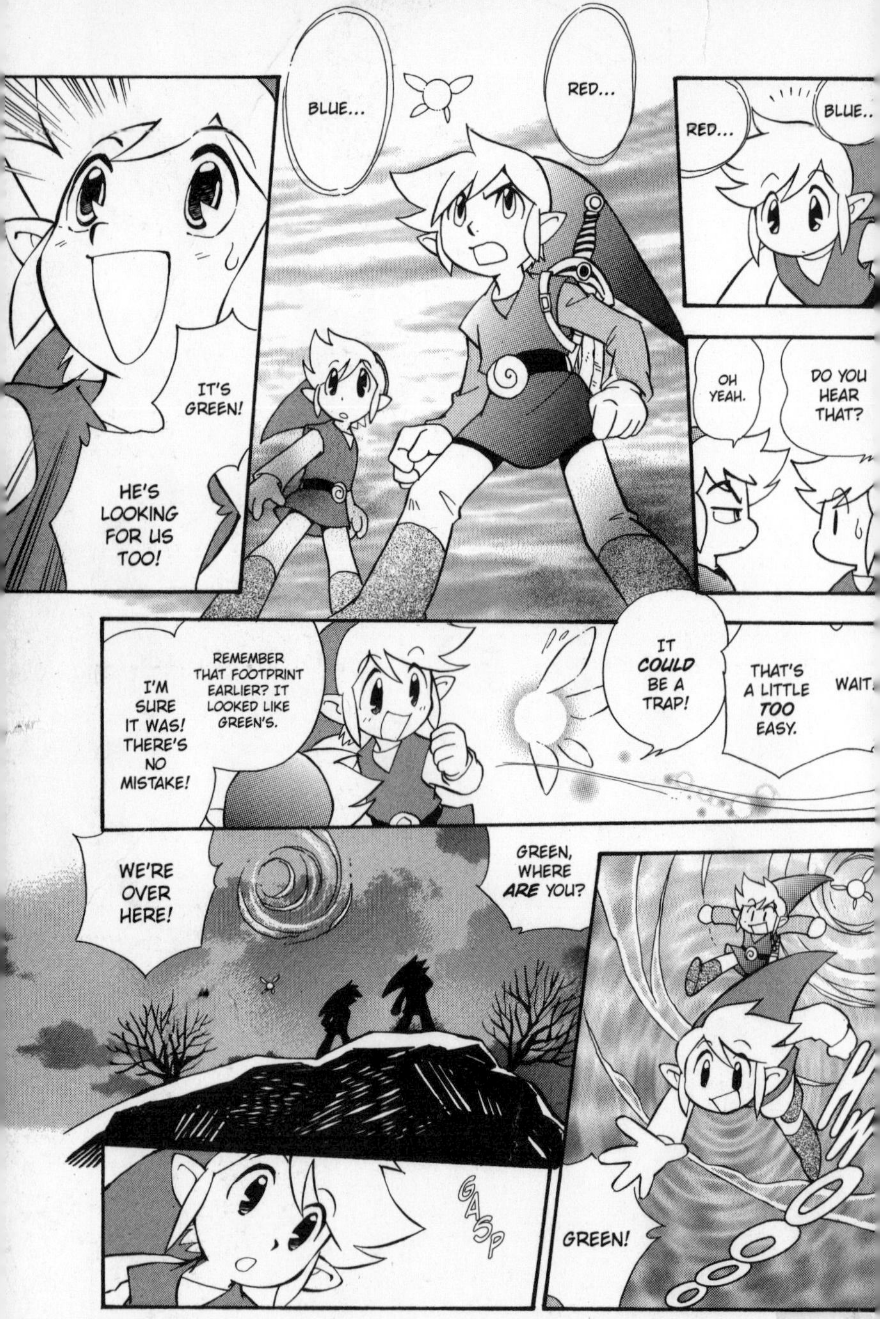
BLUE...
RED...
DO YOU HEAR THAT?
OH YEAH.
RED...
BLUE...
IT'S GREEN!
HE'S LOOKING FOR US TOO!
WAIT.
THAT'S A LITTLE **TOO** EASY.
IT **COULD** BE A TRAP!
REMEMBER THAT FOOTPRINT EARLIER? IT LOOKED LIKE GREEN'S.
I'M SURE IT WAS! THERE'S NO MISTAKE!
GREEN!
GREEN, WHERE **ARE** YOU?
WE'RE OVER HERE!
GASP

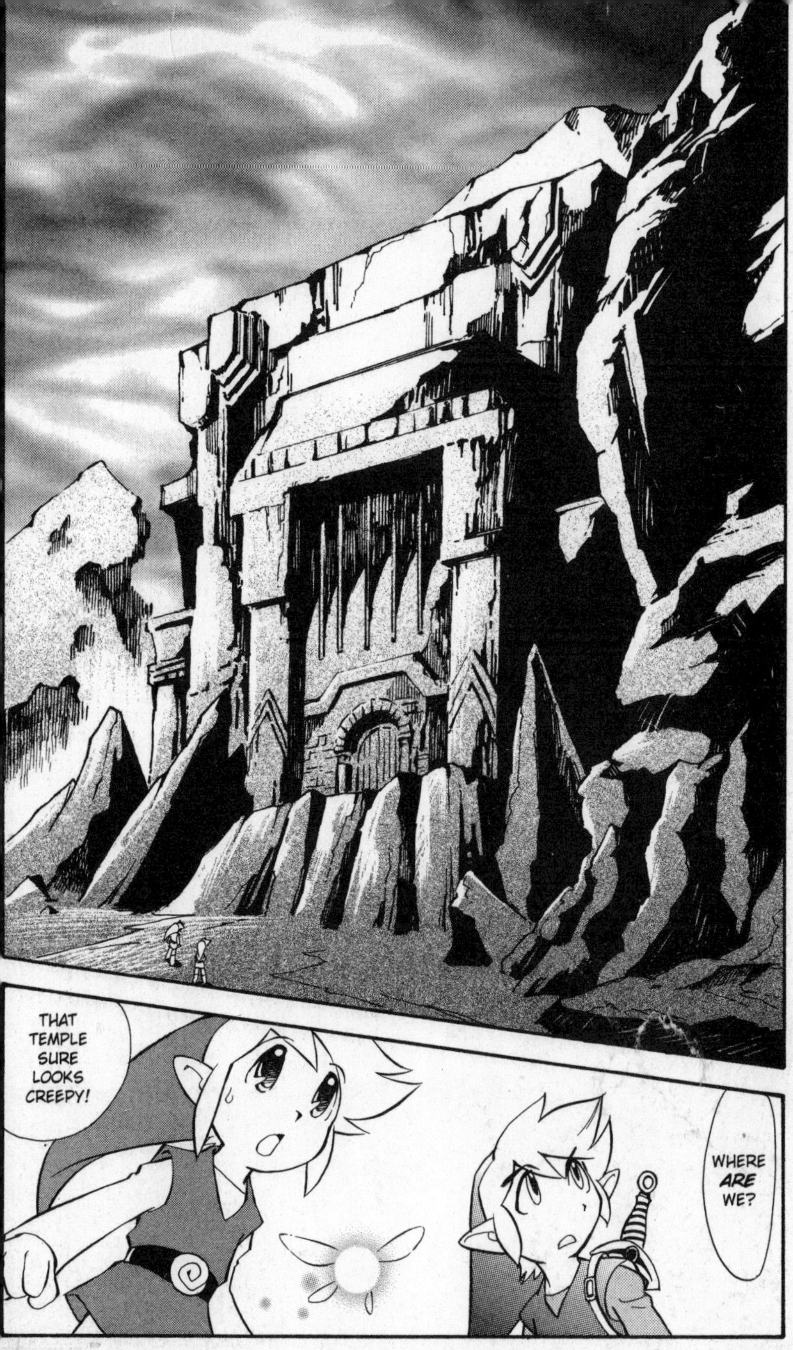
WHERE *ARE* WE?
THAT TEMPLE SURE LOOKS CREEPY!

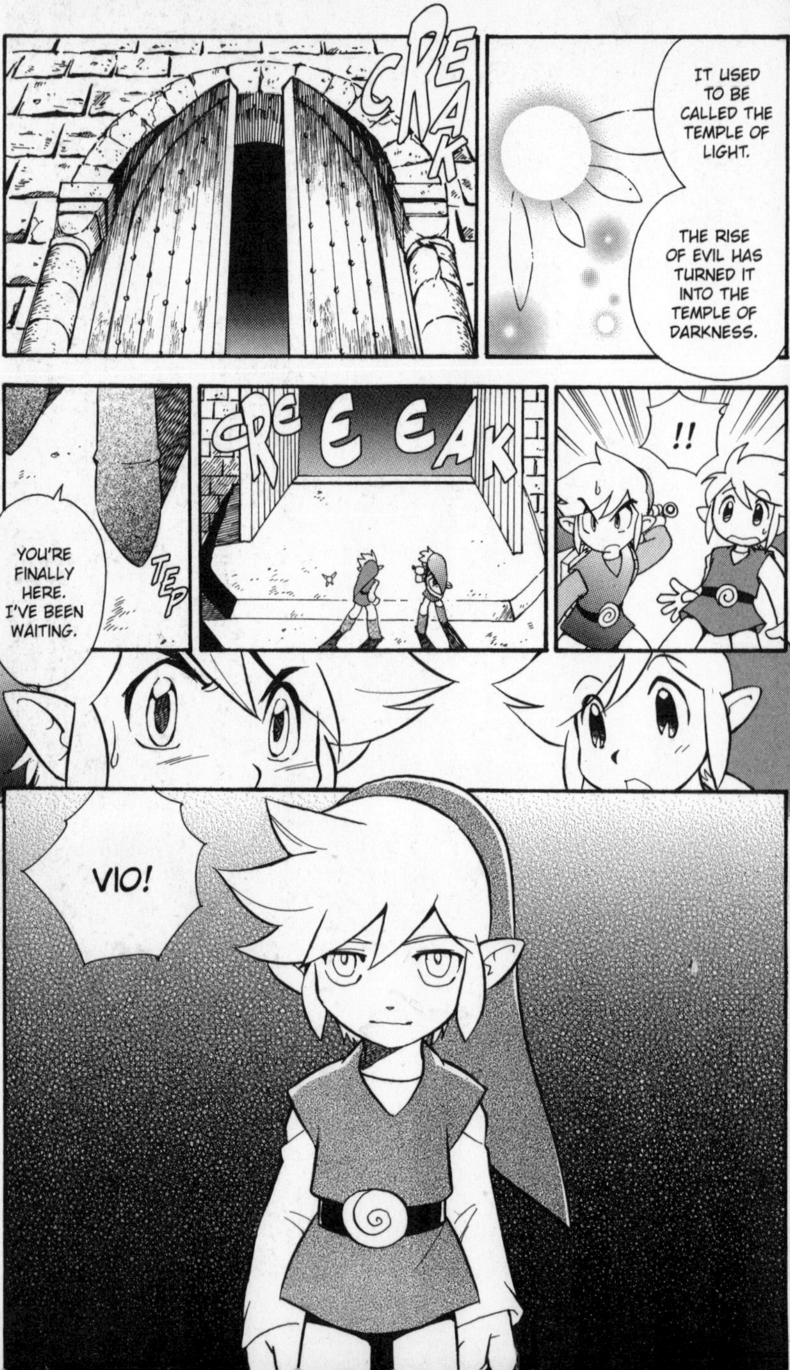
IT USED TO BE CALLED THE TEMPLE OF LIGHT.
THE RISE OF EVIL HAS TURNED IT INTO THE TEMPLE OF DARKNESS.
CREAK
!!
CRE E EAK
TEP
YOU'RE FINALLY HERE. I'VE BEEN WAITING.
VIO!

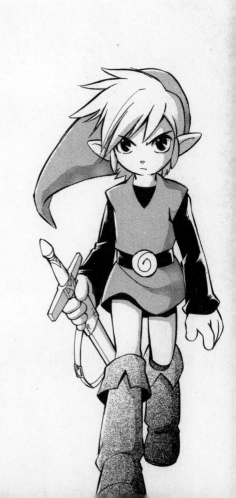

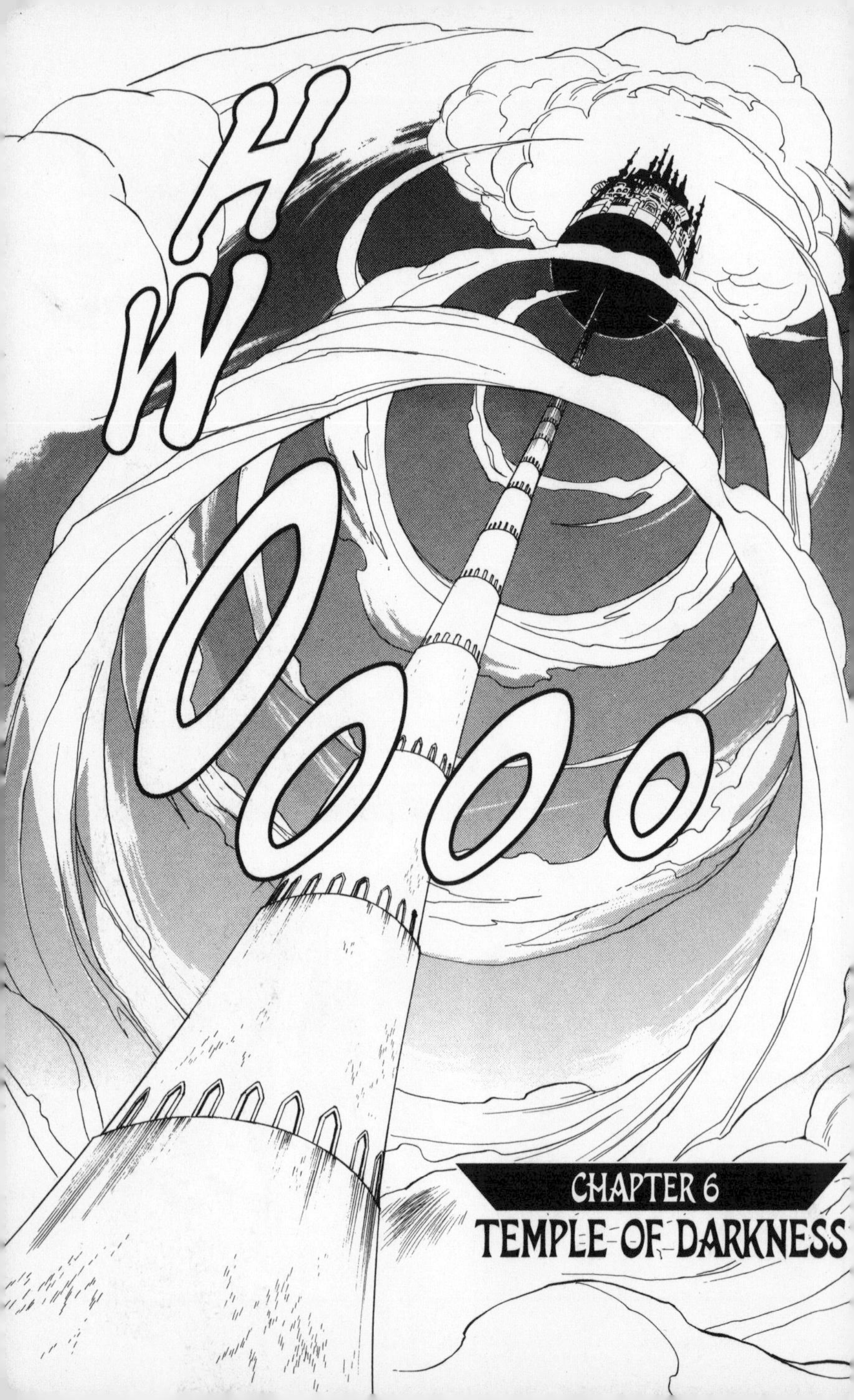
HWOOOO

CHAPTER 6
TEMPLE OF DARKNESS

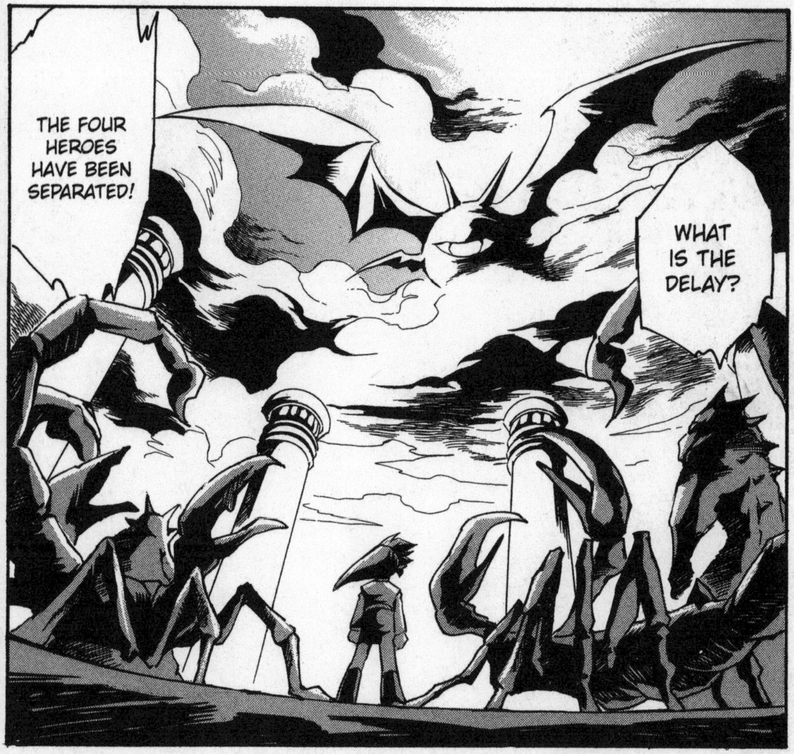
WHAT IS THE DELAY?
THE FOUR HEROES HAVE BEEN SEPARATED!

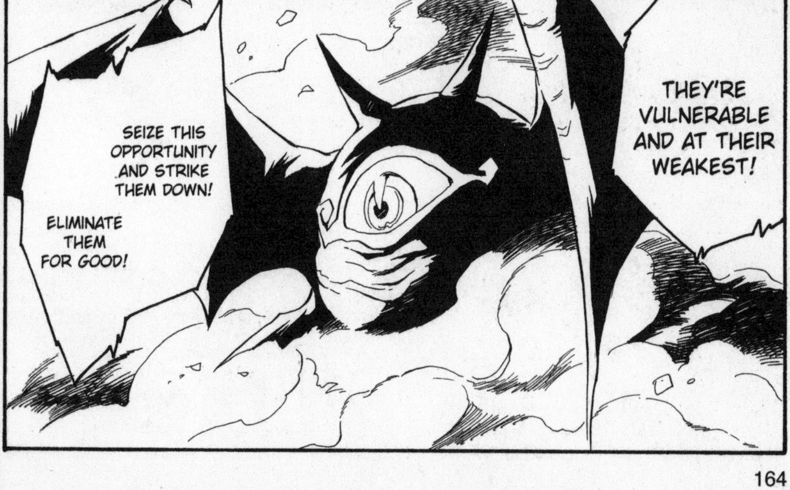
THEY'RE VULNERABLE AND AT THEIR WEAKEST!
SEIZE THIS OPPORTUNITY AND STRIKE THEM DOWN!
ELIMINATE THEM FOR GOOD!

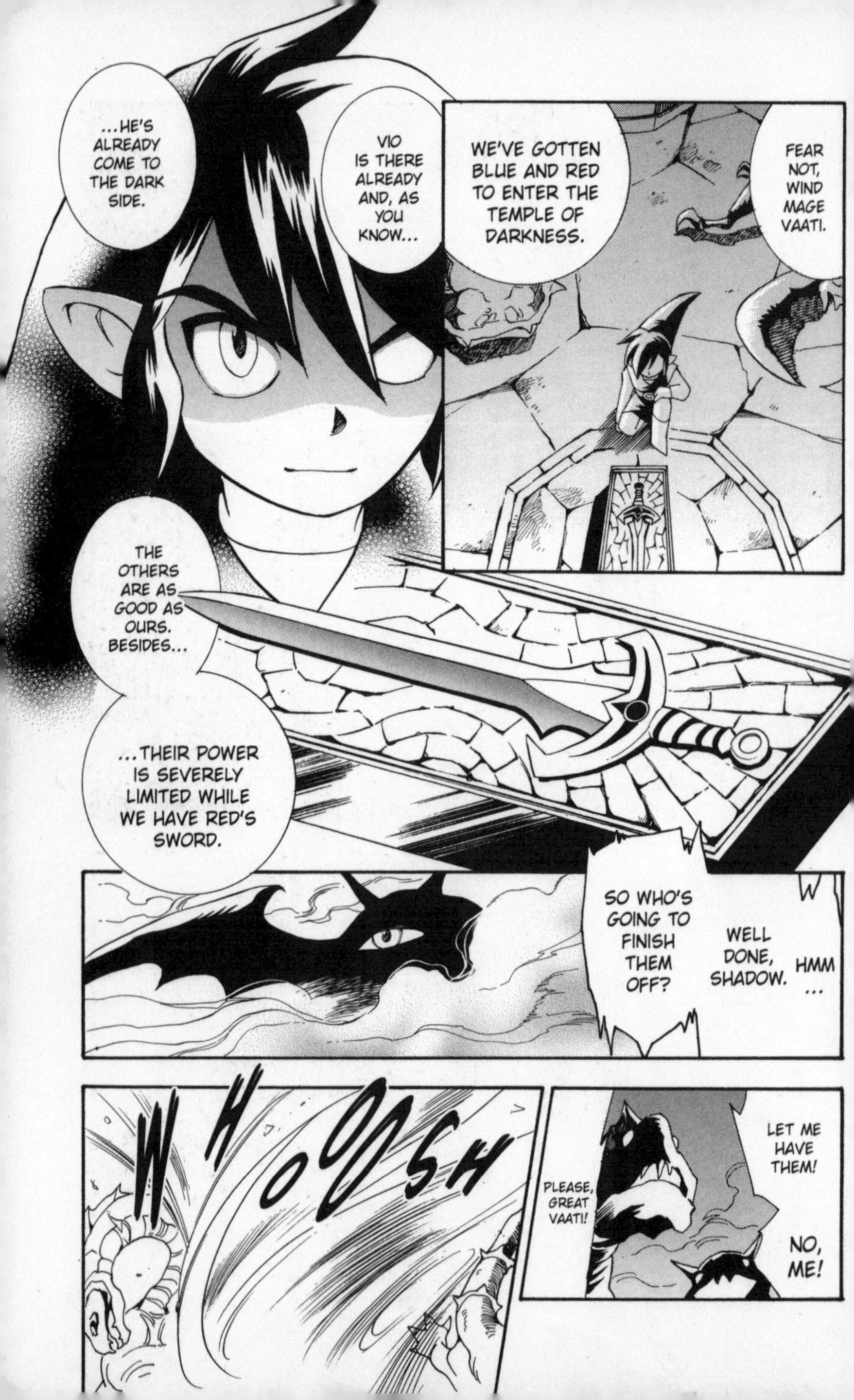
FEAR NOT, WIND MAGE VAATI.
WE'VE GOTTEN BLUE AND RED TO ENTER THE TEMPLE OF DARKNESS.
VIO IS THERE ALREADY AND, AS YOU KNOW...
...HE'S ALREADY COME TO THE DARK SIDE.
THE OTHERS ARE AS GOOD AS OURS. BESIDES...
...THEIR POWER IS SEVERELY LIMITED WHILE WE HAVE RED'S SWORD.
HMM...
WELL DONE, SHADOW.
SO WHO'S GOING TO FINISH THEM OFF?
LET ME HAVE THEM!
PLEASE, GREAT VAATI!
NO, ME!
WHOOSH

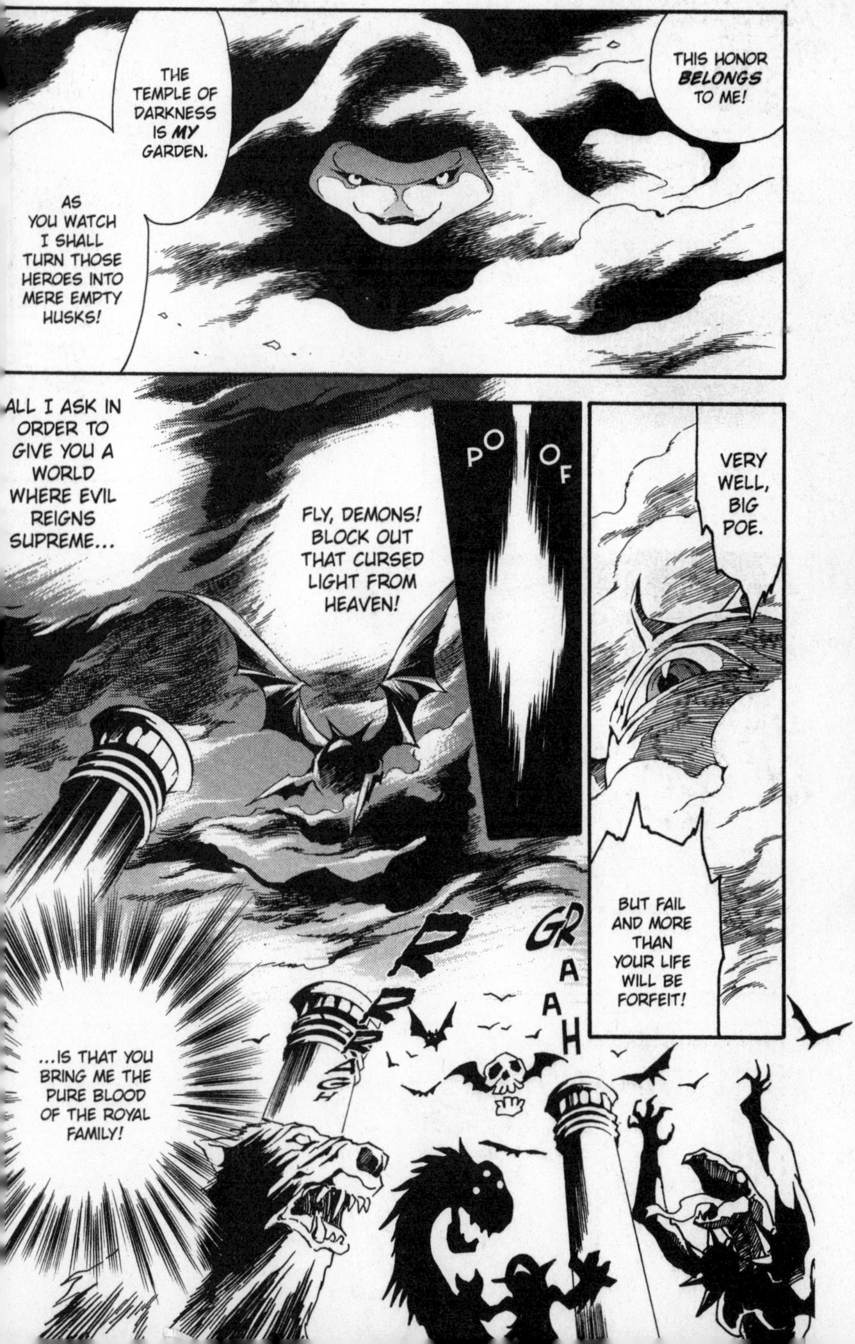
THIS HONOR BELONGS TO ME!
THE TEMPLE OF DARKNESS IS MY GARDEN.
AS YOU WATCH I SHALL TURN THOSE HEROES INTO MERE EMPTY HUSKS!
VERY WELL, BIG POE.
BUT FAIL AND MORE THAN YOUR LIFE WILL BE FORFEIT!
POOF
FLY, DEMONS! BLOCK OUT THAT CURSED LIGHT FROM HEAVEN!
ALL I ASK IN ORDER TO GIVE YOU A WORLD WHERE EVIL REIGNS SUPREME...
GRAAH
...IS THAT YOU BRING ME THE PURE BLOOD OF THE ROYAL FAMILY!

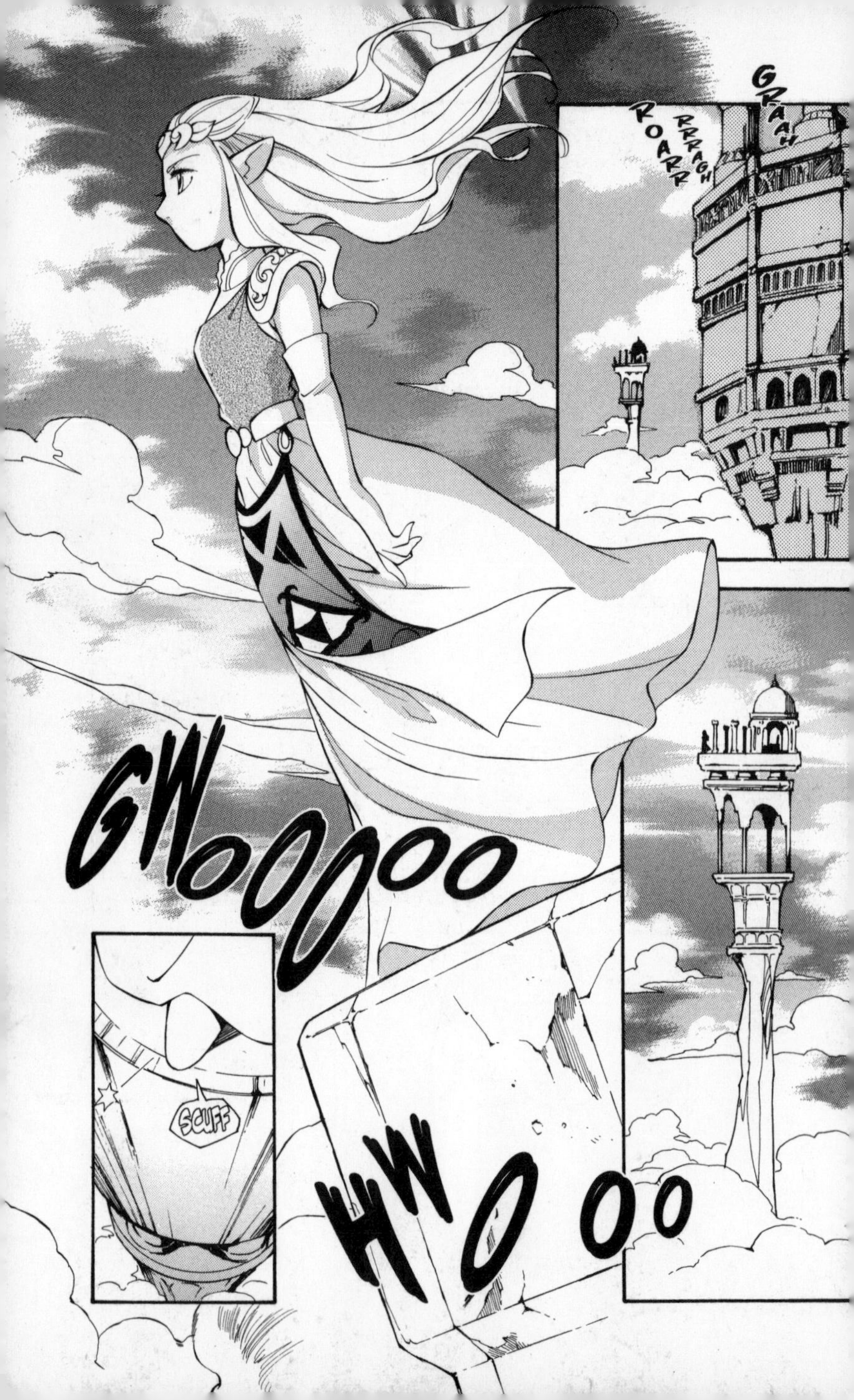
GRAAH
RRRAGH
ROARR
GWOOOOOO
HWOOO
SCUFF

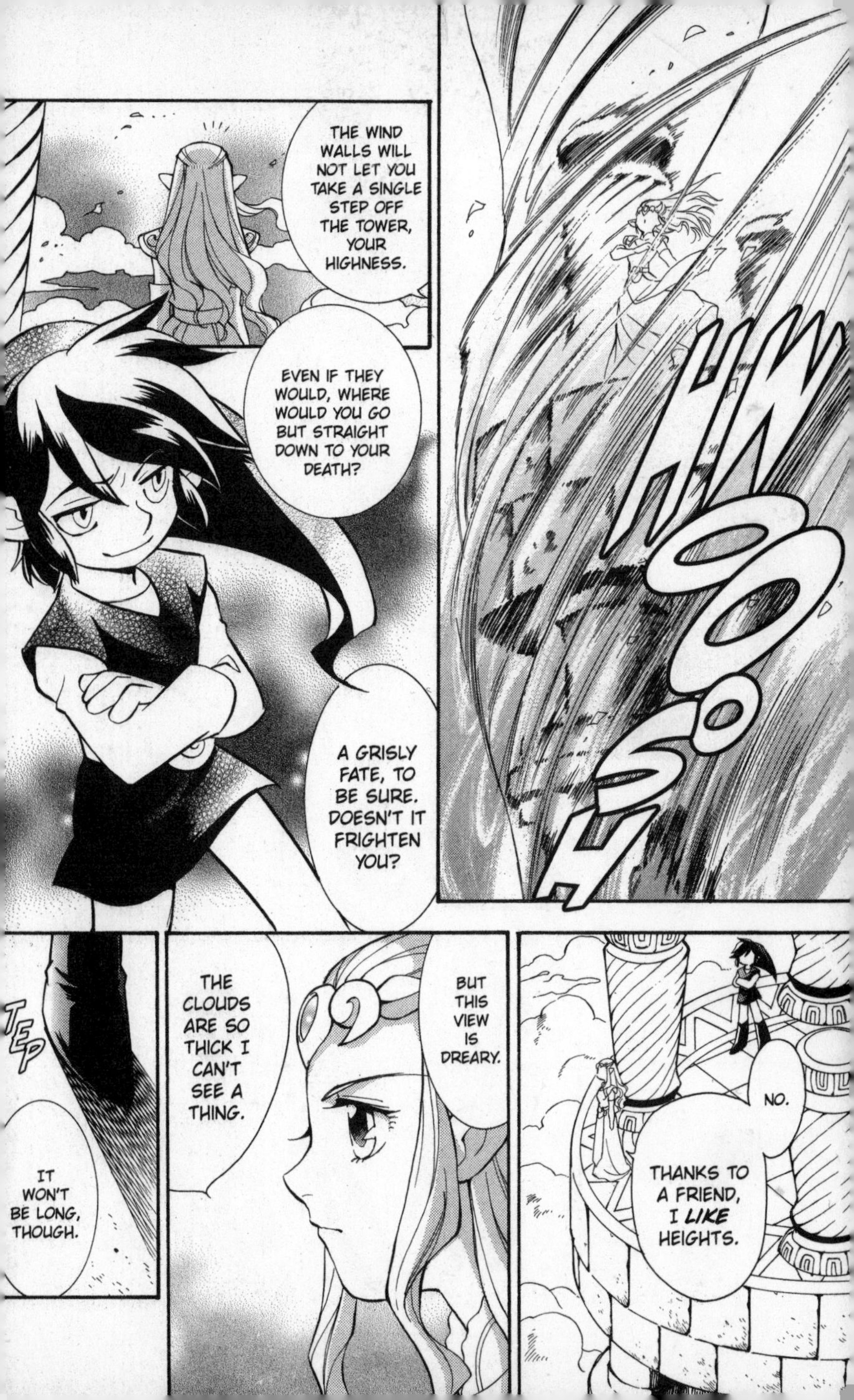
WHOOOSH
THE WIND WALLS WILL NOT LET YOU TAKE A SINGLE STEP OFF THE TOWER, YOUR HIGHNESS.
EVEN IF THEY WOULD, WHERE WOULD YOU GO BUT STRAIGHT DOWN TO YOUR DEATH?
A GRISLY FATE, TO BE SURE. DOESN'T IT FRIGHTEN YOU?
NO.
THANKS TO A FRIEND, I *LIKE* HEIGHTS.
BUT THIS VIEW IS DREARY.
THE CLOUDS ARE SO THICK I CAN'T SEE A THING.
TEP
IT WON'T BE LONG, THOUGH.

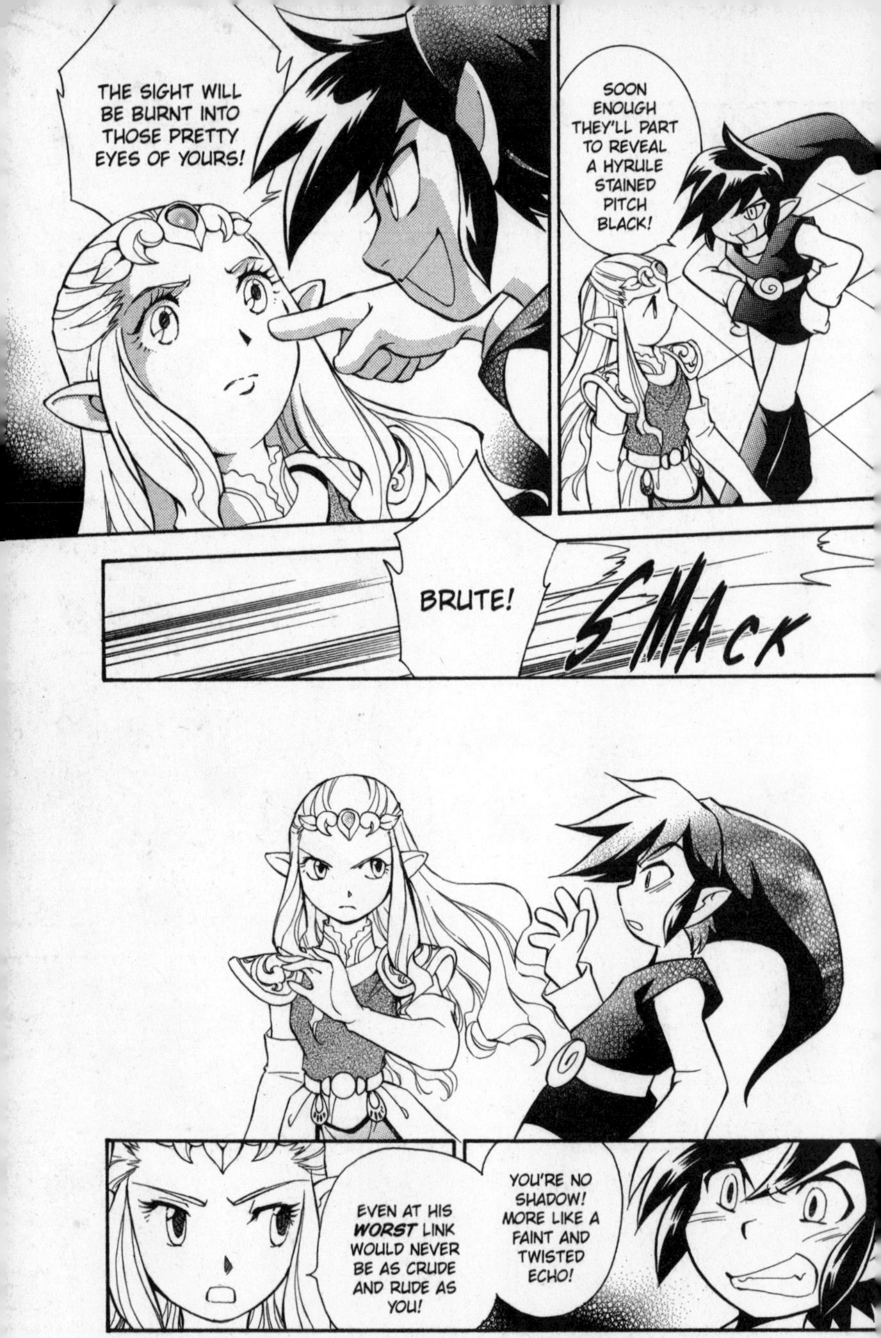
SOON ENOUGH THEY'LL PART TO REVEAL A HYRULE STAINED PITCH BLACK!
THE SIGHT WILL BE BURNT INTO THOSE PRETTY EYES OF YOURS!
SMACK
BRUTE!
YOU'RE NO SHADOW! MORE LIKE A FAINT AND TWISTED ECHO!
EVEN AT HIS *WORST* LINK WOULD NEVER BE AS CRUDE AND RUDE AS YOU!

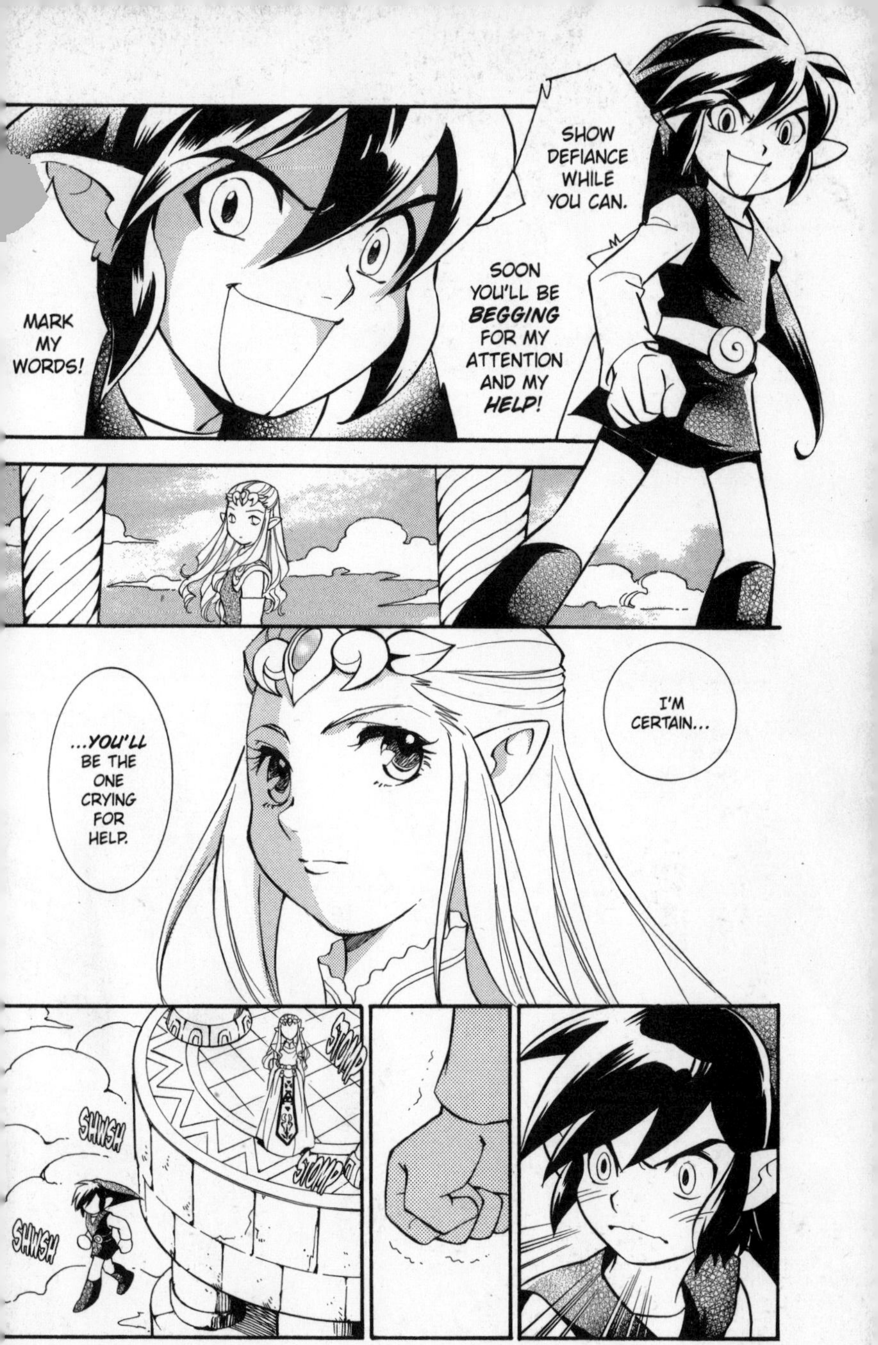
SHOW DEFIANCE WHILE YOU CAN.
SOON YOU'LL BE BEGGING FOR MY ATTENTION AND MY HELP!
MARK MY WORDS!
I'M CERTAIN...
...YOU'LL BE THE ONE CRYING FOR HELP.
STOMP
STOMP
SHWSH
SHWSH

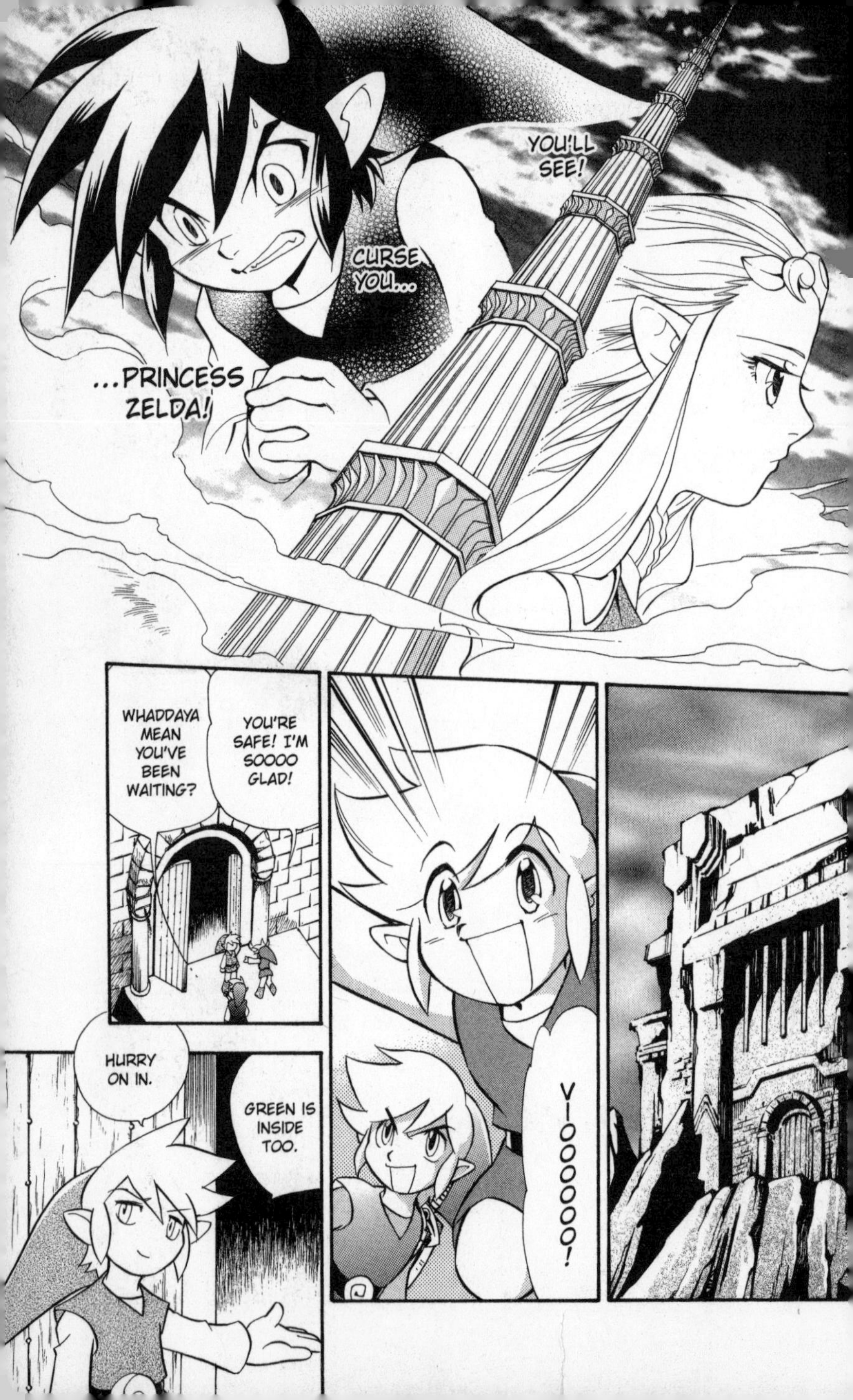
YOU'LL SEE!
CURSE YOU...
...PRINCESS ZELDA!
VIOOOOOOO!
YOU'RE SAFE! I'M SOOOO GLAD!
WHADDAYA MEAN YOU'VE BEEN WAITING?
HURRY ON IN.
GREEN IS INSIDE TOO.

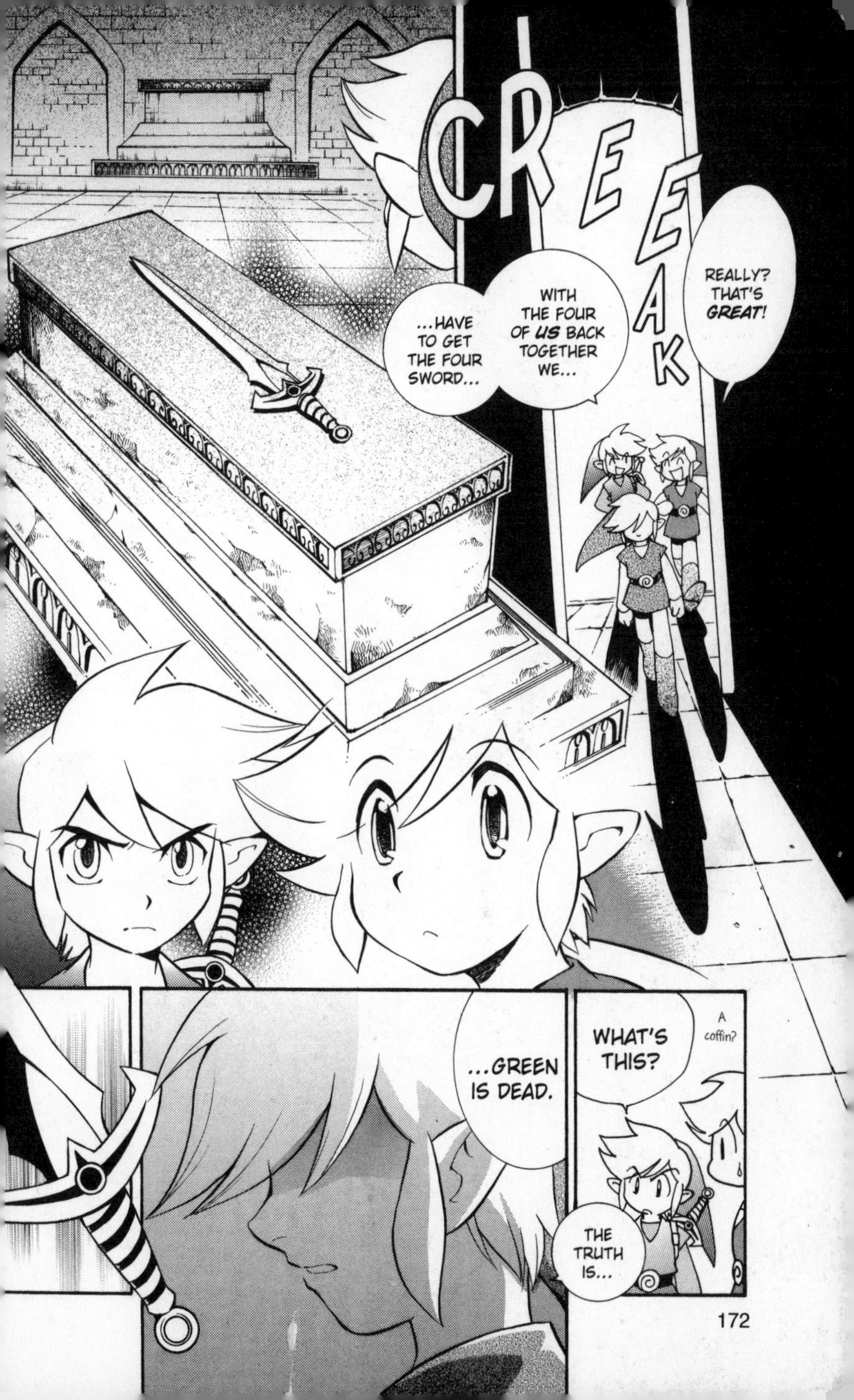
CREEEAK
REALLY? THAT'S GREAT!
WITH THE FOUR OF US BACK TOGETHER WE...
...HAVE TO GET THE FOUR SWORD...
A coffin?
WHAT'S THIS?
THE TRUTH IS...
...GREEN IS DEAD.

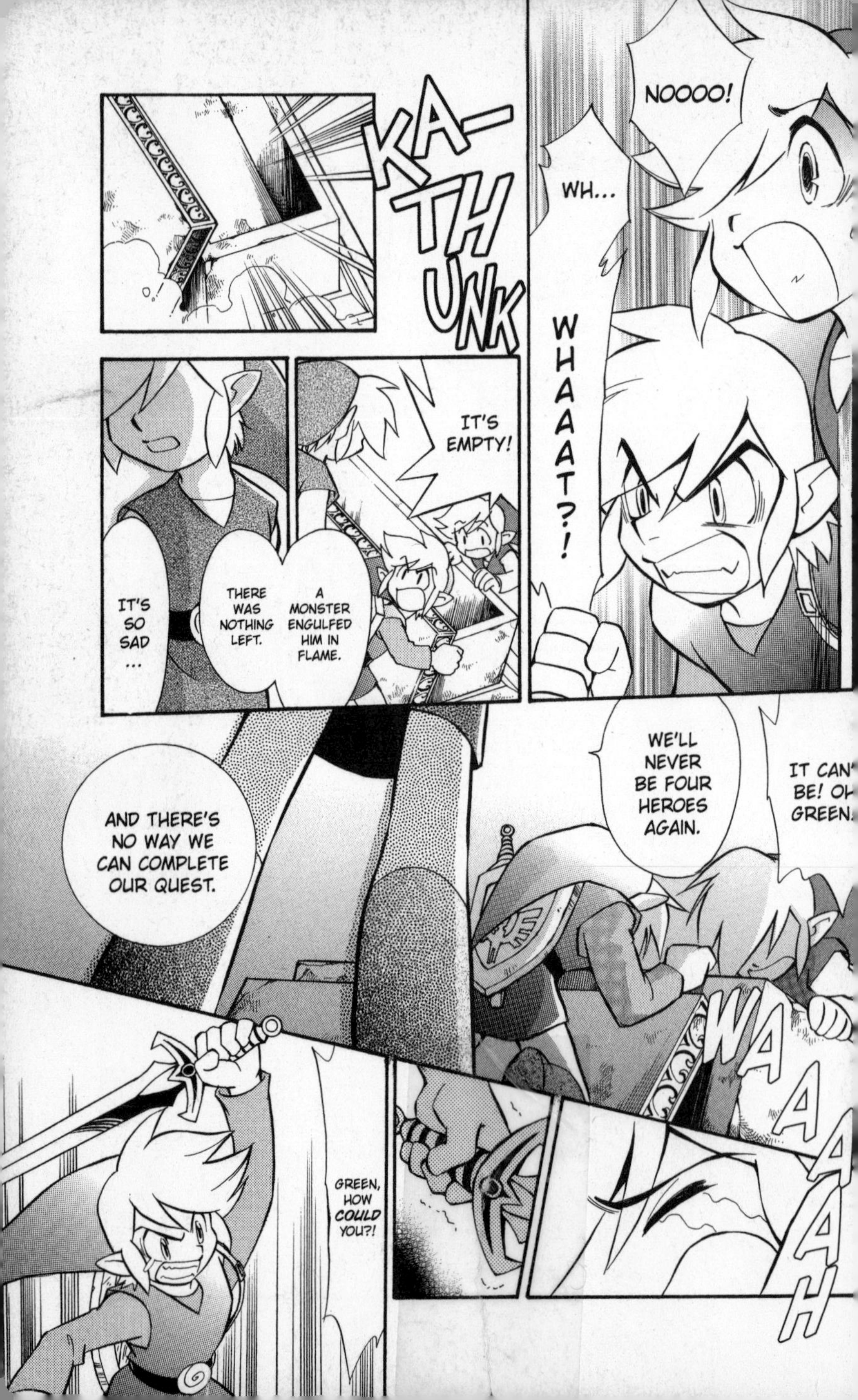
NOOOO!
WH...
WHAAAAT?!
KA-THUNK
IT'S EMPTY!
A MONSTER ENGULFED HIM IN FLAME.
THERE WAS NOTHING LEFT.
IT'S SO SAD...
IT CAN'T BE! OH GREEN...
WE'LL NEVER BE FOUR HEROES AGAIN.
AND THERE'S NO WAY WE CAN COMPLETE OUR QUEST.
WAAAAAH
GREEN, HOW *COULD* YOU?!

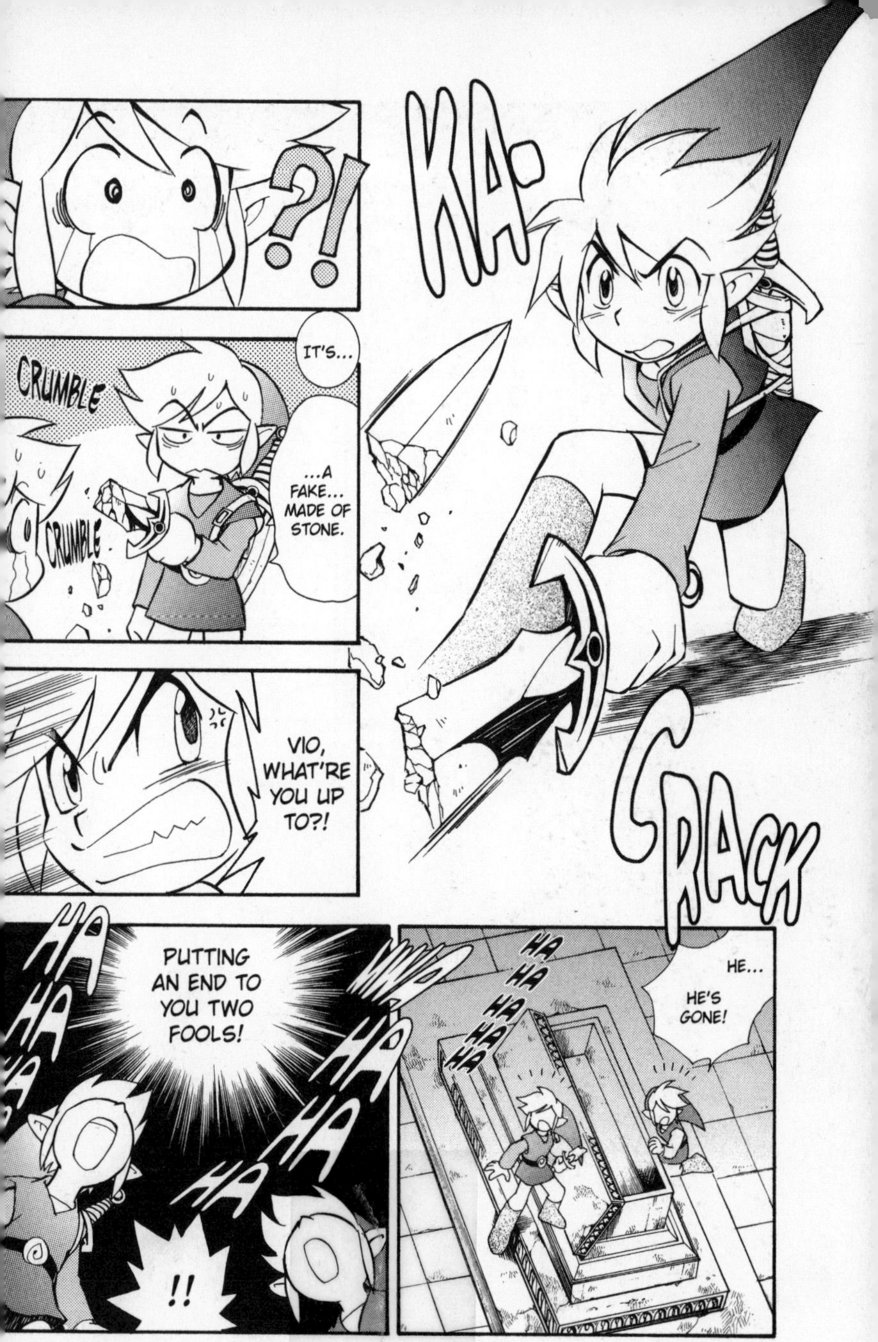
KA-
CRACK
?!
IT'S...
...A FAKE... MADE OF STONE.
CRUMBLE
CRUMBLE
VIO, WHAT'RE YOU UP TO?!
HA HA HA HA HA
HE...
HE'S GONE!
HA HA HA
PUTTING AN END TO YOU TWO FOOLS!
HA HA HA HA
!!

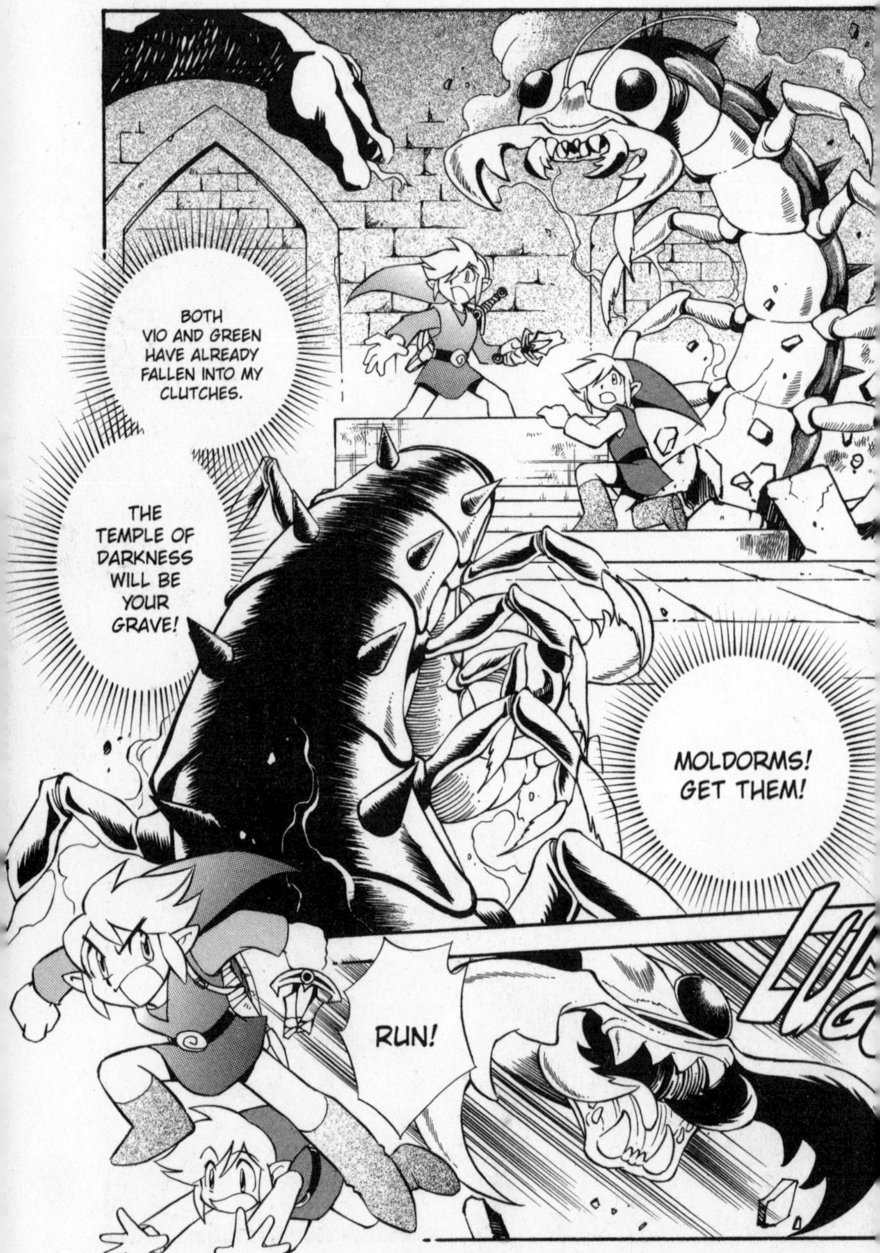
BOTH VIO AND GREEN HAVE ALREADY FALLEN INTO MY CLUTCHES.
THE TEMPLE OF DARKNESS WILL BE YOUR GRAVE!
MOLDORMS! GET THEM!
RUN!

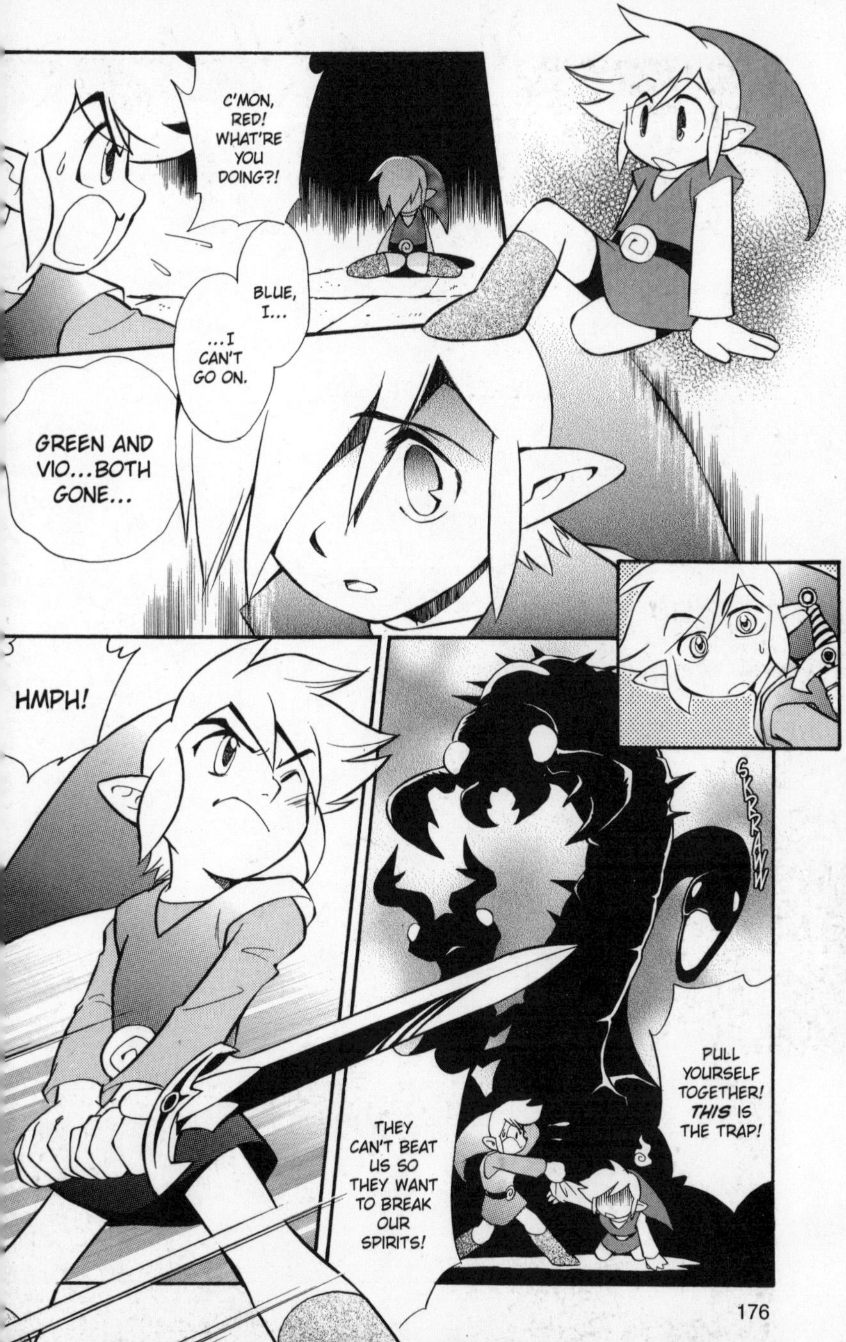
C'MON, RED! WHAT'RE YOU DOING?!
BLUE, I...
...I CAN'T GO ON.
GREEN AND VIO...BOTH GONE...
SKRAWW
PULL YOURSELF TOGETHER! *THIS* IS THE TRAP!
THEY CAN'T BEAT US SO THEY WANT TO BREAK OUR SPIRITS!
HMPH!

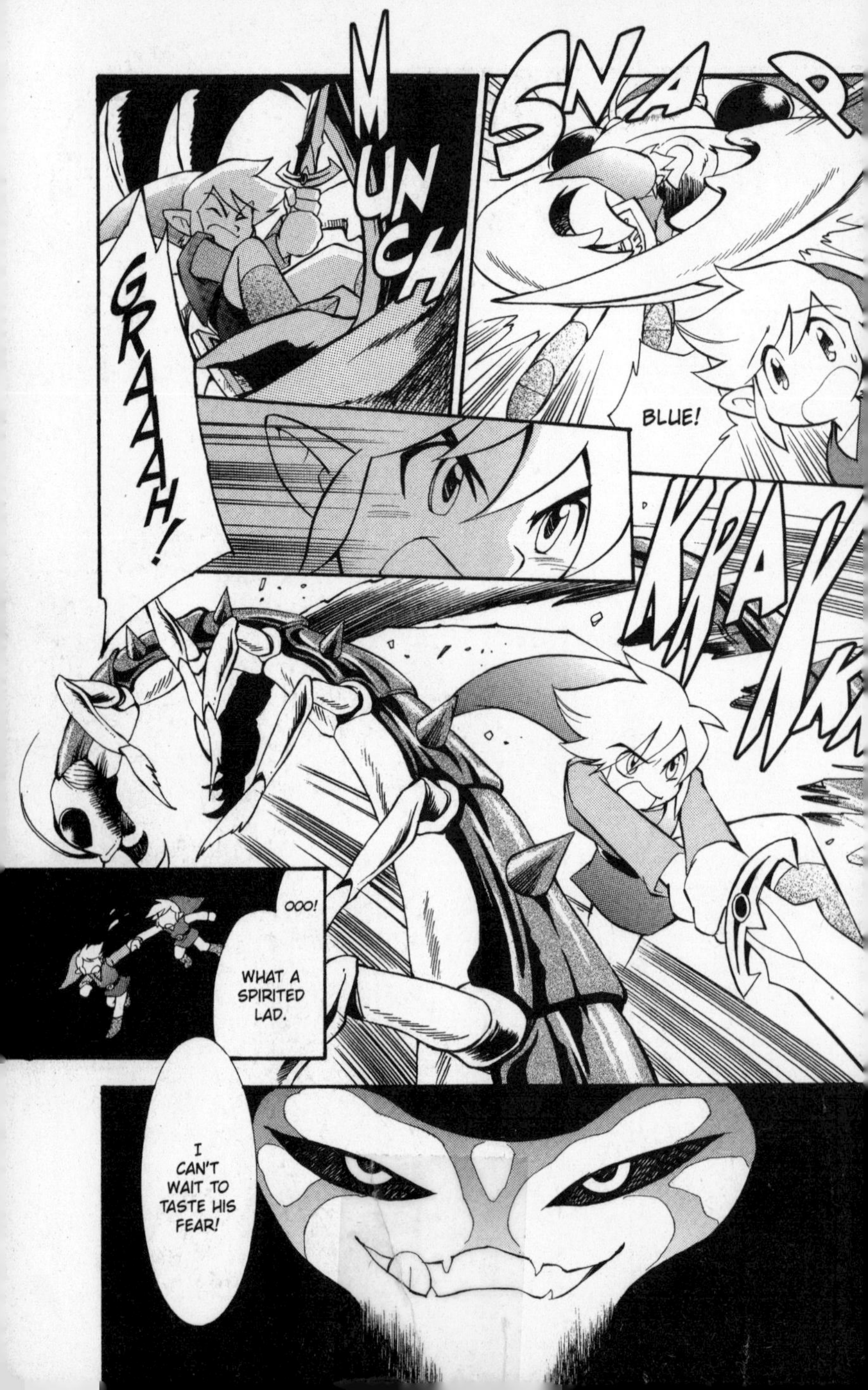
SNAP
BLUE!
MUNCH
GRAAAAH!
KRAK
OOO!
WHAT A SPIRITED LAD.
I CAN'T WAIT TO TASTE HIS FEAR!

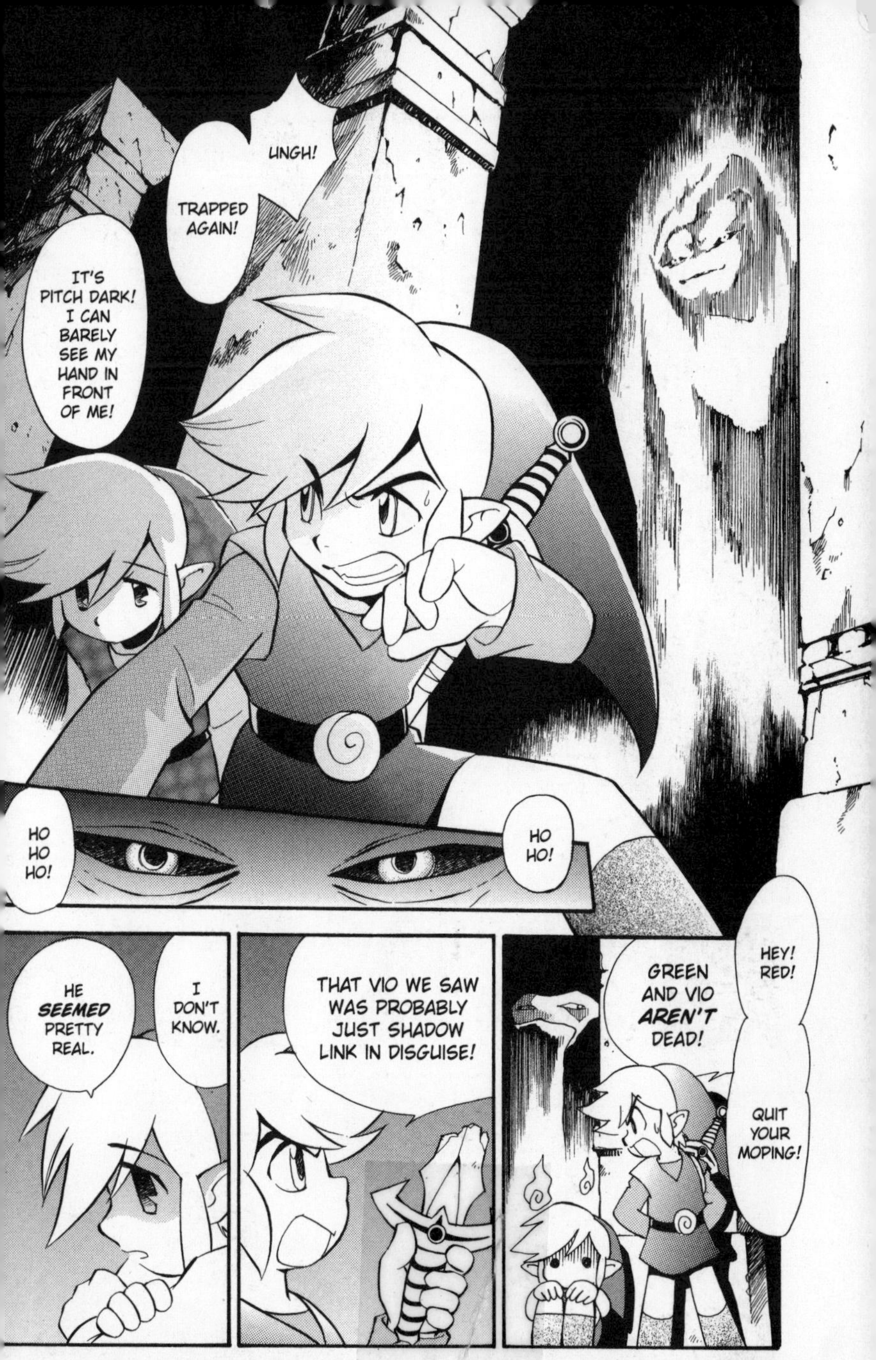
UNGH!
TRAPPED AGAIN!
IT'S PITCH DARK! I CAN BARELY SEE MY HAND IN FRONT OF ME!
HO HO!
HO HO HO!
HEY! RED!
QUIT YOUR MOPING!
GREEN AND VIO **AREN'T** DEAD!
THAT VIO WE SAW WAS PROBABLY JUST SHADOW LINK IN DISGUISE!
I DON'T KNOW.
HE **SEEMED** PRETTY REAL.

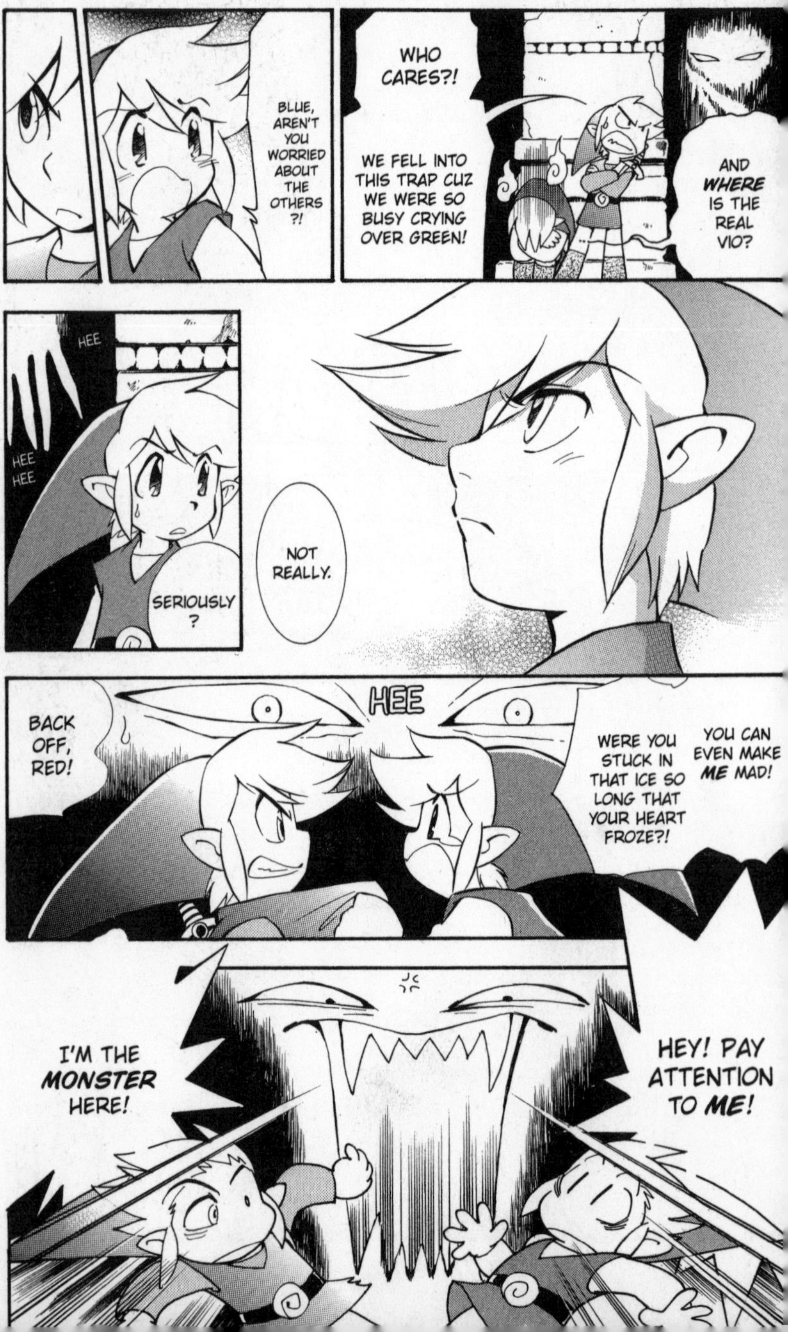
AND WHERE IS THE REAL VIO?
WHO CARES?!
WE FELL INTO THIS TRAP CUZ WE WERE SO BUSY CRYING OVER GREEN!
BLUE, AREN'T YOU WORRIED ABOUT THE OTHERS ?!
NOT REALLY.
HEE
HEE HEE
SERIOUSLY ?
YOU CAN EVEN MAKE ME MAD!
WERE YOU STUCK IN THAT ICE SO LONG THAT YOUR HEART FROZE?!
HEE
BACK OFF, RED!
HEY! PAY ATTENTION TO ME!
I'M THE MONSTER HERE!

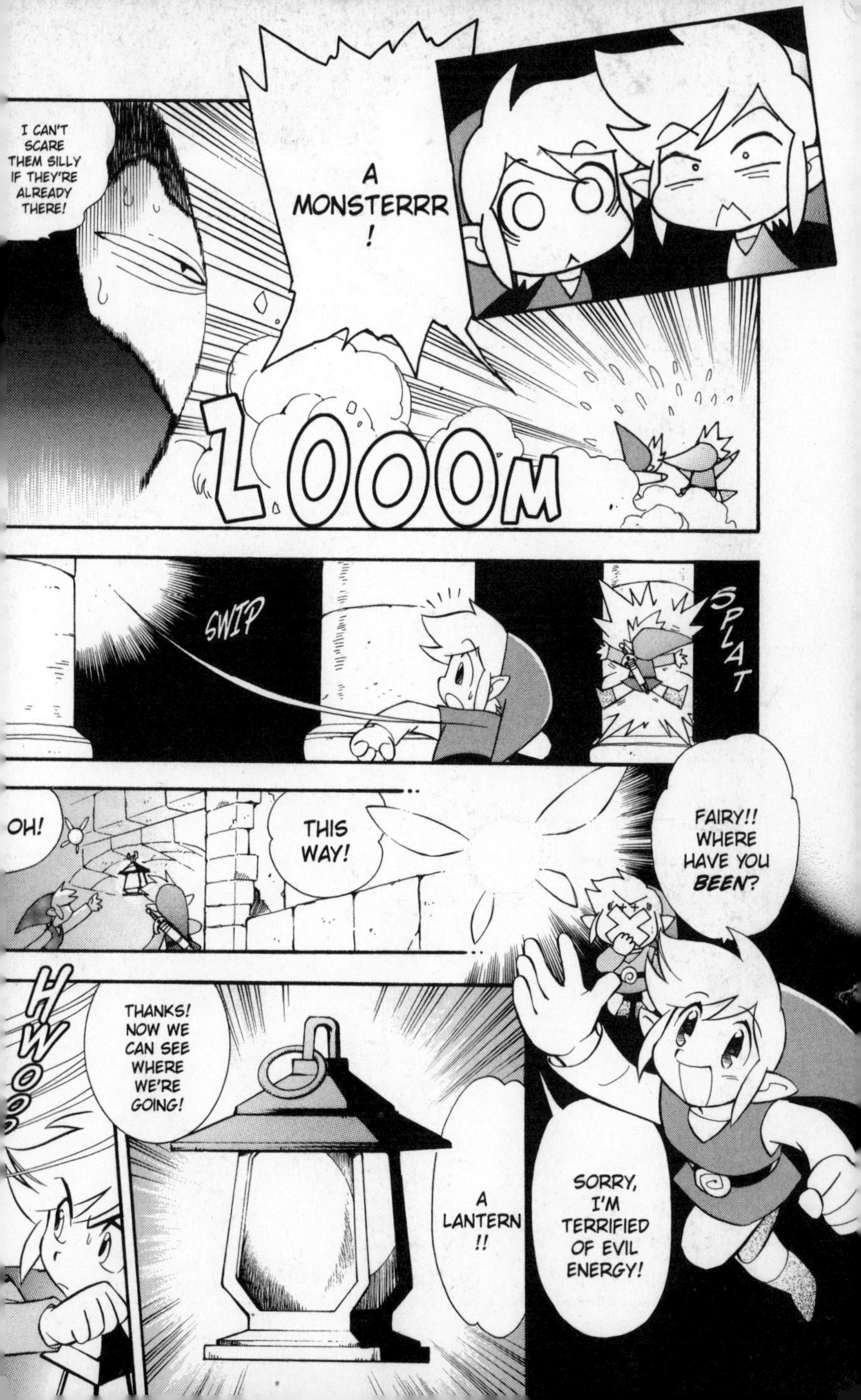

A MONSTERRR!
I CAN'T SCARE THEM SILLY IF THEY'RE ALREADY THERE!
ZOOOM
SPLAT
SWIP
FAIRY!! WHERE HAVE YOU *BEEN*?
THIS WAY!
OH!
SORRY, I'M TERRIFIED OF EVIL ENERGY!
A LANTERN!!
THANKS! NOW WE CAN SEE WHERE WE'RE GOING!
HWOOO

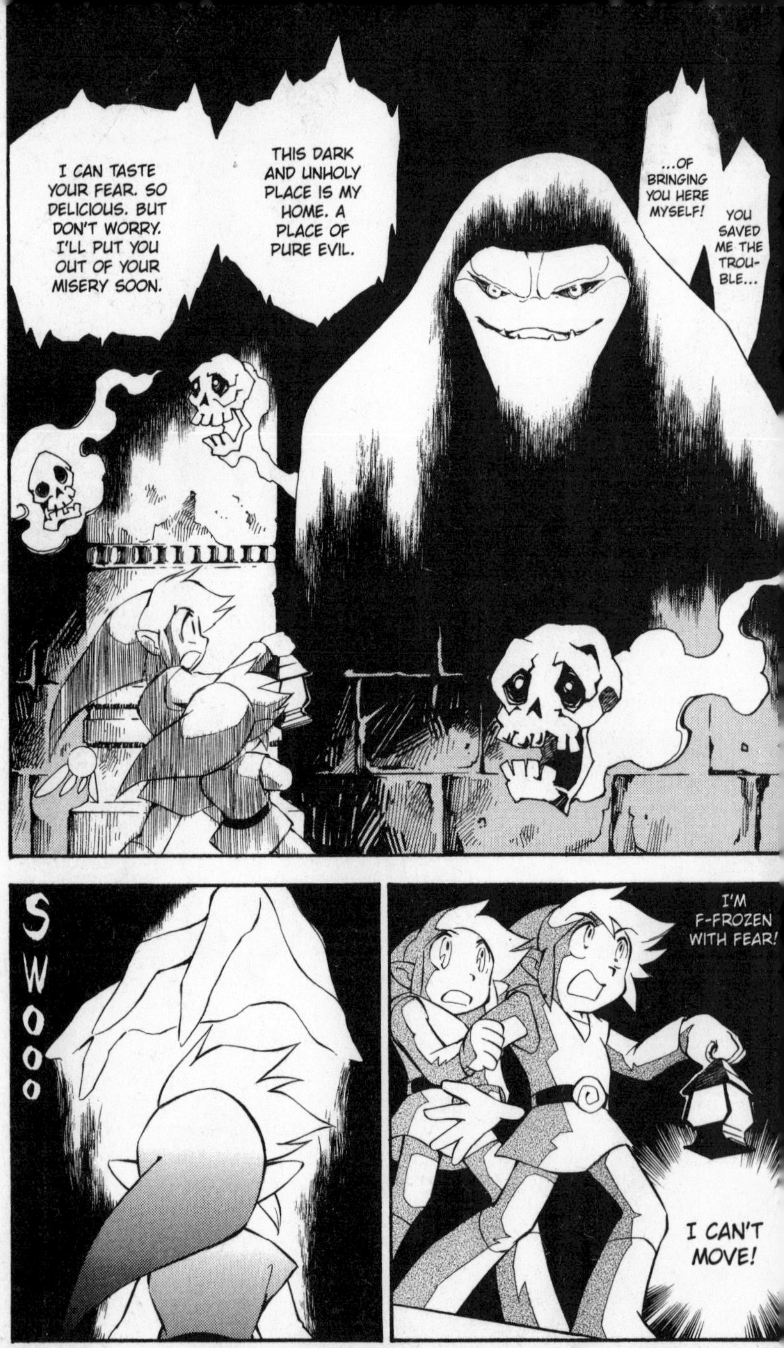
YOU SAVED ME THE TROU-BLE...
...OF BRINGING YOU HERE MYSELF!
THIS DARK AND UNHOLY PLACE IS MY HOME. A PLACE OF PURE EVIL.
I CAN TASTE YOUR FEAR. SO DELICIOUS. BUT DON'T WORRY. I'LL PUT YOU OUT OF YOUR MISERY SOON.
I'M F-FROZEN WITH FEAR!
I CAN'T MOVE!
SWOOO

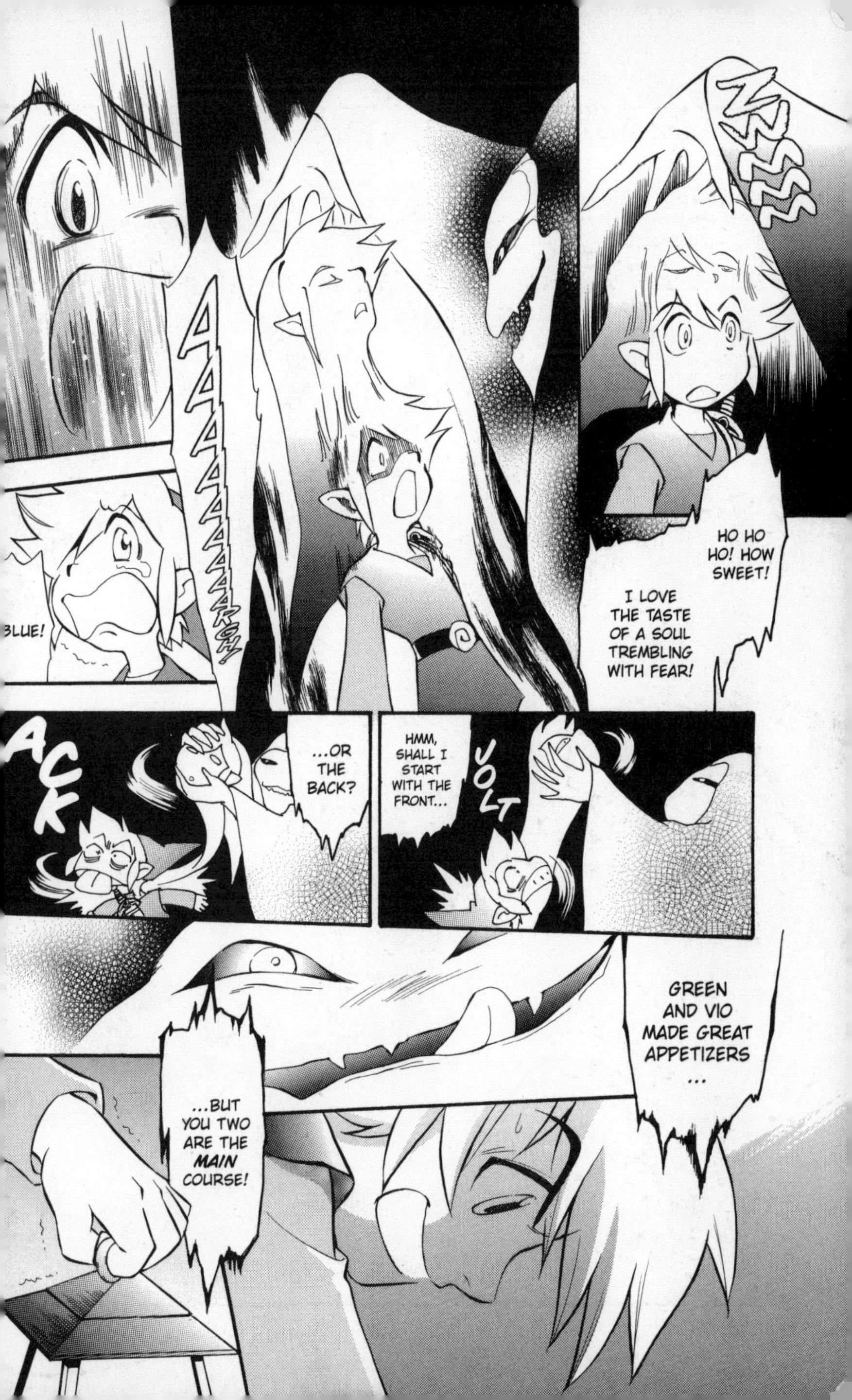
HO HO HO! HOW SWEET!
I LOVE THE TASTE OF A SOUL TREMBLING WITH FEAR!
AAAAAAAARGH!
BLUE!
HMM, SHALL I START WITH THE FRONT...
JOLT
...OR THE BACK?
ACK
GREEN AND VIO MADE GREAT APPETIZERS ...
...BUT YOU TWO ARE THE *MAIN* COURSE!

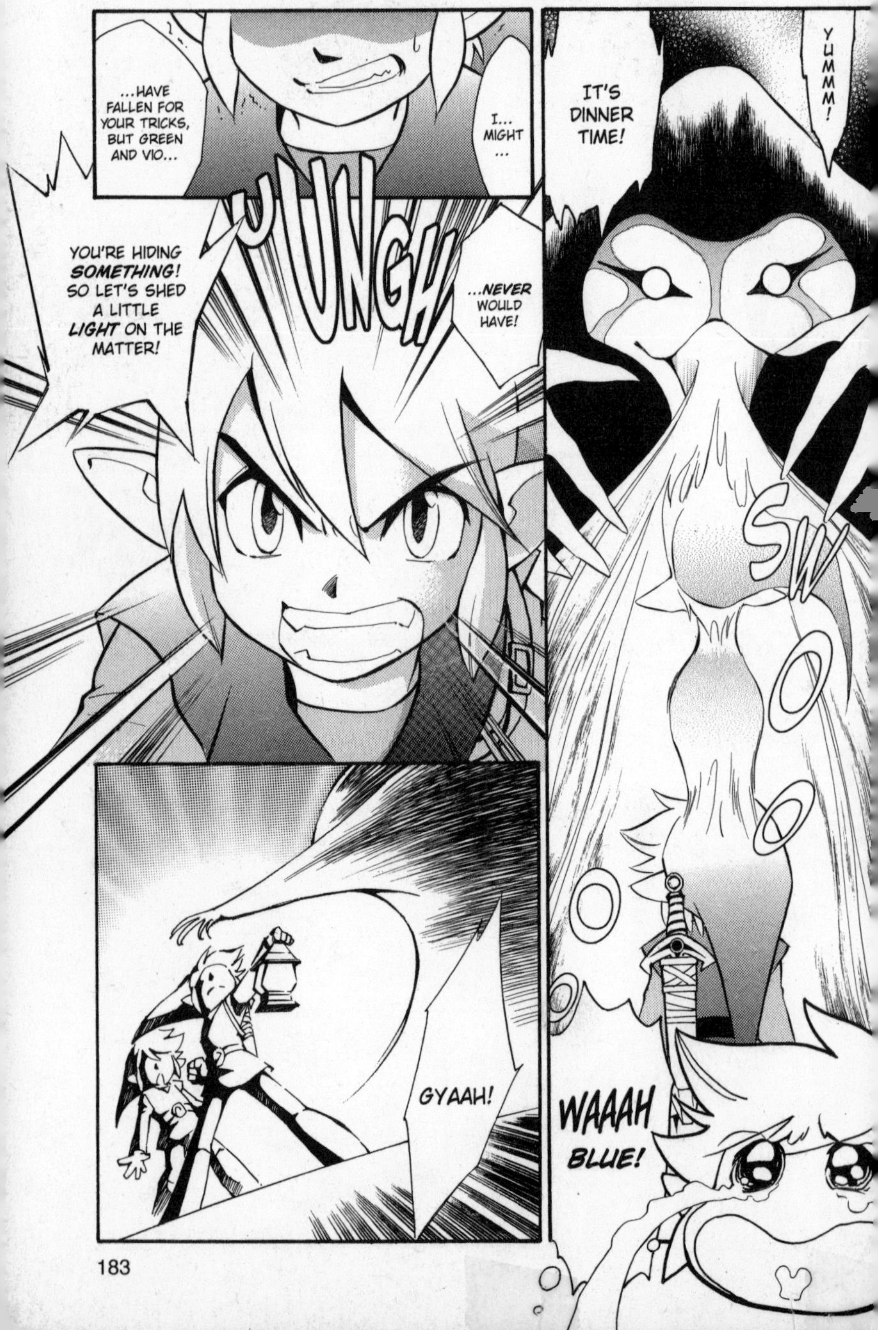
YUMMM!
IT'S DINNER TIME!
SW
WAAAH
BLUE!
I... MIGHT ...
...HAVE FALLEN FOR YOUR TRICKS, BUT GREEN AND VIO...
UNGH
...NEVER WOULD HAVE!
YOU'RE HIDING SOMETHING! SO LET'S SHED A LITTLE LIGHT ON THE MATTER!
GYAAH!

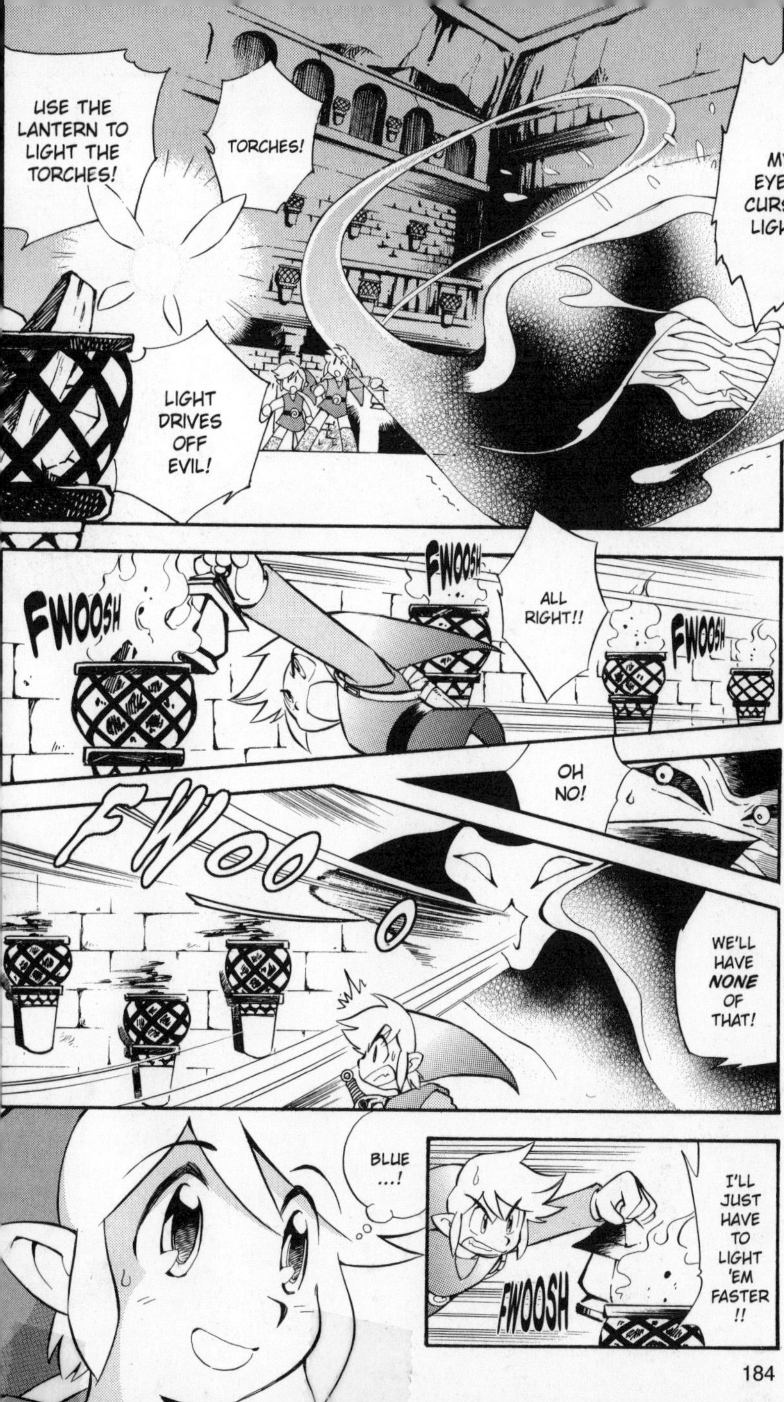
MY EYES! CURSED LIGHT!
USE THE LANTERN TO LIGHT THE TORCHES!
TORCHES!
LIGHT DRIVES OFF EVIL!
FWOOSH
ALL RIGHT!!
FWOOSH
FWOOSH
OH NO!
WE'LL HAVE *NONE* OF THAT!
FWOOO
I'LL JUST HAVE TO LIGHT 'EM FASTER!!
FWOOSH
BLUE ...!

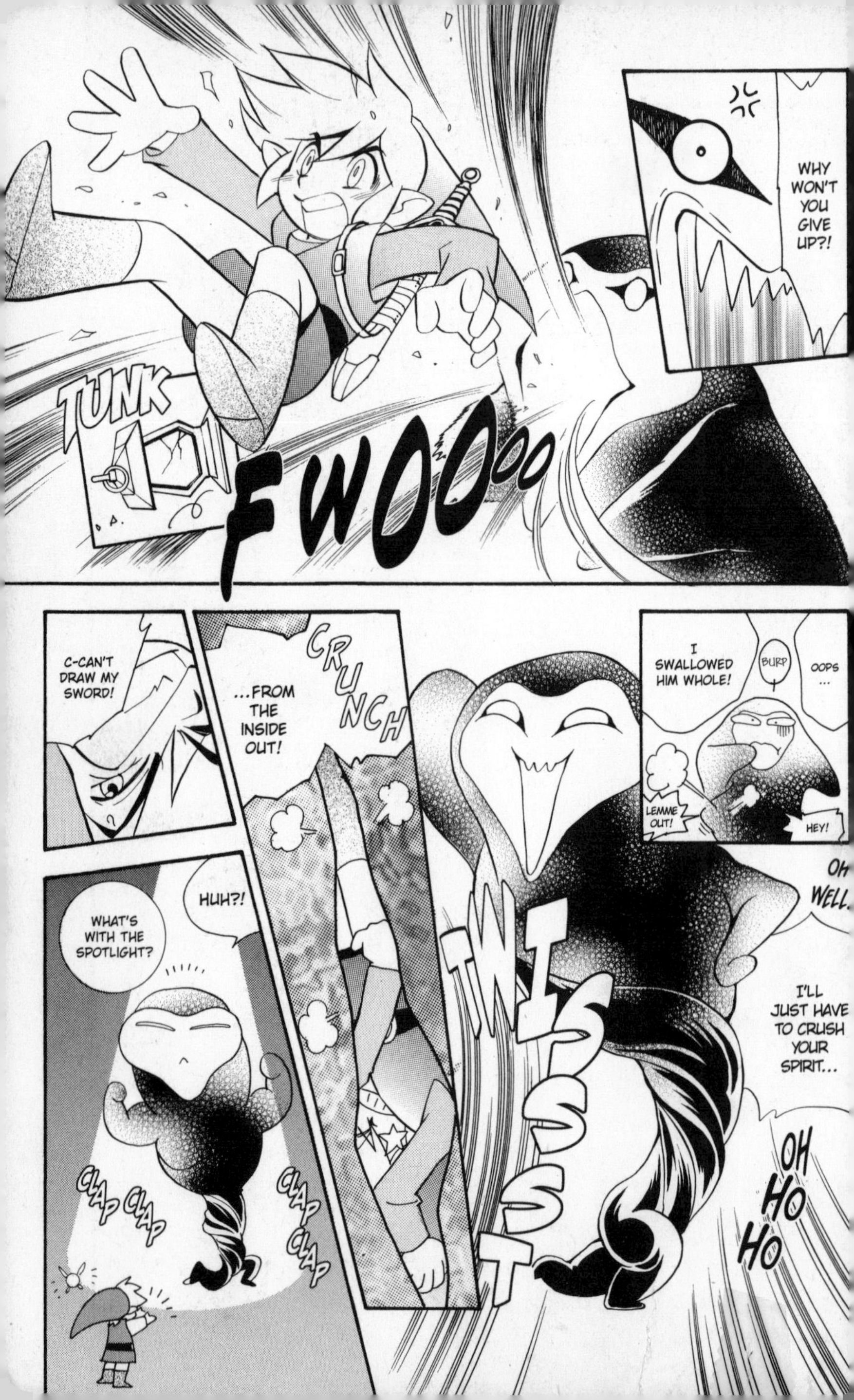
WHY WON'T YOU GIVE UP?!
TUNK
FWOOOOO
OOPS...
BURP
I SWALLOWED HIM WHOLE!
HEY!
LEMME OUT!
OH WELL.
I'LL JUST HAVE TO CRUSH YOUR SPIRIT...
OH HO HO
TWISSST
CRUNCH
...FROM THE INSIDE OUT!
C-CAN'T DRAW MY SWORD!
HUH?!
WHAT'S WITH THE SPOTLIGHT?
CLAP CLAP
CLAP CLAP

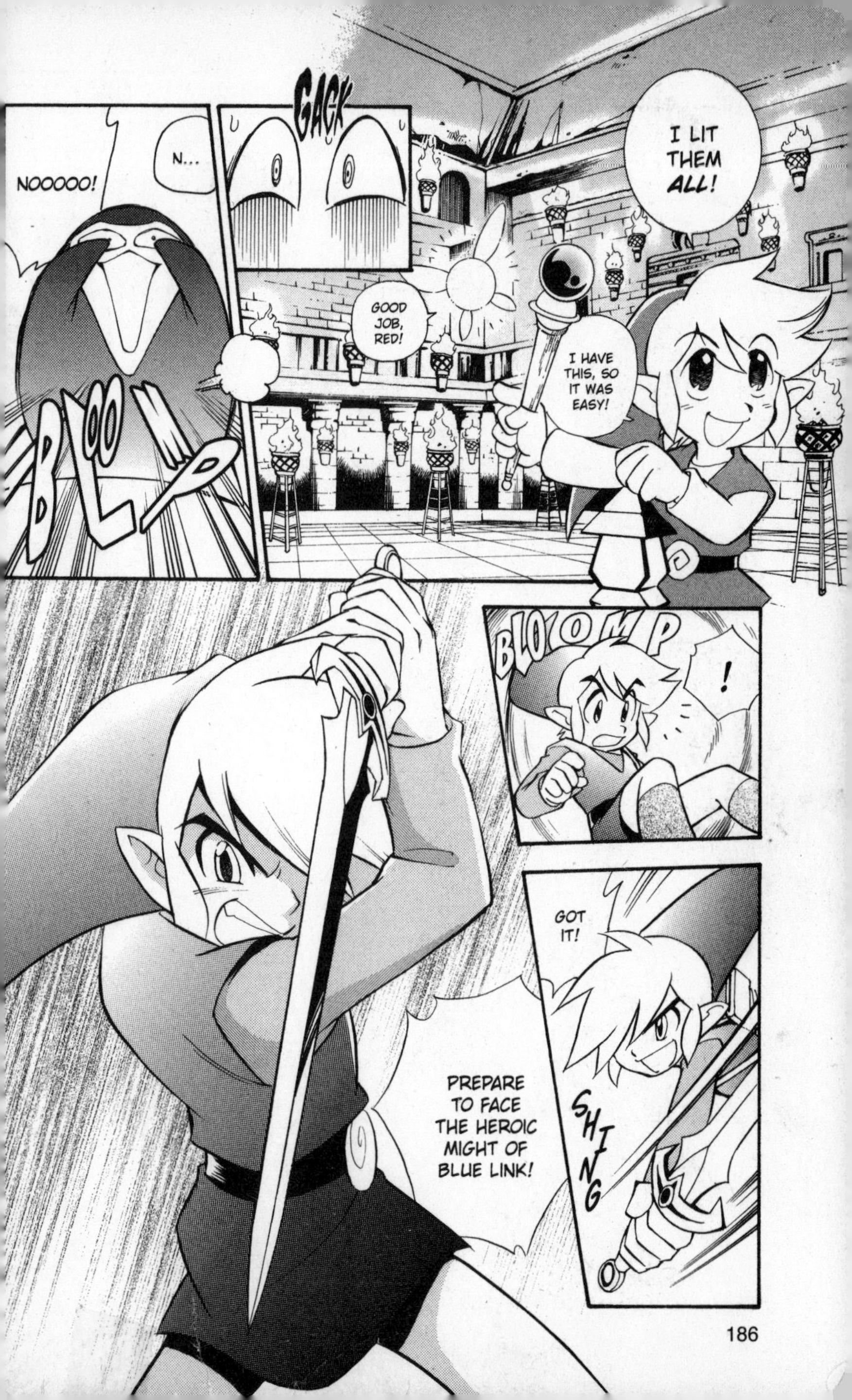
I LIT THEM ALL!
GOOD JOB, RED!
I HAVE THIS, SO IT WAS EASY!
GACK
N...
NOOOOO!
BLOOMP
BLOOMP
!
GOT IT!
SHING
PREPARE TO FACE THE HEROIC MIGHT OF BLUE LINK!

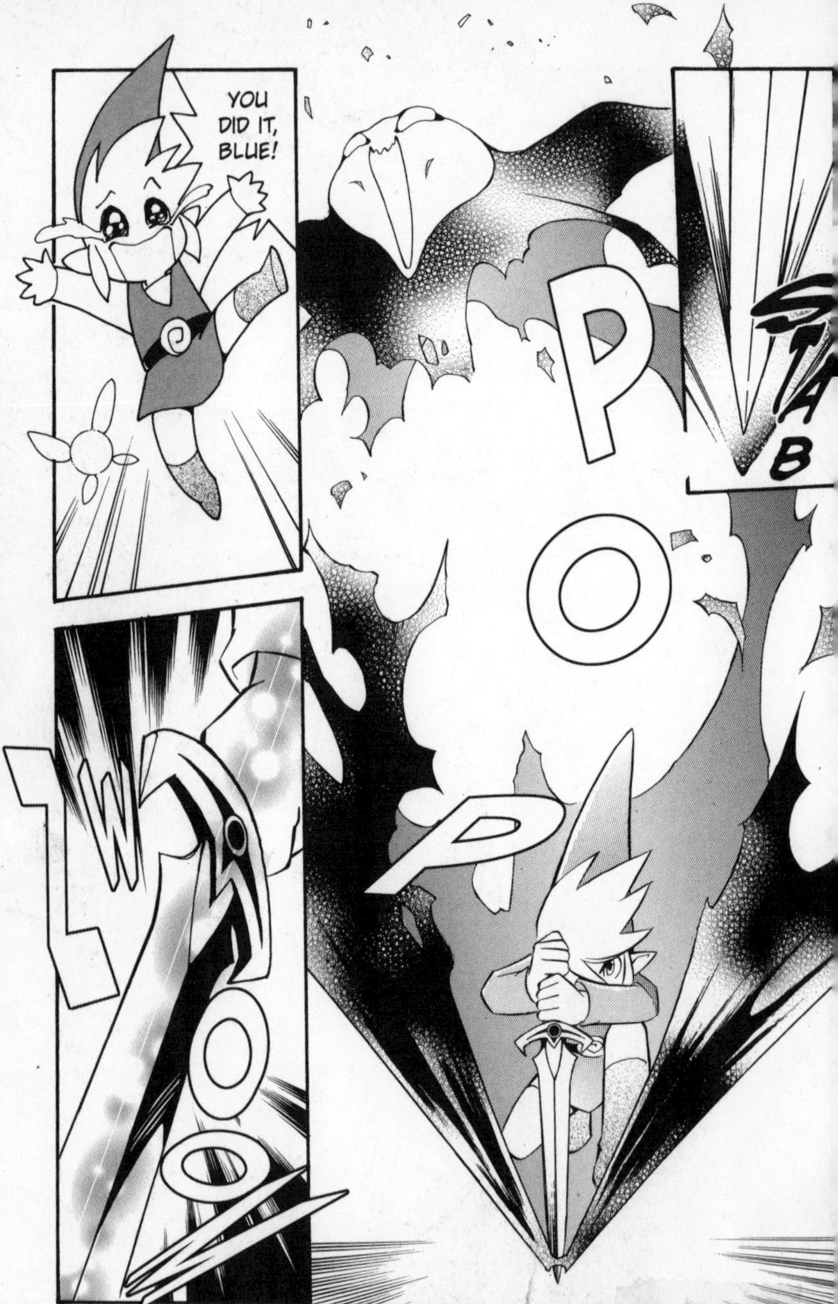
STAB
POP
YOU DID IT, BLUE!

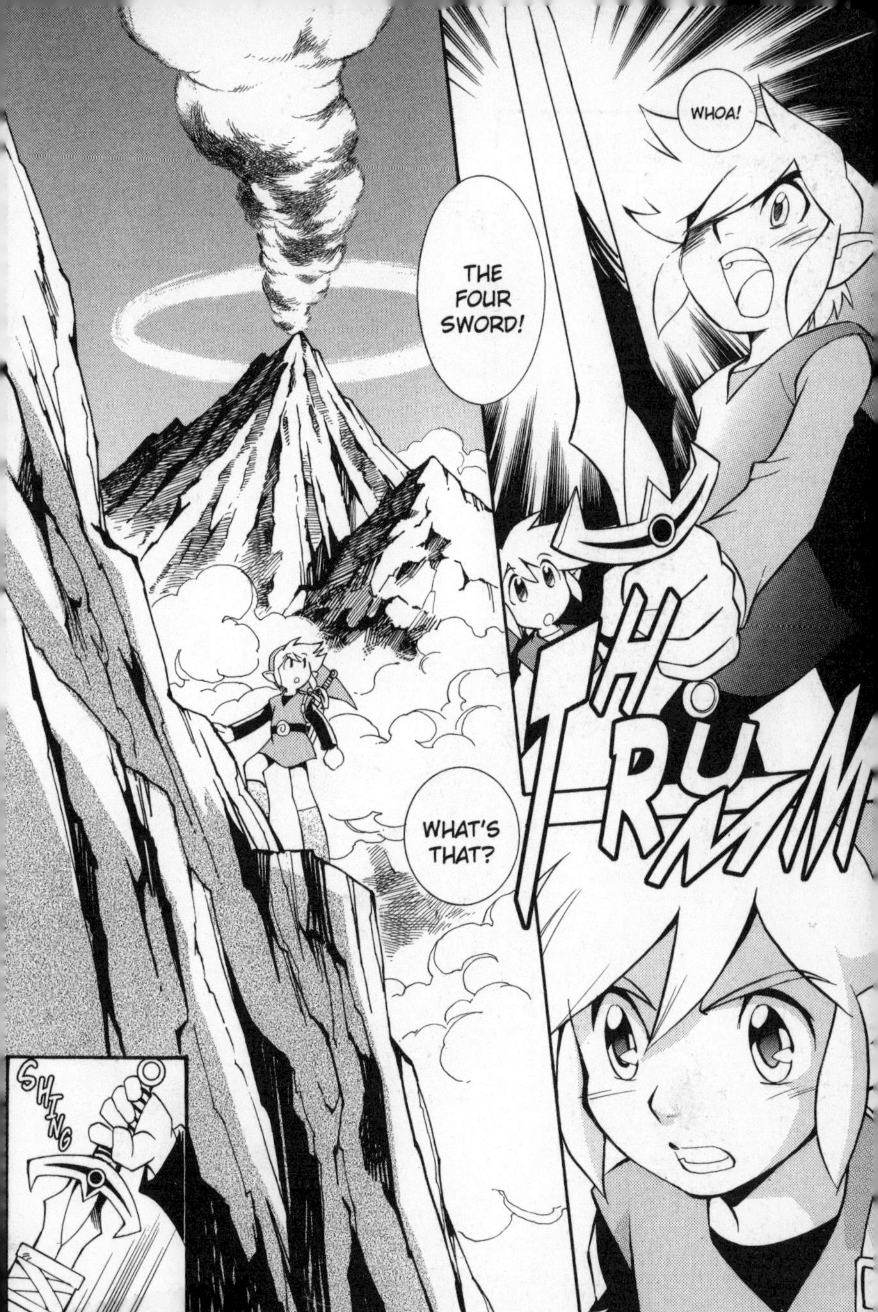
WHOA!
THE FOUR SWORD!
WHAT'S THAT?
SHING

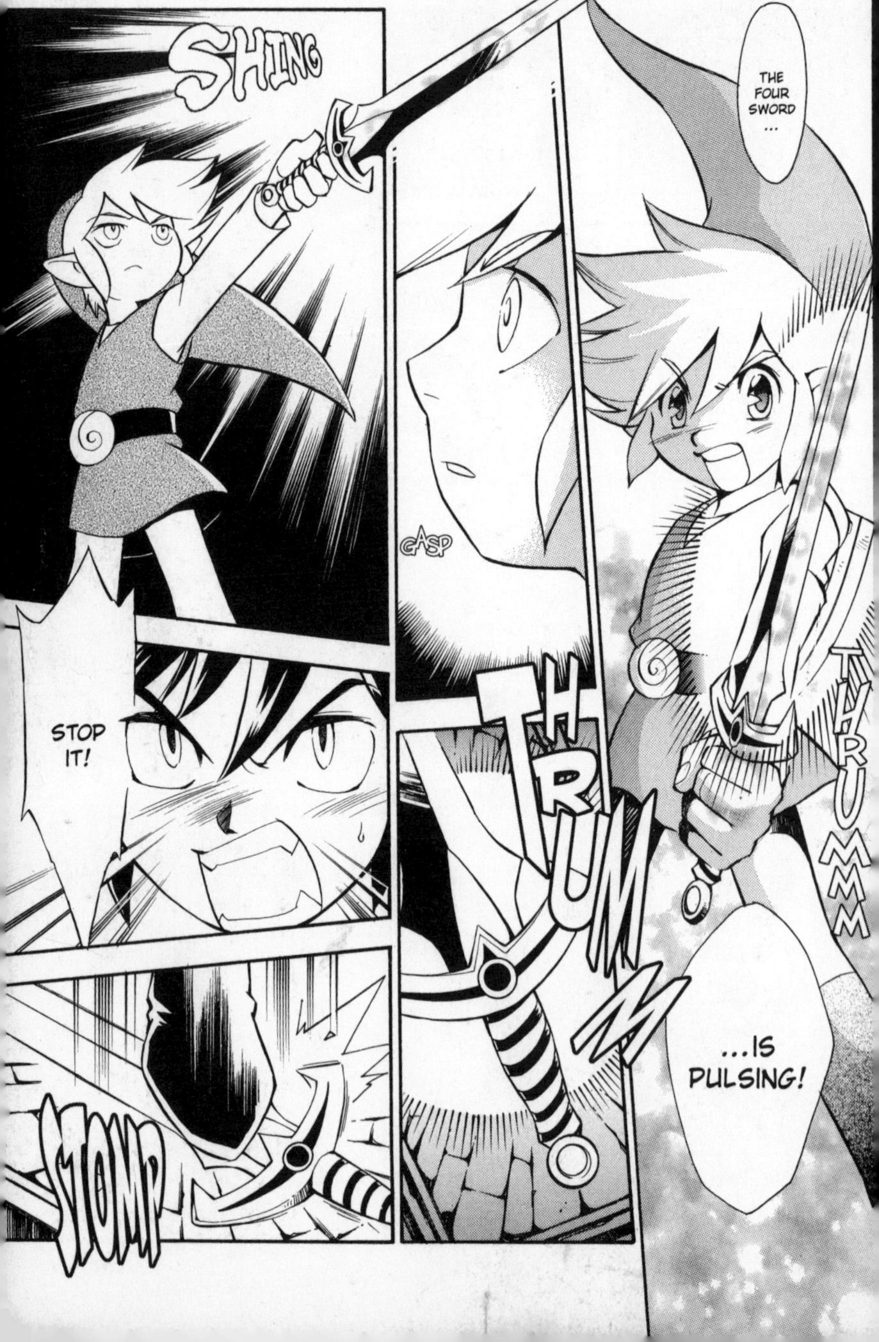
THE FOUR SWORD ...
THRUMMMM
...IS PULSING!
GASP
THRUMM
SHING
STOP IT!
STOMP

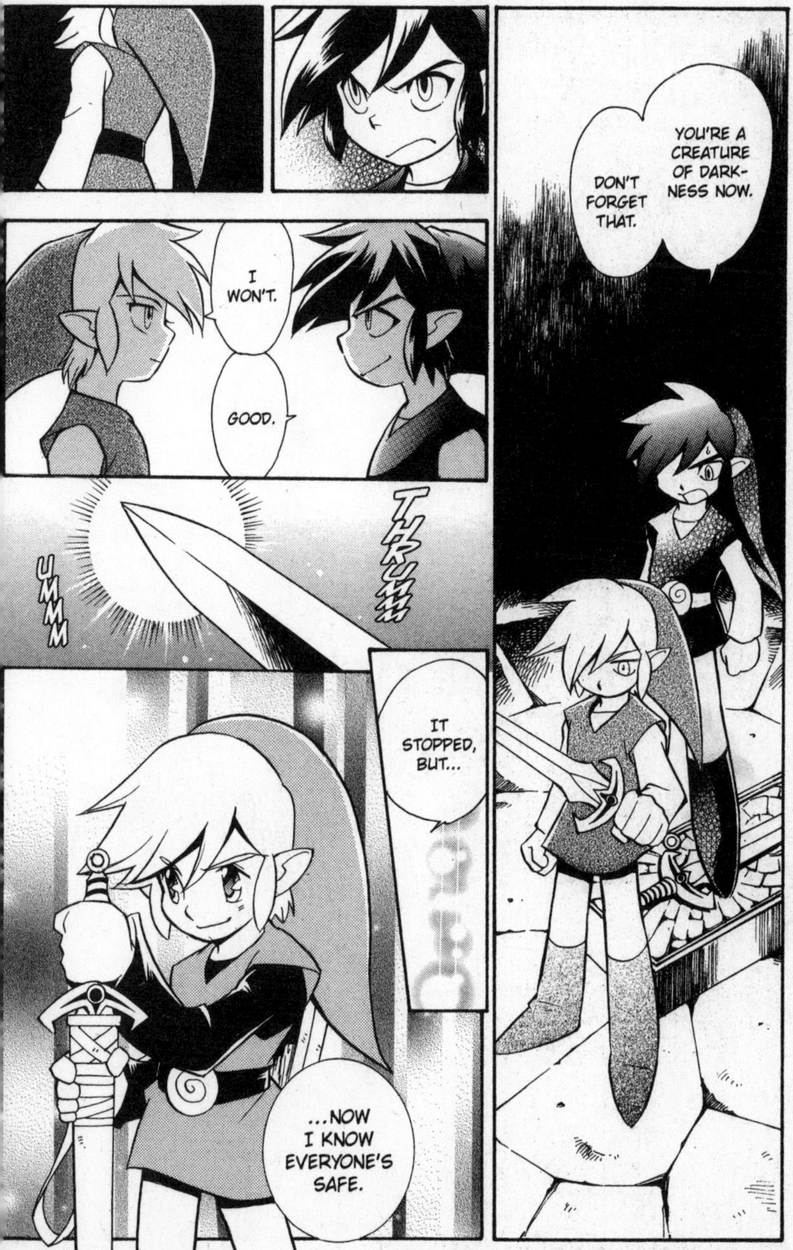
YOU'RE A CREATURE OF DARK-NESS NOW.
DON'T FORGET THAT.
I WON'T.
GOOD.
THRUMM
UMMM
IT STOPPED, BUT...
...NOW I KNOW EVERYONE'S SAFE.

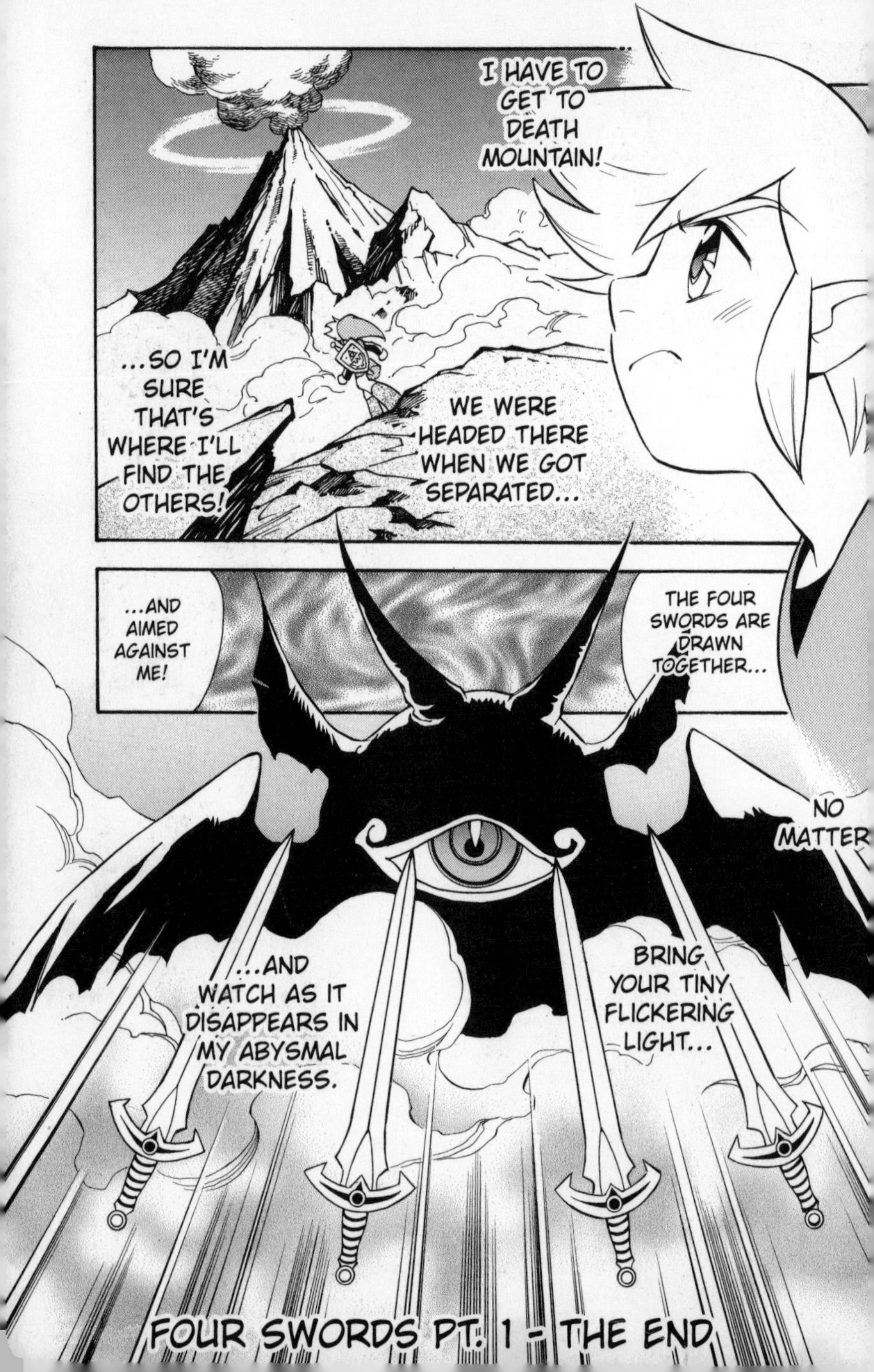
I HAVE TO GET TO DEATH MOUNTAIN!
WE WERE HEADED THERE WHEN WE GOT SEPARATED...
...SO I'M SURE THAT'S WHERE I'LL FIND THE OTHERS!
THE FOUR SWORDS ARE DRAWN TOGETHER...
...AND AIMED AGAINST ME!
NO MATTER
BRING YOUR TINY FLICKERING LIGHT...
...AND WATCH AS IT DISAPPEARS IN MY ABYSMAL DARKNESS.
FOUR SWORDS PT. 1 - THE END

Coming Next Volume

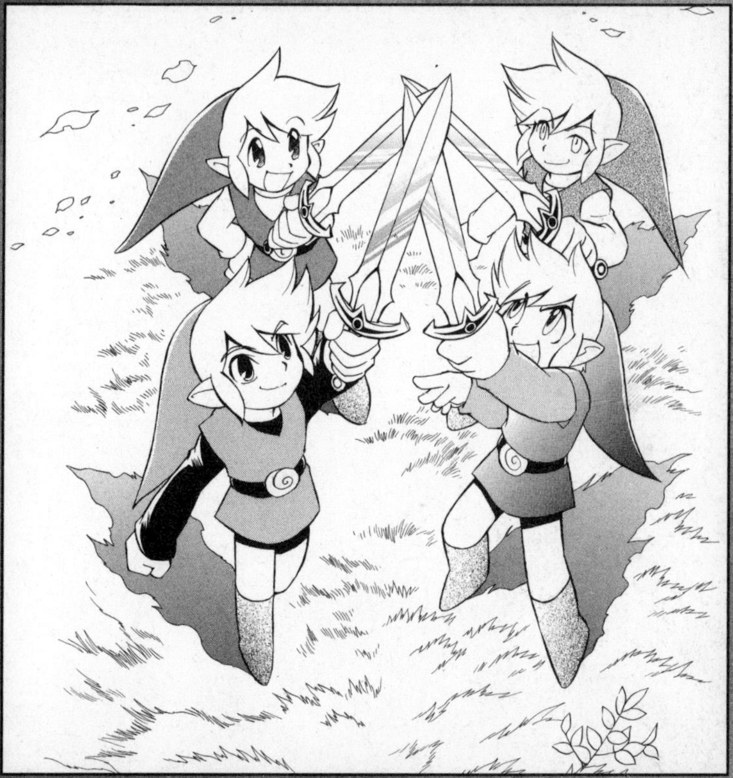

The Green, Red, and Blue Links reach Death Mountain, where they challenge Shadow Link and Violet Link in battle. Then, inside the Fire Temple they learn a terrible secret about the Dark World and the evil power behind Vaati. To defeat this great enemy, the different colored Links must find a way to become one again in order to harness the power of the Four Sword!

Available now!

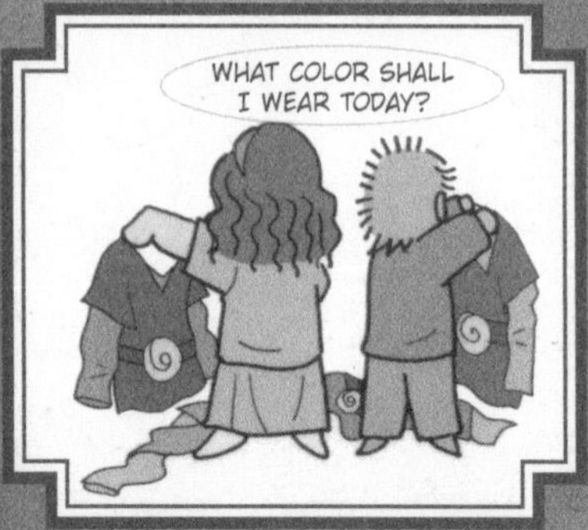
WHAT COLOR SHALL
I WEAR TODAY?

AKIRA HIMEKAWA

This time there are five Links! Four heroes and one villain! Which color are you?

Akira Himekawa is the collaboration of two women, A. Honda and S. Nagano. Together they have created nine manga adventures featuring Link and the popular video game world of *The Legend of Zelda*™, including *Ocarina of Time, Oracle of Seasons* and *Four Swords*. Their most recent work, *Legend of Zelda*™*: Phantom Hourglass,* is serialized in *Shogaku Rokunensei.*

THE LEGEND OF ZELDA™

— FOUR SWORDS —

PART 1
VIZ Kids Edition

STORY & ART BY
AKIRA HIMEKAWA

TM & © 2009 Nintendo.
© 2004 Akira HIMEKAWA/Shogakukan
All rights reserved.
Original Japanese edition
"ZELDA NO DENSETSU - YOTTSU NO TSURUGI PLUS - JOU"
published by SHOGAKUKAN Inc.

Translation/John Werry, Honyaku Center Inc.
English Adaptation/Stan! Brown
Touch-up Art & Lettering/John Hunt
Cover & Interior Design/Sean Lee
Editor/Mike Montesa

Printed in the U.S.A.

Published by VIZ Media, LLC
P.O. Box 77010
San Francisco, CA 94107

10 9 8 7 6 5 4 3
First printing, August 2009
Third printing, July 2010

PARENTAL ADVISORY
LEGEND OF ZELDA is
rated A and is suitable
for readers of all ages.
ratings.viz.com

www.viz.com

www.vizkids.com

FOUR SWORDS ADVENTURES — THE GAME

The Legend of Zelda™: *Four Swords* was released for the Nintendo Game Cube in 2004. The Game Boy Advance could also be used as a controller and connected to the Game Cube in order to play. The game was known for its multiplayer mode that allowed up to four players to take the roles of different colored Links and work together to complete the game.

THE LEGEND OF ZELDA
Manga Series

Don't miss any of Link's exciting adventures!

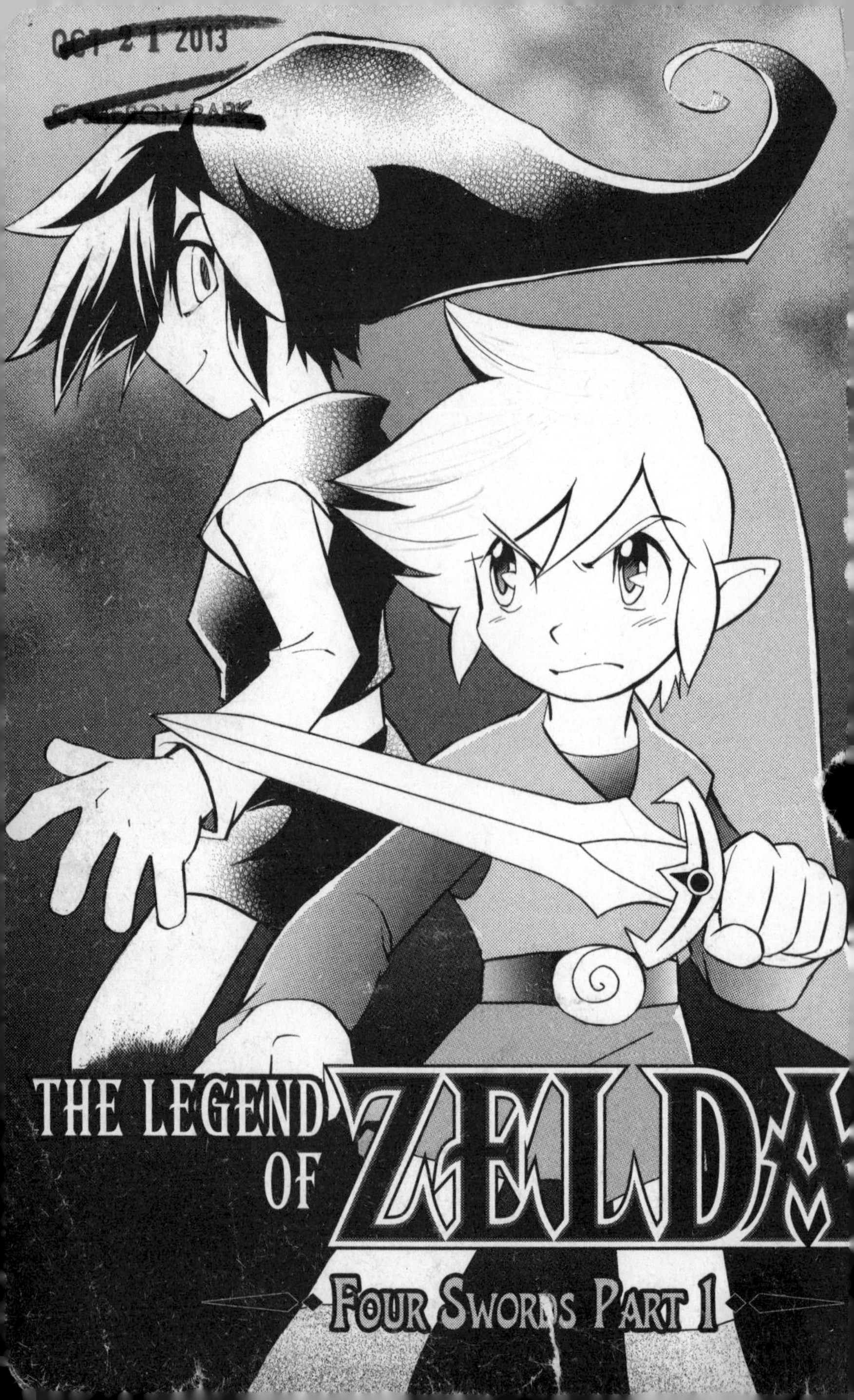
THE LEGEND OF ZELDA
Four Swords Part 1

THE LEGEND OF ZELDA
FOUR SWORDS

PART
1

CONTENTS
FOUR SWORDS PART 1

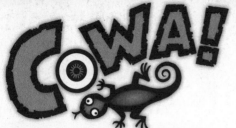

WHO'S GOT THE CURE FOR THE MONSTER FLU?

From AKIRA TORIYAMA, creator of *Dragon Ball*, *Dr. Slump*, and *Sand Land*

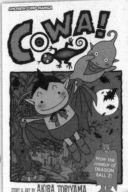

SHONEN JUMP MANGA

COWA!

STORY & ART BY AKIRA TORIYAMA

From the creator of DRAGON BALL Z!

MANGA SERIES ON SALE NOW!

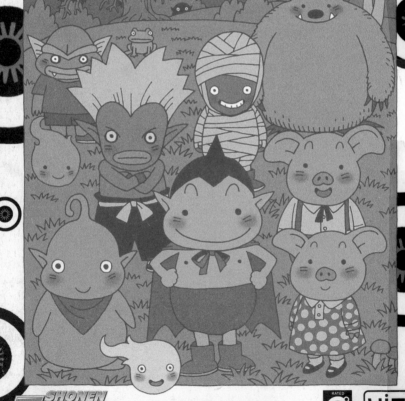

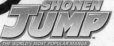

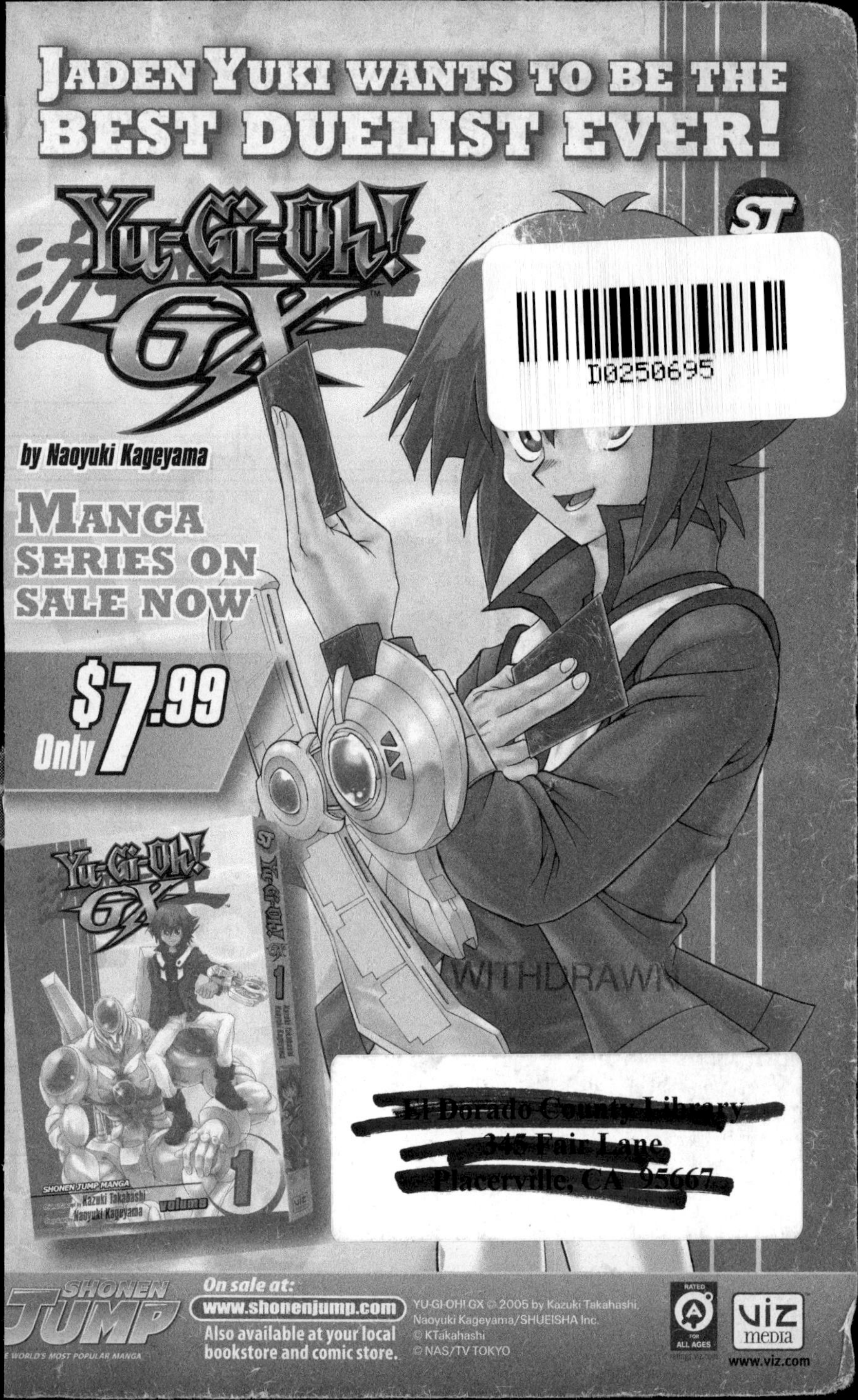
JADEN YUKI WANTS TO BE THE
BEST DUELIST EVER!
ST
YU-GI-OH! GX
by Naoyuki Kageyama
MANGA
SERIES ON
SALE NOW
Only $7.99
YU-GI-OH! GX
SHONEN JUMP MANGA
Kazuki Takahashi
Naoyuki Kageyama
volume 1
SHONEN JUMP
THE WORLD'S MOST POPULAR MANGA
On sale at:
www.shonenjump.com
Also available at your local
bookstore and comic store.
YU-GI-OH! GX © 2005 by Kazuki Takahashi,
Naoyuki Kageyama/SHUEISHA Inc.
© KTakahashi
© NAS/TV TOKYO
RATED A FOR ALL AGES
VIZ media
www.viz.com